THE CRUCIFIED KING – ENDORSEMENTS

Jeremy Treat brings together what many have rented asunder: the cross of Christ and the kingdom of God. For too long many theological tribes have *either* preached a message about the cross addressed to individuals and opted out of kingdom business *or* embarked on a campaign of kingdom work springing from Jesus' kingdom vision and then struggled to treat the cross meaningfully. Treat shows that such a division is foreign to the biblical texts and to the testimony of the historical church. In a venerable banquet of biblical exegesis, biblical theology, and systematic reflections, Treat shows that God's reign and God's redemption are both outworkings of the cross of our crucified Lord. Treat brings sanity and sensibility to a controversial topic that should not even be controversial. Judicious, balanced, informative, and compelling!

—*Michael F. Bird, Lecturer in Theology at Ridley Melbourne Mission and Ministry College, Australia*

In *The Crucified King*, Jeremy Treat makes a helpful start toward reintegrating what should never have been torn asunder: not only God's kingdom and Christ's atoning work, but also biblical theology and theological reflection.

—*Daniel J. Treier is Blanchard Professor of Theology at Wheaton College (Illinois).*

The Crucified King contributes to the current revivification of the doctrine of the atonement, exploring how the cross and kingdom are necessary and mutually interpretative realities. The cross, he argues, is the inbreaking of God's eschatological kingdom into the present, while it sums up the nature of divine and human servant-kingship. This is a delightful work of biblical and systematic theology, ripe with implications for the church's understanding of the cross of Christ as its basis and

—*A*  *Theology, University*

Jesus came proclaiming the kingdom of God but then died on the cross. The first great virtue of *The Crucified King* is that it tackles head-on this great riddle at the heart of the New Testament, clarifying how what happened to Jesus, far from contradicting his message, served rather to confirm and explain it. The book's second strength is that it reconciles two views of Jesus' death on the cross that have for too long been rivals rather than partners: the penal substitution and *Christus Victor* theories of atonement. The third strength is that it reconciles the story of redemption (biblical theology) and its logic (systematic theology). Three tensions; three proposed resolutions: blessed are the peacemakers!

—*Kevin J. Vanhoozer, Research Professor of Systematic Theology, Trinity Evangelical Divinity School*

I feel like I've witnessed a beautiful wedding where the atmosphere is just right, the visuals are perfect, and the bride and groom are perfect for one another. Pastors and theologians often manage to give the impression that the kingdom of God and the cross of the Messiah are divorced or separated. Treat's study of kingdom and cross unveils the exciting marriage between two of Scripture's central concepts.

With good writing and clear thinking of the "big picture" variety, Treat produces a dessert-quality dissertation that leaves readers enriched and satisfied. On the evidence of this work, the author will have an important voice in the theological conversations of the next generation of Christian scholars.

—*Jason Hood, St. Margaret's Anglican Church, Moshi, Tanzania*

THE
CRUCIFIED
KING

THE
CRUCIFIED
KING

ATONEMENT *and* KINGDOM IN
BIBLICAL *and* SYSTEMATIC THEOLOGY

JEREMY R. TREAT

ZONDERVAN

The Crucified King
Copyright © 2014 by Jeremy R. Treat

This title is also available as a Zondervan ebook. Visit www.zondervan.com/ebooks.

Requests for information should be addressed to:

Zondervan, 3900 Sparks Dr. SE, Grand Rapids, Michigan 49546

Library of Congress Cataloging-in-Publication Data

Treat, Jeremy R., 1980-
    The crucified king : atonement and kingdom in biblical and systematic theology / Jeremy
R. Treat.
        pages cm
    Includes bibliographical references and index.
    ISBN 978-0-310-51674-3 (softcover)
    1. Jesus Christ--Crucifixion--Biblical teaching. 2. Jesus Christ--Crucifixion. 3. Atonement--
Biblical teaching. 4. Atonement. I. Title.
    BT453.T74 2014
    232'.3--dc23   2013046045

Cover design: Michelle Lenger
Cover photography: Shutterstock.com/Mila Petkova/Hein Nouwens; iStock.com
Interior design: Matthew Van Zomeren

Printed in the United States of America

---

14 15 16 17 18 19 20 /DCI/ 22 21 20 19 18 17 16 15 14 13 12 11 10 9 8 7 6 5 4 3 2 1

To my wife, Tiffany

For the word of the cross is folly to those who are perishing, but to us who are being saved it is the power of God.

1 Corinthians 1:18

CONTENTS

DETAILED
TABLE OF CONTENTS

BIBLICAL THEOLOGY

SYSTEMATIC THEOLOGY

FOREWORD

WHAT IS THE meaning of Christ's death for us?

It is difficult to imagine a question more relevant to our personal destiny, our ecclesial identity and mission, and the hopes we hold for the future of the entire cosmos. As this book points out with care and thoroughness, kingdom and atonement were nuclear to our Lord's identity. From the beginning of his ministry, Jesus saw himself as the bringer of the end-time kingdom, with the cross as his destiny. His main *message* was the kingdom and his main *mission* was to go to Golgotha. Surely this twofold fact, defended meticulously here, should provoke us to think of kingdom and atonement together. When we do so, we discover that many of the false choices that plague this and other topics fade away.

Of course, answers to my opening question have varied widely. In the ancient church, variety was less a reflection of opposing "theologies" orbiting around a central dogma than a recognition of the far-reaching implications of our Lord's announcement, "It is finished." Many emphasized the atonement as Christ's victory over the powers of death, hell, and Satan. Others are known for underscoring its close connection with the incarnation: recapitulating (literally, "re-headshipping") Adam's race, "in Christ." Still others contemplated Christ's wounds "for us" as a death of substitution in which our guilt is transferred to Christ and his righteousness becomes ours. Yet only after centuries of refinement, categorization, and (especially in the modern era) doctoral dissertations and scholarly monographs have these been pressed neatly into mutually exclusive "atonement theories." Exaggerated contrasts are drawn between Antiochene and Alexandrian, not to mention Eastern and Western, theologies that are far less obvious in the ancient writings. In fact, those writers mixed metaphors and emphases on nearly every page.

Nor is there any basis for the repeated generalization that the sixteenth-century Reformers simply adopted Anselm's satisfaction theory and pushed to the periphery other classic emphases. Luther and Calvin, for example, moved effortlessly between what we today call *Christus Victor*, recapitulation, and penal substitution. For them, Christ is Lord, and this is conceivable only because he has dealt decisively with death at its root: namely, the debt-curse that makes it a sentence rather than a natural part of the cycle of life.

A lot of subsequent historical water went under the bridge to lead to a series of false choices:

- Old Testament (kingdom, holy war, penal sacrifices) vs. New Testament (peaceful community, nonviolence, and love)
- Jesus (kingdom) vs. Paul (atonement/justification)
- biblical vs. systematic theology
- forensic categories vs. relational, ontological-participationist, and political ones

And on I could go.

Emboldened by the ideal of "resourcement" (re-sourcing), a number of younger evangelical theologians have rediscovered the integrity of Christian conviction. Resisting central dogmas, they seek to understand the relation of the parts to the whole. Yet I am not aware of a work that has yet set out to weave broken threads back together on the specific themes of kingdom and atonement. Jeremy Treat has achieved this in *The Crucified King*. In my view at least, it is the work of a skilled scholar.

It is one thing to plead for the integration of biblical and systematic theology (among other things); quite another to actually do it. Heuristic tools—such as "the states of humiliation and exaltation"—have become too airtight, Treat argues persuasively. Treatments of Christ's royal and priestly offices, too, have often been isolated from each other. Yet Jesus Christ embraced his cross as a monarch grasps a scepter. Rather than wait until Easter to celebrate Christ's conquest, Treat not only argues the case but revels in the royal dignity of the first universal emperor whose throne was a cross. The arguments are deeply and widely informed; the conclusions range from provocative to elating.

At the same time, Treat does not run from long-standing reductionisms only to fall into his own. Without the resurrection and ascension, Christ's work is not complete. To some extent, Christ even considers his own glory incomplete until his body is raised with him and the whole cosmos shares in his everlasting Sabbath. Yet, for the eyes of faith, Christ's glory shines already in his cross.

I commend the author not only for a seminal work on the heart of the gospel, but for giving us a model for a more comprehensive vision of theological exploration. Poring over his arguments will doubtless rearrange some furniture in our thinking, but along the way it will provoke pauses to take a deep breath, to take in the vista, and to raise our hearts to heaven in praise of our gracious King.

Michael Horton

ACKNOWLEDGMENTS

THE PURPOSE OF Christian theology is to help the church speak and live in accordance with the gospel. So I begin by thanking God for the good news of what he has accomplished in his Son by the power of the Spirit. Theology, moreover, is by design a community task—we are reconciled to God and into community. The relational nature of theology is both an impetus for sharper thinking and perhaps the greatest joy of the task. Such is the case for this book, which is largely the result of tremendous mentoring, feedback, and friendship.

I would like to thank my doctoral supervisor, Kevin Vanhoozer, for shaping me as a theologian and graciously guiding me throughout this project. Doug Moo offered insightful feedback throughout the writing process and has been a great encouragement in attempting to bridge biblical and systematic theology. I am also grateful for other scholars who were kind enough to read portions of the book and offer feedback: Mike Horton, Hans Boersma, Dan Treier, Adam Johnson, Stephen Dempster, Richard Schultz, and Nick Perrin. The PhD community at Wheaton College has been incredibly helpful, especially those who set aside time specifically for my project: Hank Voss, Matthew Patton, Ben Ribbens, Daniel Owens, Stephanie Lowry, Amy Hughes, Jordan Barrett, Mike Kibbe, and Jon Hoglund.

A special thanks to my parents, Mike and Joyce Treat, for faithfully pointing me to Christ and giving unending support throughout every stage of my life. I am also forever grateful to Pastor Dave Parker and the kind people of Eastside Christian Fellowship, who raised me up and sent me out.

Finally, I dedicate this book to my beautiful wife, Tiffany. Your support and encouragement throughout this process have been remarkable, and yet are only a small reflection of your deep love for God and your commitment to me. I am thankful for the important part you played in this book, but far more for the joy that it is to be your husband, to raise our daughters, Ashlyn, Lauryn, and Evelyn, and follow Christ together.

Jeremy R. Treat
February 26, 2014

ABBREVIATIONS

AB   Anchor Bible

ABCS   Africa Bible Commentary Series

ACCS   Ancient Christian Commentary on Scripture

ACNT   Augsburg Commentary on the New Testament

ANF   *The Ante-Nicene Fathers*. Edited by A. Roberts and J. Donaldson. Buffalo, 1885–1896. Reprint, Grand Rapids, 1975.

ASTI   *Annual of the Swedish Theological Institute*

AThR   *Anglican Theological Review*

AYBC   Anchor Yale Bible Commentaries

BBR   *Bulletin for Biblical Research*

BDB   Brown, F., S. R. Driver, and C. A. Briggs. *A Hebrew and English Lexicon of the Old Testament*. Oxford, 1907.

BECNT   Baker Exegetical Commentary on the New Testament

BETL   Bibliotheca ephemeridum theologicarum lovaniensium

BLT   *Brethren Life and Thought*

BNTC   Black's New Testament Commentaries

BSac   *Bibliotheca sacra*

BST   The Bible Speaks Today

BTCB   Brazos Theological Commentary on the Bible

CBQ   *Catholic Biblical Quarterly*

CCP   Cambridge Companions to Philosophy

CIT   Current Issues in Theology

CJT   *Canadian Journal of Theology*

CTJ   *Calvin Theological Journey*

CTQ   *Concordia Theological Quarterly*

CurTM   *Currents in Theology and Mission*

DEM   *Dictionary of the Ecumenical Movement*. Edited by Nicolas Lossky. Grand Rapids, 1991.

DLNT   *Dictionary of the Later New Testament and Its Developments*. Edited by R. P. Martin and P. H. Davids. Downers Grove, 1997.

DOTHB   *Dictionary of the Old Testament: Historical Books*. Edited by Bill T. Arnold and H. G. M. Williamson. Downers Grove, 2005.

DTIB   *Dictionary for the Theological Interpretation of the Bible*. Edited by Kevin Vanhoozer. Grand Rapids, 2005.

EBC   *Expositor's Bible Commentary*

EdF   Erträge der Forschung

EDT   *Evangelical Dictionary of Theology*. Edited by Walter Elwell. Grand Rapids, 1989

ERT   *Evangelical Review of Theology*

EuroJTh   *European Journal of Theology*

EvQ   *Evangelical Quarterly*

FB   Forschung zur Bibel

FET   The Foundations of Evangelical Theology

FRLANT   Forschungen zur Religion und Literatur des Alten und Neuen Testaments

GDT   *Global Dictionary of Theology*. Edited by William A. Dyrness and Veli-Matti Kärkkäinen. Downers Grove, 2008.

HeyJ   *Heythrop Journal*

IBC   Interpretation: A Bible Commentary for Teaching and Preaching

ICC   International Critical Commentary

IDB   *The Interpreter's Dictionary of the Bible*. Edited by G. A. Buttrick. 4 vols. Nashville, 1962.

IJST   *International Journal of Systematic Theology*

JBL   *Journal of Biblical Literature*

JETS   *Journal of the Evangelical Theological Society*

JJS   *Journal of Jewish Studies*

JR   *Journal of Religion*

JSNT   *Journal for the Study of the New Testament*

JSOT   *Journal for the Study of the Old Testament*

JSOTSup   Journal for the Study of the Old Testament: Supplement Series

JTS   *Journal of Theological Studies*

KKHS   Kurzgefasster Kommentar zu den Heiligen Schriften, Alten und Neuen Testaments, sowie zu den Apokryphen

LCC   Library of Christian Classics. Philadelphia, 1953–

LW   *Luther's Works*. Philadelphia, 1955–1986

MB   Le Monde de la Bible

MQR   *Mennonite Quarterly Review*

MSJ   *The Master's Seminary Journal*

NAC   New American Commentary

NCB   New Century Bible

NDBT *New Dictionary of Biblical Theology.* Edited by T. Desmond
       Alexander and Brian Rosner. Downers Grove, 2000.
NIBC   New International Biblical Commentary
NIBCOT New International Biblical Commentary on the Old Testament
NICNT New International Commentary on the New Testament
NICOT New International Commentary on the Old Testament
NIDOTTE *New International Dictionary of Old Testament Theology and Ex-*
       egesis. Edited by W. A. VanGemeren. 5 vols. Grand Rapids, 1997.
NIGTC New International Greek Testament Commentary
NIVAC NIV Application Commentary
NovT   *Novum Testamentum*
NovTSup Novum Testamentum Supplements
NPNF*1* *Nicene and Post-Nicene Fathers,* Series 1. Edited by Philip Schaff.
       New York, 1886–1890. Reprint, Peabody, MA 1994.
NPNF*2* *Nicene and Post-Nicene Fathers*, Series 2. Edited by Philip Schaff
       and Henry Wace. New York, 1890. Reprint, Peabody, MA,
       1994.
NSBT   New Studies in Biblical Theology
NTP   New Testament Profiles
NTS   *New Testament Studies*
OECS   The Oxford Early Christian Studies
OTL   Old Testament Library
OWC   Oxford World Classics
PBTM   Paternoster Biblical and Theological Monographs
PiNTC Pillar New Testament Commentary
ProEccl *Pro ecclesia*
PSB   *Princeton Seminary Bulletin*
PTM   Paternoster Theological Monographs
PTMS   Princeton Theological Monograph Series
RTR   *Reformed Theological Review*
SBET   *Scottish Bulletin of Evangelical Theology*
SBJT   *Southern Baptist Journal of Theology*
SBLDS Society of Biblical Literature Dissertation Series
SHS   Scripture and Hermeneutics Series
SJT   *Scottish Journal of Theology*
SNTSMS Society for New Testament Studies Monograph Series
TDNT   *Theological Dictionary of the New Testament.* Edited by G. Kittel
       and G. Friedrich. Translated by G. W. Bromiley. 10 vols. Grand
       Rapids, 1964–1976.

TDOT   *Theological Dictionary of the Old Testament.* Edited by G. J. Botterweck and H. Ringgren. Translated by J. T. Willis, G. W. Bromiley, and D. E. Green. 8 vols. Grand Rapids, 1974–2006

THS   Tyndale House Studies

TJ   *Trinity Journal*

TNTC   Tyndale New Testament Commentaries

TS   *Theological Studies*

TSR   Texts and Studies in Religion

TWOT   *Theological Wordbook of the Old Testament.* Edited by R. L. Harris, G. L. Archer Jr. 2 vols. Chicago, 1980.

TynBul   *Tyndale Bulletin*

WA   Luthers Werke: Kritische Gesamtausgabe. Weimar, 1883–

WBC   Word Biblical Commentary

WSA   *Works of Saint Augustine.* Edited by John E. Rotelle. Brooklyn. 1990–2009.

WTJ   *Westminster Theological Journal*

WUNT   Wissenschaftliche Untersuchungen zum Neuen Testament

ZEB   *Zondervan Encyclopedia of the Bible*

ZECNT   Zondervan Exegetical Commentary on the New Testament

INTRODUCTION

THE KINGDOM
AND THE CROSS

PERSPECTIVES ON THE atonement have been offered from all over the world, but the voice of the man closest to the cross of Christ has rarely been heard. "Jesus, remember me when you come into your kingdom" (Luke 23:42). How could this thief view a beaten, bloodied, and crucified criminal as one who rules over a kingdom? Maybe he was confused by the title "King of the Jews" on Jesus' cross or by the crown of thorns on his head. Or perhaps, as Jesus' response indicates, this man rightly saw the kingdom of God in the *crucified* Christ.

This book seeks to provide an answer to the following basic question: What is the biblical and theological relationship between the coming of the kingdom of God and the atoning death of Christ on the cross? As we will see, the answer lies ultimately in Jesus, the crucified king, as properly understood within the story and logic of redemption.

THE KINGDOM OR THE CROSS?

Beneath the surface of this theoretical question lies the problem of the separation of the kingdom and the cross in the church as well as the academy.[1] Some champion the kingdom and others cling to the cross, usually one to the exclusion of the other.[2] Tomes are written on the kingdom with hardly a

---

1. I will generally use "kingdom and cross" as shorthand for the coming of God's kingdom and Christ's atoning death on the cross. Provisional definitions for each are given at the end of this chapter.
2. For summaries demonstrating this contemporary divide in the church, see N. T. Wright, *After You Believe: Why Christian Character Matters* (New York: HarperOne, 2010), 110–18; Jim Belcher, *Deep Church: A Third Way Beyond Emerging and Traditional* (Downers Grove, IL: Inter-Varsity Press, 2009), 105–22; Dallas Willard, *The Divine Conspiracy: Rediscovering Our Hidden Life in God* (San Francisco: HarperSanFrancisco, 1998), 42–55.

mention of Christ's cross.[3] Volumes on the cross ignore Jesus' message of the kingdom.[4] Furthermore, while some passively ignore any connection between kingdom and cross, others intentionally pit one against the other.[5] Why has such a rift developed between two of Scripture's most important motifs? There are at least six reasons.

First, and most important, the wedge driven between kingdom and cross is largely the result of reactionary debates between those who emphasize the kingdom and those who focus on the cross. The zenith of these debates was the collision between the social gospel movement of the early twentieth century and the ensuing conservative response. Walter Rauschenbusch, drawing from nineteenth-century German liberalism, advocated the kingdom of God to the exclusion of substitutionary atonement.[6] H. Richard Niebuhr's assessment of this theology is fitting: "A God without wrath brought men without sin into a kingdom without judgment through the ministrations of a Christ without a cross."[7] Conservatives reacted sharply by reclaiming the centrality of the cross, often relegating the kingdom solely to the future or ignoring it altogether,[8] thereby setting in place the defining feature of the history of this discussion: pendulum-swinging reductionism. The result is a false dichotomy—either the kingdom without the cross or the cross without the kingdom—that truncates the gospel.[9]

---

3. George Eldon Ladd, for example, in his highly influential (and overall helpful) work on the kingdom of God, never mentions atonement and only twice briefly refers to Christ's death (*The Presence of the Future: The Eschatology of Biblical Realism* [Grand Rapids: Eerdmans, 1974], 157, 324).

4. James Denney, for example, in his classic work on the atonement, mentions the kingdom on only two pages (*The Atonement and the Modern Mind* [London: Hodder & Stoughton, 1903], 12, 115).

5. Kathryn Tanner, *Christ the Key* (CIT; Cambridge: Cambridge University Press, 2010), 251; J. Denny Weaver, "Narrative *Christus Victor*," in *Atonement and Violence: A Theological Conversation* (ed. John Sanders; Nashville: Abingdon, 2006), 12; David Brondos, "Why Was Jesus Crucified? Theology, History and the Story of Redemption," *SJT* 54 (2001): 496–99.

6. Walter Rauschenbusch, *A Theology for the Social Gospel* (New York: Macmillan, 1917); see esp. ch. 19, "The Social Gospel and the Atonement." Rauschenbusch was building on the work of Friedrich Schleiermacher (*The Christian Faith* [Edinburgh: T&T Clark, 1986], 459–60) and Albrecht Ritschl (*The Christian Doctrine of Justification and Reconciliation: The Positive Development of the Doctrine* [Clifton, NJ: Reference Books, 1966], 556–63).

7. H. Richard Niebuhr, *The Kingdom of God in America* (New York: Harper & Row, 1937), 197.

8. For a historical survey of these debates, see Russell Moore, *The Kingdom of Christ: The New Evangelical Perspective* (Wheaton, IL: Crossway, 2004), 27.

9. Kingdom and cross are, of course, tied together biblically by the proclamation of the gospel, which is defined as both the coming of God's kingdom (Matt 4:23) and Christ's death and resurrection (1 Cor 15:3–4). Debates over the definition of the gospel are complex, and to enter in would require more space than is available. For an excellent approach that upholds kingdom and cross as essential to the gospel, see Simon Gathercole, "The Gospel of Paul and the Gospel of the Kingdom," in *God's Power to Save* (ed. Chris Green; Downers Grove, IL: InterVarsity Press, 2006), 138–54.

Second, the fragmentation of Scripture that has occurred since the Enlightenment has contributed greatly to the severance of kingdom and cross.[10] If the Bible is not a unified whole, then there is no need to integrate the seemingly incompatible ideas that God reigns and the Son of God dies. Furthermore, this fragmentation applies not only to the Bible as a whole, but even to individual books of the Bible. In Isaiah, the Messianic King and the Suffering Servant need not be related, for they belong to different and unrelated traditions.[11] In Mark's gospel, the kingdom ministry of Jesus need not be congruous with the Passion Narrative, for they are simply separate sources that have been brought together.[12] Clearly, such a disintegrated view of Scripture will discourage the integration of its themes.

Third, the kingdom–cross divide is widened by the "ugly ditch" between biblical studies and systematic theology.[13] Broadly speaking, systematic theology has given great attention to the doctrine of the atonement but has largely ignored the kingdom of God.[14] The field of biblical studies, on the other hand, is dominated by the theme of the kingdom of God and yet gives less attention to the doctrine of the atonement.[15] A holistic answer to the kingdom–cross divide, therefore, will bridge this gap between biblical studies and systematic theology, incorporating insights from both disciplines for both doctrines.

---

10. According to Hans Frei, historians and biblical critics of the seventeenth and eighteenth centuries brought about "the eclipse of the biblical narrative," resulting in a fragmented view of Scripture (*The Eclipse of Biblical Narrative: A Study in Eighteenth and Nineteenth Century Hermeneutics* [New Haven, CT: Yale University Press, 1974]). For the history of this fragmentation in biblical scholarship, see Michael C. Legaspi, *The Death of Scripture and the Rise of Biblical Studies* (New York: Oxford University Press, 2010), 3–26.

11. For the history of the bifurcation and eventual trifurcation of Isaiah, see Marvin Sweeney, "On the Road to Duhm: Isaiah in the Nineteenth-Century Critical Scholarship," in *"As Those Who Are Taught": The Interpretation of Isaiah from the LXX to the SBL* (ed. Claire Mathews McGinnis and Patricia Tull; Atlanta: SBL, 2006), 243–62.

12. Rudolf Bultmann, *The History of the Synoptic Tradition* (trans. John Marsh; New York: Harper & Row, 1963), 262–84.

13. Kevin Vanhoozer, "Interpreting Scripture between the Rock of Biblical Studies and the Hard Place of Systematic Theology: The State of the Evangelical (Dis)union," in *Renewing the Evangelical Mission* (ed. Richard Lints; Grand Rapids: Eerdmans, 2013).

14. Russell Moore has noted, for example, that the kingdom of God is treated in only two pages of Wayne Grudem's entire systematic theology (*Systematic Theology: An Introduction to Biblical Doctrine* [Grand Rapids: Zondervan, 1995]), both of which are in his discussion of the doctrine of the church (Moore, *The Kingdom of Christ*, 205). There are, of course, exceptions to this generalization. For example, systematic theologian Jürgen Moltmann has written extensively on the kingdom of God (*The Trinity and the Kingdom: The Doctrine of God* [New York: Harper & Row, 1981]).

15. Robert Yarbrough expresses a "serious misgiving" regarding the tendency in biblical theology to emphasize the kingdom to the point of overlooking the cross ("The Practice and Promise of Biblical Theology: A Response to Hamilton and Goldsworthy," *SBJT* 12 [2008]: 84). An exception to this general trend is New Testament scholar Leon Morris, who has contributed greatly to the doctrine of the atonement (*The Cross in the New Testament* [Exeter, UK: Paternoster, 1965]).

Fourth, kingdom and cross have not been integrated because the Gospels (the place in the canon where the kingdom theme is most explicit) have largely been withheld as a source for theology. N. T. Wright has belabored this point, saying that as a result of misreading the Gospels, "Jesus as kingdom-bringer has been screened out of the church's dogmatic proclamation."[16] The Gospel writers, once assumed to be mere historians, are now acknowledged to be theologians, interpreting Christ's ministry by the way in which they tell the story, especially as it fulfills the narrative of Israel from the Old Testament.[17]

Fifth, kingdom and cross have been difficult to relate because of the over-systematization of certain doctrines, such as the states and offices of Christ. If Christ's work is divided neatly into the two categories of humiliation and exaltation, with the cross being only in the state of humiliation, it is difficult to see how it could relate to the kingdom at all. If Christ's death is interpreted only in terms of his priestly office, then it will be difficult to connect the cross to the kingdom. Although the doctrines of the states and offices themselves are not to blame, they have often been used in a way that draws a thick doctrinal line between Christ's royal and Christ's atoning work.

Sixth, to state the obvious, if one has a mistaken view of the kingdom or the cross respectively, then properly relating the two will be impossible. For example, if the cross is understood solely in terms of personal salvation and the kingdom as future eschatology, then never the twain shall meet. Or, if the kingdom is thought to be a utopian place and the cross an eschatological event, then they will be equally difficult to relate.

The need to address this divide and clearly articulate the relationship between atonement and kingdom has grown and is pressing for such a time as this. Over fifty years ago Emil Brunner stated, "We cannot speak rightly about atonement without at the same time thinking of redemption, as the overcoming of resistance and the restoration of the rule of God."[18] Though few have taken up this task, others have joined in expressing concern over the doctrinal gap between Christ's atoning death on the cross and the kingdom of God. Herman Ridderbos laments that "there are many authors who continue to ignore the correlation of these two central data in the gospel."[19]

---

16. N. T. Wright, "Whence and Whither Historical Jesus Studies in the Life of the Church?" in *Jesus, Paul, and the People of God: A Theological Dialogue with N. T. Wright* (ed. Nicholas Perrin and Richard Hays; Downers Grove, IL: InterVarsity Press, 2011), 133.

17. Jonathan Pennington, *Reading the Gospels Wisely: A Narrative and Theological Introduction* (Grand Rapids: Baker Academic, 2012), 151–52.

18. Emil Brunner, *The Doctrine of Creation and Redemption*, vol. 2 of *Dogmatics* (Philadelphia: Westminster, 1950), 306.

19. Herman Ridderbos, *The Coming of the Kingdom* (Philadelphia: Presbyterian & Reformed, 1962), 170.

Scot McKnight claims, "Jesus' kingdom vision and atonement are related; separating them is an act of violence."[20]

HISTORY OF INTERPRETATION

Although there has always been confusion with or resistance to the paradoxical integration of kingdom and cross, such a stark division has not always been the case.[21] In the first century, Barnabas declared that "the kingdom of Jesus is based on the wooden cross" (*Epistle of Barnabas* 8:5).[22] According to Augustine, "The Lord has established his sovereignty from a tree. Who is it who fights with wood? Christ. From his cross he has conquered kings."[23] Luther chastises those who "cannot harmonize the two ideas—that Christ should be the King of Kings and that He should also suffer and be executed."[24]

These representative quotes, along with the reasons given above for the kingdom–cross divide, reveal that this division is an essentially modern (post-Enlightenment) problem.[25] Much of the church's tradition, therefore, will

---

20. Scot McKnight, *A Community Called Atonement* (Nashville: Abingdon, 2007), 13; cf. N. T. Wright, *How God Became King: The Forgotten Story of the Gospels* (New York: HarperOne, 2012), xi.

21. For example, Morwenna Ludlow demonstrates that, although Justin Martyr attributed Christ's suffering to his first coming and his kingship to his second coming, he was not representative of the early church, which had a much more unified view of Christ's suffering and kingship ("Suffering Servant or King of Glory? Christological Readings of the Old Testament in the Patristic Era," in *Christology and Scripture: Interdisciplinary Perspectives* (ed. Andrew Lincoln and Angus Paddison; London: T&T Clark, 2007], 104–19).

22. Michael Holmes, ed. and trans., *The Apostolic Fathers in English* (3rd ed.; Grand Rapids: Baker Academic, 2006), 186.

23. Augustine, *Exposition of Psalm 95* (406–407), *WSA* 18:425.

24. Luther, *Psalm 110* (1539), *LW* 13:344.

25. This reading goes against N. T. Wright, who blames the kingdom–cross divide primarily on the creeds of the early church and the theology of the Reformers (*How God Became King*, 32, 43). Regarding the creeds, David Yeago has shown that the judgments of Nicea are consistent with the New Testament ("The New Testament and the Nicene Dogma: A Contribution to the Recovery of Theological Exegesis," *ProEccl* 3 [1994]: 152–64) and that the creed's presentation of the crucifixion captures the theological ("for us") and historical ("under Pontius Pilate") shape of the creed within the broader narrative of creation and redemption (idem, "Crucified Also for Us under Pontius Pilate," in *Nicene Christianity: The Future for a New Ecumenism* (ed. Christopher Seitz; Grand Rapids: Brazos, 2001], 87–106). Regarding the Reformers, Wright's accusation of a narrow gospel of atonement and justification is simply inaccurate. Luther said, "The gospel is a story about Christ, God's and David's son, who died and was raised, and is established as Lord. This is the gospel in a nutshell" (*A Brief Instruction on What to Look For in the Gospels* [1522], *LW* 35:118). According to Calvin, the gospel has a "broad sense" that encompasses all the promises of God in redemptive history and a "higher sense" of God's grace in Christ for sinners (*Institutes of the Christian Religion* [ed. John McNeill, trans. Ford Lewis Battles, LCC; Louisville: Westminster John Knox, 2006], 2.9.2). By interacting with various stages of the tradition below, we hope to show that the kingdom–cross interplay, though largely absent today, has a rich heritage in the history of the church.

buttress my argument, though with the understanding that the kingdom–cross interplay was present but hardly explained and that our current situatedness requires not simply a reformulation of previous thought, but a fresh approach in light of contemporary questions and aided by modern advancements.

How, then, have scholars responded to the modern divide between kingdom and cross? Some have given partial answers within broader discussions on the doctrine of the kingdom or the atonement respectively. Ridderbos, in *The Coming of the Kingdom*, has an excellent six-page section titled, "The Kingdom and the Cross," where he asserts that the kingdom cannot be understood apart from the cross, nor the cross without the kingdom.[26] McKnight weighs in on the recent atonement debates, seeking to shift the emphasis of atonement from personal salvation to God's cosmic purposes for all creation. The kingdom is "the telic vision of what atonement is designed to accomplish."[27]

The doctrine of the atonement is perhaps the most important place this discussion has played out, though not necessarily in the language of kingdom and cross. Among contemporary debates, the two most controversial approaches to the atonement are penal substitution and *Christus Victor*, each offering a different view of what Christ accomplished on the cross.[28] *Christus Victor* emphasizes the cross as victory and the restoration of God's reign over the cosmos, whereas penal substitution focuses on the reconciliation of God's people. While many have attempted to use *Christus Victor* alone as a way to connect kingdom and cross,[29] others have pointed to a more holistic approach that integrates penal substitution and *Christus Victor*.[30]

---

26. Ridderbos, *The Coming of the Kingdom*, 169–74.

27. McKnight, *A Community Called Atonement*, 13.

28. For the various positions and debates, see James Beilby and Paul Eddy, eds., *The Nature of the Atonement: Four Views* (Downers Grove, IL: InterVarsity Press, 2006); Derek Tidball, David Hilborn, and Justin Thacker, eds., *The Atonement Debate: Papers from the London Symposium on the Theology of Atonement* (Grand Rapids: Zondervan, 2008); John Sanders, ed., *Atonement and Violence.*

29. Gustaf Aulén, *Christus Victor: An Historical Study of the Three Main Types of the Idea of Atonement* (New York: Macmillan, 1969); Gregory Boyd, "*Christus Victor* View," in *The Nature of the Atonement*, 23–49.

30. Henri Blocher, "*Agnus Victor*: The Atonement as Victory and Vicarious Punishment," in *What Does It Mean to Be Saved? Broadening Evangelical Horizons of Salvation* (ed. John Stackhouse; Grand Rapids: Baker Academic, 2002), 67–91; idem, *La doctrine du péché et de la rédemption* (Vaux-sur-Seine, France: EDIFAC, 2000), 95–172; Hans Boersma, *Violence, Hospitality, and the Cross: Reappropriating the Atonement Tradition* (Grand Rapids: Baker Academic, 2004); Graham Cole, *God the Peacemaker: How Atonement Brings Shalom* (NSBT; Downers Grove, IL: InterVarsity Press, 2009); Sinclair Ferguson, "*Christus Victor et Propitiator*: The Death of Christ, Substitute and Conqueror," in *For the Fame of God's Name* (ed. Sam Storms and Justin Taylor; Wheaton, IL: Crossway, 2010), 171–89.

The question of the kingdom and the cross has also been answered by a few scholars in works limited to particular books or sections of Scripture. Michael Bird addresses kingdom and cross in Mark's gospel.[31] In a recent and superb work, Mavis Leung demonstrates that there is a kingship–cross interplay throughout the gospel of John.[32] N. T. Wright's recent work focuses on reconnecting kingdom and cross in all four Gospels.[33]

There is one particular area where the relationship of the kingdom and the cross has received a great deal of attention: the quest for the historical Jesus.[34] Historical Jesus scholars have set out with vigor to discover Jesus' self-perception of his vocation, specifically regarding the relationship of his preaching of the kingdom and of his journey to the cross. This is primarily where N. T. Wright's weighty contribution falls. In *Jesus and the Victory of God*, Wright directly addresses the relationship of the kingdom and the cross in a sustained manner, arguing that "Jesus . . . believed that the kingdom would be brought about by means of his own death."[35] Wright's conclusion is compelling, and his methodological aim unmistakable: this is "the *mindset* of Jesus."[36]

When considered within the field of historical Jesus studies, however, Wright's contribution is not exactly novel. In response to Bultmann, who saw Jesus' self-perception as inaccessible to historical inquiry and therefore irrelevant to the matter, many have attempted to demonstrate that Christ's own view of his death is not only accessible but an "essential ingredient" to understanding Jesus.[37] Of those who have undertaken this task, several have noted that no theory of Jesus' own perception of his death should be taken seriously if it does not take into account the larger context of his preaching the

---

31. Michael Bird, "The Crucifixion of Jesus as the Fulfillment of Mark 9:1," *TJ* 24 (2003): 23–36. Bird elaborated on his views at the 2010 IBR annual meeting in Atlanta in a lecture titled, "The Crucicentric Kingdom and the Basileianic Cross," which was a response to N. T. Wright's plenary lecture, "The Kingdom and the Cross." Bird and Wright appealed strongly to *Christus Victor* as the way to connect kingdom and cross.

32. Mavis Leung, *The Kingship–Cross Interplay in the Gospel of John: Jesus' Death as Corroboration of His Royal Messiahship* (Eugene, OR: Wipf & Stock, 2011); see also idem, "The Roman Empire and John's Passion Narrative in Light of Jewish Royal Messianism," *BSac* 168 (2011): 426–42.

33. Wright, *How God Became King*.

34. For an extensive overview of historical Jesus research related to Jesus's death, see Scot McKnight, *Jesus and His Death: Historiography, the Historical Jesus, and Atonement Theory* (Waco, TX: Baylor University Press, 2005).

35. N. T. Wright, *Jesus and the Victory of God* (Christian Origins and the Question of God; Minneapolis: Fortress, 1996), 612. Chapter 12 is Wright's most sustained answer to the question of the kingdom and the cross. See also idem, *The Challenge of Jesus: Rediscovering Who Jesus Was and Is* (Downers Grove, IL: InterVarsity Press, 1999), 74–95; idem, "Whence and Whither Historical Jesus Studies in the Life of the Church?" 137–47; Marcus Borg and N. T. Wright, *The Meaning of Jesus: Two Visions* (San Francisco: Harper, 1999), 93–107.

36. Wright, *Jesus and the Victory of God*, 592, italics mine.

37. John Galvin, "Jesus' Approach to Death: An Examination of Some Recent Studies," *TS* 41 (1980): 713–44.

kingdom of God.[38] Jürgen Becker, in a matter-of-fact way, writes, "Since all of Jesus' activity was dedicated to the kingdom of God, it would make sense that he saw his anticipated death as having some relation to that kingdom."[39]

Perhaps the most thorough and sustained explanation of this relationship comes from German New Testament scholar Heinz Schürmann. Schürmann begins his *Gottes Reich, Jesu Geschick: Jesu ureigener Tod im Licht seiner Basileia-Verkündigung* (*God's Kingdom, Jesus' Fate: The Death of Jesus in Light of His Own Kingdom-Proclamation*) by revealing the fundamental problem to which he devoted much of his career, namely, that there appear already in the New Testament two essentially different doctrines of salvation.[40] While the post-Easter "staurological soteriology" focuses on the atoning substitutionary death of Jesus, the pre-Easter "eschatological soteriology" emphasizes the kingdom of God.[41] Schürmann insists these two conceptions of salvation, although seemingly distinct, must be understood as unified in Jesus' self-perception, which was passed on to the apostles. For Schürmann, Christ's death can only be understood "in the context of his kingdom-proclamation."[42]

What do I make of this quest for Jesus' self-perception regarding the kingdom and the cross? At the most basic level, it is simply attempting to answer a different question: How do the kingdom and the cross relate *in the mind of Jesus*? I am seeking to understand the kingdom and the cross *in the Bible and Christian theology*. Although the two questions are not unrelated, they remain different questions with different sources and presuppositions. Richard Hays's critique of N. T. Wright's method captures my concern: "Instead of attending to the distinctive portrayals of Jesus in the individual New Testament texts, [Wright] aims instead at something else: a reconstruction of the historical figure of Jesus behind the texts, including the construction of an account about Jesus' intentions and his self-understanding."[43] Though

---

38. Jacques Schlosser, *Jésus de Nazareth* (Paris: Noesis, 1999), 299–301; Helmut Merklein, "Der Tod Jesu als stellvertretender Sühnetod," in *Studien zu Jesus und Paulus* (WUNT 43; Tübingen: Mohr Siebeck, 1987), 184–85; A. Vögtle, "Todesankündigungen und Todesverständnis Jesu," in *Der Tod Jesu: Deutungen im Neuen Testament* (ed. Karl Kertelge; Herder: Freiburg, 1976), 56–57; Seyoon Kim, *The "Son of Man" as the Son of God* (WUNT 30 Tübingen: J. C. B. Mohr, 1983), 99.

39. Jürgen Becker, *Jesus of Nazareth* (New York: de Gruyter, 1998), 341.

40. Heinz Schürmann, *Gottes Reich, Jesu Geschick: Jesu ureigener Tod im Licht seiner Basileia-Verkündigung* (Freiburg, Breisgau: Herder, 1983), 11–20.

41. Ibid., 11.

42. Heinz Schürmann, "Jesu ureigenes Todesverständnis: Bemerkungen zur 'impliziten Soteriologie' Jesu," in *Jesus, Gestalt und Geheimnis: Gesammelte Beiträge* (ed. Klaus Scholtissek; Paderborn: Bonifatius, 1994), 168.

43. Richard Hays, "Knowing Jesus: Story, History, and the Question of Truth," in *Jesus, Paul, and the People of God*," 48–49. Wright's method makes interaction with him complex, if not difficult. Wright has contributed to the discussion on the kingdom and the cross as much as anyone, and although we differ in many ways, our overall theses are congruent. Because of

Scripture certainly reveals that Jesus did think and pray about his own vocation, the aim of Christian faith (and theology) is not to ascertain the self-perception of Jesus by means of historical reconstruction but to understand Jesus through the witness of Scripture.

In sum, although several have begun to ask the question of the kingdom and the cross, and some have proposed brief answers, there is little on constructively integrating kingdom and cross, and none that does so in tandem with biblical *and* systematic theology. What is needed is not only the assertion that atonement and kingdom belong together, but a biblically rooted and theologically formed articulation of *how* they relate.

BIBLICAL AND SYSTEMATIC THEOLOGY

The fact that atonement and kingdom have often been divided by a particular disciplinary wall requires this project to integrate biblical and systematic theology. Defining the relationship between the two disciplines, however, is a difficult task inasmuch as the nature of each is greatly disputed in its own right. Beginning with a brief history of this wounded relationship, I will demonstrate how biblical and systematic theology are distinct yet inseparable, thereby revealing what I mean by each and how they relate.

Biblical and systematic theology (understood in the broadest senses) have been in happy union throughout most of church history. Whether Augustine, Aquinas, Calvin, or Wesley, Christians thinking at a high level felt no obligation to pick methodological sides.[44] In 1787, however, J. P. Gabler drove a wedge between the two disciplines in his famous inaugural address at the University of Altdorf, titled, "An Oration on the Proper Distinction between Biblical and Dogmatic Theology and the Specific Objectives of Each."[45] Gabler called for a distinct separation of the two disciplines, arguing for biblical theology as a strictly historical enterprise to be conducted apart from the church's theological biases.

---

the methodological differences, I have focused my interaction on Wright's latest contribution in *How God Became King*, where he claims to be "bracketing out issues of historical referent" (xiii). However, he later acknowledges that the book as a whole is based on his previous work in *The New Testament and the People of God* (ibid., 277).

44. The following brief historical survey follows Edward Klink and Darian Lockett, *Understanding Biblical Theology: A Comparison of Theory and Practice* (Grand Rapids: Zondervan, 2012), 13–17. For a more extensive historical overview, see James Meed, *Biblical Theology: Issues, Methods, and Themes* (Louisville: Westminster John Knox, 2007), 13–60.

45. See J. Sandys-Wunsch and L. Eldredge, "J. P. Gabler and the Distinction between Biblical and Dogmatic Theology: Translation, Commentary, and Discussion of His Originality," *SJT* 33 (1980): 133–58.

This separation between biblical and systematic theology was cemented in academia by the development of the German university system and largely persists today,[46] often in line with Krister Stendahl's assertion that biblical theology focuses on "what [the Bible] meant" and systematic theology on "what it means."[47] Although the Biblical Theology Movement was declared dead in the 1960s for attempting to uphold orthodox Christian theology *and* (or *by means of*) a modernistic epistemology and methodology,[48] biblical theology itself is still alive, though its definition and relation to systematic theology is disputed.[49]

How, then, do I define biblical and systematic theology in comparison to one another? The key is that both draw from the same source of Scripture, yet have different emphases. Geerhardus Vos made a similar argument, though he is known more for his contribution to biblical theology than for defining its relationship to systematic theology. The key for Vos, contra much current thought that depicts biblical theology as closer to the text than systematic theology, is that both are equally bound to Scripture, albeit with different principles of interpretation: "There is no difference in that one would be more closely bound to Scripture than the other. In this they are wholly alike. . . . The difference arises from the fact that the principle by which the transformation is effected differs in each case. In Biblical Theology this principle is one of historical, in Systematic Theology it is one of logical construction."[50]

Biblical and systematic theology, therefore, both draw from Scripture and seek to understand its unity, albeit in different ways.[51] Biblical theology emphasizes the unity of Scripture through the unfolding history of redemption[52] or, in literary terms, the development of the plot in its

---

46. Richard Lints notes the impact of the university system on the specialization of theological disciplines (*The Fabric of Theology: A Prolegomenon to Evangelical Theology* [Grand Rapids: Eerdmans, 1993], 272).

47. Krister Stendahl, "Biblical Theology, Contemporary," *IDB*, 1:419–20.

48. Langdon Gilkey, "Cosmology, Ontology, and the Travail of Biblical Language," *JR* 41 (1961): 194.

49. For a helpful taxonomy of types of biblical theology, see Klink and Lockett, *Understanding Biblical Theology*.

50. Geerhardus Vos, *Biblical Theology: Old and New Testaments* (Grand Rapids: Eerdmans, 1948), 24–25.

51. Trevor Hart, "Systematic—In What Sense?" in *Out of Egypt: Biblical Theology and Biblical Interpretation* (ed. Craig Bartholomew et al.; Grand Rapids: Zondervan, 2004), 345.

52. I use "history of redemption" not primarily as a technical term (the concept of redemptive history was present in the early church and Reformers long before *Heilsgeschichte* spurred debates in nineteenth-century Germany) but rather as a conceptual framework for understanding the continuity of Old and New Testaments and the progressive nature of revelation. My use of this phrase is largely in line with Ridderbos (*Paul: An Outline of His Theology* [Grand Rapids: Eerdmans, 1975], 44–90) or, more recently, Brian Rosner ("Salvation, History of," *DTIB*, 714–17). Although "redemptive history" and "salvation history" are often used synonymously, I use "redemption" intentionally because, along with the idea of liberation or rescue, it includes the cost of such an exchange (see Morris, *The Apostolic Preaching of the Cross* (3rd rev. ed.; Grand Rapids: Eerdmans, 1965], 11–64).

story line.[53] Systematic theology seeks to understand the unity of Scripture through the logic of its theology and the way in which individual doctrines fit together as a coherent whole.

It is important to note, however, that these are *emphases*, not exclusive roles. In other words, biblical theology focuses on the history or story of redemption and systematic theology on its logic, but neither discipline can neglect logic or narrative respectively. John Webster goes out of his way to protect this point, fearing that Vos's definition could remove the systematic theologian's obligation and privilege of attending to the redemptive-historical shape of revelation.[54] Webster is right, along with others, to insist that redemptive history is a crucial aspect of systematic theology, not just its opening act.[55] The concerns of Vos and Webster, however, are not incompatible. Redemptive history can be emphasized in biblical theology, but still be present in systematic theology. And it should, lest one fall into what Graham Cole calls "The Peril of 'Historyless' Systematic Theology."[56]

Furthermore, biblical and systematic theology differ in their language and dialogue partners. Biblical theology's aim is to set forth the theology of the Bible in its own terms, concepts, and contexts. Systematic theology seeks not only to understand the theology of the Bible, but to bring it into conversation with the tradition of the church and contemporary theology in order to communicate sound doctrine and correct false doctrine. Therefore, although biblical and systematic theology are closely related and inseparable in practice, a distinction between the two is still valid.

In sum, I offer the following brief definitions. *Biblical theology is faith seeking understanding of the redemptive-historical and literary unity of the Bible in its own terms, concepts, and contexts. Systematic theology is faith seeking understanding of the logical coherence of the Bible in conversation with the church's tradition and contemporary theology.*

---

53. For the literary aspect of biblical theology, see Craig Bartholomew and Michael Goheen, "Story and Biblical Theology," in *Out of Egypt*, 144–71; D. A. Carson, "Systematic Theology and Biblical Theology," *NDBT*, 100. In light of the historical and literary dimensions of biblical theology I will use both "redemptive history" and "story of redemption."

54. John Webster, "Principles of Systematic Theology," *IJST* 11 (2009): 70; cf. idem, "Biblical Theology and the Clarity of Scripture," in *Out of Egypt*, 361.

55. Michael Horton, *Covenant and Eschatology: The Divine Drama* (Louisville: Westminster John Knox, 2002); Kevin Vanhoozer, *The Drama of Doctrine: A Canonical-Linguistic Approach to Christian Theology* (Louisville: Westminster John Knox, 2005); Hart, "Systematic—In What Sense?" 350; Michael Williams, "Systematic Theology As a Biblical Discipline," in *All For Jesus: A Celebration of the 50th Anniversary of Covenant Theological Seminary* (ed. Robert Peterson and Sean Michael Lucas; Fearn, UK: Christian Focus, 2006), 167–96.

56. Graham Cole, "The Peril of a 'Historyless' Systematic Theology," in *Do Historical Matters Matter to Faith? A Critical Appraisal of Modern and Postmodern Approaches to Scripture* (ed. James Hoffmeier and Dennis Magary; Wheaton, IL: Crossway, 2012), 55–70.

Having stated the similarities and distinctions between biblical and systematic theology, their relation can now be addressed. The key here, contra much current thought that assumes a simple linear step from biblical to systematic theology, is that their relationship is bidirectional. The two disciplines, while remaining distinct in their emphases, should enrich one another in the broader task of Christian theology.

Vern Poythress rightly acknowledges this bidirectional relationship and offers several practical ways in which the disciplines interact. Biblical theology enriches systematic theology by reminding it of (1) the redemptive-historical nature of revelation, (2) the need for actual exegesis of the texts used, and (3) the systematizing process already beginning to take place within Scripture.[57] The "reverse influence of systematic theology on biblical theology" is that biblical theology presupposes the central truths of orthodox theology.[58] The basic idea here is that one need not check their theological convictions at the exegetical door in order to give Scripture the final authority.[59] Although using the best tools available from the guild, biblical theology remains faith seeking understanding.[60] In sum, systematic theology draws from, further develops, and informs biblical theology.

How does this mutually enriching, bidirectional approach to biblical and systematic theology play out in practice? While the order of authority clearly goes from Scripture to theology, the fact that one cannot simply set aside their theological presuppositions means that the order of practice is caught up in a hermeneutical spiral.[61] Though there is interplay throughout, the natural order is that theology emerges from the narrative of Scripture. As Alister McGrath explains, "Doctrine is generated by, and subsequently interprets the Christian narrative."[62]

---

57. Vern Poythress, "Kinds of Biblical Theology," *WTJ* 70 (2008): 132.

58. Ibid., 133.

59. The most obvious example is that biblical theology as a whole rests on a particular doctrine of Scripture. As Webster says, "Biblical theology is a corollary of the unity of Scripture as the church's canon" ("Biblical Theology and the Clarity of Scripture," 352).

60. This point reveals that I see much overlap between biblical theology and the movement known as theological interpretation of Scripture. Although biblical theology seems to place more emphasis on the unfolding nature of redemptive history, I equally resonate with the recurring themes in theological interpretation of Scripture, such as embracing theological presuppositions, awareness of the tradition, and interpreting in community. For a general introduction to this movement, see Daniel Treier, *Introducing Theological Interpretation of Scripture: Recovering a Christian Practice* (Grand Rapids: Baker Academic, 2008); J. Todd Billings, *The Word of God for the People of God: An Entryway to the Theological Interpretation of Scripture* (Grand Rapids: Eerdmans, 2010). For a taxonomy of the relationship between biblical theology and theological interpretation of Scripture, see Daniel Treier, "Biblical Theology and/or Theological Interpretation of Scripture?" *SJT* 61 (2008): 16–31.

61. Grant Osborne, *The Hermeneutical Spiral: A Comprehensive Introduction to Biblical Interpretation* (Downers Grove, IL: InterVarsity Press, 2006).

62. Alister McGrath, *The Genesis of Doctrine: A Study in the Foundations of Doctrinal Criticism* (Grand Rapids: Eerdmans, 1997), 37.

Therefore, in this book I will define the relationship between the kingdom and the cross, beginning with the theology of the Bible in its own terms, concepts, and context, with an emphasis on the unfolding history/story line of redemption (biblical theology), and then broaden the conversation by engaging with voices from church history and contemporary theology, with the aim of further coherence, correction of unbalanced/unbiblical depictions of kingdom and cross, and formulating doctrines in a way that will communicate in today's context.

THE KINGDOM *AND* THE CROSS

This book will not only demonstrate the inseparability of kingdom and cross, but will also define the way in which they relate. Part 1 traces the relationship between the kingdom and the cross as it unfolds in the story line of Scripture. Chapter 1 focuses on the Old Testament, for the kingdom and the cross can only be understood as the culmination of themes developed throughout the story of Israel. I offer a panoramic sweep of the Old Testament, tracing the way in which the victory and suffering promised to the seed (Gen 3:15) develop into the royal victory and atoning suffering of the Messiah. Chapter 2 then zooms in on Isaiah as the high point of Old Testament prophecy, where these themes converge in the figure of the servant, who brings the kingdom through his atoning suffering.[63]

Chapters 3 and 4 look at atonement and kingdom as they are fulfilled in Christ from the perspective of the New Testament authors. According to the gospel of Mark, Jesus proclaims his kingdom mission (Mark 1:1–8:21), explains its paradoxical nature (8:22–10:52), and then establishes the kingdom on the cross (11–16:8). In Colossians, the "kingdom of his beloved Son" (Col 1:13) and the "blood of his cross" (1:20) are woven into the same story of eschatological transference into the kingdom, reconciliation to God, and defeat of evil powers. The book of Revelation explicitly says that king Jesus "has freed us from our sins by his blood and made us a kingdom" (Rev 1:5–6)—later described as a lion-like victory through lamb-like means (5:5–6) that entails the defeat of Satan by Christ and his followers (12:10–11).

---

63. The goal here is to capture breadth *and* depth. I therefore touch briefly on key passages as I move throughout the canon, but go deep into the two books that are arguably the most relevant for this discussion (Isaiah with the Davidic king and the Suffering Servant, and Mark with Jesus' proclamation of the kingdom and journey to the cross). I focus on Mark (as opposed to the other gospels) because of the explicit connection with Isaiah and the clear emphasis on both kingdom and cross.

Chapter 5 summarizes my findings and furthers the argument through four key points for understanding kingdom and cross in biblical theology.

First, the Old Testament (and especially Isaiah 40–55) is the proper context for understanding the kingdom and the cross. The Old Testament background includes the story of victory through sacrifice as well as concepts such as covenant and temple, and leads to the observation that the promises of the kingdom in the Old Testament are fulfilled (in an "already/not yet" sense) in the cross of Christ in the New Testament.

Second, kingdom and cross play distinct and yet inseparable roles in the story of redemption. The kingdom is *telic* (the goal toward which everything moves) and the cross is *central* (the climax and turning point of the story), and they intersect as the end-time kingdom breaks into history through the cross.

Third, the cross does not merely fall in between the ages of redemptive history; it causes the shift from one to the other. In other words, the great exchange on the cross effects the great transition to the age of the kingdom of God.

Finally, and as the main thesis of Part I, the kingdom of God is established on earth by Christ's atoning death on the cross. Within the broader spectrum of all Christ's work (incarnation, life, resurrection, ascension, Pentecost, parousia), Christ's death is the decisive moment in the coming of God's kingdom.

Part 2 extends the study from biblical to systematic theology, turning the focus to the logic of kingdom and cross in conversation with the tradition and contemporary theology. At the most basic level, the kingdom and the cross are held together by the Christ. Therefore, I focus on each of the doctrines of Christology, atonement, and kingdom. Chapter 6 presents an argument for the kingship of Christ on the cross, which thereby demands a reconsideration of the often overly categorized states and offices of Christ. In place of a strictly successive view of the states of Christ (exaltation *after* humiliation), I propose exaltation *in* humiliation within the broader movement of exaltation *through* humiliation. The rethinking of the *munus triplex* rejects sharp lines drawn between Christ's offices and thereby seeks to resituate Christ's death not only as a priestly act, but as a kingly one as well. Far from doing away with these doctrines, my argument actually calls for a return to their original forms.

After discussing the necessity of a proper approach to the doctrine of the atonement in chapter 7, chapter 8 enters into contemporary atonement debates, specifically addressing the hostile relationship between penal substitution and *Christus Victor*. This chapter is especially significant for this project because *Christus Victor* has often been used as a connector between the kingdom and the cross, though usually to the exclusion of penal substitution. I will first discuss the common approach of pitting *Christus Victor* against penal substitution and then argue that Christ's penal-substitutionary death is the means for his victory on the cross—*Christus Victor* through penal substitution. *Christus Victor* is important for connecting kingdom and cross, but only if properly integrated with penal substitution. On the cross, Jesus bears the penalty for sin by taking the place of sinners, thereby defeating Satan and establishing God's kingdom on earth.

Chapter 9 shifts the attention from the royal nature of the cross to the cruciform shape of the kingdom. By applying Luther's theology of the cross to the kingdom of God, I offer a constructive proposal for a kingdom that is hidden in this age beneath the foolishness of the cross but understood through faith to be the power and wisdom of God. I then engage Jürgen Moltmann who, as a systematic theologian, has dealt extensively with the kingdom of God and argues for its cruciform nature. Unfortunately, in his zeal for understanding God through the revelation of the cross, Moltmann redefines (if not denies altogether) the kingship of God. According to Moltmann, God rules *only* through saving and serving. In response, I present a doctrine of God that recognizes the Lord as the compassionate *and* just king, who rules through saving *and* judging. The chapter closes with a brief discussion of the way in which God advances his kingdom—namely, through Christians who have been united to Christ and are being conformed to his cross by the power of his resurrection.

Before moving on to the already begging question of how I define kingdom and atonement respectively, I offer one final qualification. My discussion of Christ's *atoning death* in relation to God's kingdom is meant to be received in harmony with (not in exclusion to) the other aspects of Christ's work, such as his life, resurrection, ascension, sending of the Spirit, and second coming. All the aspects are inseparable, and yet they play different roles theologically. The link between the cross and resurrection is especially significant for the coming of God's kingdom. Although I will address this connection throughout, I cannot put it better than N. T. Wright, who says that "the resurrection is precisely the resurrection of the kingdom-bringer, the crucified kingdom-bringer, and that these elements are not left behind in the resurrection but rather fulfilled."[64]

---

64. Wright, "Whence and Whither Historical Jesus Studies in the Life of the Church?" 147.

DEFINING KEY TERMS

THE KINGDOM OF GOD

The kingdom of God is widely acknowledged as the primary theme of Jesus' preaching, and many argue that it is the unifying motif of the Old Testament, New Testament, and even the Bible as a whole.[65] However, despite ten thousand scholarly publications on the kingdom of God in the last century, there has been little consensus on its definition.[66]

At the most basic level, ἡ βασιλεία τοῦ θεοῦ refers to the concept of God's reign.[67] In broader terms, the kingdom of God entails the fulfillment of all the promises of God for salvation.[68] Somewhere in between these two approaches, I offer a practical working definition of the kingdom of God that certainly does not say everything, but attempts to capture its essence. I offer this definition in two phases: the design of the kingdom in creation and the coming of the kingdom in redemption.[69] After defining the kingdom of God, I will then explain the entailments of the kingdom of God.

THE DESIGN OF THE KINGDOM IN CREATION

As we will see in the next chapter, Genesis 1–2 presents the *telos* of creation as *God's reign through his servant-kings over creation*—that is the design of the kingdom of God. I will make two observations about this design, followed by a phrase-by-phrase explanation. First, the order of the sentence reveals the order of significance in defining God's kingdom. The kingdom is foremost about *God's* reign; then, human vicegerency; and then, the realm of God's reign. Second, while ἡ βασιλεία τοῦ θεοῦ primarily refers to the reign of God, the elements of people and place have been acknowledged broadly. Gerhard

---

65. For example, John Bright, *The Kingdom of God: The Biblical Concept and Its Meaning for the Church* (Nashville: Abingdon, 1957), 7; Ladd, *The Presence of the Future*, xi.

66. Lesław Chrupcała, *The Kingdom of God: A Bibliography of 20th Century Research* (Jerusalem: Franciscan, 2007). An updated version of this bibliography (2012) is available online at http://198.62.75.4/opt/xampp/custodia/?p=2259 (accessed 27 August 2012). For a brief historical survey of the kingdom of God in theology, see Stephen Nichols, "The Kingdom of God: The Kingdom in Historical and Contemporary Perspectives," in *The Kingdom of God* (ed. Christopher Morgan and Robert Peterson; Theology in Community; Wheaton, IL: Crossway, 2012), 25–48. For a more in-depth study, see Benedict Viviano, *The Kingdom of God in History* (Wilmington, DE: Glazier, 1988).

67. R. T. France, "Kingdom of God," *DTIB*, 420.

68. Ladd, *The Presence of the Future*, 205.

69. There has been a long time consensus that "kingdom of heaven" in Matthew is synonymous with "kingdom of God" elsewhere. However, Jonathan Pennington has added the important qualification that Matthew's use of "kingdom of heaven" is part of his broader theology regarding the tension and eventual resolution between heaven and earth (*Heaven and Earth in the Gospel of Matthew* [NovTSup 126; Boston: Brill, 2007]).

von Rad says these twin themes "run through the whole canon like a *cantus firmus*."[70] Stephen Dempster articulates the concepts of place and people with the terms "dominion and dynasty," as well as geography and genealogy, land and lineage, Zion and scion.[71]

God's Reign

The kingdom of God is first and foremost a statement about God—who he is (king) and what he does (reign). Although this divine focus should be obvious (it is, after all, the kingdom *of God*), recent history proves otherwise. The social gospel movement spoke of the kingdom as the realization of human potential in making the world a better place. A more recent definition of the kingdom observes that "the notion of the kingdom as an ideal society, characterized by equality, justice, and freedom, has gradually been accepted."[72] The problem with both of these definitions is that they simply leave out God, the king who makes the kingdom what it is. If one defines the kingdom as a utopian world without mentioning God, they miss the whole point of the kingdom, which redefines the world in terms of God's kingship. R. T. France puts it well, "'The kingdom of God' is not making a statement about a 'thing' called 'the kingdom,' but about *God*, that he is king."[73] The eschatological hope of Israel was not a godless paradisiacal world but rather that "the LORD will be king over all the earth" (Zech 14:9).

The kingdom of God does not refer merely to a general or abstract concept of God's sovereignty (God *is* king), but to his active, dynamic reign in history. God's dynamic reign was evident even before the fall when God was busy expanding his blessing—bringing dominion over all the earth through his image bearers (Gen 1:26–28; 2:15; cf. Psalm 8). While the reign versus realm debate of past generations was certainly polarized, there is now a scholarly consensus that ἡ βασιλεία τοῦ θεοῦ refers primarily (though not solely) to God's dynamic *reign*.[74] Therefore, the message of the kingdom is not simply

---

70. Gerhard von Rad, "Typological Interpretation of the Old Testament," in *Essays on Old Testament Hermeneutics* (ed. Claus Westermann; Atlanta: John Knox, 1963), 31.

71. Stephen Dempster, *Dominion and Dynasty: A Biblical Theology of the Hebrew Bible* (NSBT; Downers Grove, IL: InterVarsity Press, 2003).

72. D. J. Smit, "Kingdom of God," *DEM*, 567.

73. France, "Kingdom of God," 420, italics his.

74. Gustaf Dalman set the standard in the early twentieth century by claiming מלכות and βασιλεία always mean reign and never realm (*The Words of Jesus* [trans. D. M. Kay; Edinburgh: T&T Clark, 1902], 94). By 1962, however, the influential work of Ladd demonstrated that the kingdom refers primarily to God's dynamic reign and derivatively to its realm ("The Kingdom of God: Reign or Realm?" *JBL* 81 [1962]: 236). For a discussion of contemporary nuances to this consensus, see Pennington, *Heaven and Earth in the Gospel of Matthew*, 254–55, 281–85.

that God *is* king, but that God will come *as* king and set right what human sin has made wrong.

Through His Servant-Kings

Human vicegerency entails three significant points. First, God the creator-king reigns *over* all of his creatures, but he also reigns *through* his image-bearing servant-kings.[75] This theme has often been overlooked, but it is crucial to understanding the kingdom of God. Second, the relationship between the divine king and human servant-kings is a *covenant*. The covenantal/relational aspect of the kingdom provides the proper context for understanding God's kingship. Third, the scope of God's eschatological kingdom is as wide as creation, but the focus is on his people. In other words, while the kingdom of God captures the comprehensive nature of God's work, it still maintains the special place of humanity.

Over Creation

God's reign over and through his servant-kings requires a realm.[76] In Genesis 1–2, the realm of God's rule is Eden, but the eschatological goal is for God's reign to be over all the earth. The message of the kingdom is not an escape from earth to heaven, but the very renewal of the heavens and the earth. It was for this reason that Jesus prayed for God's kingdom to come "on earth as it is in heaven" (Matt 6:10). Bonhoeffer expressed well the *this-worldliness* of the kingdom, saying that only those "who love both earth and God at the same time, can believe in the kingdom of God."[77]

THE COMING OF THE KINGDOM IN REDEMPTION

After the fall, God's kingdom remained the eschatological goal, although now in the form not only of eschatology but of redemption. It was this kingdom—the *redemptive* reign of God—that Jesus proclaimed throughout his ministry. Jesus'

---

75. I use "servant-kings" as a parallel to what scholars often refer to as "vice-regents." For two excellent articles on the importance of human vicegerency in creation and therefore the restoration of vicegerency in the kingdom of God, see Dan McCartney, "*Ecce homo*: The Coming of the Kingdom as the Restoration of Human Vicegerency," *WTJ* 56 (1994): 1–21; Roy Ciampa, "The History of Redemption," in *Central Themes in Biblical Theology: Mapping Unity in Diversity* (ed. Scott Hafemann and Paul House; Grand Rapids: Baker Academic, 2007), 254–308.

76. As Ladd says, "The kingdom is primarily the dynamic reign or kingly rule of God, and derivatively, the sphere in which the rule is experienced" (*A Theology of the New Testament* [Grand Rapids: Eerdmans, 1974], 109).

77. Dietrich Bonhoeffer, "Thy Kingdom Come: The Prayer of the Church For God's Kingdom on Earth," in *Preface to Bonhoeffer: The Man and Two of His Shorter Writings* (ed. John Godsey; Philadelphia: Fortress, 1965), 28.

proclamation of the kingdom was radical not because of its content, but because he announced its fulfillment in himself. Jesus is the servant-king through whom God establishes his reign over all the earth. Therefore, the redemptive nature of God's kingdom did not change its core character but rather expanded it to include this new way of bringing God's kingdom on earth. The following is my summative working definition of the kingdom of God:

The design of God's kingdom in creation: God's reign through his servant-kings over creation.
The coming of God's kingdom in redemption: God's *redemptive* reign through *Christ* and his *reconciled* servant-kings over the *new* creation.

THE ENTAILMENTS OF THE KINGDOM

In the Old Testament, the coming of the kingdom for redemption entailed, among other things, victory over evil, forgiveness of sins, and a new exodus.[78] I will briefly look at each, and will eventually demonstrate how they are interrelated in Christ's bringing the kingdom.

Victory over Evil

The coming of God's reign on earth entails the dethroning of the "ruler of this world" (John 12:31).[79] In the Old Testament, God's reign is first explicitly mentioned after the destruction of the Egyptians in redeeming Israel (Exod 15:18), and the prophetic hope for God's eternal kingdom includes the shattering of all earthly kingdoms (Dan 2:44). Jesus considered his exorcisms of demons evidence for the coming of God's kingdom (Matt 12:28–29), and in his exemplary prayer for the disciples (Matt 6:9–13), as Ridderbos observes, "the deliverance from the Evil One is the conclusion of the prayer for the coming of the kingdom."[80]

---

78. Jonathan Lunde lists the following entailments of the coming kingdom: "the judgment of Israel's enemies (e.g., Isa. 9:4–7; 11:1–9; 16:5; 32:1–5, 14–20; 42:1–9; 61:1–3; Jer. 30:21–22; 33:15–26; Ezek. 37:21–25; Joel 3:2, 12–13; Amos 9:11; Zech. 3:8; 6:12–13; 9:9–10 . . .); the return of the exiles (e.g., Isa. 11:1, 10–16; Mic. 4:6–8); the renewal of the land (e.g., Amos 9:13–15); the rebuilding of the temple (e.g., Ezek. 43:1–7); the coming of the Messiah (e.g., Ezek. 37:21–25); the establishment of a New Covenant (Jer. 31:31–34); the outpouring of the Spirit (e.g., Joel 2:28–29); the healing and purification of the people (e.g., Isa. 62:1–3; Jer. 33:6–8); and the inclusion of the nations in the blessings of the kingdom (e.g., Zech. 8:20–23)" (*Following Jesus, the Servant King: A Biblical Theology of Covenantal Discipleship* [Grand Rapids: Zondervan, 2010], 49).

79. For evidence in Second Temple Judaism and in Scripture, see Craig Evans, "Inaugurating the Kingdom of God and Defeating the Kingdom of Satan," *BBR* 15 (2005): 49–75.

80. Ridderbos, *The Coming of the Kingdom*, 108.

Forgiveness of Sins

The forgiveness of sins (inseparably linked with atonement in Leviticus) is a crucial element in the coming of the kingdom.[81] In the Old Testament, the key prophetic texts for God's kingdom include the promise of forgiveness (Isa 33:24; 40:2; 43:25; 44:22; Mic 7:18–20; Zech 13:1); Daniel 9:24 declares that the kingdom will come "to put an end to sin, and to atone for iniquity."[82] At the heart of the promised new covenant—also crucial to the kingdom—is the assurance of forgiveness of sins (Jer 31:31–34; Ezek 18:31; 36:22–28).[83]

In the New Testament, Jesus characterizes the coming of the kingdom with a parable of a king who forgives the servants of their debts (Matt 18:23–27). For Paul, it is significant that the two passages where he speaks most clearly of being transferred from the kingdom of Satan to the kingdom of God both include the forgiveness of sins (Acts 26:18; Col 1:13–14). Scholars have recognized this crucial aspect of the coming of the kingdom, calling the forgiveness of sins the central feature[84] or "heart and sum"[85] of the coming of the kingdom.[86]

New Exodus

From Eden to Canaan, land has been an essential ingredient in the kingdom of God. As Graeme Goldsworthy says, "If God rules, he rules somewhere."[87] The place of land in the kingdom of God is clearly evident in the pattern of redemption set forth in the exodus. God as king delivers Israel from bondage so that he might lead them to the promised land. Isaiah transforms this past redemption into future hope, as he prophesies how God as king might deliver his people again through a *new* exodus, resulting not only in a new land but in a new heavens and new earth (Isa 52:11–12; 65:17). Finally, Mark presents Jesus' ministry in terms of a new exodus (Mark 1:2–3), which Jesus then summarizes by saying, "The kingdom of God is at hand" (1:15). The

---

81. Hence, the oft-repeated phrase in Leviticus: "The priest shall make atonement for him for the sin which he has committed, and he shall be forgiven" (Lev 4:35; cf. 4:20, 26, 31; 5:10, 13, 16, 18; 6:7; 19:22).
82. See Dempster, *Dominion and Dynasty*, 218.
83. Peter Gentry and Stephen Wellum, *Kingdom through Covenant: A Biblical-Theological Understanding of the Covenants* (Wheaton, IL: Crossway, 2012), 650.
84. Ladd, *A Theology of the New Testament*, 77.
85. Ridderbos, *The Coming of the Kingdom*, 214; cf. Michael Horton, *The Christian Faith: A Systematic Theology for Pilgrims on the Way* (Grand Rapids: Zondervan, 2011), 545, 947.
86. George Buchanan demonstrates in the Old Testament and first-century Judaism that "sins had to be taken seriously and legally removed before kingdom could come" ("The Day of Atonement and Paul's Doctrine of Redemption," *NovT* 32 [1990]: 237).
87. Graeme Goldsworthy, "The Kingdom of God as Hermeneutic Grid," *SBJT* 12 (2008): 7.

kingdom entails God's deliverance *from* foreign oppressors and *for* the realm of God's new creation.

THE TIMING OF THE KINGDOM

The timing of the kingdom is perhaps the most shocking feature of Jesus' announcement: "The *time* is fulfilled, and the kingdom of God is *at hand*" (Mark 1:15, italics mine). While Dodd's "realized eschatology" defined the kingdom as wholly present in Jesus' ministry and Schweitzer's "consistent eschatology" relegated the kingdom solely to the future, there is a present scholarly consensus that the kingdom is *already* present and *not yet* consummated (inaugurated eschatology).[88]

ATONEMENT

The word "atonement" is a distinctively English word that has been used since the sixteenth century to describe the at-one-ment of parties formerly alienated.[89] Since Tyndale's use of the word to translate the Hebrew כפר (Lev 23:28) and the Greek καταλλαγή (2 Cor 5:18–19), "atonement" has become a technical term in theology, usually referring to the way in which Jesus' death reconciles God and sinners by removing sin and its effects.[90] While there has never been one "orthodox" view of the atonement, the traditional atonement theology since the Reformation has recently been questioned and even outright rejected by many.[91] In light of the various viewpoints within these debates, I offer my own brief definition of the atonement:

> The doctrine of the atonement is faith seeking understanding of the way in

---

88. Ladd, *A Theology of the New Testament*, 56.

89. For the history of the etymology "atonement," see Stephen Sykes, *The Story of Atonement* (London: Darton, Longman & Todd, 1997), 2–3.

90. The linguistic issues in the doctrine of the atonement are complex. Tyndale's translation of כפר as "atonement" has been rendered accurate, but καταλλαγή is better translated "reconciliation." The Greek ἱλαστήριον is the closest to כפר and debates have ensued as to whether it should be translated as propitiation (ESV), expiation (RSV), or sacrifice of atonement (NIV). For a helpful discussion of כפר, see Jay Sklar, *Sin, Impurity, Sacrifice, Atonement: The Priestly Conceptions* (Sheffield: Sheffield Phoenix, 2005). For ἱλαστήριον, see Morris, *The Apostolic Preaching of the Cross*, 144–213. Beyond the biblical languages, interaction with modern languages is difficult as well, for the English "atonement" can be translated into French as *redemption* or *expiation* and into German as *Versöhnung, Sühne,* or *Erlösung* (see Henri Blocher, "Atonement," *DTIB*, 72).

91. See, e.g., S. Mark Heim, *Saved from Sacrifice: A Theology of the Cross* (Grand Rapids: Eerdmans, 2006); Darrin W. Snyder Belousek, *Atonement, Justice, and Peace: The Message of the Cross and the Mission of the Church* (Grand Rapids: Eerdmans, 2012). For a survey of the doctrine of the atonement in modern theology, see Kevin Vanhoozer, "Atonement," in *Mapping Modern Theology: A Thematic and Historical Introduction* (ed. Kelly Kapic and Bruce L. McCormack; Grand Rapids: Baker Academic, 2012), 175–202.

which Christ, through all of his work but primarily his death, has dealt with sin and its effects in restoring the broken covenant relationship between God and humans and thereby brought about the turn of the ages. At its core, the doctrine of the atonement is the attempt to understand the meaning of Christ's death as "for our sins in accordance with the Scriptures" (1 Cor 15:3).

I will explain this definition by clarifying how the atonement includes outcome and means, a broad and narrow sense, vertical and horizontal dimensions, and is expansive and particular.

OUTCOME AND MEANS

The word *atonement* is often used in two different senses, which, neither right nor wrong, need to be clarified. On the one hand, atonement is referred to as the outcome of Christ's work (at-one-ment), and on the other hand, as the means of Christ's accomplishment (*making* atonement).[92] In the *outcome* approach, atonement is often synonymous with reconciliation or focuses on other effects of Christ's work such as peace[93] or community.[94] In the *means* approach, the focus is on the way in which such a state of reconciliation is achieved (e.g., sacrifice). In my estimation, most contemporary discussions of atonement focus on the outcome, whereas historically the emphasis has been on the means.[95] I believe both aspects are necessary for the doctrine of the atonement.[96] Theologically, atonement entails both at-one-ment *and* the means by which it is achieved.

---

92. Many have questioned the validity of attempting to explain the "how" of the atonement altogether. C. S. Lewis provides a classic statement: "We are told that Christ was killed for us, that His death has washed out our sins, and that by dying He disabled death itself. That is the formula. That is Christianity. That is what has to be believed. Any theories we build up as to how Christ's death did all this are, in my view, quite secondary; mere plans or diagrams to be left alone if they do not help us, and, even if they do help us, not to be confused with the thing itself" (*Mere Christianity: Comprising The Case for Christianity, Christian Behaviour, and Beyond Personality* [New York: Touchstone, 1996], 54–55). I believe in the validity of the "how" question for the following reasons: (1) Scripture does not merely stop at the fact of atonement, but does at least begin to explain the "how," which requires, or at least permits, theologians to do the same. (2) Historically, the "how" aspect has been a central part of atonement discussions.
93. Cole, *God the Peacemaker*.
94. McKnight, *A Community Called Atonement*.
95. For example, Gregory's fishhook theory ("An Address on Religious Instruction," in *Christology of the Later Fathers* (ed. Edward Hardy, LCC; Philadelphia: Westminster, 1954], 301), or Augustine's mouse-trap theory (*Sermon 263: On the Fortieth Day, The Ascension of the Lord* [396–97] *WSA* 7:220). Stephen Long says, "The atonement is the doctrine that seeks to show how Christ's life, death, and resurrection reconcile sinful creatures to God" ("Justification and Atonement," in *The Cambridge Companion to Evangelical Theology*, ed. Daniel Treier and Timothy Larsen [Cambridge: Cambridge University Press, 2007], 81).
96. See Henri Blocher, "The Sacrifice of Jesus Christ: The Current Theological Situation," *EuroJTh* 8 (1999): 31.

BROAD AND NARROW

To further specify the means of atonement, a distinction must be made between a broad and narrow sense of Christ's work. Robert Yarbrough helpfully distinguishes between all of Christ's work (the broad sense) and Christ's death (the narrow sense): "While in one sense the meaning of atonement is as broad and diverse as all of God's saving work throughout time and eternity, in another it is as particular and restricted as the crucifixion of Jesus. For in the final analysis Scripture presents his sacrificial death as the central component of God's reconciling mercy."[97] Both senses are necessary and must be properly related. In other words, Christ's atoning work refers primarily to his death on the cross, but includes the spectrum of Christ's work in his life, resurrection, ascension, sending of the Spirit, and second coming.

This distinction relates to the outcome/means distinction above, for all of Christ's work is atoning in the sense of reconciliation (at-one-ment), but inasmuch as atonement also includes the sacrificial means, the cross is of particular importance. Based on the Old Testament background, where atonement deals with sin through the shedding of blood, it is difficult to deny the strong connection between the cross and atonement.[98] This point does not take away from the broader spectrum of Christ's work, but ties Christ's *atoning* work especially to the cross. Atonement is centered on Christ's death within the broader spectrum of all of his work.[99]

VERTICAL AND HORIZONTAL

The doctrine of the atonement seeks to understand the meaning of Christ's death as "for our sins in accordance with the Scriptures" (1 Cor 15:3). While "for our sins" has provided the primary meaning of Christ's death in the history of atonement theology, the "in accordance with the Scriptures" adds a much-needed redemptive-historical and eschatological shape to the atonement.[100] In short, atonement entails vertical (*ordo salutis*) and horizontal (*historia salutis*) dimensions. The meaning of Christ's atoning death is not only the way in which it affects the vertical relationship between God and humanity, but also how it impacts the horizontal shape of redemptive history as it move toward the last days.

---

97. Robert Yarbrough, "Atonement," *NDBT*, 388.
98. The resurrection, for example, is certainly atoning in the sense of at-one-ment, but in terms of making atonement, Scripture makes no such connection.
99. See also Cole, *God the Peacemaker*, 25. For a more thorough discussion of the centrality of the cross in the doctrine of the atonement, see below, pp. 217–20.
100. Richard Gaffin, "Atonement in the Pauline Corpus: 'The Scandal of the Cross,'" in *The Glory of the Atonement: Biblical, Theological, and Practical Perspectives* (ed. Charles Hill and Frank James III; Downers Grove, IL: InterVarsity Press, 2004), 143.

The redemptive-historical aspect of the atonement has been recognized by a small number of scholars.[101] McGrath helpfully observes that "Christ's death did not take place in some sort of vacuum, but in the context of a tradition of recognizing the redemptive acts of God in human history."[102] McKnight claims that Jesus himself, by explaining his death in terms of the Passover and exodus, "storifies" his own death.[103] David Yeago commends the early church's crafting of the Nicene Creed in a way that upholds the meaning of Christ's death as "for us" within its proper historical narrative "under Pontius Pilate."[104]

Despite this great tradition, it seems that today many theologians have neglected the significance of redemptive history for the doctrine of the atonement. Contemporary atonement theology, for example, has been criticized for being de-historicized,[105] de-dramatized,[106] and decontextualized.[107] N. T. Wright's criticism is both representative and stinging: "So many popular presentations are far too abstract: they take the whole event out of its context in history, in the story of God and his people, and imagine it simply as a non-historical transaction between God and Jesus into which we can somehow be slotted."[108]

At what point did this error of detaching the cross from the story line of Scripture take place? Thomas Torrance claims that the allegorizing of the early church led to a depreciation of history and elevation of timeless truth.[109] Hans Boersma traces "de-historicizing tendencies" from the Augustinian tradition through Protestant scholasticism, and finally in John Owen's emphasis on Christ's death as a commercial transaction.[110] J. I. Packer says that the Reformed scholastics, while attempting to respond to the criticism of the Socinians, tried to beat them at their own game and, in their zeal to prove themselves rational, became rationalistic. The sad result, according to Packer, was that "they made the word of the cross sound more like a conundrum

101. See, e.g., D. C. Allison, *The End of the Ages Has Come* (Philadelphia: Fortress, 1985).
102. Alister McGrath, *The Mystery of the Cross* (Grand Rapids: Zondervan, 1988), 43.
103. McKnight, *A Community Called Atonement*, 83.
104. Yeago, "Crucified Also for Us under Pontius Pilate," 87–106.
105. Boersma, *Violence, Hospitality, and the Cross*, 168.
106. Vanhoozer, *The Drama of Doctrine*, 383.
107. Thomas Torrance, *Divine Meaning: Studies in Patristic Hermeneutics* (Edinburgh: T&T Clark, 1995), 22–25.
108. N. T. Wright, *The Crown and the Fire: Meditations on the Cross and the Life of the Spirit* (Grand Rapids: Eerdmans, 1995), 122; see also Jenson, "On the Doctrine of Atonement," *Reflections* (2006), available at www.scribd.com/doc/148066225/On-the-Doctrine-of-Atonement; Cole, *God the Peacemaker*, 13.
109. Torrance, *Divine Meaning*, 105.
110. Boersma, *Violence, Hospitality, and the Cross*, 168–70.

than a confession of faith—more like a puzzle, we might say, than a gospel."[111] Lastly, while Boersma and Packer critique aspects of the penal substitution tradition for decontextualizing the atonement, J. Denny Weaver makes a similar critique of Gustaf Aulén, accusing him of "having stripped away the narrative of Jesus and retaining only the image of cosmic triumph."[112]

We must understand the atonement in terms of its vertical and horizontal dimensions. The cross represents not only the great exchange (substitutionary atonement), but also the great transition (the eschatological turn of the ages). Paul says Christ "gave himself for our sins to deliver us from the present evil age" (Gal 1:4). This one verse includes the great exchange ("for our sins") and the great transition ("deliver us from the present evil age"). Based on this verse, we must not merely uphold both aspects of the cross, for they are integrated in Scripture itself: the great exchange effects the great transition.

EXPANSIVE AND PARTICULAR

Christ's death on the cross is a gloriously multifaceted work, the scope of which could never be exhausted but only admired. There are two polar opposite errors that arise from the many-splendored nature of Christ's work: reductionism and relativism. Reductionism focuses on one aspect of the atonement to the exclusion of the others, whereas relativism upholds all aspects, often at the expense of order and integration.[113] We seek to avoid reductionism and relativism by embracing the *expansive* nature of Christ's atoning work, while still giving proper attention to *particular* aspects through order and integration.[114]

CONCLUSION

The division between the kingdom and the cross should not be. Jesus is the king who atones for our sins, and we must not only seek to understand his cross but to stand under him as our king. Indeed, even my provisional

---

111. J. I. Packer, "What Did the Cross Achieve? The Logic of Penal Substitution," *TynBul* 25 (1974): 5.

112. J. Denny Weaver, "The Nonviolent Atonement: Human Violence, Discipleship and God," in *Stricken by God? Nonviolent Identification and the Victory of Christ* (ed. Brad Jersak and Michael Hardin; Grand Rapids: Eerdmans, 2007), 324.

113. Adam Johnson offers a concise and helpful distinction between an aspect and a theory of the atonement: "An aspect of the atonement refers to the thing itself—the reality of this particular dimension of Christ's saving work. A theory of the atonement is a conceptually unified account of an aspect of Christ's death and resurrection, which explains the problem (sin), the characters (God, Christ, humankind) and an explanation of the solution by means of which to remove the problem" (*God's Being in Reconciliation: The Theological Basis of the Unity and Diversity of the Atonement in the Theology of Karl Barth* [New York: T&T Clark, 2012], 20).

114. For a fuller explanation of this approach, see below, pp. 177–89.

definitions above of kingdom and atonement beg for more integration, for one cannot understand the kingdom of God apart from Christ's atoning work, nor can one understand the atonement apart from the coming of God's kingdom. Integrating major doctrines such as atonement and kingdom is certainly a formidable task, but a necessary one nonetheless. To this task I now turn, and I begin "in the beginning . . ." (Gen 1:1), for the connection between atonement and kingdom unfolds progressively in the story line of Scripture.

BIBLICAL
THEOLOGY

CHAPTER ONE

VICTORY THROUGH SACRIFICE IN THE OLD TESTAMENT

WHAT IS THE relationship between Christ's atoning death on the cross and the coming of God's kingdom? The unity of Scripture as one grand story of redemption is a good place to start, for the coming of God's kingdom and the crucifixion of his Son both transpire within the same overarching story of redemptive history. Yet while part of the *same* story, kingdom and cross clearly play *different* roles. The kingdom is *telic*—oriented to the end-time hope that God will put all things right by reigning on earth as he does in heaven. The cross is *central*, in that all history moves toward it and unfolds from it.[1]

How, then, do kingdom and cross relate in the story of redemption? I will ultimately argue that the kingdom of God is established on earth by the atoning death of Jesus on the cross. However, while the end-time reign of God shockingly breaks into the middle of history in the death of the Messiah, I will also demonstrate that it was God's design from the beginning, revealed in the first hint of good news (Gen 3:15). In this chapter, I will provide a panoramic view of the unfolding themes of victory and suffering in the Old Testament; then in the next chapter I will zoom in on the book of Isaiah, where victory and suffering not only develop but most clearly converge.

THE IMPORTANCE OF THE OLD TESTAMENT

The "kingdom of God" (Mark 1:15) and Christ's death "for our sins" (1 Cor 15:3) may emerge in the New Testament as fully blossomed concepts, but

---

1. Gal 1:3–4; 6:14–16; 2 Cor 5:14–17; Eph 2:14–16.

they are truly the fruit of roots that have grown in the soil of the Old Testament, constantly intertwined and ultimately stemming from the same "seed" (Gen 3:15). Therefore, when Jesus said, "Thus it is written, that the Christ [Messiah] should suffer" (Luke 24:46), he was not merely proof-texting Isa 52:13–53:12 or some other elusive individual prophecy of a suffering Messiah. He was interpreting his life, death, and resurrection as the fulfillment of a *pattern* in the story of Israel, a pattern characterized by humiliation and exaltation, shame and glory, suffering and victory.[2] As Jewish scholar Jon Levenson says, "The story of humiliation and exaltation of the beloved son reverberates throughout the Bible because it is the story of the people about whom and to whom it is written."[3] I will trace this pattern as it emerges in the Old Testament, demonstrating that the victory and suffering introduced in the *protoevangelium* develop into *royal* victory and *atoning* suffering throughout the story of Israel. From the bruised heel of Genesis (3:15) to the reigning lamb of Revelation (22:1), the Bible is a redemptive story of a crucified Messiah who will accomplish a royal victory through atoning suffering.

Although a full-fledged biblical theology of victory through sacrifice would take more space than is available, I hope to accomplish two purposes in this chapter: (1) to demonstrate that the coming of the kingdom and the death of Christ in the New Testament are the culmination of themes that have been intertwined in their Old Testament development, and (2) to provide a redemptive-historical context for the more exegetical sections that follow. In order to understand the development of victory and suffering in *redemptive* history, one must first have a clear picture of God's design for *creation* as well as its demise.

CREATION

The beginning of any story will greatly determine the shape of its narrative. The biblical story begins with God, and what Psalms states explicitly is expressed in Genesis 1–2 through narrative: God is king over his creation (Ps

---

2. This interpretation of Luke 24:46 is corroborated by its context, where Jesus is speaking of "the Law of Moses and the Prophets and the Psalms" (Luke 24:44). Clearly, Jesus believes he is fulfilling the entirety of the Old Testament, not simply a few isolated prophecies. Such an interpretation does not mean that Jesus does not fulfill particular prophecies of suffering, but rather those are exceptional pictures of a more embedded pattern. The idea that the Christ must suffer in accordance with the Old Testament is also seen in Mark 9:12; Luke 22:37; 24:26; Acts 3:18; 26:22–23. For the argument that the New Testament authors cited and alluded to the Old Testament in a contextual rather than atomistic way, see C. H. Dodd, *According to the Scriptures: The Sub-Structure of New Testament Theology* (London: Nisbet, 1952).

3. Jon Levenson, *The Death and Resurrection of the Beloved Son: The Transformation of Child Sacrifice in Judaism and Christianity* (New Haven, CT: Yale University Press, 1993), 67.

93:1–2; 95:3–6; 96:10; 104; 136:1–9). While other ancient Near Eastern creation narratives depict creation as a process of conflict and struggle, Genesis 1 portrays God as simply speaking, and it is so. God is presented, in other words, as a king who reigns through his word.[4]

Humanity as the pinnacle of God's creation further reveals the design of God's rule over the earth. Adam and Eve are, along with the rest of creation, under the rule of God; they are servants. Yet, unlike the rest of creation, they are made in God's image and given the commission to "be fruitful and multiply and fill the earth and subdue it" (Gen 1:28).[5] They are servants of God, but rulers of the earth: servant-kings. God not only reigns *over* people; he also reigns *through* them.

God's reign over and through his servant-kings is the means by which he accomplishes his ultimate goal of revealing the glory of his majestic name and establishing his kingship over all the earth.[6] In Genesis 2, Adam is placed in the garden of Eden and given the task of serving and guarding it (Gen 2:15). The Hebrew words for "serve" (עבד) and "guard"(שׁמר) are combined elsewhere in the Old Testament only to describe the priests' role in the temple (Num 3:7–8; 8:26; 18:5–6), therefore depicting Eden as a temple and Adam its priest-king.[7] He is to rule (Gen 1:26–28) *by* serving in the Edenic temple and guarding it from intruders (Gen 2:15).[8]

The logical implication, if one combines the general commission to "fill the earth and subdue it" (Gen 1:28) with the more specific task of "serving and guarding" Eden (Gen 2:15), is that humanity was to Edenize the entire

---

4. For the kingship of God in creation, see John Goldingay, *Israel's Faith* (Old Testament Theology; Downers Grove, IL: InterVarsity Press, 2006), 2:60; Ciampa, "The History of Redemption," 257.

5. Although the meaning of the image of God is greatly debated and certainly includes multiple aspects, the emphasis in Gen 1:26–28 is the functional role of exercising dominion as God's representative. See Dempster, *Dominion and Dynasty*, 59; G. K. Beale, *A New Testament Biblical Theology: The Unfolding of the Old Testament in the New* (Grand Rapids: Baker Academic, 2011), 30–31, 381–84.

6. As important as the theme of the kingdom of God is in redemptive history, I concur with Beale's contention that it is a "penultimate means to divine glory" (*A New Testament Biblical Theology*, 16; cf. Ridderbos, *The Coming of the Kingdom*, 20–21).

7. Gordon Wenham, *Genesis 1–15* (WBC; Waco, TX: Word, 1987), 67. Regarding the most appropriate translation for עבד and שׁמר, the following choose "serve" and "guard": Umberto Cassuto, *A Commentary on the Book of Genesis* (Jerusalem: Magnes, 1989), 1:122; John Sailhamer, *Pentateuch as Narrative* (Grand Rapids: Zondervan, 1992), 100–101; Scott Hafemann, *The God of Promise and the Life of Faith: Understanding the Heart of the Bible* (Wheaton, IL: Crossway, 2001), 228. Beale prefers "work" and "keep" (*The Temple and the Church's Mission: A Biblical Theology of the Temple* [NSBT; Downers Grove, IL: InterVarsity Press, 2004], 67).

8. Beale, *A New Testament Biblical Theology*, 32; Stephen Dempster, "The Servant of the Lord," in *Central Themes in Biblical Theology*, 136; John Walton, *Genesis* (NIVAC; Grand Rapids: Zondervan, 2001), 174.

creation, expanding God's royal presence from the garden to the ends of the earth. Psalm 8 interprets Genesis 1 in this way, recounting how in creation God crowned humanity with glory and honor and gave them dominion over the earth (Ps 8:3–8); all of this is bracketed by the first and last verse of the psalm: "O Lord, our Lord, how majestic is your name in all the earth!" (Ps 8:1, 9).

The salient point is that God's reign through humanity over all the earth is the *telos* of Genesis 1–2, not the reality. In other words, before the fall and redemption ever entered the picture, there was a creation-consummation story line aimed at God's glorious reign over all the earth through his servant-kings. Eschatology precedes soteriology.[9] Genesis 1–2, therefore, does not technically present a picture of the "kingdom of God" but rather a project moving in that direction, as well as the pattern by which it will be achieved. God reigning through his servant-kings over all the earth to the glory of God's name—that is the project toward which Genesis 1–2 is aimed.

FALL

Genesis 3, of course, records that Adam and Eve, rather than ruling over the earth, submit to one of its craftiest creatures—the serpent—and thereby corrupt the goodness of creation and collapse humanity's mission to "fill the earth and subdue it" to the glory of God (Gen 1:28; cf. Psalm 8). Rather than going forth from Eden to expand the blessing of God's royal presence, they are banished from the garden to a wandering existence that instead spreads the curse. This banishment from Eden, however, reveals not only humanity's failure to carry out their royal commission but also that their sin has separated them from their Creator, fracturing the once harmonious relationship between God and his people. Hosea's parallel between Adam and Israel is illuminating:

> For I desire steadfast love and not sacrifice,
>> the knowledge of God rather than burnt offerings.
> But like Adam they [Israel] transgressed the covenant;
>> there they dealt faithlessly with me. (Hos 6:6–7)

The implications are immense. Hosea had been comparing God's covenant with Israel to the most intimate relationship available to people—marriage. Here, Hosea implies that Adam and Eve similarly shared a (marital-like) covenant relationship with God, characterized by knowing and loving God (Hos 6:6). By giving in to the serpent rather than ruling over it, Adam and Eve "transgressed the

---

9. Michael Horton, *Lord and Servant: A Covenant Christology* (Louisville: Westminster John Knox, 2005), 79–80.

covenant," which resulted for them—as it did for Israel—in God saying, "You are not my people, and I am not your God" (Hos 1:9). Although the concept of covenant is not formally introduced until Noah and Abraham, the parallel in Hosea makes clear that while the aim of Genesis 1–2 is God's reign being spread over the earth through his servant-kings, the heart of this kingdom vision is the covenant relationship between the divine king and his servant people.[10]

THE *PROTOEVANGELIUM*

From the cursed dirt of Genesis 3, redemptive history sprouts forth with the promise of the seed (*zerah*) of a woman who will bruise the head of the serpent and suffer a bruised heel in the process (Gen 3:15). The key is that the victory of the seed is the divine response to the sin-induced corruption of creation and derailment of the royal mission in Genesis 3. In other words, the *protoevangelium* points forward to a recovery of the prefall condition of blessed goodness *and* the prefall mission of filling and subduing the earth for God's majestic glory. As Dempster says, "The seed of the woman will restore the lost glory. Human—and therefore divine—dominion will be established over the world."[11]

The fall does not prompt God to abandon his original intention of filling the earth with the glory of his name through image-bearers that rule on his behalf. Hence, the royal commission to "be fruitful and multiply and fill the earth and subdue it" (Gen 1:28) is repeated throughout the story of Genesis and the rest of the Old Testament. Adam failed at his task, and the essence of his commission is then passed on to Noah (9:1, 7), Abraham (12:2–3; 17:2, 6, 8, 16; 22:18), Isaac (26:3–4, 24), Jacob (28:3–4, 14; 35:11–12; 48:3, 15–16), and corporate Israel (47:27; Deut 7:13).[12] The distinct feature of the commission given after the fall is that, while Adam and Eve were given a *command* ("be fruitful and multiply" Gen 1:28), the commission is transformed for the patriarchs into a *promise* (*I will . . . make you* fruitful and multiply you" Lev 26:9, italics mine). "This promise was that a 'seed' would finally bring about the blessing that Adam should have."[13]

The end-time goal remains: the kingdom of God is the *telos* of creation *and* redemption. The presence of sin, however, means that a new route to this goal must be devised. Genesis 3:15 provides the key, for the promise of victory

---

10. For further discussion on how Hos 6:7 sheds light on Genesis 1–2, see Gentry and Wellum, *Kingdom through Covenant*, 217–20, 612–13.

11. Dempster, *Dominion and Dynasty*, 69; cf. idem, "The Servant of the Lord," 177.

12. See Beale's excellent discussions in *The Temple and the Church's Mission*, 93–121; idem, *A New Testament Biblical Theology*, 46–58.

13. Beale, *A New Testament Biblical Theology*, 914.

includes the price of suffering. As Bruce Waltke says, "Salvation history tells the story of Eve's elect seed reversing the chaos Adam introduced by suffering for righteousness in the war against Satan's kingdom."[14] Therefore, with the victory *and suffering* of the *protoevangelium*, "a new way of arriving at the consummation was introduced."[15]

Suffering will be a key ingredient in God's victorious plan of redeeming his people and their royal task. Herman Bavinck explains the place of suffering in the coming kingdom of God: "From this point on, the road for the human race will pass through suffering to glory, through struggle to victory, through the cross to a crown, through the state of humiliation to that of exaltation. This is the fundamental law that God here proclaims before the entrance into the kingdom of heaven."[16] Furthermore, the interplay between suffering and victory, humiliation and exaltation, is a pattern seen in individuals (e.g., Joseph, Gideon, David, Daniel, Jehoiachin, the righteous sufferer of the Psalms, the servant of Isaiah), corporate Israel (exodus and return from exile), institutions (kingdom and temple), and offices (priest and king).

Granted, the connection between suffering and victory in Gen 3:15 is ambiguous, but this is precisely where the unfolding nature of God's revelation in Scripture presses the reader forward in the story. "Although complex," says Daniel Block, "the Old Testament picture of the messiah gains clarity and focus with time."[17] As the story unfolds, we will see that the victory develops into *royal* victory and the suffering into *atoning* suffering, with the final result of royal victory *through* atoning suffering.

The victory is a *royal* victory because the seed of the woman who will crush the serpent's head is progressively revealed in a lineage of kings.[18] The suffering of the seed takes various forms, but the implementation of the sac-

---

14. Bruce Waltke, "The Kingdom of God in the Old Testament: Definitions and Story," in *The Kingdom of God* (ed. Christopher Morgan and Robert Peterson; Theology in Community; Wheaton, IL: Crossway, 2012), 78.

15. Geerhardus Vos, *The Pauline Eschatology* (Grand Rapids: Eerdmans, 1961), 325.

16. Herman Bavinck, *Sin and Salvation in Christ*, vol. 3 of *Reformed Dogmatics* (ed. John Bolt; trans. John Vriend; Grand Rapids: Baker Academic, 2003), 199.

17. Daniel Block, "My Servant David: Ancient Israel's Vision of the Messiah," in *Israel's Messiah in the Bible and the Dead Sea Scrolls* (ed. Richard Hess and Daniel Carroll R.; Grand Rapids: Baker Academic, 2003), 56.

18. The royal lineage of the seed has been demonstrated extensively by T. Desmond Alexander ("Genealogies, Seed and the Compositional Unity of Genesis," *TynBul* 44 [1993]: 25–70; idem, "Royal Expectations in Genesis to Kings: Their Importance for Biblical Theology," *TynBul* 49 [1998]: 191–212). According to Alexander, "This line of 'seed' . . . is the beginning of a royal dynasty through whom God will bring his judgment upon the 'seed of the serpent.' That the one who will bring this judgment and reverse the consequences of the first couple's disobedience will be of kingly standing is not surprising when we bear in mind the vice-regent status earlier conferred on Adam and Eve" (*The Servant King: The Bible's Portrait of the Messiah* [Vancouver: Regent College, 2003], 18).

rificial system provides the grid to eventually see the suffering as atoning.[19] Though Gen 3:15 does not necessarily entail atoning suffering, Graham Cole is right to say that "with regard to the unfolding story of the divine project as canonically presented, post the fall the foundation of atonement lies in the *protoevangelium* of Genesis 3:15."[20]

ABRAHAM

If the *protoevangelium* is a glimmer of hope in a world darkened by the curse, God's promise to and covenant with Abraham is a flood of light from the starlit heavens. The threefold promise to Abraham includes land, descendants, and blessing (Gen 12:1–3)—a promise so foundational that John Stott says, "It may truly be said without exaggeration that not only the rest of the Old Testament but the whole of the New Testament are an outworking of these promises of God."[21] Yet, how do these promises relate to the original reign of humanity (1:26–28) and the victory of the seed (3:15)?

The call of Abraham clearly reveals the divine intention to reverse the curse of Genesis 3, for the fivefold "blessing" in Gen 12:1–3 is a direct response to the fivefold "curse" in Genesis 3–11 (3:14, 17; 4:11; 5:29; 9:25).[22] Moreover, echoing the *protoevangelium's* inclusion of suffering with victory, the mention of cursing in 12:3 "implies that there will be opposition to the plan of blessing but that this attack will be defeated: 'I will bless those who bless you and curse those who curse you.'"[23]

Genesis 12:1–3 not only provides a remedy to the problem of Genesis 3 but sets out to recover the trajectory of Genesis 1–2. As William Dumbrell says, "Gen 12:1–3 is the rejoinder to the consequences of the fall and aims

---

19. Although unquestioned throughout most of church history, there has been a recent resistance to the idea of redemptive suffering/violence. See Walter Wink, *Engaging the Powers: Discernment and Resistance in a World of Domination* (Minneapolis: Fortress, 1992), 7; Steve Chalke and Alan Mann, *The Lost Message of Jesus* (Grand Rapids: Zondervan, 2003), 125–29; Joanne Carlson Brown and Rebecca Parker, "For God So Loved the World," in *Christianity, Patriarchy, and Abuse: A Feminist Critique* (ed. Joanne Carlson Brown and Carole Bohn; New York: Pilgrim, 1989), 2. For defenses of redemptive suffering, see Boersma, *Violence, Hospitality, and the Cross*; Mary VandenBerg, "Redemptive Suffering: Christ's Alone," *SJT* 60 (2007): 394–411; Henri Blocher, *Evil and the Cross: Christian Thought and the Problem of Evil* (Downers Grove, IL: InterVarsity Press, 1994), 102–4; S. Jeffery, Michael Ovey, and Andrew Sach, *Pierced for Our Transgressions: Rediscovering the Glory of Penal Substitution* (Wheaton, IL: Crossway, 2007), 235–39.

20. Cole, *God the Peacemaker*, 91.

21. John Stott, *Understanding the Bible* (Grand Rapids: Zondervan, 1984), 51.

22. Michael Fishbane argues that the promise of land, seed, and blessing is "a typological reversal of the primordial curses in Eden: directed against the earth, human generativity, and human labour" (*Biblical Interpretation in Ancient Israel* [New York: Clarendon, 1985], 372–73).

23. Dempster, *Dominion and Dynasty*, 77.

at the restoration of the purposes of God for the world to which Gen 1–2 directed our attention."[24] It is no surprise, then, that Abraham's calling is rich with royal overtones.[25] As Gordon Wenham notes, "What Abram was promised was the hope of many an oriental monarch."[26]

Once again, Abraham's call is reminiscent of Adam's commission, with the command being transformed into a promise. Whereas Adam is commanded to "be fruitful and multiply and fill the earth" (Gen 1:28), Abraham is promised that *God* will make him a great nation (12:2) and *God* will give him the land (12:7). And while Abraham does go on to accomplish great royal acts (Genesis 14 tells of his defeating kings), the story once again presses forward to a "seed" who will accomplish what no other has been able to do.

God's mission to bless all the families of the earth through Abraham is further clarified by the promises that Abraham will bear *royal* descendants— "kings shall come from you" (Gen 17:6)—and that the mission will ultimately be accomplished by Abraham's seed—"in your [seed] shall all the nations of the earth be blessed" (22:18). How does the "seed" of Abraham (22:18) relate to the "seed" of the woman (3:15)? T. Desmond Alexander has demonstrated that "the linear genealogies in Genesis 5 and 11 trace the 'seed of the woman' to Abraham."[27] Christopher J. H. Wright notes that after the promise of 3:15, "attentive readers will have been wondering who this serpent crusher will be. From Genesis 12:1–3 onward we know it will be one of the seed of Abraham. A son of Abraham will be a blessing for the sons of Adam."[28] These promises are explicit instances where the ambiguous victory of the seed in 3:15 is developing into a royal victory.

COVENANT

In Genesis 15 and 17, God's promise to Abraham is formalized relationally through a series of covenants that "function as administrative instruments of God's kingly rule."[29] A covenant is a binding agreement between

24. William Dumbrell, *Covenant and Creation: A Theology of the Old Testament Covenants* (Grand Rapids: Baker, 1993), 68.

25. Dempster, *Dominion and Dynasty*, 76.

26. Wenham, *Genesis 1–15*, 275.

27. Alexander, "Royal Expectations in Genesis to Kings," 205.

28. Christopher J. H. Wright, *The Mission of God: Unlocking the Bible's Grand Narrative* (Downers Grove, IL: InterVarsity Press, 2006), 212.

29. Meredith Kline, *Kingdom Prologue: Genesis Foundations for a Covenantal Worldview* (Overland Park, KS: Two Age, 2000), 4; see also Peter Gentry, "Kingdom through Covenant: Humanity as the Divine Image," *SBJT* 12 (2008): 16–42.

a suzerain king and subordinate vassal kings (servant-kings) that is sealed by a sacrifice.[30] Covenant, therefore, is an essential aspect of the kingdom of God—"it is *through the biblical covenants* that God's kingdom comes to this world."[31]

This covenant-kingdom connection introduces a significant feature for my argument. Not only does covenant provide the proper categories for king and servant, but it binds together the concepts of kingship and sacrifice. Paul Williamson explains the sacrificial ritual of Genesis 15 in light of Jer 34:18: "Those obligating themselves to the covenant pass between the cleaved animals, essentially declaring the same fate for themselves should they fail to carry out their responsibilities."[32] The fact that only the Lord walks through the animals (Gen 15:17) reveals that if the covenant promises are not kept, God himself commits to bearing the curse. In sum, at the heart of the kingdom of God is a covenant, the sacrifice-sealed relationship between the divine king and his servants.

We have seen that the promise to and covenant with Abraham is a continuation of the trajectory of spreading God's royal blessing throughout the earth in Genesis 1–2 and 3:15. What, then, is the significance of the strange sacrificial narrative of Genesis 22? While God promised to make Abraham a great dynasty, his only son goes through a near-death and resurrection experience, where God provides a substitutionary sacrifice in place of Isaac. The portended suffering of Isaac—the seed of Abraham—echoes the suffering of the seed of the woman and attaches to it the idea of substitutionary atonement that would eventually be institutionalized in the sacrificial system. Dempster observes that Genesis 22

> contains very specific terminology and symbolism that are used later in the canon. The fact that it is Jerusalem where this sacrifice is offered is hardly incidental. It is certainly also significant that the sacrifice functions as a substitute for the child of promise. Similar sacrificial terminology occurs in only two other places: the first sacrifice at the tabernacle (Lev. 8–9) and the annual sacrifices used for the Day of Atonement (Lev. 16). It [is] as

---

30. O. Palmer Robertson succinctly defines a covenant as "a bond in blood sovereignly administered" (*The Christ of the Covenants* [Grand Rapids: Baker, 1980], 4). For a recent and thorough study of covenant see Scott Hahn, *Kinship by Covenant: A Canonical Approach to the Fulfillment of God's Saving Promises* (New Haven, CT: Yale University Press, 2009).

31. Gentry and Wellum, *Kingdom through Covenant*, 591, italics theirs; cf. Kline, who says, "To follow the course of the kingdom is to trace the series of covenants by which the Lord administers his kingdom" (*Kingdom Prologue*, 1).

32. Paul Williamson, *Sealed with an Oath: Covenant in God's Unfolding Purpose* (NSBT; Downers Grove, IL: InterVarsity Press, 2007), 86. Williamson notes that while this interpretation has not gone unchallenged, it remains the current consensus.

if the Day of Atonement institutionalizes for the public community this private experience of Abraham and Isaac.[33]

Alongside this development of suffering is the development of victory. For the first time since Gen 3:15 the seed—now known to be a royal seed—is promised to "possess the gate of his enemies" (22:17–18). In other words, by Genesis 22 the text has drawn together the seed, royalty, and victory; and all this is interwoven with an account of substitutionary atonement. Although it is still not clear how the substitutionary atonement relates to the royal victory, the connection will become manifest as they develop respectively into the Davidic kingdom and the sacrificial system. The death and resurrection of the beloved son becomes a pattern embedded into the fabric of God's coming kingdom.[34]

JOSEPH AND JUDAH

The story of Joseph is both the crescendo of the pattern of humiliation and exaltation developed thus far and the preenactment of Israel's destiny in Egypt.[35] Roy Ciampa draws out the connection to the opening pages of Genesis: "By the time we get to the end of the book of Genesis, we find Joseph functioning as vice-regent over the mighty nation of Egypt and bringing salvation (dare we say blessing?) both to the nation and to his own family in the process."[36] Joseph's ascension to royalty is characterized by suffering and is his reign exercised over his brothers with forgiveness.

However, although Joseph develops the pattern of suffering and victory, it is from the line of his brother Judah that the royal seed will emerge: "The scepter shall not depart from Judah" (Gen 49:10). The royal line, traced from the seed of the woman in 3:15 and throughout Genesis, will bring about a kingly figure from the tribe of Judah, who will bring God's blessing to all the nations of the earth (cf. Num 24:14–19).[37]

---

33. Dempster, *Dominion and Dynasty*, 85. "The Hebrew words for 'Burnt offering,' 'appear,' and 'ram' appear together only in Lev. 8–9, 16 and Gen. 22" (ibid., fn. 47).

34. According to Levenson, the ritual sacrifice of Genesis 22 is embedded as a pattern in Israel's story by means of its narrative equivalence: the death and resurrection of the beloved son. He asserts, "The beloved son is marked for both exaltation and humiliation. In his life the two are seldom far apart" (*The Death and Resurrection of the Beloved Son*, 59). This pattern applies not only to Jacob and Joseph but to Israel as a whole and ultimately to Jesus who, as the beloved son, fulfills the pattern in his death and resurrection.

35. Ibid., 143, 150.

36. Ciampa, "The History of Redemption," 267.

37. Alexander, *The Servant King*, 31–33. Numbers 24 further clarifies that the scepter of Judah in Gen 49:10 is the seed of the woman in Gen 3:15, for this scepter from Israel not only will have dominion over the earth (Num 24:19) but shall crush the head of his enemy (24:17). See James Hamilton, "The Skull Crushing Seed of the Woman: Inner-Biblical Interpretation of Genesis 3:15," *SBJT* 10 (2006): 49 n. 45.

EXODUS

The opening of the book of Exodus reports that while Israel had received the blessing of multiplication as a people, they were in the wrong land, under the wrong king, and experiencing the toilsome labor and ruthless slavery of a cursed world (Exod 1:7–14). Yet, God remembered his covenant promises to Abraham, Isaac, and Jacob (2:23–25; 6:1–8) and redeemed his people from slavery by pouring out his judgment on Egypt. The salient feature is that the suffering of the Passover lamb plays a key role in the victory of God and his people.[38] In fact, if the wrath of God were not averted from Israel by the spotless lambs, their fate would be no different than that of the Egyptians. Atonement (at least in the sense of averting the wrath of God) is a key ingredient in the victory.[39] Furthermore, because the victory over the Egyptians is attributed to God's kingship (Exod 15:7), it is appropriate to say that this is an instance of royal victory through atoning suffering.

The exodus results in the declaration that God is king and Israel a kingdom of priests (Exod 15:18; 19:6). As Dempster says, "The covenant at Sinai marks a people that manifests God's intentions for creation from the beginning. . . . This kingdom of priests is to manifest God's rule to the world. . . . Israel is being called to a restoration of the creation rule of Genesis 1–2."[40] Before the fall, Adam was in right relationship with God and unhindered by sin in witnessing to God's reign. However, for Israel, the presence of sin requires that they be "a kingdom of priests . . . a *holy* nation" (Exod 19:6, italics mine); they must receive atonement for sin. The purification of God's people and land will prove to be a central tenet in God's kingdom. Hence, after becoming a kingdom of priests (19:6), they are given the sacrificial system to uphold the purity of the kingdom.[41]

DAVID

The idea of God reigning through a mediatorial man over his creation began with Adam, was promised in the seed of Abraham, and found its Old Testament pinnacle in David. As another Adam figure—a seed of a woman—David's résumé of victory speaks for itself (2 Samuel 8). If David is

---

38. Christopher J. H. Wright, "Atonement in the Old Testament," in *The Atonement Debate*, 73.

39. For a defense of the view that the Passover lamb was atoning, see ibid.; also, see Morris, *The Apostolic Preaching of the Cross*, 131–32.

40. Dempster, *Dominion and Dynasty*, 103.

41. See Matthew Levering and Michael Dauphinais, *Holy People, Holy Land: A Theological Introduction to the Bible* (Grand Rapids: Brazos, 2005), 75–76.

the victorious seed (Gen 3:15) from the tribe of Judah (49:10), what role then does suffering play in his rise to power and establishment of the kingdom?

David's rise to power clearly entails the well-established pattern of humiliation and exaltation, suffering and victory. Though anointed king as a boy, David's life was filled with trials, persecution, and defeat before he ascended the throne. One unique feature that David brings out in this pattern is the idea of power through weakness. Although David certainly grew in stature, his story is not so much one of weakness *to* power but rather power *through* weakness.

Take, for example, the occasion of his being chosen as king (1 Sam 16:1–13). While some saw a weak, ruddy, young shepherd-boy, dwarfed by his majestic brothers, God saw a powerful king. The most profound example of power through weakness is David's defeat of Goliath (1 Samuel 17). While the strongest men in the country stood by in fear, the young, overlooked boy defeated the great enemy through the power of faith. This theme of power through weakness echoes throughout Scripture: the victory of Gideon's three hundred-man army (Judges 7), Samson destroying one thousand men with a donkey's jaw bone (Judg 15:15), Haman outwitted by a young Jewish girl (Esther), and so on. The theme is always that God's power works through human weakness for God's glory.

Lastly, David is especially significant because God's covenant with him (2 Sam 7:12–14) clarifies and narrows the lineage and mission of the royal seed.[42] James Hamilton argues for continuity in the story line because "the promises to Abraham, which answer the curses following Adam's sin, are passed on to David."[43] The promise to Abraham of land and people under a royal seed is now framed in terms of God establishing the kingdom of the seed of David, who is also a son of God.

TEMPLE

The temple is an essential element in the kingdom, for when God established the Davidic kingdom, the son of David was to build a temple for God (2 Sam 7:13). Echoes of Eden abound, to the tune of a priest-king who will expand God's rule over the earth.[44] Just as the tabernacle traveled with the

---

42. Although 2 Sam 7:12–14 does not use the word "covenant," Scripture elsewhere attests that God is indeed making a covenant with David (2 Sam 23:5; Ps 89:35; 132:12; Isa 55:3).

43. James Hamilton, "The Seed of the Woman and the Blessing of Abraham," *TynBul* 58 (2007): 269; cf. Williamson, *Sealed with an Oath*, 144; Wright, *The Mission of God*, 345.

44. Ciampa, "The History of Redemption," 276.

people of Israel on their way to the promised land (Num 2:17), the temple is the permanent center around which the kingdom is organized.[45] What is the significance of the temple for the kingdom?

The temple functions not only as the dwelling place of God, but also as the means by which unholy people can dwell with the holy God (i.e., the sacrificial system). The royal overtones are especially significant. Just as the palace is the "house" of the human king, the temple is the "house" of the divine king (2 Sam 7:13). As N. T. Wright says, "It is the Temple that joins heaven and earth together and so makes possible the sovereign rule of God on earth as in heaven."[46] The very footstool of king YHWH's throne is the ark in the Most Holy Place (1 Chr 28:2; Ps 99:5; 132:7), the place for the climactic sacrificial offering on the Day of Atonement.

Perhaps the clearest picture of the interconnectedness between God's kingship and the temple is Isaiah's vision of God enthroned in the temple (Isaiah 6). The thrice holy song of the seraphim reveals that God's kingship is inseparable from his holiness, which is why Isaiah's response before the holy king is to acknowledge his uncleanliness (6:5). The only hope for Isaiah before the holy king is that his sins would somehow be atoned for and his guilt taken away, which is exactly what happens by the grace of God (6:7). Isaiah's encounter with God demonstrates, as does the role of the temple in general, that to be under the saving rule of God, one must have their sins atoned for. Atonement and kingdom are inseparable.[47]

THE RIGHTEOUS SUFFERER OF THE PSALMS

The righteous sufferer of the Psalms further reveals the interplay between kingship and suffering in the Old Testament.[48] Although the righteous sufferer is broadly representative of Israel throughout the Psalms, it is primarily applied to David as *the* righteous sufferer (see Psalms 7; 22; 69; 109).[49] The notable feature is that the righteous one who suffers is *King* David—the

---

45. Christian Grappe, *Le royaume de dieu: avant, avec et après Jésus* (MB; Genève: Labor et Fides, 2001), 208–14.
46. Wright, *How God Became King*, 173.
47. For the place of forgiveness of sins in the kingdom in the Old Testament, see Ladd, *The Presence of the Future*, 213.
48. For the tradition of the righteous sufferer in biblical and extrabiblical Jewish writings, see Lothar Ruppert, *Der leidende Gerechte: Eine motivgeschichtliche Untersuchung zum Alten Testament und zwischentestamentlichen Judentum* (FzB; Würzburg: Echter, 1972).
49. For understanding the righteous sufferer as a corporate identity (Israel) and individual figure (David), see Jerome Creach, *The Destiny of the Righteous in the Psalms* (St. Louis: Chalice, 2008), 7–9.

righteous *royal* sufferer. David is not only *a* king but in the Psalms he is *the* king; David is the only king mentioned in the Psalms, other than two brief references to Solomon's kingship in the titles to Psalms 72 and 127.

The attachment of suffering to his royal identity, therefore, revolutionizes the notion of kingship. Jerome Creach attests, "Kingship is transformed in the Psalter by its exclusive association with David and, in turn, by the characterization of David as God's servant who bears the shame of the people."[50] The failed monarchy, however, dashed the expectations of David's reign and gave rise to an eschatological reinterpretation of the Psalms that looked forward to a new David who *as king* would suffer for his people.[51] It is no surprise, therefore, that many scholars have observed that the righteous/royal sufferer of the Psalms is picked up and developed in Isaiah's Suffering Servant (Isa 52:13–53:12).[52]

ISAIAH

Following the era of the united kingdom, Israel steadily declines into exile, but the vision of the kingdom of God soars through the prophets. The striking feature is that just as with the victory of the seed, the advancement of the kingdom is intertwined with suffering. The book of Isaiah represents the apex of the development of suffering and victory that began in Gen 3:15. Although I will return to Isaiah for an in-depth treatment in the next chapter, the key point here, within the unfolding story of Israel, is that Isaiah not only clarifies the seed's suffering as *atoning* and the victory as *royal*, but that the royal victory will come *through* atoning suffering. John Bright explains the place of vicarious suffering in the coming of the kingdom: "For suffering is not merely the consequence of the Servant's task—it is the organ of it. . . . The victory of the Kingdom of God is achieved through the vicarious sacrifice of the Servant."[53] The coming of the kingdom of God hinges on the suffering of the servant.

ZECHARIAH

The latter part of Zechariah (chapters 9–14) focuses on an eschatological Davidic ruler who will bring the long-hoped-for reign of God on earth.

---

50. Ibid., 109.
51. Joshua Jipp, "Luke's Scriptural Suffering Messiah: A Search for Precedent, a Search for Identity," *CBQ* 72 (2010): 258.
52. Joel Marcus, *The Way of the Lord: Christological Exegesis of the Old Testament in the Gospel of Mark* (Louisville: Westminster John Knox, 1992), 190; J. Stewart Perowne, *The Book of Psalms* (Grand Rapids: Zondervan, 1976), 419.
53. Bright, *The Kingdom of God*, 152.

Recalling Gen 49:10 and expanding on Isa 52:13–53:12, Zechariah presents the royal victory of this ruler through the shocking means of suffering and even death.[54] Zechariah 9:9–10 tells of the coming of a humble king who will speak peace to the nations, rule from sea to sea, and set captives free.

How does this king accomplish such redemption? "Because of the blood of my covenant with you" (Zech 9:11). This ruler is later said to be "pierced" (Zech 12:10), which will result in the opening of a fountain that will cleanse God's people of their sins (Zech 13:1). Finally, this shepherd-king will be *stricken*, which brings about a restoration of the covenant relationship with God (Zech 13:7).[55] Zechariah corroborates the Isaianic message that suffering is instrumental in the coming of God's kingdom.

The above sweep of Israel's unfolding story reveals that the victory *and* suffering of the *protoevangelium* gradually develop into royal victory *through* atoning suffering. Though much more could be added in terms of breadth,[56] I will instead seek depth in the book of the Old Testament that most clearly reveals the link between atoning suffering and the coming kingdom of God—Isaiah.

---

54. Zechariah's dependence and development of Isaiah is demonstrated by Anthony Peterson, *Behold Your King* (New York: T&T Clark, 2009), 240–42; David Mitchell, *The Message of the Psalter: An Eschatological Programme in the Book* (JSOTSup 252; Sheffield: Sheffield Academic, 1997), 207–9.

55. For the unity of these three passages and their respective figures, see Douglas Moo, *The Old Testament in the Gospel Passion Narratives* (Eugene, OR: Wipf & Stock, 2008), 174.

56. Other passages that could supplement this biblical theology of victory through sacrifice are Psalms 2; 72; 89; 110:1–4; Jer 23:5–8; 31–34; Ezek 4:1–6; 37:24–28; Daniel 7; 9:24–27.

CHAPTER TWO

THE SUFFERING SERVANT AND HIS KINGDOM CONTEXT IN ISAIAH

OUR JOURNEY THROUGH the Old Testament revealed an unfolding pattern of royal victory through atoning suffering. Approaching the book of Isaiah, we find ourselves on the mountaintop, not only as a climax to the story of Israel, but as a viewpoint to look forward into the New Testament. The Isaianic song of the Suffering Servant (Isa 52:13–53:12) has perhaps the greatest potential in all of Scripture for connecting atoning suffering and the coming of God's kingdom. Unfortunately, the song has often been torn from its royal context and turned instead into another barrier between atonement and kingdom.

This problem—Isa 52:13–53:12 being interpreted apart from its canonical context—is twofold. First, the bifurcation (and eventual trifurcation) of the book of Isaiah by nineteenth-century German historical criticism isolated Isa 52:13–53:12 from its broader context of chapters 1–39 and 56–66. Second, within Isaiah 40–55 itself, Bernhard Duhm's delineation of the so-called "servant songs" lifted Isa 52:13–53:12 out of its immediate context.[1] In line with the recent recovery of the unity of the book of Isaiah,[2] I will address this twofold problem for interpreting Isa 52:13–53:12 with a twofold solution: (1) interpreting Isa 52:13–53:12 in light of its broader context of chapters 1–39

---

1. Bernhard Duhm, *Das Buch Jesaia* (KKHS; Göttingen: Vandenhoeck & Ruprecht, 1892).
2. Jacques Vermeylen, "L'unité du livre d'Isaïe," in *The Book of Isaiah* (ed. Jacques Vermeylen; BETL; Leuven: Leuven University Press, 1989), 11–53; H. G. M. Williamson, "Recent Issues in the Study of Isaiah," in *Interpreting Isaiah: Issues and Approaches* (ed. David Firth and H. G. M. Williamson; Downers Grove, IL: InterVarsity Press, 2009), 21–30.

(especially chs. 9; 11; 32) and 56–66, and (2) its immediate context of chapters 40–55 (especially chs. 51–54).

While there is a vast amount of literature interpreting the Suffering Servant in light of the other servant songs (Isa 42:1–9; 49:1–7; 50:4–9),[3] I will focus on the equally important, yet neglected, aforementioned contexts. The aim is to provide a biblically rooted and theologically informed answer to the following question: How does re-placing the Suffering Servant in these particular contexts contribute to our understanding of the identity of the servant and the nature of his accomplishment in Isa 52:13–53:12? We will find that the servant is the Davidic king who will bring about a new exodus and thereby establish God's kingdom by means of his sacrificial suffering.[4]

THE SUFFERING SERVANT AND THE MESSIANIC KING (ISAIAH 1–39)

IDENTIFYING THE SERVANT AND THE KING

The rediscovered unity of the book of Isaiah has re-opened the door for scholars to explore the relationship between the Messianic King of Isaiah 1–39 and the servant of Isaiah 40–55, many of them concluding that the two titles refer to one messianic figure.[5] I will briefly list the strongest and most

---

3. See, e.g., Henri Blocher, *Songs of the Servant: Isaiah's Good News* (Downers Grove, IL: InterVarsity Press, 1975); Otto Kaiser, *Der königliche Knecht: Eine traditionsgeschichtlich-exegetische Studie über die Ebed-Jahwe-Lieder bei Deuterojesaja* (FRLANT; Göttingen: Vandenhoeck & Ruprecht, 1959).

4. The title "servant" of Yahweh is given both to unfaithful corporate Israel (Isa 42:18–20; 44:1–2) and to a faithful individual representative of Israel (42:1; 49:3, 5; 52:13; 53:11). However, the nation of Israel cannot be the servant of Yahweh in the servant songs because the servant is said to be sinless (Isa 53:9) and to have a mission to restore Israel (Isa 49:5–6). Despite the distinction between the two servants, however, they are held together closely because the latter is the faithful remnant of the former. For the most comprehensive studies of the identity of the servant, see Christopher North, *The Suffering Servant in Deutero-Isaiah: An Historical and Critical Study* (London: Oxford University Press, 1948); Herbert Haag, *Der Gottesknecht bei Deuterojesaja* (EdF 233; Darmstadt: Wissenschaftliche Buchgesellschaft, 1985).

5. The following scholars identify the servant with the messianic king: Oswald Thompson Allis, *The Unity of Isaiah: A Study in Prophecy* (Philadelphia: Presbyterian & Reformed, 1950), 87–101; Ernst Wilhelm Hengstenberg, *Christology of the Old Testament: And a Commentary on the Messianic Predictions* (Edinburgh: T&T Clark, 1861), 2:264; Edward Young, *The Book of Isaiah* (NICOT; Grand Rapids: Eerdmans, 1965), 3:342; Kaiser, *Der königliche Knecht*; Richard Schultz, "The King in the Book of Isaiah," in *The Lord's Anointed: Interpretation of Old Testament Messianic Texts* (ed. P. Satterthwaite, Richard Hess, and Gordon Wenham; THS; Carlisle, UK: Paternoster, 1995), 154–59; Block, "My Servant David," 43–55; Alexander, *The Servant King*, 108–12; Dempster, "The Servant of the Lord," 154–60; Peter Gentry, "The Atonement in Isaiah's Fourth Servant Song (Isaiah 52:13–53:12)," *SBJT* 11 (2007): 24. As an example of a counterargument, G. Hugenberger claims that the servant is a new Moses ("The Servant of the LORD in the 'Servant Songs' of Isaiah: A Second Moses Figure," in *The Lord's Anointed*, 105–40); for a refutation of this thesis, see Block, "My Servant David," 45–46.

common arguments for identifying the servant and the king, and then build on this foundation by focusing on often-unnoticed connections between the first stanza of the Suffering Servant song and Isaiah 1–39.[6]

SUMMARY OF ARGUMENTS THAT IDENTIFY THE SERVANT AND THE KING

(1) *The title "servant."* The fact that the key figure of Isa 52:13–53:12 is called "my servant" (52:13; 53:11) provides "overwhelming" evidence that he is identified with the Davidic Messiah.[7] The exact title "my servant" is applied to David more than to any other figure (23x for David, 13x for Jacob, 8x for Moses) and the title "servant," when considered with its possessive pronouns, is dominated by references to David (66x for David, 19x for Moses).[8] Isaiah's explicit reference to King David as "my servant" in Isa 37:35 suggests that for Isaiah the Davidic king and the Suffering Servant are not mutually exclusive figures.

(2) *Anointed for specific tasks.* Both the king and the servant are anointed with the Spirit of Yahweh for the tasks of establishing justice (מִשְׁפָּט) (Isa 9:7 [6]; 42:1–4),[9] bringing light to the nations (9:2; 42:6–7), and opening the eyes of the blind (32:3; 42:7).[10]

(3) *Botanical imagery.* The king and the servant are described with botanical imagery, both being called a "root" (שֹׁרֶשׁ) (Isa 11:10; 53:2).[11] The LXX translates "root" (שֹׁרֶשׁ) in Isa 53:2 as "child," indicating that the translators identified the Suffering Servant with the son given in Isaiah 9 who is revealed as a king in chapter 11.[12]

(4) *Davidic covenant and kingdom.* The Messianic King and the servant are both connected to God's promises to David (Isa 9:7; 55:3).[13]

---

6. I assume J. A. Motyer's general outline of Isa 52:13–53:12 in his *The Prophecy of Isaiah: An Introduction & Commentary* (Downers Grove, IL: InterVarsity Press, 1993), 423:
   A: The Servant's Exaltation (Isa 52:13–15)
   　B: The Rejection/Suffering of the Servant (Isa 53:1–3)
   　　C: Significance of the Servant's Suffering (Isa 53:4–6)
   　B': The Rejection/Suffering of the Servant (Isa 53:7–9)
   A': The Servant's Exaltation (Isa 53:10–12)
7. Block, "My Servant David," 47.
8. Dempster, "The Servant of the Lord," 131–33.
9. "Both in the Old Testament and in the ancient Near East, establishing justice was consistently regarded as one of the primary responsibilities of the king" (H. G. M. Williamson, *Variations on a Theme: King, Messiah and Servant in the Book of Isaiah* [Carlisle, UK: Paternoster, 2000], 136).
10. See Schultz, "The King in the Book of Isaiah," 156.
11. Botanical imagery was often used to describe kings in the Old Testament. See Gentry, "The Atonement in Isaiah's Fourth Servant Song," 31–32 and especially n. 36.
12. Ibid., 32.
13. The meaning of Isa 55:3 is disputed, but interpreting it within its context links it to the servant. See Gentry and Wellum, *Kingdom through Covenant*, 445; Schultz, "The King in the Book of Isaiah," 155; Motyer, *Isaiah*, 13.

(5) *Royal characteristics.* The promise of victory (Isa 52:12–13), response of the kings (52:14–15; cf. 49:7), and burial with the rich (53:9) suggest a royal interpretation for the servant.[14]

(6) *Early Jewish interpretation.* The *Targum of Isaiah* adds "the messiah" after "my servant" in Isa 52:13, showing that early interpreters identified the Suffering Servant with the Messianic King.[15]

As a final note, the fact that the servant is never explicitly referred to as "king" is of little significance, for even the messiah of Isaiah 1–39 was not called "king" (מֶלֶךְ) until 32:1. The "royal prerogatives and characteristics,"[16] as well as the other evidence above, make clear that the servant is a royal, Davidic, messianic figure.[17]

THE SERVANT'S ROYAL EXALTATION (ISAIAH 52:13–15)

The song opens in the same way that it closes, with the exaltation of the servant. Therefore, although the suffering of the servant is central to the song, his exaltation provides the framework. The first stanza to this song is immeasurably important for understanding the identity and accomplishment of the servant, yet has often been neglected. The first stanza, however, makes clear that the servant is also a royally exalted figure.

"HIGH AND LIFTED UP" (ISAIAH 6:1 AND 52:13)

The emphasis on exaltation in the first stanza is immediately apparent from the three successive and largely synonymous verbs used to describe the servant ("he shall be high and lifted up, and shall be exalted," Isa 52:13). The *degree* of exaltation, however, is greatly heightened when the reader discovers that this language of exaltation is only used elsewhere to describe Yahweh, the divine king (Isa 6:1; 33:10; 57:15). Isaiah 6, acknowledged by scholars to have a major impact on the entire book of Isaiah,[18] is especially relevant for the introduction to the song of the Suffering Servant:

> Isaiah 6:1: In the year that King Uzziah died I saw the Lord sitting upon a throne, high and lifted up [וְרָם וְנִשָּׂא]; and the train of his robe filled the temple.

---

14. Block, "My Servant David," 50.

15. Brevard Childs, *Isaiah* (OTL; Louisville: Westminster John Knox, 2001), 408.

16. Gerard Van Groningen, *Messianic Revelation in the Old Testament* (Grand Rapids: Baker, 1990), 611.

17. Although my focus is on the royal nature of the servant's accomplishment, it in no way implies that royalty is the only aspect of his identity or achievement. Many have noted that the servant fulfills each of the messianic roles of the threefold office: prophet, priest, and king (e.g., Richard Schultz, "Servant/Slave," *NIDOTTE*, 4:1196).

18. Williamson, *Variations on a Theme*, 9.

Isaiah 52:13: Behold, my servant shall act wisely;
 he shall be high and lifted up [יָרוּם וְנִשָּׂא],
 and shall be exalted.

The exact phrase used to portray Yahweh as king in Isa 6:1 ("high and lifted up") is applied in Isa 52:13 to describe the servant of Yahweh.

How, then, in light of this intratextual link between Isa 6:1 and 52:13, can we describe the connection between the divine king and the Suffering Servant? The fact that Yahweh crushes the servant (Isa 53:10) means that they cannot simply be the same figure, although it does relate the servant and Yahweh in an unprecedented way. Perhaps the answer lies in the description of the Suffering Servant as the "arm of the LORD" (Isa 53:1). Yahweh is king (Isa 6:1), but in the prologue to Isaiah 40–55, God's kingship is said to be enacted through mediatorial means: "Behold, the LORD God comes with might, and his arm rules for him" (Isa 40:10). The "arm of the LORD" seems to be an extension of Yahweh's own power, and yet somehow distinct from Yahweh himself.[19] Isaiah 53:1 declares this "arm of the LORD" to be the servant of Yahweh, and therefore the mediatorial agent for enacting his kingship.[20]

How does this contribute to the task at hand of identifying the *Messianic King* and the servant? First, the servant and the Messianic King are both closely identified with Yahweh (Isa 9:6; 53:1) and are said to act on his behalf (9:7; 53:1). Additionally, the implications of Isaiah 6 for understanding the exaltation of the servant are vast. While 52:13–15 shows the exaltation of the servant on its own, the background of Isaiah 6 greatly enriches our understanding in two primary ways. First, the identity of the servant is confirmed as royal. The servant is a king. Second, Isaiah 6 reveals that the servant is exalted to the highest possible level, divine royalty. In short, Isa 52:13 reveals the exaltation of the servant; Isaiah 6 reveals the extent of the exaltation.

REVERSAL OF HARDENING (ISAIAH 6:9–10 AND 52:15)

The "high and lifted up" reference from Isa 6:1 unveils the royal identity of the Suffering Servant, but the connection to the hardening theme in 6:9–10 reveals an aspect of his mission and accomplishment. The connection between reversal of the hardening in 6:9–10 and the victory of the servant in

---

19. According to John Goldingay and David Payne, "[The arm] is a revelation of a part of Yhwh in some sense representing Yhwh and distinguishable from Yhwh" (*A Critical and Exegetical Commentary on Isaiah 40–55* (ICC; London: T&T Clark, 2006], 298).

20. The identity of the "arm" is contested, but the following scholars identify the "arm" with the Suffering Servant: John Oswalt, *The Book of Isaiah: Chapters 40–66* (NICOT; Grand Rapids: Eerdmans, 1998), 375; Motyer, *Isaiah*, 427; Williamson, *Variations on a Theme*, 164.

52:15 is initially evident in the verbal parallels. In Isaiah 6, Yahweh hardens Israel "lest they see [פֶּן־יִרְאֶה] with their eyes, and hear [יִשְׁמָע] with their ears, and understand [יָבִין] with their hearts, and turn and be healed" (6:10). In 52:13–53:12 the servant's effect on the kings is the opposite as that in the hardening passage: "That which has not been told them they see [רָאוּ], and that which they have not heard [לֹא־שָׁמְעוּ] they understand [הִתְבּוֹנָנוּ]" (Isa 52:15). The hardening motif is a unifying theme throughout the book of Isaiah, but it is ultimately in the person and work of the servant that the reversal takes place.[21] Torsten Uhlig explains how this informs the identity of the servant:

> The individual servant appears as someone who has experienced the oppo-
> site of hardening in order to achieve his mission: his ear is awakened and
> opened so that he can sustain the weary (Isa 50:4–5). As those who listen
> to the voice of this servant (Isa 50:10) a group is speaking about the servant
> and the change of mind they have experienced (Isa 52:13–53:12).[22]

The suffering of the servant reverses the hardening because it deals with the source and cause of the hardening in the first place—the sin of the people. "He has died for them, their transgressions were laid upon him so that the people can have peace and be healed (cf. Isa 53:4–6)."[23] The redemption proclaimed in Isaiah 40–55 is aimed at overcoming the hardening from 6:9–10, and the climactic suffering of the servant effects its reversal.

The link between the reversal of hardening and Isa 52:13–53:12 also contributes to the identification of the Suffering Servant with the Messianic King. Uhlig observes that it has remained widely unnoticed that the motif of hardening occurs in many of the messianic passages of Isaiah 1–39.[24] The Messianic King will have a spirit of wisdom, understanding, and knowledge (11:2), and the effect of his reign will be the opposite of the previous hardening:

> Then the eyes of those who see will not be closed,
>   and the ears of those who hear will give attention.
> The heart of the hasty will understand and know,
>   and the tongue of the stammerers will hasten to speak distinctly.
>   (Isa 32:3–4)

---

21. Torsten Uhlig, "Too Hard to Understand? The Motif of Hardening in Isaiah," in *Interpreting Isaiah: Issues and Approaches* (ed. David Firth and H. G. M. Williamson; Downers Grove, IL: InterVarsity Press, 2009), 74.
22. Ibid., 80.
23. Ibid.
24. Ibid., 79.

Like that of the Messianic King, the mission of the servant is also "to open the eyes that are blind" (Isa 42:7). Identity is intricately related to mission, and the mission of the Messianic King is to establish a kingdom (9:7). The means of establishing this kingdom, however, is not present in Isaiah 1–39 but points forward to 52:13–53:12, where the king fulfills his mission as a servant through his victorious suffering.

DISTINCTIONS BETWEEN THE SERVANT AND THE KING

We have seen that there are strong links between the Suffering Servant of Isa 52:13–53:12 and the Messianic King of Isaiah 1–39. However, although the servant and the king share many similarities, one must also take into account their differences. While the king is said to establish "his kingdom" (Isa 9:7), the servant is described as having "no . . . majesty that we should look at him" (53:2). The king is called "Wonderful Counselor, Mighty God" (Isa 9:6); the servant, "a man of sorrows" (53:3). Of the king Scripture says, "The government shall be on his shoulder" (Isa 9:6); yet the servant only "carried our sorrows" (53:4). The king is said to "strike the earth with the rod of his mouth" (11:4), but the servant "opened not his mouth" (53:7). The king will rise up to "kill the wicked" (11:4), but the servant is "cut off out of the land of the living" (53:8). Finally, it is "the zeal of the LORD of hosts" that will accomplish the Messiah's victory (Isa 9:7); yet for the servant, "it was the will of the LORD to crush him" (53:10). Furthermore, the Messianic King of Isaiah 9, 11, and 32 is never said to serve, suffer, and certainly not die. Rather than ignoring these differences and leaning solely on the similarities found above, perhaps we ought to see them precisely as the key to understanding the unique identity of the servant-king.

DEVELOPMENT OF THE ROYAL SERVANT'S MISSION

If the Davidic king and the Suffering Servant are the same figure, then how does one account for the way in which they are presented differently? The answer lies in the chronological and thematic development within the book of Isaiah. In other words, the story line of the book includes a variety of contexts that respectively highlight different aspects of God's interaction with his people at different times—preexilic (Isaiah 1–39) and exilic (Isaiah 40–55)—and result in different portrayals of God's agent in his unchanging purpose of establishing his kingdom. According to Daniel Carroll, "The person that the people of God must wait for, then, is a composite figure, whose ultimate identity keeps pushing the reader forward through a series of historical eras yet without final closure."[25] Isaiah 52:13–53:12, therefore, represents not a contradiction in the Isaianic expectation of the Messiah but rather a new development regarding the *means* of the Messiah's mission to establish the kingdom.[26]

Many reject the idea of a suffering messiah because of a lack of precedence thus far in Scripture. Although I have demonstrated this pattern in the story of Israel, Isaiah's presentation of the suffering Messianic King is certainly unique in that it is far more explicit and developed. The suffering of the Messianic King is not an anomaly but rather the shocking apex of development in the messianic understanding. Interpreting Isa 52:13–53:12 in light of the context of Isaiah 1–39 has shown that the Suffering Servant is to be identified with the Messianic King, who will establish his kingdom through the surprising means of sacrificial suffering.

THE SUFFERING SERVANT AND THE NEW EXODUS REIGN OF GOD (ISAIAH 40–55)

Having identified the Suffering Servant with the king (and coming kingdom) of Isaiah 1–39, I will now briefly describe the context of Isaiah 40–55 and then zoom in on the most immediate context of the song of the Suffering Servant, the units bracketing each side (Isa 51:1–52:12; 54:1–17).

THE NEW EXODUS AND THE REIGN OF GOD

Amidst God's judgment of Israel and the nations in Isaiah 1–39, there was hope in the coming of the Messianic King who would establish God's kingdom on earth. Turning from the "book of judgment" (Isaiah 1–39) to the "book of comfort" (Isaiah 40–66), however, there is a notable shift in emphasis from a king establishing a kingdom to a servant bringing about a new exodus.[27] While I have focused on the identity of the king and the servant, we must also ask: How does this work of bringing about a new exodus relate to the kingdom of God? In other words, does the mission of the messianic king drop out when one comes to Isaiah 40–55 and particularly to 52:13–53:12?

---

25. M. Daniel Carroll R., "The Power of the Future in the Present: Eschatology and Ethics in O'Donovan and Beyond," in *A Royal Priesthood? The Use of the Bible Ethically and Politically: A Dialogue with Oliver O'Donovan* (ed. Craig Bartholomew; SHS; Carlisle, UK: Paternoster, 2002), 132.

26. Alexander, *The Servant King*, 112.

27. For the new exodus theme in Isaiah 40–55, see Bernhard Anderson, "Exodus Typology in Second Isaiah," in *Israel's Prophetic Heritage: Essays in Honor of James Muilenburg* (ed. Bernhard Anderson and W. Harrelson; New York: Harper, 1962), 177–95. For the influence of the exodus throughout Scripture, see Richard Patterson and Michael Travers, "Contours of the Exodus Motif in Jesus' Earthly Ministry," *WTJ* 66 (2004): 25–47.

There are three reasons why the context of the coming of the kingdom in Isaiah 1–39 does not drop out (and is in fact developed) in Isaiah 40–55.[28] First, as mentioned above, the different contexts of Isaiah 1–39 (monarchy) and 40–55 (exile) require different emphases and even language to express God's actions and unchanging purposes within each respective period. The vision of a messianic kingdom is set forth in Isaiah 1–39, but in the context of an exiled people (Isaiah 40–55), God's reign assumes an especially redemptive mode.

Second, the background of the exodus itself upholds the unity of the new exodus and the reign of God. The song of Moses (Exod 15:1–18) opens by attributing Yahweh's redemptive victory to his majesty (15:7) and concludes with a description of Yahweh bringing his people into the promised land, where "the LORD will reign forever and ever" (15:18; this is significantly the first explicit mention of the reign of Yahweh in the Bible). In short, Israel is redeemed *from* bondage, *for* a kingdom, and *by* the king. Furthermore, this kingdom entails not only the kingship of God over his people in the promised land, but the Edenic restoration of God's people as a "kingdom of priests" (Exod 19:6).

Third—and most important—Isaiah 40–55, laden with allusions to a new exodus (Isa 40:3–5; 41:17–20; 42:14–16; 43:1–3, 14–21; 48:20–21; 49:8–12; 51:9–10; 52:11–12; 55:12–13), is strategically framed by references to the reign of God (40:9–11; 52:7). In the ever-important prologue of Isaiah 40–55, a herald proclaims the "good news" that "the LORD comes with might, and his arm rules for him" (40:9–10). As a great shepherd-king, he will "tend his flock" and "gather the lambs in his arms" (40:11). Yahweh *is* king (41:21; 43:15; 44:6; 52:7), and he will once again majestically lead his people out of bondage by means of his "arm" (40:10; cf. 43:15–19).

Just as Isaiah 40–55 opens with a declaration of God's kingship, it reaches its apex with another herald announcing the "good news" that "Your God reigns!" (52:7). Yahweh has been proclaiming royal deliverance of his people from bondage, but in this announcement the *aim* of the new exodus is revealed: the kingdom of God.[29] In the exodus, God delivered his people from slavery to the Egyptians in order that they might live in the promised land under his reign through King David. In the new exodus, God will

---

28. I use the phrase "coming of the kingdom" loosely to mean the future establishing of God's reign through his Davidic Messiah (Isaiah 9; 11; 32; cf. Mic 4:8).

29. Rikki Watts, "Consolation or Confrontation: Isaiah 40–55 and the Delay of the New Exodus," *TynBul* 41 (1990): 34; William Dumbrell, *The Faith of Israel: A Theological Survey of the Old Testament* (2nd ed.; Grand Rapids: Baker Academic, 2002), 108; Bright, *The Kingdom of God*, 140.

redeem his people from slavery to sin in order that they might live eternally in the new creation under his reign through the Davidic Messiah.

GREAT AND GREATER DELIVERANCE (ISAIAH 40–48 AND 49–55)

The theme of Isaiah 40–55 is presented in the first words of the introduction: "Comfort, comfort, my people" (40:1). Like "a red thread that extends from 40:1," the promise of God's comfort and deliverance remains in the midst of his righteous judgment.[30] This deliverance takes on two distinct forms: the "Great Deliverance" (Isaiah 40–48) presents Israel as the blind and rebellious servant who is delivered physically from Babylon by Cyrus. The "Greater Deliverance" (Isaiah 49–55) is an eschatological deliverance from the captivity of sin through the individual servant who restores Israel.[31] Oswalt's structure is helpful for tracing the thematic flow of Isaiah 49–55:

Anticipation of Salvation (Isa 49:1–52:12)
Proclamation of Salvation (Isa 52:13–53:12)
Invitation to Salvation (Isa 54:1–55:13)

The fourth song has commonly been interpreted in light of the other servant songs, so this section will add to that context by focusing particularly on the passages that bracket the song (Isa 51:1–52:12 and 54:1–17), which have played a much lesser role in interpretation.[32]

ANTICIPATION OF SALVATION (ISAIAH 51:1–52:12)

The triumph of the servant in Isa 52:13–53:12 can only be understood as the climactic act that 51:1–52:12 anticipates. The unfolding account builds toward victorious salvation (52:7) and then astonishingly reveals the means to this great accomplishment: "Behold, my servant" (52:13). The entire section is held together by eight initial imperatives, the last five of which are double imperatives. All of these flow together to form one anticipatory unit proclaiming the deliverance of Israel through the "arm of the LORD."

---

30. Childs, *Isaiah*, 402.

31. Oswalt, *Isaiah 40–66*, 286; Gary V. Smith, *Isaiah 40–66* (NAC 15b; Nashville: Broadman & Holman, 2009), 336. Although Motyer only considers Isaiah 44–48 the "Great Deliverance," I retain his terms because they succinctly express the continuity and distinction between the two sections (*Isaiah*, 421).

32. According to J. Ross Wagner, the apostle Paul interpreted Isa 52:13–53:12 within its immediate context ("The Heralds of Isaiah and the Mission of Paul: An Investigation of Paul's Use of Isaiah 51–55 in Romans," in *Jesus and the Suffering Servant: Isaiah 53 and Christian Origins* (ed. W. H. Bellinger and William Reuben Farmer [Harrisburg, PA: Trinity Press International, 1998], 220–22).

The unfolding story can be summarized as follows: Yahweh tells Israel three times to listen (Isa 51:1, 4, 7), for his salvation is coming. Israel then calls on the "arm of the LORD" to awaken and bring about this salvation (51:9–11), to which God responds with three doublets of his own, each calling the people to awaken to a new situation that the Lord has brought about: the comfort of his people (51:12–16), the removal of God's wrath (51:17–23), and the reign of God (52:1–12). Finally, with one last double imperative God commands his people to "depart, depart" from that to which they were enslaved and into the newly achieved reality (52:11).

Isaiah 51:1–8 is structured around the threefold use of the imperative to listen, each followed by words of assurance for God's coming salvation.[33] The statement "the LORD comforts Zion" (51:3) clearly refers to the opening promise of Isaiah 40, showing that this unit (51:1–52:12) is not the beginning of anticipation but the culmination of what has built from 40:1 onward. The context of the servant's accomplishment is broadened even further by the references to the Abrahamic covenant (51:2) and God's desire for Israel—to "make her wilderness like Eden" (51:3). These references place the coming deliverance of Yahweh in the broader Old Testament context of creation, fall, and restoration through the "seed" of Abraham.

One of the clearest connections between Isaiah 40 and 51:1–8 is the "arm of the LORD," which also proves to be a key theme throughout the rest of 51:1–52:12 and 52:13–53:12. After the proclamation of comfort in 40:1, the means of this salvation is declared in 40:10, "Behold, the LORD God comes with might, and his arm rules for him." It is no surprise, then, that in 51:5 Israel is presented as waiting in expectation on the "arm" of Yahweh. Motyer observes the importance of the "arm of the LORD" motif throughout Isaiah 40–55, demonstrating that the reference to the arm in 51:5 builds on 40:10 and "prepares for 51:9, a call for a new-exodus activity of the Lord; for 52:10, where the Lord's arm is bared for universal revelation of saving power; and for 53:1, where we meet the arm of the Lord in person."[34] The increasing longing for salvation from the "arm of the LORD" thrusts the reader forward to the eventual announcement of "arm of the LORD" as "the servant of the LORD" (Isa 53:1).

Isaiah 51:9–16 consists of two sections: a double imperative from Israel calling the "arm of the LORD" to "awake, awake" (51:9–11), and a response

---

33. Smith, *Isaiah 40–66*, 389.

34. Motyer, *Isaiah*, 404. The "arm of the LORD" is not only a unifying theme in Isa 51:1–53:12, but a key theme for connecting this unit with the rest of the book of Isaiah (30:30; 40:10; 48:14; 51:5; 52:10; 53:1; 59:16; 62:8; 63:5, 12).

from Yahweh with the double pronoun "I, I am he," that he will be faithful to his promises and that their anticipation will not be in vain (51:12–16). This passage coheres well with the previous one, for it is "a proper response to divine promises" that were presented in 51:1–8.[35] Yahweh has promised comfort and salvation through his arm, and Israel is now crying out in anticipation for that salvation to come quickly. He responds with the reassurance that "I, I am he who comforts you" (51:12) and "you are my people" (51:16). He will hold true to his promise; deliverance is coming.

Isaiah 51:17–23 addresses the wrath of God in terms of Israel's problem (51:17–20) and God's solution (51:21–23). Yahweh calls Israel to "awaken" to the state of their sinful condition: "You . . . have drunk from the hand of the LORD the cup of his wrath" (Isa 51:17). Israel's "captivity" goes beyond their oppression under other nations and the brokenness from sin; they need to be saved from the wrath of God.

The presence of God's wrath is clearly a major component of Israel's problem, and therefore, the removal of God's wrath is absolutely essential for their salvation. Astonishingly, God then declares, "Behold, I have taken from your hand the cup of staggering; the bowl of my wrath you shall drink no more" (Isa 51:22). As the anticipation of 51:1–52:12 begins to be depicted as an achieved reality, the removal of God's wrath is a key aspect to this new state of being. God's wrath, however, is not merely erased, for God declares that he has removed his wrath from Israel and "put it into the hand of your tormentors" (51:23). According to Oswalt, the averting of God's wrath confirms his justice, because he does not merely forget the due penalty for sin, but transfers the punishment to Israel's tormentors.[36]

Motyer interprets the removal of God's wrath in light of the new exodus theme, so prevalent in Isaiah 49–55:

> At the exodus, the Lord's Passover redemption of his people coincided with his just visitation upon Egypt for refusing his word and afflicting his people. It was not the visitation of just punishment on Egypt that redeemed the people (else why was the Passover sacrifice required?), but the removal of wrath from the one and the infliction of wrath on the other were two sides of the same divine action.[37]

Remembering that Isa 51:1–52:12 is pointing forward to the accomplishment of the servant in 52:13–53:12, this specific passage reveals that averting the

---

35. Ibid., 408.
36. Oswalt, *Isaiah 40–66*, 356.
37. Motyer, *Isaiah*, 415.

wrath of God is an essential part of Israel's deliverance and therefore a crucial aspect of the servant's accomplishment.

Isaiah 52:1–12, although one unit describing the reality of Yahweh's redemption, is often divided into three sections (52:1–6, 7–10, 11–12). The first words of Isa 52:1–6 are almost identical to the words of 51:9. The double imperative "awake, awake, put on strength," used in 51:9 by Israel to beckon the "arm of the LORD" for deliverance, is used here to call the people to respond to the deliverance that the "arm of the LORD" has secured. This transformed reality is defined by purity (52:1), freedom (52:2), and, finally, redemption (52:3–6), which recalls as a framework God's deliverance of Israel from captivity in Egypt.

Isaiah 52:7–10 is incredibly significant because it represents the pinnacle of anticipation for the servant's accomplishment and the fullest portrayal of the new reality it has created. The achieved new reality is characterized by the reign of God and is expressed in highly lyrical form through the scene of a messenger returning from battle with news of the results. The "good news" of victory is summed up in the one phrase—"Your God reigns" (52:7)—to which the people respond with singing because they know it means the "return of the LORD to Zion" (52:8). Oswalt argues that the summative statement of salvation—"Your God reigns"—is defined by the previous threefold description of good news: "peace," "happiness," and "salvation" (Isa 52:7).[38]

"Peace" (שָׁלוֹם) describes a condition of welfare or wholeness, where all things are in their proper relation to each other; "happiness" (טוֹב) refers to the goodness of creation purposes restored; and "salvation" (יְשׁוּעָה) entails a condition of freedom from every bondage, particularly that of sin. The riveting declaration "Your God reigns" not only indicates the kingdom context of Isaiah 40–55 but recalls the messianic vision of the establishment of a kingdom, which would be brought about by "the zeal of the LORD" (Isa 9:7).

The last section, Isa 52:11–12, contains the final double imperative of this unit. While the previous double imperative called Israel to "awaken" to the new reality achieved by the servant, this last double imperative commands them to "depart" from their captivity and into that reality. Although this section appeals to the exodus narrative and surely calls Israel to a new exodus, it also makes clear that the new exodus is no duplication of the deliverance from the Egyptians. They are not told to "go out in haste" like the Israelites in the exodus, but as Goldingay says, it is "a procession under the protection of that victorious king of verses 7–10."[39]

---

38. Oswalt, *Isaiah 40–66*, 368.

39. John Goldingay, *Isaiah* (NIBCOT 13; Peabody, MA: Hendrickson, 2001), 299.

To summarize, as a unit Isa 51:1–52:12 reveals the pinnacle of anticipation for God's redemption, for in between promise ("comfort, comfort, my people," Isa 40:1) and prophecy of fulfillment ("the LORD has comforted his people," Isa 52:9) lies the increasing desire for God's great act of bringing about a new exodus and establishing his reign in Zion.[40] As Motyer says, "The LORD has *bared his holy arm in the sight of all nations*—but as to the act itself, we are still in suspense!"[41]

PROCLAMATION OF SALVATION: THE SONG OF THE SUFFERING SERVANT (ISAIAH 52:13–53:12)

The song of the Suffering Servant provides the resolution to what has led up to it and the foundation for what follows. Here we are at the heart of God's *means* of accomplishing salvation and the eschatological hinge-point between bondage and redemption. Because my aim is not to provide an in-depth exegesis of Isa 52:13–53:12 itself but to locate it within its proper context, I will cut to the heart of the matter: the suffering of the servant is depicted in terms of substitutionary atonement.

This aspect of the servant's accomplishment has been the dominant interpretation of the song throughout the history of the church and, though questioned by recent critics,[42] has been successfully defended by many.[43] Motyer's structure of the song shows that the *meaning* of the servant's suffering is primarily revealed in the center of the song (Isa 53:4–6).[44] First, the suffering was substitutionary: "he has borne our griefs and carried our sorrows"; "he was pierced for our transgressions; he was crushed for our iniquities"; and "the LORD has laid on him the iniquity of us all." While 53:3 makes clear that he suffered as a "man of sorrows," 53:4–6 reveals that his suffering was not for his own doing but rather in the place of others. The servant takes the chastisement of the many, who in exchange receive peace (53:5).

Second, his suffering is atoning. Although the word "atonement" is not used in the song, the concept is strongly present.[45] The language of bearing guilt and iniquity (Isa 53:4–6) and sin itself (53:12), coupled with the lan-

---

40. For the similarities between Isa 40:1–21 and 52:7–10, see Childs, *Isaiah*, 406; Goldingay, *Isaiah*, 299.

41. Motyer, *Isaiah*, 416, emphasis his.

42. R. N. Whybray, *Isaiah 40–66* (NCB; Greenwood, SC: Attic, 1975), 175; Harry Orlinsky, "The So-Called 'Servant of the Lord' and 'Suffering Servant' in Second Isaiah," in *Studies on the Second Part of the Book of Isaiah* (ed. Harry Orlinsky and N. Snaith; Leiden: Brill, 1967), 1–133.

43. Alan J. Groves, "Atonement in Isaiah 53: For He Bore the Sins of Many," in *The Glory of the Atonement* (ed. Charles Hill and Frank James III; Downers Grove, IL: InterVarsity Press, 2004), 61–89; Oswalt, *Isaiah 40–66*, 384–89; Motyer, *Isaiah*, 423–26; Blocher, *Songs of the Servant*, 72.

44. See above, p. 70, fn.6..

45. Groves, "Atonement in Isaiah 53," 64–68.

guage of substitution, recalls the entire sacrificial system of Israel. The servant is portrayed as both the priest who makes an offering of atonement (52:15; 53:10) and the sin-bearing, sacrificial lamb himself (53:4–7). He is the guilt offering (53:10), which according to the law of Moses would effect atonement and therefore restore a covenant relationship with God (Lev 5:14–6:7; 7:1–10).[46] In short, the suffering of the servant provides a substitutionary atonement for "the many," removing sin as well as its consequences and restoring a right relationship with God. Within the broader *goal* of the new exodus reign of God, we have now discovered the *agent* (the royal servant) and the *means* (substitutionary, atoning suffering).

INVITATION TO SALVATION (ISAIAH 54:1–17)

The triumph of the suffering servant is anticipated in Isa 51:1–52:12, proclaimed in 52:13–53:12, and offered through an invitation in 54:1–17. This last passage assumes the restoration of God's people and metaphorically describes the "heritage of the servants of the LORD" (Isa 54:17). Westermann makes a key distinction for understanding this passage: "The subject of the promise is again not deliverance and restoration, but the new condition of salvation."[47] Although the entire passage focuses on the description of this condition of salvation, the first segment (54:1–10) emphasizes the source of the restoration as the gracious character of God by using the metaphor of marriage, while the second segment (54:11–17) highlights the benefits of restoration by using the metaphor of a city.

Especially important to understanding the work of the servant is the way in which Isa 52:13–53:12 relates to 54:1–17. The state of being in Isa 54:1–17 is created by, and dependent on, the work of the servant in 52:13–53:12. According to Motyer, "In his saving work, the servant has done everything, removing sin, establishing in righteousness, creating a family. The way is therefore open for response, pure and simple: to sing over what someone else has accomplished."[48]

Although the connection between Isa 52:13–53:12 and 54:1–17 has often been called into question,[49] the literary and thematic links prove their inseparability in the canon. First, the two passages share key vocabulary: "peace" (שָׁלוֹם) in 53:5 and 54:10, 13; "offspring" (זֶרַע) in Isa 53:10 and 54:3; and

---

46. Barry Webb, *The Message of Isaiah: On Eagles' Wings* (BST; Downers Grove, IL: InterVarsity Press, 1996), 213.

47. Claus Westermann, *Isaiah 40–66: A Commentary* (OTL; Philadelphia: Westminster, 1969), 277.

48. Motyer, *Isaiah*, 444.

49. For a discussion of the positions, see Oswalt, *Isaiah 40–66*, 413.

"many" (רַבִּים) in 53:11, 12 and 54:1. Second, the two passages share a similar focus in subject matter. Whereas certain portions of Isaiah, such as chapters 40–48, focus on the physical deliverance, 52:13–53:12 and 54:1–17 share a common emphasis on the issues of sin, righteousness, mercy, pardon, and relationship with God.[50] Third, in light of the broader context of Isaiah 49–55, the two passages cohere thematically to form a congruent whole. If Isa 52:13–53:12 is understood as the means by which God's people are reconciled to him, it serves logically as a foundation for the new condition of salvation presented in Isaiah 54. Muilenburg expresses the fittingness of the Suffering Servant song well: "Precisely at the juncture of the coming of the kingdom and the inauguration of the new covenant he [the writer] finds it necessary to place the poem of the suffering Servant."[51]

Isaiah 54:1–10 invites Israel to "Sing!" and embrace the restoration achieved by the servant in 52:13–53:12. The ransomed people of God are described metaphorically as a barren woman who can now sing over her multitude of children (54:1–3) and as a widow who will lose the reproach of widowhood because her Maker is now her Husband (54:4–5). This is the achieved reality that Israel is being invited into, a restored relationship with her Creator that is described in the most intimate terms available.

While we have seen anticipation (Isa 51:1–52:12), proclamation (52:13–53:12), and invitation (54:1–17), Isa 54:7–8 reveals the motivation behind God's salvation: "For a brief moment I deserted you . . . but with everlasting love [חֶסֶד] I will have compassion on you." The astonishment of a king being subjected to suffering on behalf of others begs the question: *Why* would he do this? That question is answered in 54:8 with one of the richest Hebrew words (חֶסֶד), expressing the gracious love and covenant devotion of Yahweh for his people. Isaiah 54:10 then introduces another key theme that is directly related to the song of the Suffering Servant, describing the achieved reality in chapter 54 as Yahweh's covenant of peace (שָׁלוֹם). The שָׁלוֹם enjoyed by the redeemed in Isaiah 54 is the very שָׁלוֹם achieved by the servant in Isa 53:5: "Upon him was the chastisement that brought us peace" (שָׁלוֹם).

Isaiah 54:11–17 continues to describe the achieved reality of salvation, now speaking of Israel in terms of a city being established in righteousness. The flow of the metaphor moves from the magnificence of the city (54:11–12) to the blessedness of its citizens (54:13–14) to Yahweh's protection and governance of the city (54:15–17). The city motif is prevalent throughout the

---

50. Ibid., 414.
51. Quoted in ibid.

book of Isaiah,[52] but it is only on the foundation of the servant's accomplishment that this city is built. The city, marked by peace (54:13, שָׁלוֹם), is a picture of the new reality achieved by the servant in 52:13–53:12.

The last verse offers a fitting conclusion: "This is the heritage of the servants of the LORD" (Isa 54:17). Oswalt avers that the "this" includes not only the content of Isaiah 54 but the restored relationship with Yahweh, which has been the entire focus of chapters 49–55.[53] Furthermore, the recipients of the servant's accomplishment are now declared "servants of the LORD." As will be discussed further below, the atoning work of the servant of Yahweh has restored the servants to Yahweh.

THE SUFFERING SERVANT AND THE NEW CREATION (ISAIAH 56–66)

Though my primary aim is to understand the place of the servant's suffering in the context of the coming kingdom of the Messiah, I would be remiss not to mention at least briefly the significance of Isaiah 56–66. There is a scholarly consensus that Isaiah 56–66 presupposes and even develops Isaiah 40–55,[54] once again in light of a new context (postexilic) and with an especially eschatological focus (the new heavens and new earth).

The key feature of Isaiah 56–66 is the effect of the work of the servant on the servants, as God's reign is extended from Jerusalem to the ends of the earth. Hence, the servant (singular) in Isaiah 49–53 shifts to the servants (plural) in Isaiah 54–66. W. A. M. Beuken has argued convincingly that the promise of "offspring" to the servant in 53:10 is fulfilled in the "servants" of 54:17, and it becomes the dominant theme throughout Isaiah 56–66.[55] Schultz captures the thematic development well: "The work of the individual servant restores the national servant so that individuals within Israel once again serve God."[56] The servant's priestly offering of himself (52:15; 53:10) results in the democratization of the priesthood to all of God's servants: "You shall be called the priests of the LORD" (Isa 61:6; cf. 54:11–17; 56:1–8;

---

52. Motyer, *Isaiah*, 449.

53. Oswalt, *Isaiah 40–66*, 431.

54. Jake Stromberg, *Isaiah after Exile: The Author of Third Isaiah as Reader and Redactor of the Book* (Oxford: Oxford University Press, 2011), 2; Williamson, "Recent Issues in the Study of Isaiah," 37.

55. W. A. M. Beuken, "The Main Theme of Trito-Isaiah 'the Servants of Yhwh,'" *JSOT* 15 (1990): 67–87. This thesis has been affirmed by the following scholars: Motyer, *Isaiah*, 445; Childs, *Isaiah*, 444–52; Joseph Blenkinsopp, *Isaiah 56–66: A New Translation with Introduction and Commentary* (AB; New York: Doubleday, 2003).

56. Schultz, "Servant/Slave," 1195.

59:21–60:3; 66:21). The new exodus is truly being fulfilled, for the LORD has redeemed his people and made them "a kingdom of priests" (Exod 19:6).

SUMMARY: THE SERVANT-KING AND THE KINGDOM OF SERVANTS

How does re-placing the Suffering Servant in the proper context contribute to the interpretation of the *identity* of the servant and the nature of his *accomplishment* in Isa 52:13–53:12? I have demonstrated that such re-placing reveals that he is the Messianic King (Isaiah 1–39), who will bring about a new exodus (Isaiah 40–55) and thereby establish God's kingdom by the surprising means of his atoning death. In other words, the context of 52:13–53:12 portrays an act of salvation that is *by a servant-king* (identity) and *for a kingdom of servants* (accomplishment).

The *identity* of the servant is characterized by his connection to both the Messianic King and the divine king. Throughout all of Scripture, Yahweh is king, though from the beginning of the story his kingship is mediated through humans (Gen 1:28). Yet while humanity failed at properly representing God's reign, God promised to anoint one human, in the line of David, through whom he would reign for all of eternity (Isa 9:1–7). The hope of God's reign being restored on earth moves from the Messianic King in Isaiah 1–39 to a surprisingly new presentation of God's mediated rule: "Behold, my servant" (52:13). The servant is the Messianic King, the "arm of the LORD" (53:1) which "rules for him" (40:10). The servant-king is the mediatorial means of establishing God's kingship.

The nature of the servant's *accomplishment* is greatly enriched by its context of the coming kingdom of God (Isaiah 1–39), new exodus (Isaiah 40–55), and new creation (Isaiah 56–66). The substitutionary atonement of the servant not only reconciles sinners to Yahweh but also effects the new exodus and Yahweh's reign on earth, restoring unfaithful servants into proper service of the king. The immediate context of the Suffering Servant song reveals that the anticipation of God's reign (Isa 51:1–52:12) finds its resolution in the suffering of the servant (52:13–53:12), which is then celebrated in a great song of restoration (54:1–17). In other words, in between the promise of redemption (51:1–52:12) and the fulfillment of redemption (54:1–17) lies the great achievement of the Redeemer (52:13–53:12).[57]

---

57. William Dumbrell, "The Role of the Servant in Isaiah 40–55," *RTR* 48 (1989): 105–13; idem, *The Faith of Israel*, 109–10; Watts, "Consolation or Confrontation," 52.

The context of the fourth servant song also reveals the comprehensive nature of the servant's work, perhaps best seen in Isaiah's use of *šālôm* to describe the fruit of the servant's work and the ensuing state of God's reign. *Šālôm* was predicted as part of the messianic hope (Isa 9:6), anticipated as good news (52:7) and achieved by the servant as a defining feature of the new reality (54:8).[58] God's "shalom-producing rule"[59] (Isa 52:7), however, is displayed in its fullest in the majestic suffering of the servant: "Upon him was the chastisement that brought us *šālôm*" (53:5). Therefore, if the reign of the Messiah is characterized by unending *šālôm* (9:7), and he is predicted "to establish it and uphold it . . . from this time forth and forevermore" (9:7), then the atoning death of the servant is the means for this establishment of the kingdom and its foundation into eternity.

The paradoxical nature of the servant-king's suffering and exaltation is at the heart of his glorious accomplishment. He who was "lifted up" (נִשָּׂא) and exalted (Isa 52:13) is the very one who "has borne [נָשָׂא] our griefs" (53:4) and "bore [נָשָׂא] the sin of many" (53:12). In English, one simply misses the wordplay, but the irony could not be any greater. The one who is "lifted up" in exaltation is the one who has "lifted up" our sins onto himself in order that we may be reconciled to God and share in his victory. Although exaltation and humiliation seem to be extreme opposites, the servant is exalted through humiliation and victorious through suffering. Re-placing the song of the Suffering Servant in its canonical context provides a kingdom framework for the sin-bearing, sorrow-carrying, punishment-averting, guilt-offering, place-taking, atoning death of the servant-king. The significance could not be more *crucial*: the servant-king brings about a kingdom of servants through his atoning and victorious suffering.

And yet, all of this is prophetic—lunging the reader forward in search of fulfillment. While the kingdom vision of Isaiah was majestic and lofty, the Old Testament ends modestly, with partial fulfillment and certainly no king ushering in a new era of salvation. But the promise remains. The anticipation builds. To the New Testament we must turn.

---

58. Webb, *Isaiah*, 214.
59. Dempster, *Dominion and Dynasty*, 175.

CHAPTER THREE

THE CRUCIFIED KING IN MARK

THE NEW TESTAMENT presents Jesus as the continuation and fulfillment of the Old Testament story of Adam and Israel. In this chapter, I will follow Mark's portrayal of Jesus; then, in the next chapter I will interpret two other key New Testament passages that are linked together by the "blood" of the cross and "kingdom" of Christ (Col 1:13–20; Rev 5:5–10).

Mark's integration of the kingdom and the cross in Jesus' fulfillment of Israel's story suggests that interpreters miss the mark when focusing solely on *either* the kingdom *or* the cross. As perilous as this bifurcation is, a simple reading of Mark's gospel could (and often does) further the divide. The first half of Mark seemingly highlights Jesus' victorious proclamation and demonstration of the kingdom, whereas the latter half emphasizes his service and apparent defeat on the cross. How do the kingdom and the cross relate in Mark's gospel?[1] The relationship between the kingdom and the cross in Mark has been construed in various ways:

1. Kingdom despite cross (Jesus' life and resurrection, not death, bring the kingdom)[2]
2. Cross despite kingdom (Jesus' death is what really matters)[3]

---

1. Scholars have employed a variety of methods in answering this question. While form critics tore the kingdom and the cross apart by attributing each to different sources (i.e., Bultmann, *The History of the Synoptic Tradition*, 262–84), certain historical Jesus scholars seek to bring the two back together in the mind of Jesus himself (Schürmann, *Gottes Reich, Jesu Geschick*; Wright, *Jesus and the Victory of God*, 540–611; McKnight, *Jesus and His Death*). I will address Mark's construal of the kingdom and the cross, not by reconstructing the origins of Mark's gospel or rediscovering the aims of the historical Jesus but rather by apprehending Mark's theological portrayal of Jesus in the final form of his narrative, especially in light of Mark's use of the Old Testament.
2. Brondos, "Why Was Jesus Crucified?" 496–99.
3. Reflected in the still common sentiment of the gospels as "passion narratives with extended introductions" (Martin Kähler, *The So-Called Historical Jesus and the Historic, Biblical Christ* [Philadelphia: Fortress, 1964)], 80).

3. Kingdom then cross (Jesus' kingdom mission cut short by death)[4]
4. Cross then kingdom (Jesus' death as precursor to the kingdom)[5]
5. Kingdom qualifies cross (theology of glory corrects theology of suffering)[6]
6. Cross qualifies kingdom (theology of suffering corrects theology of glory)[7]

I propose that the proper relationship is defined as "kingdom by 'way' of cross." While there is certainly an emphasis on Jesus' kingdom ministry in Galilee (Mark 1:1–8:21) and on the cross in Jerusalem (11:1–16:8), a closer reading of the "way" section (8:22–10:52) reveals there is no contradiction between the kingdom and the cross, nor is there simply a progression from one to the other; rather, there is a mutually enriching relationship between the two that draws significantly from the story of Israel and culminates in the crucifixion of Christ the king.[8] The kingdom is redefined by suffering and the cross is portrayed as an act of kingly power.

The kingdom–cross interplay is implicitly proclaimed in Galilee, explicitly explained on "the way," and effectively established at Golgotha. I will demonstrate that one need not choose between Mark's gospel as "a passion narrative"[9] *or* a kingdom "manifesto"[10] because it is a coalescence of these themes in Jesus, who brings the kingdom by way of the cross. Below, I will trace the development of the kingdom–cross interplay throughout Mark, observing how the kingdom mission of Jesus culminates on the cross.

---

4. Regarding the coming of the kingdom, Rudolf Bultmann says, "This hope of Jesus and of the early Christian community was not fulfilled. The same world still exists and history continues" (*Jesus Christ and Mythology* [New York: Scribner, 1958], 14); cf. idem, *The History of the Synoptic Tradition*, 262–84.

5. Johannes Weiss, *Die Predigt Jesu vom Reiche Gottes* (Göttingen: Vandenhoeck & Ruprecht, 1900); Albert Schweitzer, *The Mystery of the Kingdom of God: The Secret of Jesus' Messiahship and Passion* (trans. Walter Lowrie; New York: Macmillan, 1950).

6. Robert Gundry, *Mark: A Commentary on His Apology for the Cross* (Grand Rapids: Eerdmans, 2000), 1–14, 1022–26.

7. "The regnant view has it that Mark corrects the theology of glory with the theology of suffering" (ibid., 2).

8. The following works support the thesis that Mark is portraying the crucifixion as enthronement: Joel Marcus, "Crucifixion as Parodic Exaltation," *JBL* 125 (2006): 73–87; T. E. Schmidt, "Mark 15:16–32: The Crucifixion Narrative and the Roman Triumphal Procession," *NTS* 41 (1995): 1–18; Norman Perrin, "The High Priest's Question and Jesus' Answer (Mark 14:61–62)," in *The Passion in Mark: Studies on Mark 14–16* (ed. Werner Kelber; Philadelphia: Fortress, 1976), 91–94; Howard Jackson, "The Death of Jesus in Mark and the Miracle from the Cross," *NTS* 33 (1987): 25.

9. Kahler, *The So-Called Historical Jesus and the Historic, Biblical Christ*, 80.

10. Werner Kelber, *The Kingdom in Mark: A New Place and a New Time* (Philadelphia: Fortress, 1974), 139.

THE KINGDOM IN THE SHADOW OF THE CROSS (MARK 1:1–8:26)

THE BEGINNING OF THE GOSPEL

In keeping with ancient literary convention, Mark's prologue reveals key themes for the entirety of his work. Mark's first word (ἀρχή) is not simply telling the reader where to begin, but is rather a reference to Gen 1:1 (ἐν ἀρχῇ LXX), which places Mark's story about Jesus within the story of the world from creation (Genesis 1–2) to new creation (Isa 65:17–25), and more specifically (as is clear in the next verse) within the story of Israel.[11] Mark's explicit Old Testament citation in Mark 1:2–3, although attributed to Isaiah, is actually a conflation of Exod 23:20; Mal 3:1; and Isa 40:3. The key to this citation is that, by referencing Isaiah, Mark is not merely proof-texting John's ministry of preparation, but is recalling the entire context of Isaiah 40–55: the long-awaited Isaianic new exodus, culminating in God's reign over the earth.

Although the influence of Isaiah 40–55 on Mark has been recognized broadly, Rikki Watts and Joel Marcus in particular have shed light on how the Isaianic new exodus provides a conceptual and hermeneutical framework for the entirety of Mark's gospel.[12] The Isaianic new exodus context includes a dual perspective of salvation and judgment: salvation in terms of the Isaianic new exodus and judgment in terms of Malachi's warning of its delay. For Mark, therefore, the beginning of Jesus' ministry represents the beginning of the Isaianic new exodus and the establishment of God's reign on earth.[13] While at one level Mark's structure is simply geographic (Galilee, journey, Jerusalem), theologically it aligns with the pattern of redemption established in the exodus and prophesied in the Isaianic new exodus (deliverance from evil, journey along "the way," enthronement in Jerusalem).[14] Especially pertinent is the fact that the influence of Isaiah 40–55 on Mark includes not only the Isaianic new exodus, which culminates in God's enthronement in Jerusalem (Isa 52:7), but also its agent and means—the servant and his atoning death (Isa 52:13–53:12).[15]

Once the stage for the Isaianic new exodus has been set, the drama immediately unfolds in two opening acts: John's preparation (Mark 1:4–8) and Jesus'

---

11. Nicholas Perrin, "Where to Begin with the Gospel of Mark," *CurTM* 35 (2008): 413.
12. Rikki Watts, *Isaiah's New Exodus in Mark* (Grand Rapids: Baker Academic, 2001); Marcus, *The Way of the Lord*.
13. Watts, *Isaiah's New Exodus in Mark*, 4.
14. Ibid., 81.
15. Watts, "Consolation or Confrontation," 49–59.

ministry (1:9–15). John "prepares the way" for Jesus not only by proclaiming his coming but by foreshadowing his career. John preaches (κηρύσσω, 1:4, 7) and is handed over (παραδίδωμι, 1:14) to be killed; then Jesus preaches (κηρύσσω, 1:14) and is handed over (παραδίδωμι, 15:15) to be killed.[16] The main point of John's introduction, however, is his proclamation of Jesus as the "stronger one" (ὁ ἰσχυρότερος, Mark 1:7). Whereas Isa 40:9–10 has Yahweh coming in "strength" (ἰσχύς LXX), with his arm ruling for him, John announces Jesus as coming in strength to rule on behalf of God. This background "exalts Jesus as a royal figure"[17] and likely reveals John's understanding of Jesus to be messianic, especially considering Isa 11:2, which speaks of a Davidic descendant on whom "the Spirit of the LORD shall rest" and will have a spirit of "strength" (ἰσχύς LXX).[18]

The baptism of Jesus is pivotal in Mark because it looks back to the Old Testament to describe Jesus' mission and forward to the cross as its climax. Within Mark's gospel itself, the baptism (Mark 1:9–11) forms an inclusio with the crucifixion (15:37–39).[19] In the baptism, the heavens are torn, a voice comes from heaven, and Jesus is declared to be the Son of God (1:9–11). In the crucifixion, a cry is voiced from the cross, the curtain is torn, and Jesus is declared to be the Son of God (15:37–39). For Mark, Jesus' *anointing* at his baptism anticipates the climactic event of his *enthronement* on the cross.[20]

Yet how can Mark combine the seemingly contradictory kingship and suffering of Jesus? The answer lies not in Mark's synthesis of abstract concepts (kingship and suffering) but in interweaving Old Testament traditions and figures. The Old Testament is the interpretive world from which Mark draws, and scholars have shown that Mark cites/alludes to the Old Testament primarily in a contextual (rather than atomistic) way,[21] and even merges Old Testament traditions at crucial points in his argument.[22] In Jesus' baptism, the voice from heaven declares, "You are my beloved Son; with you I am

---

16. The pattern is the same for the disciples, who are to preach (κηρύσσω, Mark 3:14) and then be handed over (παραδίδωμι, 13:9) to be killed.

17. Adela Yarbro Collins, *Mark: A Commentary* (Hermeneia; Minneapolis: Fortress, 2007), 146.

18. In Second Temple Judaism, the Messiah was associated with strength (ἰσχύος) (*Pss. Sol.* 17:37; *1 En.* 49:3).

19. Stephen Motyer, "The Rending of the Veil: A Markan Pentecost?" *NTS* 33 (1987): 155–57.

20. Ardel Caneday, "Christ's Baptism and Crucifixion: The Anointing and Enthronement of God's Son," *SBJT* 8 (2004): 70–85.

21. Holly Carey, *Jesus' Cry from the Cross: Towards a First-Century Understanding of the Intertextual Relationship Between Psalm 22 and the Narrative of Mark's Gospel* (New York: T&T Clark, 2009), 172; Watts, *Isaiah's New Exodus in Mark*, 111.

22. Howard Clark Kee, "The Function of Scriptural Quotations and Allusions in Mark 11–16," in *Jesus und Paulus* (ed. E. Ellis and E. Grässer; Göttingen: Vandenhoeck & Ruprecht, 1975), 173.

well pleased" (Mark 1:11), which combines the Old Testament figures of the Davidic Messiah (Ps 2:7) and Isaianic Servant (Isa 42:1).[23]

Based on Mark's contextual use of the Old Testament, these allusions refer not merely to Jesus' sonship or his pleasing of the Father, but to the entire contexts of the Old Testament passages. Jesus is therefore declared to be the servant of Isaiah 40–55 whose suffering (52:13–53:12) will bring about the new exodus and reign of God. Likewise, the Ps 2:7 allusion refers not only to Jesus' sonship, but to his anointing (2:2), enthronement (2:6), and victory over enemies (2:9); all of these draw from the tradition of 2 Sam 7:12–14.

Mark's presentation of the kingdom–cross interplay, therefore, is not primarily conceptual but redemptive-historical. In other words, Mark seeks not to synthesize kingship and suffering in the abstract but to weave together prophetic strands such as the Davidic king and the suffering servant. While coalescing the concepts of "authority and servanthood" or "power and weakness" is helpful (Paul does this as well), it is not the primary way Mark explains this paradox.[24] Rather, Mark does so by revealing Jesus as the Davidic/Danielic king who reigns by taking on the suffering of the servant. In sum, just as Mark's opening composite citation (Mark 1:2–3) revealed the broader context of the Isaianic new exodus and the coming kingdom of God, this merged allusion (1:11) reveals the identity of the one who will bring it about.

As a new Israel bringing about a new exodus, Jesus comes through the water and into the wilderness for forty days, keeping the covenant where Israel did not. The main thrust of the temptation story is to show the "deep background" of the cosmic conflict between the kingdom of God and the kingdom of Satan—a conflict that intensifies until it culminates in the cross.[25] Overcoming the temptation of Satan foreshadows the momentary victories in Jesus' miracles, healings, and exorcisms, and the ultimate victory in his death and resurrection.

---

23. For a survey of the interpretation of this allusion, see Rikki Watts, "Mark," in *Commentary on the New Testament Use of the Old Testament* (ed. G. K. Beale and D. A. Carson; Grand Rapids: Baker Academic, 2007), 122.

24. For studies of these concepts in Mark, see Narry Santos, *Slave of All: The Paradox of Authority and Servanthood in the Gospel of Mark* (JSNT 237; London: Sheffield Academic, 2003); Frederick Houk Borsch, *Power in Weakness: New Hearing for Gospel Stories of Healing and Discipleship* (Philadelphia: Fortress, 1983); Theodore Weeden, "Cross as Power in Weakness (Mark 15:20b–41)," in *The Passion in Mark*, 115–34; Dorothy Lee-Pollard, "Powerlessness as Power: A Key Emphasis in the Gospel of Mark," *SJT* 40 (1987): 173–88.

25. Elizabeth Struthers Malbon, *Mark's Jesus: Characterization as Narrative Christology* (Waco, TX: Baylor University Press, 2009), 45. Malbon also helpfully distinguishes between (1) the background conflict with the transcendent characters, (2) the middle-ground conflict with the authorities, and (3) the foreground conflict with the disciples (ibid.).

Jesus' opening proclamation—"The kingdom of God is at hand" (Mark 1:15)—summarizes the content of his teaching, the power of his miracles/healings/exorcisms, and the eschatological goal that defines his mission. But what exactly is the kingdom of God in Mark's gospel? Linguistically, most scholars agree that ἡ βασιλεία τοῦ θεοῦ means the dynamic reign or kingship of God.[26] Theologically, however, God's reign entails all the eschatological hopes of the Old Testament, especially those emphasized by Isaiah, encompassing both judgment and salvation (Isa 40:1–11; 52:7–12). Although God is sovereign over all, the "kingdom of God" is the eschatological hope of God's rule being established on earth through his Messiah (9:1–7). The promises of the kingdom (i.e., victory over enemies and forgiveness of sins) direct the messianic mission of Jesus to the cross.

OPPOSITION TO THE KINGDOM

The body of the narrative begins with Jesus demonstrating (Mark 1:16–45) what he just proclaimed (1:14–15): the nearness of the reign of God. Yet how do these demonstrations of the kingdom (miracles, healings, exorcisms) relate to Jesus' ensuing death? According to Peter Bolt, they act as a "foretaste" or a "microcosm" of the salvation that Christ ultimately provides in his death and resurrection.[27] "Jesus was demonstrating in individual cases what he had come to do on the grand scale."[28]

Though Jesus proclaimed and demonstrated the kingdom with great success, the plot truly begins to unfold as the kingdom comes into conflict with the religious leaders. Mark 2:1–3:6 consists of five conflict stories in the form of a chiasm, ultimately showing the increasing resistance to the kingdom and the inevitable outcome of the cross.[29] Within the overall framework of conflict, the center of the chiasm is the first overt allusion to the death of Christ ("the bridegroom is taken away" 2:20).[30] Based on Mark's literary use of chiasms, Joanna Dewey argues that the center of the chiasm is especially significant and often introduces an antithetical idea into the story.[31] The

---

26. R. T. France, *Divine Government: God's Kingship in the Gospel of Mark* (London: SPCK, 1990), 8–15.

27. Peter Bolt, *Jesus' Defeat of Death: Persuading Mark's Early Readers* (Cambridge: Cambridge University Press, 2003), 271.

28. Ibid., 272.

29. Joanna Dewey, "Literary Structure of the Controversy Stories in Mark 2:1–3:6," *JBL* 92 (1973): 394–401; idem, *Markan Public Debate: Literary Technique, Concentric Structure, and Theology in Mark 2:1–3:6* (SBLDS 48; Chico, CA: Scholars, 1979).

30. "Taken away" (ἀπαίρω) is also used twice to describe the destiny of the servant (Isa 53:8 LXX).

31. Dewey, "Literary Structure of the Controversy Stories in Mark 2:1–3:6," 398.

allusion to Jesus' death in 2:20 "is for Mark a suitable literary climax," revealing that "Jesus' ministry is shown to be under the shadow of the cross from the beginning."[32] Early on, therefore, it is clear that the Markan Jesus has a mission to bring the kingdom of God and yet is set on a path to the cross. How do these two aims relate? Before answering that question, the narrative heightens the tension by showing the ever-increasing opposition to Jesus' kingdom that will lead to his cross.

If the Pharisees' setting out to destroy Jesus was in essence a declaration of war, then this next section shows the gathering of troops on each side in preparation for the inevitable collision. While the Markan Jesus calls his twelve disciples to himself (Mark 3:13–19), the opposition also grows, spreading even to Jesus' own family (3:20–35). The height of the opposition and Jesus' most explicit explanation of it come from the Pharisees' accusing Jesus of being possessed by Beelzebub. If the opposition between God's kingdom and Satan's kingdom has been the background to the increasing conflict, this encounter brings it to the fore. Though Satan is certainly a "strong man" (ὁ ἰσχυρός Mark 3:27), Jesus is the "stronger man" (ὁ ἰσχυρότερος, 1:7) who is establishing God's kingdom and therefore destroying Satan's.[33] Though the battle continues to escalate, this encounter demonstrates Jesus' authority over Satan and identifies each exorcism as "an eschatological event which served to prepare God's creation for his coming rule."[34] It is also noteworthy that in this encounter Jesus connects the defeat of Satan with the forgiveness of sins (3:27–28), both of which were part of Isaiah's vision of God's coming kingdom (Isa 40:2).

THE MYSTERY OF THE KINGDOM

With such growing opposition (which will ultimately lead to Jesus' death), how can Jesus continue to proclaim the presence and victory of the kingdom of God? Jesus answers this question with four parables (Mark 4:1–35), revealing that despite all appearances the kingdom *is* advancing, though its presence is hidden and its nature misunderstood. Though Jesus proclaims the kingdom publicly in parables (explained by the reference to Isa 6:9–10), he explains in private to his disciples that they have been given the "secret of the kingdom of God" (Mark 4:11). The secret or mystery is not simply that

---

32. Ibid., 400.

33. The connection between the prologue and the "strong man" saying is corroborated by the fact that these are the only two places in Mark which bring together "Satan," "spirit," and "strong" terminology.

34. Howard Clark Kee, "The Terminology of Mark's Exorcism Stories," *NTS* 14 (1968): 243.

the kingdom is in fact present, but the *paradoxical way* in which it is advancing and will ultimately be established. The disciples do not understand the teaching of a powerful kingdom coming through surprisingly humble means (4:13), which foreshadows their rejection of the idea when Jesus teaches it explicitly on "the way" (8:32; 9:32; 10:35–40).

The theme of food binds Mark 6:6b–8:21 together, portraying Jesus as the provider of manna in the wilderness and the disciples as the not-yet-understanding wanderers on the way.[35] Although the disciples participate in Jesus' ministry by preaching, healing, and casting out demons (6:6b–13), their relative success is paralleled by their doubtfulness, lack of understanding, and hardness of heart (6:35–37, 52; 7:17–18; 8:14–21). It is the identity of Christ, however, that dominates this section, as is evident in Mark's intentional juxtaposing of the two feasts provided by Herod (6:14–29) and Jesus (6:30–44).

Though Herod and his companions discuss the varying options for Jesus' identity (Mark 6:14–16), Mark reveals Jesus' identity by comparing it to the "kingship" of Herod. Whereas Herod's reign is characterized by fear, uncontrollable desire, and domination, Jesus' reign is one of compassion, shepherding, and service. This section ends with Jesus' question, "Do you not yet understand?" (8:21), implying the blindness of the disciples and anticipating Jesus' revealing the mystery of the kingdom on "the way" to Jerusalem.

THE KINGDOM REDEFINED BY THE CROSS (MARK 8:27–10:52)

The nature of the kingdom's coming, mysteriously hidden in Jesus' early ministry, is revealed and explained on "the way" to Jerusalem (Mark 8:27; 9:33, 34; 10:52). In other words, what is geographically a mere journey from Galilee to Golgotha (the way *to* the cross) is also theologically God's wise means for establishing his kingdom (the way *of* the cross). Mark's widely recognized redactional use of ἡ ὁδός (half of Mark's uses of ἡ ὁδός are in the "way" section) recalls the double-mention of ἡ ὁδός in the prologue (Mark 1:2–3), which lays out the broad context of the Isaianic new exodus and more specifically the "way of the LORD" (Isa 40:3; 43:16–21; 51:9–10; 52:1–12; 62:10–12).[36] "The way" in Isaiah is Yahweh's triumphant processional march

---

35. Joel Marcus, *Mark 1–8: A New Translation with Introduction and Commentary* (AYBC; New York: Doubleday, 2000), 381.

36. William Swartley, "The Structural Function of the Term 'Way' in Mark," in *The New Way of Jesus: Essays Presented to Howard Charles* (ed. W. Klassen; Newton, KS: Faith and Life, 1980), 73–86.

to enthronement in Jerusalem, by which he leads his people out of bondage and into his kingdom (Isa 40:1–11; 52:1–12), opening their eyes along the way (35:1–7; 42:16).[37] Just as Isaiah prophesied that the end of the exile and coming of the kingdom (40:1–52:12) would be effected by the means of the servant's atoning death (52:13–53:12), the Markan Jesus establishes God's kingdom not in spite of the cross, but by "way" of the cross.

In addition to the structural location of the "way" section between Christ's proclamation of the kingdom and his death on the cross, its internal structure also has great significance for interpreting Mark. Along with the repeated use of ἡ ὁδός, the section is framed by Mark's only two sight-giving stories (Mark 8:22–26; 10:46–52) and includes three passion-resurrection predictions, each of which follows the threefold pattern of (1) Jesus predicting his death and resurrection (8:31; 9:30–32; 10:32–34), (2) the disciples misunderstanding (8:32–33; 9:33–34; 10:35–41), and (3) Jesus clarifying by teaching about discipleship (8:34–38; 9:35–37; 10:42–45). While each of the predictions includes the same basic elements, there is a progression in clarity of details and meaning.

The bracket stories of sight-giving show that although the disciples are blind to God's way of bringing the kingdom (the suffering of the Messiah), their eyes will be opened. The first healing story (Mark 8:21–26) specifically foreshadows that this giving of sight will happen incrementally. In the second, just as Bartimaeus initially only sees in part and then is given a fuller revelation, Peter will rightly acknowledge Jesus as the Messiah, but misunderstand the nature of his messiahship.

THE FIRST PASSION-RESURRECTION PREDICTION

The first prediction unifies Mark's narrative as a whole by making explicit what has been implicit up to this point (Mark 2:20; 3:6, 19) and foretelling what is to come (chs. 14–16). The structure of the pericope itself is revealing, forming a chiasm that highlights Jesus' messiahship and suffering:

A *Messianic* identity (8:27–30)
   B *Suffering* to come for Jesus (8:31–33)
   B′ *Suffering* to come for disciples (8:34–37)
A′ *Messianic* power and glory to come (8:38–9:1)[38]

Along with the commonly held notion that Mark qualifies Jesus' messiahship with the suffering of the cross, the converse is also true: Jesus' death on the cross is motivated and shaped by his mission of bringing the kingdom.

---

37. Marcus, *The Way of the Lord*, 35.

38. Joel Marcus, *Mark 8–16: A New Translation with Introduction and Commentary* (AYBC; New Haven, CT: Yale University Press, 2009), 623.

The first prediction happens on "the way" to Jerusalem when Jesus asks his disciples, "Who do people say that I am?" (Mark 8:27). Peter correctly identifies Jesus' *identity* as the Messiah, but Jesus silences Peter so that he can explain the *nature* of his messiahship: "The Son of Man must suffer many things and be rejected by the elders and the chief priests and the scribes and be killed, and after three days rise again" (Mark 8:31).[39]

Once again, the Markan Jesus draws heavily from the Old Testament to interpret the nature of his messiahship. The reference to "Son of Man," end-lessly disputed as a term in the mouth of the historical Jesus,[40] is more easily discerned as used by Mark. Although not mutually exclusive with the generic Old Testament meaning of "human being" (Num 23:19; Ps 8:4; 144:3; Isa 51:12; Jer 50:40; and thirty-nine references in Ezekiel), Mark explicitly refer-ences the Danielic background at least three times (Mark 8:38; 13:26; 14:62), and it is therefore the primary referent. In Daniel, the "one like a son of man" (Dan 7:13) is a human figure described in divine language who is given dominion to defeat the kingdoms of the world and restore the "saints" into their place in the kingdom.

The remarkable feature of Jesus' reference is that the "Son of Man must suffer." Could the one who brought victory over the suffering of others (Mark 5:26) now become a victim to suffering himself? The fact that the "son of man" never suffers in Daniel 7, along with the absence of a suffering son of man in Jewish interpretation, raises the question of the background of the Markan Jesus' mission.[41] A significant answer lies in the small term δεῖ (Mark 8:31). The divine "must" implies that "the Son of Man must suffer" because it is the will of God; Christ's death is a part of God's plan.

The divine will is not merely known secretly to Jesus, but it is revealed in the Old Testament, evident in Jesus' later saying that it is "written of the Son of Man that he should suffer many things" (Mark 9:12). Since the "son of man" never suffers in Daniel 7, the Markan Jesus is clearly draw-ing elsewhere from the Old Testament to qualify the nature of his Danielic

---

39. Jesus' encounter with Peter is one instance of the "messianic secret" motif made famous by William Wrede. Although he was right to highlight the significance of this theme for Mark, Wrede was wrong to argue on the basis of the church's later justification of Jesus' seemingly nonmessianic identity (*The Messianic Secret* [trans. J. C. G. Greig; Cambridge: Clarke, 1971]). As made clear below, the messianic secret is used by Mark to show that Jesus' identity is only truly understood through the cross.

40. See Morna Hooker, *The Son of Man in Mark: A Study of the Background of the Term "Son of Man" and Its Use in St. Mark's Gospel* (Montreal: McGill University Press, 1967). For a recent survey, see James Dunn, *Jesus Remembered* (Grand Rapids: Eerdmans, 2003), 724–58.

41. It is possible, as some have argued, that the son of man suffers in Daniel 7 because he is so closely identified with the "saints" who suffer (Hooker, *The Son of Man in Mark*, 27–30; Gun-dry, *Mark*, 446).

authority and messianic identity.[42] Although there are several possible places that Jesus could potentially be drawing from, the most likely referent is Isa 52:13–53:12.[43]

Whereas Mark previously combined the Old Testament images of the Davidic Messiah and the Suffering Servant, here the Markan Jesus combines the Old Testament images of the Danielic son of man and the Suffering Servant. While in Daniel 7 the one like a son of man uses his authority "to judge sins, Jesus, the suffering Son of Man, uses his authority to forgive sins (Mark 2:10). What was hinted at in Galilee—the kingdom is present, but is advancing in an unexpected way—is now affirmed and clarified by Jesus: the "way" of the kingdom's coming is by means of the suffering of the Son of Man.

With an ironic reversal of roles, Peter then takes Jesus aside and rebukes him. Jesus' response ("Get behind me, Satan!" Mark 8:33) reveals not only his determination to accomplish the divine plan whatever the cost, but the source of its opposition. Whereas the divine plan has been revealed as the kingdom by way of the cross, Satan's counterplan is also revealed: the kingdom without a cross. Peter, however, was thinking in terms that were common in the Judaism of his day: the Messiah was expected to defeat the Romans and politically reestablish the kingdom of Israel.[44]

In fact, one could even say that the logic of victory through power is universally preferable to that of victory through suffering. This human logic, however, is precisely the problem according to Jesus: "For you are not setting your mind on the things of God, but on the things of man" (Mark 8:33). In other words, from a (fallen) human perspective, victory through suffering is foolishness. But from God's perspective, the cross is the power and wisdom of God (1 Cor 1:18).

In each prediction, Jesus clarifies his teaching by discussing discipleship. The message remains the same: the kingdom by way of the cross. Although Mark focuses primarily on Christ's way of establishing God's kingdom (Christology) and derivatively the disciples' way of entering it (discipleship),

---

42. Collins argues that Messiah and Son of Man are synonymous in Mark (*Mark*, 402); Watts demonstrates that there is at least considerable overlap ("Mark," 136).

43. Watts, summarizing Hooker and Barrett, lists five reasons: "(1) Isa. 53 is the only explicitly eschatological text in the OT that contains not only the suffering and vindication, but also the death . . . of Yahweh's agent; (2) Isa. 53 is the linchpin of Isaiah's new-exodus hope . . . which itself is central to Mark's understanding of Jesus; (3) Isa. 53:10's explicit statement of the divine will explains Mark 8:31's *dei*; (4) the servant will be vindicated and highly exalted . . . not unlike Dan. 7's son of man; (5) since both Isa. 53 and Dan. 7 address the issue of Israel's restoration from exile, their association here, though novel, is not incongruent" ("Mark," 176); cf. Moo, *The Old Testament in the Gospel Passion Narratives*, 86–111.

44. Collins, *Mark*, 407.

the two are inseparable. Furthermore, Jesus' "follow me" (Mark 8:34) echoes his kingdom mission in Galilee, where he proclaimed the kingdom (1:14–15) and then immediately extended the same invitation to his future disciples (1:16–17). Jesus has not abandoned his kingdom mission in order to go to the cross; the kingdom mission continues. Just as Jesus would paradoxically establish the kingdom through suffering, the disciples would only enter and advance the kingdom by taking up their cross. This uncanny logic of the kingdom—"whoever loses his life . . . will save it" (Mark 8:35)—will be determinative for Christ and his followers.

Mark 8:38–9:1 has proven to be a difficult passage. While Mark 8:38 is a clear reference to the son of man in Daniel 7, the precise timing of the kingdom coming "with power" has made this a *crux interpretum*.[45] Does the kingdom come with power at the second coming, the ascension, Pentecost, the resurrection, the transfiguration, the cross? Is it, as France argues, an incremental process that envelops each of these stages?[46] The second coming of Christ has been a popular choice, but this requires the belief that Jesus was wrong about the timing. Although in the history of interpretation the cross has not been a strong candidate, perhaps this reasoning is based on the type of logic that Jesus denounced (τὰ τῶν ἀνθρώπων Mark 8:33), which assumes royal power is antithetical to the cross.

The Isaianic context has already shown that the victorious new exodus and coming kingdom are not antithetical to the death of a suffering servant, but rather hinge on it. The immediate context of the logion (Mark 8:27–9:1) also strongly attests to the connection between the powerful coming of the kingdom and the cross. Jesus' prediction that the royal Son of Man must suffer, followed by his paradoxical statement about saving life by losing it, flow seamlessly into an interpretation of the kingdom's power coming at the cross. The triumphal entry and crucifixion (discussed below) further this evidence, putting Jesus forth as a humble king who reigns from the cross. In sum, although the coming of the kingdom is certainly an incremental process (prophesied, near, established, consummated), the decisive moment is the death of the Messiah.[47]

The transfiguration (Mark 9:2–13) is significant for the kingdom–cross

---

45. For a survey of the history of interpretation of Mark 9:1, see Martin Künzi, *Das Naherwartung-slogion Markus 9.1* (Tübingen: J. C. B. Mohr, 1977).

46. R. T. France, *The Gospel of Mark: A Commentary on the Greek Text* (NIGTC; Grand Rapids: Eerdmans, 2002), 345.

47. For a defense of this position, see Kent Brower, "Mark 9:1: Seeing the Kingdom in Power," *JSNT* (1980): 17–41; Michael Bird echoes and builds on many of Brower's arguments in "The Crucifixion of Jesus as the Fulfillment of Mark 9:1."

interplay because the declaration of Jesus as the Son of God (9:7) is strategically located in the middle of an inclusio consisting of the same declaration at Jesus' baptism and crucifixion (1:11; 15:39). The continuity of these three scenes reveals Mark's clear purpose of not only identifying Jesus as the royal Son of God but specifically illustrating that his royalty is most clearly displayed on the cross.[48] While the religious leaders oppose this idea and the disciples misunderstand it, it is only on the cross that Jesus will be properly recognized as the Son of God. Within this broad framework of continuity between the baptism, transfiguration, and cross, Mark also contrasts the *reality* portrayed in the transfiguration and the *appearance* of the cross:[49]

Transfiguration	Crucifixion
Unearthly light (9:2–3)	Supernatural darkness (15:33)
Jesus' clothes are luminous (9:2–3)	Jesus' clothes are stripped off (15:24, 26)
Two Old Testament saints (9:4)	Two criminals (15:27, 32)
Conversation with Elijah (9:4)	Apparent conversation with Elijah (15:35)
Disciples are present (9:5)	Disciples flee (14:50)
God speaks (9:7)	God is silent

While the continuity reveals that Jesus truly is the Messiah who reigns from the cross, the contrast reveals that his glorious kingship is paradoxically hidden in his gruesome death. The radiance of his glory is seen as darkness, his power as weakness, and his kingship as servanthood. In other words, between his anointing (baptism) and enthronement (crucifixion), Mark provides a glimpse (transfiguration) of the majestic glory of Christ that will be hidden paradoxically in his suffering—a revelation that is vindicated in Christ's resurrection. The transfiguration anticipates the resurrection because both reveal what is truly happening in the crucifixion.

THE SECOND PASSION-RESURRECTION PREDICTION

The second prediction (Mark 9:30–37) continues to unfold the necessity and meaning of Jesus' death in his mission to establish the kingdom. Whereas the first prediction has Jesus being "rejected" (Mark 8:31; cf. Ps 118:22), here Jesus says he will be "delivered" (παραδίδωμι, 9:31), likely drawing from the Isaianic servant (Isa 53:6, 12 LXX) and the Danielic son of man (Dan

---

48. The continuity is primarily found in the declaration of Jesus as God's Son, but for more allusions, see Caneday, "Christ's Baptism and Crucifixion," 78.

49. Adapted from Marcus, *Mark 8–16*, 641.

7:25–27 LXX). The disciples' misunderstanding this time results in silence, but their conversation "on the way" (Mark 9:34) to Capernaum provides Jesus with another opportunity to clarify the nature of his kingdom and the disciples' way of following. Whereas before he had spoken of the logic of the kingdom in terms of saving life by losing it, here he addresses the disciples' misguided search for greatness by declaring that true greatness comes through serving.

THE THIRD PASSION-RESURRECTION PREDICTION

The third prediction (Mark 10:32–45) represents the pinnacle of the "way" section, in that it not only offers the most historical detail for Jesus' death and resurrection but also speaks explicitly of its meaning. Jesus interprets his death as an act of service and as a "ransom for many" (10:45), which, although heavily disputed, at least means that it is redemptive and substitutionary.[50] By interpreting his death as a "ransom," the Markan Jesus recalls Israel's redemption from slavery in Egypt. "Isaiah picks up this language to speak of a NE [new exodus], ultimately to be brought about by the Servant of the Lord."[51]

Although Isa 52:13–53:12 LXX does not use the word λύτρον ("ransom"), the saying of Jesus provides "a perfect summary of the servant's vicarious death on behalf of many others [and] the language of ransom does appear in the context."[52] Furthermore, Jesus' redemptive death "for many" (Mark 10:45) echoes the work of the servant who "bore the sin of many" (Isa 53:12). The background of the Suffering Servant, therefore, reveals Jesus' interpretation of his death to be redemptive and substitutionary within the broader aim of bringing about the new exodus.

The immediate context of the pericope (Mark 10:32–45) reveals that Jesus has not set aside his kingdom mission when interpreting his death. Rather, Jesus' ransom saying is in response to James's and John's request to sit at Jesus' right and left hand in glory—imagery that clearly recalls royalty. While the disciples correctly assume Jesus' coming enthronement and their sharing of his royal power, his response indicates that they do not understand the cost involved: "Are you able to drink the cup that I drink . . . ?" (10:38).

---

50. The strongest support for this claim, as I will discuss below, is that the song of the Suffering Servant provides the background for Jesus' death as a ransom for many. For further discussion, see Rikki Watts, "Mark," 203–6. According to Watts, "It was in the past almost universally assumed that [Mark] 10:45 derived from the suffering of the servant in Isa. 53:10–12. . . . Even critics recognize that it is difficult to deny some parallelism with Isa. 53:12" (203).
51. Peter Bolt, *The Cross from a Distance: Atonement in Mark's Gospel* (NSBT; Downers Grove, IL: InterVarsity Press, 2004), 72.
52. Ibid.

After the other disciples become indignant with James and John, Jesus further explicates the nature of his kingdom by contrasting it with the rulers of this world. The contrast, however, aims not to reject the notion of greatness or preeminence, but to qualify it by service. Jesus' message is not "do not reign, serve!" but rather "reign, by serving!" In short, the kingdom context of Jesus' death reveals he reigns by ransoming.

The kingdom context of the ransom saying is further supported by the broader context of the gospel as a whole. Watts draws attention to the similar literary function of Mark 10:45 and Isa 52:13–53:12: "Mark 10:45b functions as the final explanatory capstone to Mark's 'Way' section. This, it might be noted, is entirely congruent with the literary function of Isaiah 53 within Isaiah 40–55 which . . . indicates the way in which Israel's INE [Isaianic new exodus] is to be accomplished."[53] Although Isaiah provides the hermeneutical framework for Mark, the ransom saying is clearly another case of Mark weaving together Old Testament strands. The "son of man" (Daniel 7) serves by giving his life "for many" (Isa 52:13–53:12). Though there are many connections between the two background passages,[54] it is more important to focus on the way in which Jesus combines these two figures. While the Isaianic servant clearly serves, the Danielic son of man is said to *be served* (Dan 7:14). It appears, therefore, that Mark is using the servant to qualify the way in which the Son of Man establishes God's kingdom.[55]

Lastly, Jesus' third prediction further corroborates the important role of God's wrath in establishing the kingdom on the cross. Jesus' prediction that the leaders of the people will "deliver him over to the Gentiles" (Mark 10:33), usually read purely as a historical assertion, is "theologically loaded" when read against the backdrop of the Old Testament.[56] To be handed over to the Gentiles is to be handed over to the wrath of God (Lev 26:32–33, 38; Hos 8:10 LXX; cf. Ps 106:41; Ezra 9:7).[57] Even more explicit is Jesus' reference to his death as drinking "a cup," a common Old Testament symbol of God's wrath (Ps 11:6; 75:8; Hab 2:16; Ezek 23:31–34), especially for the Isaianic new exodus (Isa 51:17). Based on this context, Bolt is right to conclude that "the servant's death . . . has exhausted the cup of God's wrath on behalf of

---

53. Watts, *Isaiah's New Exodus in Mark*, 270.

54. See Marcus, *Mark 8–16*, 742, 753.

55. Jesus' serving is primarily redemptive (the disciples do not ransom) and secondarily exemplary (they do serve by giving of themselves). The individual/corporate interplay fits with the Isaianic servant and the Danielic son of man—both of which act as individual and corporate figures. In Isaiah the individual servant restores Israel to be servants (Isa 54:17). In Daniel, the "son of man" shares the throne with the saints (Dan 7:27).

56. Bolt, *The Cross from a Distance*, 56.

57. See ibid., 56–58.

Israel. Jesus now predicts that, as the servant of the Lord, he will drink the cup of God's wrath."[58]

THE KINGDOM ESTABLISHED BY THE CROSS (MARK 11:1–16:8)[59]

APPROACHING THE CROSS

Having explained the way of the kingdom, Jesus is now ready to establish it. According to Mark, Jesus enters Jerusalem as the fulfillment of Yahweh's new exodus return to Zion to be enthroned as king over the earth. Jesus' kingly authority is evident not only in the crowd's acclamation of the "coming kingdom of our father David" (Mark 11:10), but also in the background provided by Zech 9:9–11 (cf. Gen 49:10–11; 1 Kgs 1:33–34, 38–39; 2 Kgs 9:12–13). Jesus is the humble king who has come to establish his kingdom by humble means—"the blood of my covenant" (Zech 9:11).

The direct quotation of Ps 118:26 on the lips of the crowd (Mark 11:9) further presents Jesus as the messianic king. Psalm 118 speaks of a victorious Davidic king who is blessed as he enters into the temple. This connection between the coming king and the temple (cf. 2 Sam 7:12–14), along with the common cultural practice of kings having a formal processional entrance followed by a ceremonial visit to the temple, prepares the reader for Jesus, the humble king, entering into the temple.

Mark frames the central action of Jesus' cleansing the temple with the interpretive story of cursing the fig tree, revealing that Jesus, in fulfillment of Mal 3:1 (cf. Mark 1:2), is bringing judgment to the temple.[60] While Jesus had been preaching the kingdom, it is in this section (11:1–13:37) that Mark lays out the ever-important role of the temple in the coming kingdom of God.[61] The key Old Testament background for the relationship of the kingdom and the temple is 2 Sam 7:12–14, which speaks of God establishing the kingdom of David's son, who in turn will build a temple for God.[62] The temple— the dwelling place for the holy God and the place of sacrifice for unholy

---

58. Ibid., 67. Bolt also argues that Psalm 69 is the background for Jesus' baptism statement and therefore includes the idea of Jesus bearing the wrath of God.

59. I concur with the majority of Markan scholars that Mark's original gospel concluded at 16:8. See Joel Williams, "Literary Approaches to the End of Mark's Gospel," *JETS* 42 (1999): 21–35.

60. Watts, *Isaiah's New Exodus in Mark*, 316.

61. Of Mark's nine uses of ἱερόν, eight are in this section.

62. In the ancient Near East, there was a strong connection between kings and temples, especially kings building temples. It was also common in Second Temple Judaism to expect the Messiah to be a temple builder (Marcus, *Mark 8–16*, 791, 1015).

people—is an essential aspect of the kingdom of God. There is no kingdom unless the king is present. There can be no people in the kingdom unless they are made holy through atonement for sins. As the messianic bringer of the kingdom, Jesus clearly gives the temple a central role. But against expectations, the temple will be purged through destruction and restored in his own body. Jesus himself is replacing the temple as the dwelling place of God and the place where atonement is made for sins; this is "the groundwork for the passion narrative."[63]

In response to the Pharisees questioning his authority, Jesus tells the parable of the tenants (Mark 12:1–12), clearly drawing on earlier themes of his life, such as his identity as the "beloved Son" (12:6; cf. 1:11; 9:7) and his messianic mission being "rejected" by the religious leaders (12:10; cf. 8:31). What Jesus had predicted to his disciples, he is now explaining to his antagonists. Jesus interprets the parable by quoting Ps 118:22–23, referring to himself as the cornerstone of a new temple. While Jesus had just spoken of God's judgment of the temple, in this parable he shows how it will be restored in his own resurrected body.

Markan scholars have been so preoccupied with the timing of the events of Mark 13 (AD 70 or the parousia?) that the context of Jesus' teaching is often overlooked in interpretation. According to Bolt, however, when Mark 13 is read in the context of Mark's narrative, it is primarily about the death and resurrection of Christ—"an apocalyptic preparation for the passion."[64] Mark 13 does not insert a detached future-eschatology lecture into the middle of a passion narrative, but rather fills the unfolding historical events with eschatological meaning and locates the death and resurrection of Christ within God's cosmic purposes. This interpretation is significant for the kingdom–cross interplay because it places the cross on an eschatological plane, the same plane on which the kingdom is usually understood. The cross represents the end of the ages and is the turning point in redemptive history.

FULFILLMENT OF THE SCRIPTURES

Mark's use of the Old Testament is especially pertinent for the Passion Narrative proper (Mark 14–15). In short, the Old Testament is the script for it. In the words of the Markan Jesus himself, "The Son of Man goes as it is written of him" (Mark 14:21) in order that "the Scriptures be fulfilled" (14:49). There are four primary Old Testament backgrounds from which

---

63. Ibid., 770.
64. Bolt, *The Cross from a Distance*, 91; see also idem, "Mark 13: An Apocalyptic Precursor to the Passion Narrative," *RTR* 54 (1995): 10–32; Allison, *The End of the Ages Has Come*, 169.

Mark draws: (1) the righteous sufferer of the Psalms, (2) the servant of Isaiah 40–55, (3) the son of man of Daniel 7, and (4) the shepherd of Zechariah 9–14.[65] In fact, the Psalms and Isaiah traditions are inseparable and together constitute the dominant influence on Mark's portrayal of the passion.[66] It is also significant that, as noted above, each of these four traditions combine (or at least hint at combining) kingship and suffering.[67]

On the day "when they sacrificed the Passover lamb" (Mark 14:12), Jesus declared "This is my body" and "This is my blood" (14:22–24), in effect claiming to be the Passover lamb himself, bringing about the long-awaited new exodus. Building on the ransom saying in 10:45, this is one of Jesus' most explicit statements regarding the meaning of his death and is also placed in the context of the kingdom of God (14:25).

Even more significant than the explicit reference to the kingdom, however, is the assumed connection between exodus, covenant, and kingdom, all of which are being drawn together and reconstituted around Jesus. In one simple phrase—"This is my blood of the covenant, which is poured out for many" (Mark 14:24)—the Markan Jesus characteristically combines two Old Testament traditions: Exod 24:8 (and its derivative, Zech 9:11) and Isa 53:12. In Exodus, after the Passover and redemption of Israel (Exodus 12), a covenant was made between God and his people (Exodus 19–23), which was then sealed by the sacrifice of animals and dashing of blood on the people (24:8). The primary function of the "blood of the covenant," therefore, was to seal the covenant between God the king and his people, who were to be a kingdom of priests (19:6). Jesus uniquely combines the events of Passover and covenant-sealing in himself, interpreting his death as redemption *from* sin and *for* a new covenant with the king.

The second half of Mark 14:24 ("poured out for many") further clarifies the meaning of Jesus' death, as it recalls the Isaianic context and specifically

65. Moo, *The Old Testament in the Gospel Passion Narratives*; Marcus, *The Way of the Lord*, 153–98. Though I concur with much recent scholarship that emphasizes the significant influence of Psalms (especially Psalm 22), I disagree with those who dismiss the influence of the Isaianic servant. For example, Kelli O'Brien, *The Use of Scripture in the Markan Passion Narrative* (London: T&T Clark, 2010). There are three primary reasons why the Isaianic background should not be dismissed: (1) Mark's Passion Narrative repeatedly alludes to Isaiah (see Marcus, *The Way of the Lord*, 187–89). (2) The Isaianic new exodus framework and Mark's dominant usage of Isaiah in the rest of the gospel (esp. Mark 8:27–10:52) make it highly unlikely that this background would drop out completely in the Passion Narrative. (3) The Isaianic Suffering Servant and the righteous sufferer of the Psalms are closely related, for, as scholars have recognized, the servant is a prophetic adaptation of the righteous sufferer (ibid., 190).
66. Rikki Watts, "The Psalms in Mark's Gospel," in *The Psalms in the New Testament* (ed. Steve Moyise and Maarten Menken; London: T&T Clark, 2004), 25; Marcus, *The Way of the Lord*, 190.
67. See above, pp. 65–67, 96 fn. 41..

the "for many" of Isa 53:12 and Mark 10:45. Zechariah 9:11, which directly builds on Exod 24:8 and likely is informed by Isaiah 40–55, offers further background to Jesus' interpretation of his death. The message of Exod 24:8 remains, but in Zechariah, the "blood of [the] covenant" (Zech 9:11) is a key part of the coming of the humble messianic king (9:9–10). Whereas Exod 24:8 looks back to Israel's deliverance, Zech 9:11 transforms the past redemption into future hope. The blood of the covenant seals the relationship between the coming king and his ransomed people.

By foretelling Peter's denial (Mark 14:26–31), Jesus further interprets his own death as the shepherd-king of Zech 13:7 being stricken (by God), resulting in the scattering of his disciples. Gethsemane (Mark 14:32–42) heightens the irony of Jesus' royal identity and human frailty, repeatedly using vocabulary concerning ability (14:35, 36), strength (14:37), and weakness (14:38). Whereas in the transfiguration Jesus took aside (παραλαμβάνω, 9:2) the three to reveal his transcendent glory, here he takes aside (παραλαμβάνω, 14:33) the three to show his human frailty. Marcus says, "In Mark there is the closest possible connection between these two aspects of Jesus," a type of "paradoxical coexistence."[68]

The trial of Jesus before the Sanhedrin (Mark 14:53–65) heightens the irony that has been building: Jesus' proclamation as the messianic Son of Man who will be seated at the right hand of God is bracketed by false accusation and mocking/beating. Despite all appearances and accusations, Jesus is king. According to S. J. Donahue, "In the trial narrative Mk uses the royal Christology to interpret the trial and death of Jesus as the suffering of the crucified King."[69] Amidst other Old Testament backgrounds, the Isaianic servant is especially alluded to in Jesus' silence (Mark 14:61; cf. Isa 53:7) and the guards' spitting on and striking Jesus (Mark 14:65; cf. Isa 50:6). Marcus concludes that this background "may suggest that this absorption of abuse is actually effecting the defeat of the rulers of this world. Jesus, then, is not being vanquished but triumphing in his very humiliation."[70]

THE CRUCIFIXION OF THE KING

Finally we come to the climax itself: the crucifixion of the Messiah. The surprising and salient feature of the account is that it is here, in the crucifixion, that Mark intentionally highlights the kingship of Jesus. Six times in Mark

---

68. Marcus, *Mark 8–16*, 983.

69. S. J. Donahue, "Temple, Trial, and Royal Christology (Mark 14:53–65)," in *The Passion in Mark*, 78.

70. Marcus, *Mark 8–16*, 1018.

15 Jesus is called "king" (half of the uses of βασιλεύς in the entire gospel). As Frank Matera has noted, "The gospel makes its first public proclamation of Jesus' kingship only when the passion has begun and there can be no mistaking the nature of that kingship. The King of Israel is a suffering and rejected Messiah."[71] Matera, therefore, argues that the main theme of Mark 15 is the kingship of Jesus, which is structured around the six uses of βασιλεύς (15:2, 9, 12, 18, 26, 32) and three mockery scenes (15:16–20a, 27–32, 35–36) that highlight the irony of the event: the one mocked as king, truly is king.[72] According to Matera, "In every instance then, Mark unfolds the royal theme as he presses on to his story's climax, the death of Jesus and the centurion's confession."[73]

Jesus, the one who came to "bind" (δέω) the strong man (Mark 3:27), has now been bound (δέω) by the religious leaders and handed over (παραδίδωμι) to Pilate (15:1). Pilate's opening question to Jesus—"Are you the King of the Jews?" (15:2)—introduces Mark's theme of the chapter: the kingship of Jesus. The Markan Jesus answers in the affirmative, but "by rendering Jesus' answer in an ambiguous manner, Mark not only allows the narrative to continue, but he also presents a problem which must be resolved. In what sense is this man the King of the Jews?"[74] When Pilate questions Jesus further, Mark notes Jesus' silence and Pilate's amazement, both actions that echo Isaiah's Suffering Servant (Isa 52:14; 53:7).

The first mockery scene (Mark 15:16–20a) is perhaps the starkest, for Jesus is not only mocked with words, but he is dressed, praised, and kneeled before as a king wearing a crown of thorns. Beyond the Old Testament background of the mocking of the servant (Isa 50:6) and the righteous sufferer (Ps 22:7), T. E. Schmidt has argued that these details evoke a Roman triumphal procession.[75] While Mark has used irony throughout his gospel,[76] this historical background corroborates Mark's paradoxical presentation of Jesus' way to the cross as a royal procession.

---

71. Frank Matera, *The Kingship of Jesus: Composition and Theology in Mark 15* (SBLDS; Chico, CA: Scholars, 1982), 121.

72. Ibid., 4, 61.

73. Ibid., 63.

74. Ibid., 16.

75. Schmidt, "Mark 15:16–32."

76. "The smallest seed produces the largest plant (4:31–32). Saving life means losing it, and losing life results in saving it (8:35). The first are last and the last, first (9:35; 10:31). Greatness comes by being a slave of all (10:43–44). The stone rejected by the builders is the chief cornerstone (12:10–11). The one who gave the least gave the most (12:41–44). The crucified Christ is the King of the Jews (15:25–26, 32). The one who cannot save himself saves others (15:31). The one forsaken by God is the Son of God (15:34, 39)" (Joel Williams, "Is Mark's Gospel an Apology for the Cross?" *BBR* 12 [2002]: 103); cf. Jerry Camery-Hoggatt, *Irony in Mark's Gospel: Text and Subtext* (SNTSMS 72; Cambridge: Cambridge University Press, 1992).

In the crucifixion scene itself (Mark 15:20b–26), Marcus draws similar conclusions from Roman backgrounds and Mark's use of parody. In his article "Crucifixion as Parodic Exaltation," Marcus explores Roman perceptions of crucifixion, arguing that the "lifting up" on the cross was a parody of the victim's own self-exaltation.[77] In other words, crucifixion was a mock enthronement. Marcus claims that by employing such irony, Mark is mocking the mockery and thereby revealing that the one crucified as a pretender king truly is king. Marcus's summary is compelling:

> Ensconced on the royal seat of the cross, the crucified person was a king of fools; but the supreme irony for Mark is that in the present instance this laughingstock of a "king" is indeed being installed as the monarch of the universe. Having been clothed, crowned, and hailed as a king in the previous section, Jesus is now royally enthroned—on a cross.[78]

According to the second group of mockers (Mark 15:27–32), in order for Jesus to display his kingship, he must "save himself" and "come down . . . from the cross" (15:31–32). Clearly these mockers had not been present when Jesus had turned such worldly logic on its head by teaching that one must "take up his cross" and that he who "loses his life" will save it (8:34–35). Jesus reveals his kingship not by coming down from the cross to save himself, but by staying on the cross to save others. Jesus reigns by saving, and he saves by giving his life.

It is also significant that the mockers ask Jesus to come down from the cross "that we may see and believe" (Mark 15:32). This mocking request ironically recalls when Jesus taught the "secret of the kingdom" to the disciples but said others "may indeed see but not perceive" (Mark 4:12). These mockers are now looking directly at the mystery of the kingdom—the crucified king—and they do not understand. They are blind "to the upside-down way in which God's purposes work themselves out in a world where a cross may truly become a throne."[79] The divine revelation of kingship through the cross is only comprehended by the human counterpart of faith. Fallen human logic sees a defeated messianic pretender on the cross. Faith sees and understands that Christ's cross is truly the throne from which he is ransoming his people from the kingdom of Satan into the kingdom of God. The messianic secret remains intact. Jesus' claim to messiahship is public, but the nature of his messiahship is yet to be understood.

---

77. Marcus, "Crucifixion as Parodic Exaltation."
78. Marcus, *Mark 8–16*, 1049–50.
79. Ibid., 1052.

The crucifixion of Christ brings about "darkness over the whole land" (Mark 15:33), an eschatological sign of God's judgment (Exod 10:21; Mark 13:24) and more specifically the day of the Lord (Amos 8:9–10). What was anticipated in Mark 2:20—the bridegroom being taken away on "that day"—is now taking place. As a key element in the coming of the kingdom, "the judgment predicted by the prophets has fallen on the crucified Jesus."[80]

The interpretive question regarding Jesus' "cry of dereliction" is whether it refers only to Ps 22:1 (emphasizing Jesus' human weakness) or the entire psalm (emphasizing Jesus' confidence in God's vindication). Holly Carry surveys the options in this debate, concluding that it presumes a false dichotomy and that there is a necessary tension between the suffering and vindication of the righteous sufferer in Psalms and in Mark.[81] The severity of Ps 22:1 cannot be escaped: Jesus truly is forsaken by God. He suffers under the wrath of God on the cross. Yet, it is Mark's habit when quoting the Old Testament to refer to the entire context, and within the Passion Narrative he has already shown that the rest of Psalm 22 is on his mind (Mark 15:24, 29; cf. Ps 22:6–8, 18).[82] When the entirety of Psalm 22 is taken into account, the cry fits well within Markan theology that has been unfolding. While it begins with the cry of lament, the rest of the psalm is framed by references to the kingship of God (22:3, 28). The cry of forsakenness therefore reveals not only the severity of Jesus' physical and spiritual suffering but also God's sovereign plan to accomplish his purposes through these very means.

After announcing the death of Jesus (Mark 15:37), Mark reports a divine (15:38) and human (15:39) response. Regarding the divine, the tearing of the curtain signifies both judgment (on the temple) and revelation (of God's majestic glory). Jesus earlier declared the temple obsolete as a dwelling place for God and predicted its downfall (13:2). His death now reveals that its corruption has led to its destruction (which is physically consummated in AD 70) and ultimately to a new era in redemptive history.

The tearing of the curtain likewise has a revelatory meaning. The temple curtain functioned primarily to veil the majesty of God, in order that sinful people might not be destroyed by such radiant splendor. The tearing of the curtain, therefore, signifies that the majestic glory of the Lord now shines forth from the crucified Christ. The veil is no longer needed because "in Jesus' death on the cross, God's majesty becomes manifest."[83] Such divine

---

80. Ibid., 1062.
81. Carey, *Jesus' Cry from the Cross*, 5.
82. Ibid., 70–93.
83. Eta Linnemann, *Studien zur Passionsgeschichte* (Göttingen: Vandenhoeck & Ruprecht, 1970), 163 (translation mine); quoted in Moo, *The Old Testament in the Gospel Passion Narratives*, 338.

reactions of both judgment and salvation at the death of Christ imply one thing: "The kingdom has arrived in the crucifixion of Jesus."[84]

The divine action from above (darkness and torn curtain) brings about a human response from below: "Truly this man was the Son of God" (Mark 15:39). A title that had royal connotations in Jewish and Roman backgrounds, "Son of God" was applied to Jesus by Mark in the prologue, but not yet by a person in the narrative. But here, a Gentile, in fulfillment of the Isaianic new exodus vision of reaching the nations (Isa 49:6), looks at the crucified Christ and declares him to be the royal Son of God. What Jesus had kept secret and what Mark had shown through irony, the centurion declares publicly: Jesus is the crucified king.

Seeing/believing has been a major theme in Mark's gospel, always as a human correlate to the good news of *God's* kingdom (Mark 1:15; 4:12). Just as the Isaianic new exodus envisioned Yahweh healing the blind on his royal procession to Jerusalem, Jesus had been revealing the mystery of the kingdom to his disciples, who—like Bartimaeus—were understanding in stages. At the cross, God revealed the mystery of the kingdom to the centurion, "for the secret of the kingdom of God is that Jesus must die as the crucified Messiah."[85] Whereas the mockers looked at Jesus and thought his kingship was laughable, the centurion saw "truly" (15:39) that Jesus' kingship is laudable. The mockers could "see but not perceive" (4:12) because they were looking at Jesus from a worldly perspective (8:33). The centurion was seeing and believing:

> The seeing of unbelief . . . remains wedded to human notions of rule and power, and the seeing of faith . . . perceives in apparent powerlessness the hidden, saving power of God. Faith alone can penetrate the ultimate paradox of the gospel: that the kingly power of God is manifest in the suffering and death of Jesus on the pagan cross, transforming the cross into a power that is infinitely greater than any human power.[86]

The centurion stood at the foot of the cross and, seeing the crucified Jesus, declared him to be king. The women also were "looking," although "from a distance" (Mark 15:40). They, too, would see the glory of God in the crucified Christ, though one more thing was necessary—the resurrection.

---

84. Bird, "The Crucifixion of Jesus as the Fulfillment of Mark 9:1," 30.

85. Richard Hays, *The Moral Vision of the New Testament: Community, Cross, New Creation: A Contemporary Introduction to New Testament Ethics* (San Francisco: HarperSanFrancisco, 1996), 76; see also Joel Marcus, "Mark 4:10–12 and Marcan Epistemology," *JBL* 103 (1984): 571.

86. Christopher Marshall, *Faith as a Theme in Mark's Narrative* (SNTSMS; Cambridge: Cambridge University Press, 1994), 207–8.

Just as Mark describes his entire account as the "beginning of the gospel" (Mark 1:1), much is left open-ended. The kingdom was established on the cross, but the empty tomb emphatically points forward to its revelation, advancement, and consummation. In the same way that God's kingdom came through the cross, the disciples are to enter into the kingdom by way of the cross. But they are not to move forward in darkness. The Son has risen.

THE KINGDOM BY WAY OF THE CROSS

Having analyzed Mark's unfolding narrative, we have seen that within the various stages of the coming of the kingdom, the cross is the decisive moment. The kingship of Christ on the cross, the signs of the cross as an eschatological turning point, and the Isaianic background of the suffering of the servant as the hinge of the new exodus and reign of God all point to the cross as the decisive moment in Jesus' mission. Although it may sound reasonable to attribute victory to the resurrection and *not* to the cross, the Markan Jesus exposes such reasoning as fallen human logic and proposes instead a divine paradoxical wisdom (Mark 8:33). For Mark, the cross is not a defeat but the divinely willed means for God to bring about his kingdom through his Messiah.

To be sure, the cross and resurrection of Jesus are absolutely inseparable—τὸν ἐσταυρωμένον ἠγέρθη (Mark 16:6). The perfect passive participle here emphasizes that Jesus remains the crucified one after the resurrection. He is the crucified-resurrected one. The resurrection is the confirmation that Jesus is who he said he was and that on the cross he truly was reigning as king. The resurrection (and ascension and session) are crucial for Christ's kingship, but they are not its beginning. For Mark, the empty tomb represents not Christ's resurrection *in order to be* king, but the resurrection *of* the king.

In sum, the kingdom comes by "way" of the cross. In fulfillment of the Isaianic new exodus culminating in God's reign over all the earth, the Markan Jesus proclaims his kingdom mission (Mark 1:1–8:21), explains its paradoxical nature (8:22–10:52), and then establishes the kingdom on the cross (11–16:8). While kingdom and cross are often set at odds, Mark reveals that the messianic mission culminates at Golgotha, where the crucified king establishes his kingdom by way of the cross. The "secret of the kingdom" (4:12) is that it paradoxically comes through the crucifixion of "the King" (15:26)—misunderstood by fallen human logic (8:33), yet perceived through faith (1:15).

CHAPTER FOUR

THE BLOOD OF THE CROSS AND THE KINGDOM OF CHRIST

I HAVE DEMONSTRATED that Mark's portrayal of Jesus entails the kingdom of God being established on the cross. Although Mark does so in a unique way with particular emphases, the kingdom–cross interplay is present in the other gospels as well.[1] Perhaps John's account is the most explicit,[2] where Jesus speaks of the cross as the hour of glory (John 12:23) and the beginning of his exaltation (12:32–33; cf. 3:14, 8:28), and is then delivered by Pilate to be crucified with the introduction, "Behold your King!" (19:14). Furthermore, the Gospels and Paul, once thought to be theologically incompatible, have proven in recent scholarship to have a high level of continuity,[3]

---

1. **Matthew**: W. D. Davies and D. C. Allison, *A Critical and Exegetical Commentary on the Gospel According to Saint Matthew* (ICC; Edinburgh: T&T Clark, 1988), 3:598–606; D. A. Carson, *Matthew* (EBC; Grand Rapids: Zondervan, 1995), 573; Paul Meyer, "An Exegetical Reflection on Matthew 21:1–11," in *The Word in This World: Essays in New Testament Exegesis and Theology* (ed. J. T. Carroll; Louisville: Westminster John Knox, 2004), 280–81. **Luke**: Yong-Sung Ahn, *The Reign of God and Rome in Luke's Passion Narrative: An East Asian Global Perspective* (Leiden: Brill, 2006); Jipp, "Luke's Scriptural Suffering Messiah," 260; Mark Strauss, *The Davidic Messiah in Luke-Acts: The Promise and Its Fulfillment in Lukan Christology* (Sheffield: Sheffield Academic, 1995), 317–36. **John**: Leung, *The Kingship-Cross Interplay in the Gospel of John*; Wilhelm Thüsing, *Die Erhöhung und Verherrlichung Jesu im Johannesevangelium* (Münster: Aschendorff, 1959), 30–33; D. A. Carson, *The Gospel According to John* (PiNTC; Grand Rapids: Eerdmans, 1991), see comments on John 18:33–37, 39; 19:3, 12, 15, 19–22. N. T. Wright claims that all four Gospels emphatically intertwine kingdom and cross (*How God Became King*, 225).
2. See Martin Hengel, "The Kingdom of Christ in John," in *Studies in Early Christology* (Edinburgh: T&T Clark, 1995), 343–44.
3. See the essays in Michael Bird and Joel Willitts, eds., *Paul and the Gospels: Christologies, Conflicts and Convergences* (London: T&T Clark, 2011).

especially between Paul and Mark.[4] The kingdom–cross interplay is present across various authors and genres of the New Testament. Although space does not allow for a full survey, I will highlight two explicit references that link the "kingdom" of Christ and the "blood"[5] of his cross from different authors and genres: Col 1:13–20 and Rev 5:5–10.[6]

COLOSSIANS 1:15–20

The Christ hymn of Col 1:15–20, though much disputed in background and structure, is straightforward in its message: Christ reigns supreme over creation and redemption.[7] One of the most remarkable features of the hymn is that the scope of reconciliation ("all things," which appears seven times in 1:15–20) is matched only by the particularity of its means ("the blood of his cross" 1:20).[8] While the hymn by itself has yielded great discussion on the person of Christ and the cosmic nature of his redemption, placing it in the broader context of Colossians enriches its interpretation and is particularly relevant to the question of the kingdom and the cross.

Paul inserted this hymn not as detached theology but as part of his greater purpose of encouraging the Colossians to "walk in [Christ]" (Col 2:6) and to know his sufficiency in the face of the "philosophy" deceiving the Colossians (2:8). I will discuss the relationship between the hymn and two particularly relevant passages that make up its context (1:12–14; 2:13–15). While 1:12–14 places the hymn in the redemptive-historical context of Christ's kingdom, 2:13–15 elaborates on Christ's reconciling death in relation to the powers of Satan's kingdom.[9]

---

4. Michael Bird, "Mark: Interpreter of Peter and Disciple of Paul," in *Paul and the Gospels*, 30–61; Joel Marcus, "Mark—Interpreter of Paul," *NTS* 46 (2000): 473–87; idem, *Mark 1–8*, 74–75; William Telford, *The Theology of the Gospel of Mark* (Cambridge: Cambridge University Press, 1999), 164–69; Fenton, "Paul and Mark," in *Studies in the Gospels: Essays in Memory of R. H. Lighfoot* (ed. D. E. Nineham; Oxford: Blackwell, 1967), 89–112.

5. For the theological significance of blood in Scripture, see Morris, *The Apostolic Preaching of the Cross*, 112–28; more recently, Sklar, *Sin, Impurity, Sacrifice, Atonement*.

6. I will also look in the next chapter at 1 Cor 1:18–2:5; Gal 1:3–4; Heb 2:5–10.

7. For the history of interpretation, see Matthew Gordley, *The Colossian Hymn in Context: An Exegesis in Light of Jewish and Greco-Roman Hymnic and Epistolary Conventions* (Tübingen: Mohr Siebeck, 2007), 3–25.

8. Richard Bauckham, "Where Is Wisdom to Be Found? Colossians 1:15–20 (2)," in *Reading Texts, Seeking Wisdom: Scripture and Theology* (ed. David Ford and Graham Stanton; Grand Rapids: Eerdmans, 2004), 134.

9. I understand the στοιχεῖα (Col 2:8) and the ἀρχαί and ἐξουσίαι (1:16; 2:10, 15) to be evil spiritual "powers." For a defense of this position, see Clinton Arnold, *The Colossian Syncretism: The Interface between Christianity and Folk Belief at Colossae* (Grand Rapids: Baker, 1996), 158–94, 251–55.

THE KINGDOM OF THE SON AND RECONCILIATION BY HIS CROSS (COL 1:12–14 AND 1:15–20)

Colossians 1:12–14 and 1:15–20 both belong to Paul's extended introduction (1:1–2:5), and more particularly to the prayer for the Colossians (1:9–23), following his customary introductory thanksgiving (1:3–8). Within this prayer (1:9–23), Paul implores the Colossians to give thanks (1:12) and then presents a basis for their thanksgiving by recounting the many blessings they have been given "in Christ" (1:12–23).[10]

The fact that the hymn begins with ὅς (Col 1:15) provides the structural link between the two passages. As Moo claims, "If Paul is quoting a 'hymn,' he has probably replaced the original noun with the relative pronoun to connect the hymn to the context."[11] This ὅς, therefore, is the beloved Son who rules over his kingdom and in whom is found redemption and forgiveness (1:13–14). Though 1:12–14 and 1:15–20 are distinct units, there is great overlap thematically,[12] and within the flow of the letter one "passes almost imperceptibly" into the other.[13] Yet while there is clearly a strong connection between the two units,[14] 1:12–14 properly belongs with what precedes (1:9–11), yet is transitional and inseparable from what follows (1:15–20).[15]

What, then, is the meaning of Col 1:12–14? First, the background for this passage is Israel's past redemption in the exodus and prophetic hope for future redemption in a new exodus.[16] Being "transferred . . . to the kingdom of his beloved Son" (1:13), therefore, does not refer primarily to individuals entering the realm of God's reign (although it certainly includes this) but to the eschatological reality that the church has been transferred into a new era

---

10. N. T. Wright, *The Epistles of Paul to the Colossians and to Philemon: An Introduction and Commentary* (TNTC; Grand Rapids: Eerdmans, 2002), 48–49.

11. Douglas J. Moo, *The Letters to the Colossians and to Philemon* (PiNTC; Grand Rapids: Eerdmans, 2008), 117.

12. Dunn notes especially the conceptual proximity of redemption in Col 1:14 and reconciliation/making peace in 1:20 (*The Epistles to the Colossians and to Philemon: A Commentary on the Greek Text* [NIGTC; Grand Rapids: Eerdmans, 1996], 102).

13. Peter O'Brien, *Colossians, Philemon* (WBC; Waco, TX: Word, 1982), 20.

14. For a survey of various proposals regarding the relationship between the two units, see Dunn, *Colossians*, 68; Thomas Sappington, *Revelation and Redemption at Colossae* (Sheffield: JSOT, 1991), 193–97.

15. Sappington, *Revelation and Redemption*, 197.

16. Colossians 1:12–14 uses the same terminology as the LXX to describe the exodus ("inheritance," Deut 19:10; 12:12; "deliver, save" Exod 6:6; 14:30) and the new exodus ("ransom, redemption," Isa 51:11, 52:3; "servant" 42:1; cf. "Son," Ps 2:7). The exodus background has been recognized since Augustine (*On the Psalms, NPNF[1]* 8:377). For the influence of the new exodus on Col 1:12–14, see G. S. Shogren, "Presently Entering the Kingdom of Christ: The Background and Purpose of Col 1:12–14," *JETS* 31 (1988): 176–77; Arnold, *The Colossian Syncretism*, 291.

defined by God's reign through Christ, freedom from evil, and the forgiveness of sins.

Second, within the Pauline framework of "already and not yet," this passage clearly emphasizes the finished work of Christ (realized eschatology).[17] While what "is described here would elsewhere be thought of as reserved for the end of history/time,"[18] the aorist tenses of the verbs make clear that redemption has already been accomplished and need only to be applied.

Third, the forgiveness of sins is a central element in the kingdom of Christ. Many interpret "redemption" as apposite to "forgiveness."[19] It is possible, however, that "redemption" retains the meaning of freedom from hostile enemies (as in the exodus) and is therefore distinct. Assuming this distinction, Sappington observes that "redemption from spiritual forces is closely tied in with the blessing of forgiveness" and suggests "on the basis of 1:14 that redemption consists of and/or comes about through the forgiveness of sins."[20] Either way, forgiveness (and possibly redemption through forgiveness) is a central element in the kingdom of Christ. As Eduard Lohse says, "the sovereign rule of Christ is present where there is forgiveness of sins."[21]

How, then, does Col 1:12–14 inform the interpretation of the hymn? First and foremost, it provides a redemptive-historical framework for the reconciliation of all things. The cosmic redemption of 1:15–20 is not a timeless reality but rather the ultimate *telos* of Israel's hope that has broken into the middle of the story through the blood of Christ's cross (1:20) and his resurrection (1:18). Furthermore, 1:12–14 sets forth a macroview of salvation that is elaborated in 1:15–20. The scope of redemption is "all things," and the means for this redemption is the blood of Christ's cross. The influence of Isaiah 40–55 is again present, as the cosmic scope of redemption recalls the expansive Isaianic vision for the kingdom of God (49:6), and the "making peace by the blood of his cross" (Col 1:20) echoes the servant whose suffering "brought us peace" (Isa 53:5). According to Morna Hooker, the hymn "give[s] us Christological statements which back up the reality of what Paul has said about the Colossians' redemption in verses 12–14."[22]

---

17. Although many commentators correctly observe the emphasis on the "already" realized eschatology in Colossians, Paul still maintains the tension with the "not yet." See Moo, *Colossians*, 68–69.

18. Dunn, *Colossians*, 77.

19. O'Brien, *Colossians*, 28.

20. Sappington, *Revelation and Redemption*, 211.

21. Eduard Lohse, *Colossians and Philemon: A Commentary on the Epistles to the Colossians and to Philemon* (Hermeneia; Philadelphia: Fortress, 1971), 40.

22. Morna Hooker, *From Adam to Christ: Essays on Paul* (Cambridge: Cambridge University Press, 1990), 128.

THE BLOOD OF THE CROSS AND THE KINGDOM OF DARKNESS (COL 1:15–20 AND 2:13–15)

After an extended introduction (Col 1:1–2:5), Paul opens the body of his letter with his main charge, "walk in him" (2:6–7)—which summarizes his teaching thus far and serves as the positive basis for the attack on the Colossian heresy.[23] Colossians 2:8–23 then engages the "philosophy," offering a positive argument of what the believer already has "in Christ" (2:8–15), followed by a direct attack on the philosophy (2:16–23). Colossians 2:13–15, therefore, is part of the larger unit of 2:8–15, which brings the main theological teaching of the letter (1:15–20) to bear on the pastoral purpose of the letter—"walk in him" (2:6–7). In other words, Paul applies his lofty christological teaching to the specific situation in Colossae, particularly addressing the "philosophy" threatening to take the Colossians captive (2:8).

While many have attempted to reconstruct the precise nature of the Colossian philosophy, the results are unavoidably speculative and cannot be determinative for interpreting Paul's letter.[24] However, despite Colossians leaving the reader wanting for specifics, the letter does make clear the main components of the philosophy. The philosophy (1) depends on "human tradition" (Col 2:8) and "human precepts and teachings" (2:22) that promote asceticism (2:18, 20–23); (2) depends on "the elemental spirits of the world" (2:8) and "worship of angels" (2:18); and (3) does not depend on Christ (2:8, 19).[25] In response to this philosophy, therefore, Paul declares that "in Christ" the Colossian Christians have the fullness of God (2:9–10) and complete victory over spiritual powers (2:10, 15).[26]

The connection between Col 2:8–15 and 1:15–20 can be seen verbally and theologically. In both passages, Christ is the dwelling place for the "fullness" of God (1:19; 2:9), "the head" (1:18; 2:10), supreme over "rulers and authorities" (1:16; 2:10, 15), and victorious through the "cross" (1:20; 2:14–15). Theologically, in 2:13–15 Paul is elaborating on 1:19–20 and applying it specifically to the Colossian philosophy concerning "the powers," that is, how Christ's reconciliation of "all things" entails their defeat.[27]

---

23. On the centrality of Col 2:6–7 in Paul's structure and purposes, see Wright, *Colossians*, 98; O'Brien, *Colossians*, 104–5; Moo, *Colossians*, 176.

24. For a survey of these reconstructions, see O'Brien, *Colossians*, xxx–xli; Moo, *Colossians*, 46–60. While most scholars agree that the "philosophy" was syncretistic, I am most convinced by Arnold's amalgamation of different backgrounds (*The Colossian Syncretism*, 226–27).

25. For a more thorough treatment of the basic components of the philosophy, as derived from the text, see Moo, *Colossians*, 50–52.

26. In Col 2:10–13 alone, there are three references to being "in him" (2:10, 11, 12) and three συν-compounds (2:12–13). O'Brien is correct, therefore, to say that the "in Christ" motif, "runs like a scarlet thread through the whole passage" (*Colossians*, 104).

27. Wright says the message of Col 1:19–20 is "considerably amplified" in 2:13–15 (*Colossians*, 76). Dunn says that Paul seeks "to explain . . . the full significance of what he earlier declared regarding the cross (Col 1:19–20)" (*Colossians*, 145). O'Brien calls 2:8–15 an "explanatory resumption of chapter 1:15–20" (*Colossians*, 104).

THE MEANING OF COLOSSIANS 2:13–15

Despite relative consensus in translation, Col 2:13–15 is fraught with exegetical difficulties. The passage is structured around the main verb συνεζωοποίησεν, which is then developed by three aorist participles explaining the basis for this new life:

> συνεζωοποίησεν ὑμᾶς σὺν αὐτῷ
>
> χαρισάμενος ἡμῖν πάντα τὰ παραπτώματα
>
> ἐξαλείψας τὸ καθ᾽ ἡμῶν χειρόγραφον τοῖς δόγμασιν . . .
>
> ἀπεκδυσάμενος τὰς ἀρχὰς καὶ τὰς ἐξουσίας. . . (Col 2:13–15)[28]

The first two aorist participles are probably causative,[29] making the basic flow of the text as follows: God made you alive with Christ by forgiving your sins, based on your record of debt being cancelled through Christ's work on the cross. Yet what is this "record of debt . . . with its legal demands" (χειρόγραφον τοῖς δόγμασιν)? The χειρόγραφον was a legal document acting as a "note of indebtedness,"[30] or, in modern terms, an IOU. Δόγμασιν is more difficult to translate, yet based on Paul's use of the word in Eph 2:15, it likely refers to "decrees" that are an expression of the commandments of the Mosaic law. The "decrees," therefore, provide the reason why the "record of debt" was "against us."[31] As Dunn says, "Although the written record against us cannot be identified with the law as such . . . behind it lie the decrees of the law giving the *cheirographon* its condemnatory force."[32]

Colossians 2:15 is the climax of this section, as Paul further develops his argument by applying it to the "rulers and authorities." While the forgiveness of sins and victory over evil are clearly linked in Paul's thought, there are exegetical hurdles that obfuscate the precise nature of that relationship. Although the middle voice of ἀπεκδυσάμενος has led interpreters—from the early church to Lightfoot—in the direction of Christ divesting himself of his flesh or the "rulers and authorities,"[33] the context of the verb has led most contemporary scholars to agree that Christ strips the rulers and authorities, thereby disarming them of their power.[34]

The irony here is thick, for while the centurions had stripped Jesus and exposed him as powerless before the crowd (Mark 15:20), Paul says that it was

28. Arnold, *The Colossian Syncretism*, 275.

29. O'Brien, *Colossians*, 123; Moo, *Colossians*, 207–8.

30. Eduard Lohse, "χειρόγραφον," in *TDNT*, 9:435.

31. Markus Barth and Helmut Blanke, *Colossians: A New Translation with Introduction and Commentary* (AB; New York: Doubleday, 1994), 329–30; Lohse, *Colossians*, 109.

32. Dunn, *Colossians*, 165.

33. J. B. Lightfoot, *Saint Paul's Epistles to the Colossians and to Philemon* (New York: Macmillan, 1900), 187–89.

34. O'Brien, *Colossians*, 127–28; Lohse, *Colossians*, 111–12; Moo, *Colossians*, 213.

the "rulers and authorities" who were truly being stripped of their power. Moreover, this disarming was a defeat, for Christ was "triumphing" (θριαμβεύσας) over the "rulers and authorities," a clear reference to Roman triumphal processions.[35] Just as a Roman general would celebrate a military victory by parading through the streets with his defeated enemies shackled in a procession behind him, Jesus had destroyed the forces of evil and was making a public spectacle of them as he revealed the divine wisdom of Christ crucified (1 Cor 2:6–8).

The last exegetical difficulty of this passage raises one of the most significant theological questions: Is Christ's triumph over the "rulers and authorities" located specifically "in the cross" or more generally "in him"? While translators and commentators are divided over this issue,[36] the exegetical outcome is not determinative for the theological conclusion. For even if the triumph is "in him," the "him" is the crucified Christ who has brought reconciliation to all things (including the powers) by the blood of the cross.

This is not to say that the cross is the only element, but that the context of this passage (Col 2:13–15) is discussing the forgiveness that comes through Christ's death on the cross. In his commentary on this passage, Calvin argued that the context requires the reader to attribute Satan's downfall (Col 2:15) to Christ's debt-cancelling work on the cross (2:13–14).[37] O'Brien agrees: "The context of Colossians 2:15 demands that we understand the removal of power or authority which the principalities exercised over the lives of men by holding the certificate of indebtedness in their grip."[38]

The debt-cancelling work of the cross and the victory over the powers, however, are not held together merely by context, but also by the development of the passage. As Paul expounds on the blood of the cross and applies it to the rulers and authorities, "verse 15 draws out the effect of verse 14."[39] If the "record of debt" and its "decrees" were the instruments of the evil forces in accusing sinners, then cancelling the record disarms them of their power to condemn.[40] Lohse summarizes the logic of Christ's forgiving and victorious work:

35. David Williams, *Paul's Metaphors: Their Context and Character* (Peabody, MA: Hendrickson, 1999), 257–60.

36. The prepositional phrase ἐν αὐτῷ (Col 2:15) could mean "in him" (RSV, NASB, ESV), referring to Christ, or "in it" (KJV, NRSV), referring to the "cross" (NIV, NIB, NET).

37. John Calvin, *Calvin's Commentaries* (trans. Calvin Translation Society; Grand Rapids: Baker, 1999), comment on Col 2:15.

38. O'Brien, *Colossians*, 127.

39. Wright, *Colossians*, 117.

40. Sappington, *Revelation and Redemption*, 212; R. P. Martin, "Reconciliation and Forgiveness in the Letter to the Colossians," in *Reconciliation and Hope: New Testament Essays on Atonement Presented to L. L. Morris on his 60th Birthday* (ed. Robert Banks; Carlisle, UK: Paternoster, 1974), 123–24.

The author of Col appropriated this confession because it clearly expressed what was for him the essential connection between forgiveness of sins and victory over the powers and principalities. . . . With the forgiveness of sins each and every claim of the "elements of the universe" . . . was nullified. This stresses even more forcefully that both affirmations form an indissoluble pair: on the cross of Christ the certificate of indebtedness is erased; on the cross of Christ the powers and principalities are disempowered. Consequently, where there is forgiveness of sins, there is freedom from the "powers" and "principalities," there is life and salvation![41]

Furthermore, outside of the logic of this passage itself, Sappington argues that the connection to Col 1:12–14 corroborates this interpretation as well.[42] Inasmuch as forgiveness is a key element in being transferred from the domain of darkness to the kingdom of the beloved Son (1:12–14), then it is similarly through forgiveness (wiping out the "record of debt") that Christ is victorious over the powers of the domain of darkness (2:13–15).

RECONCILING ALL THINGS AND DEFEATING THE POWERS

The primary overlap between Col 1:15–20 and 2:13–15 is in the connection between the cross (1:20; 2:14) and the powers (1:16; 2:15). At one level, we can simply say that the reconciliation of all things entails the defeat of the powers. The difficulty, however, is that 1:15–20 implies that the powers themselves are reconciled. The way we interpret the reconciliation of the powers in 1:20 should be determined by the elaboration of the powers in 2:15. The powers are not restored to friendship with their Creator but continually seek to take captive the people of God (2:8). A way forward is to recognize that the "reconciliation" in 1:20 includes Christ's "making peace" on the cross. Some scholars, therefore, have helpfully referred to the "reconciliation" of the powers as "pacification": "the imposing of peace, something brought about by conquest."[43]

SUMMARY

Paul unfolds his argument in Col 1:12–14, 15–20, and 2:13–15 progressively, each passage further elaborating on the previous one. Col 1:12–14 provides a redemptive-historical macroview of salvation in terms of being transferred from the domain of darkness to the kingdom of the beloved Son. Col 1:15–

---

41. Lohse, *Colossians*, 107.
42. Sappington, *Revelation and Redemption*, 222.
43. F. F. Bruce, "Christ as Conqueror and Reconciler," *BSac* 141 (1984): 293; cf. Arnold, *The Colossian Syncretism*, 269.

20 reveals that this eschatological redemption is also cosmic reconciliation to God through the blood of Christ's cross. Finally, 2:13–15 demonstrates that this eschatological transference into the kingdom and reconciliation to God entails the defeat of the powers. In short, the colossal accomplishment of transferring sinners to the kingdom of the beloved Son, which includes reconciliation to God and defeat of the powers, is brought about by the blood of Christ's cross. Calvin highlights the paradoxical nature of Christ's victory in Colossians: "Paul magnificently celebrates the triumph which Christ obtained upon the cross, as if the cross, the symbol of ignominy, had been converted into a triumphal chariot."[44]

The theological development in Colossians reveals that the victory over the powers, while incredibly important for Paul, fits within the broader aims of reconciliation to God and entering into his kingdom. Being reconciled to the king is the ultimate goal; defeating the powers is an integral step in this process. As Chrysostom said, "It is a great thing indeed to have been delivered from darkness; but to have been brought into a kingdom too is far greater."[45]

In sum, Christ reigns over the reconciled new creation, which entails forgiveness and redemption for God's people and disarming and destruction for his enemies. The context of the Christ hymn informs its meaning and provides great insight into the question of the kingdom and the cross. As Moo says, "Through the work of Christ on the cross, God has brought his entire rebellious creation back under the rule of his sovereign power."[46]

REVELATION 5:5–10

If the Bible is one grand narrative, one would expect many threads to come together at the end of the story. This is precisely what happens in Revelation, which presents an apocalyptic vision of God's consummation of all things. The heart of the book (Revelation 4–5) offers a visual that captures my entire argument with one image: a slain Lamb on the throne (5:6), as well as another clear exegetical link between the "kingdom" of God and the "blood" of the cross (5:9–10). While primary attention will be given to 5:5–10, I will begin with 1:5b–6, which introduces the themes on which 5:5–10 expands, and conclude by discussing 12:10–11, which offers further clarity and applies the previous christological statements to Christ's followers.

---

44. Calvin, *Institutes*, 2.16.6.
45. Chrysostom, *Homilies on Colossians*, NPNF[1] 13:266.
46. Moo, *Colossians*, 137.

THE BLOOD AND THE KINGDOM (REV 1:5B–6)

In Revelation, theology is set forth within the broader context of doxology. It is no wonder, then, that before John can even get through his initial greeting he bursts into a hymn, praising Jesus, "who loves us and has freed us from our sins by his blood and made us a kingdom, priests to his God and Father" (Rev 1:5b–6). For John, the redeeming work of Christ on the cross is at the heart of the eschatological vision for the kingdom. While the book of Revelation certainly is concerned with the future, the past tense of the key verbs makes clear that redemption has decisively been accomplished (λύσαντι) and God's people have already been made (ἐποίησεν) a kingdom on earth. The consummation of the kingdom, therefore, will not be a new work but an outworking of what has already been won on the cross. Although this doxological description of Christ's redeeming work is expanded throughout Revelation, there are four key elements from this passage that lay a foundation for what lies ahead.

First, the story of Israel provides the context for the Messiah's work. What was promised to Israel at Sinai ("You shall be to me a kingdom of priests," Exod 19:6) has been fulfilled on Gologtha ("To him who loves us and has freed us from our sins by his blood and made us a kingdom, priests to his God and Father," Rev 1:5b–6).

Second, Christ's sin-forgiving, kingdom-making work on the cross is motivated by his love. The grammatical shift between "him who loves us" (present participle) and "has freed us from our sins" (aorist participle) and "made us a kingdom" (aorist indicative) suggests that "Christ's love for us is a continuing reality that in point of time expressed itself in the redemptive act of Calvary."[47]

Third, dealing with sin is at the heart of Christ's bringing the kingdom. While Revelation will have much to say regarding the defeat of Satan (esp. Rev 12:7–12), the emphasis here is on "the atoning effects of [Christ's] death" for the coming of the kingdom.[48] Kingdom, therefore, is not only about victory but about reconciliation (cf. Exod 19:4).

Fourth, the kingdom of God on earth entails the restoration of human vicegerency. The kingdom is characterized primarily by *Christ's* throne; he is "the ruler of kings on earth" (Rev 1:5). But he has made *us* a kingdom, meaning that those who are under his reign will also reign with him on his throne (3:21; cf. Gen 1:28).

---

47. Robert Mounce, *The Book of Revelation* (NICNT; Grand Rapids: Eerdmans, 1977), 49; cf. Robert Wall, *Revelation* (NIBC; Peabody, MA: Hendrickson, 1991), 58.

48. Grant Osborne, *Revelation* (BECNT; Grand Rapids: Baker Academic, 2002), 64.

THE LION AND THE LAMB (REV 5:5–10)

Revelation 5:9–10 expands on 1:5b–6, once again in the form of a hymn: "For you were slain, and by your blood you ransomed people for God . . . and you have made them a kingdom and priests to our God." While the basic concept is the same (Christ ransoms people by his blood and makes them a kingdom and priests), the context of this passage greatly enhances its meaning. Revelation 4–5 constitutes a vision of the heavenly throne room, providing "the focal vision" from which the rest of the book flows and "the theological center which expresses John's basic convictions."[49] While the two chapters are one unit, Revelation 4 praises God for his reign in creation and Revelation 5 praises the Lamb for his reign in redemption.

The throne is the "central theological image" in Revelation.[50] In Revelation 4, however, "John intentionally withholds any description of the central figure on the throne, leaving a blank center in the picture to be filled in by the figure of the Lamb—yet another means of affirming that God is the one who defines himself by Christ."[51] After a glorious description of the throne (4:3–7) and a hymn of worship to the king (4:8–11), John sees a scroll in the right hand of the one on the throne and hears an angel proclaiming, "Who is worthy to open the scroll . . . ?" (5:1–2), which contains God's sovereign plan for the destiny of the world (revealed in chapters 6–22 and summarized in 4:1 as "what must take place after this"). To *open* the scroll means not only to reveal, but also to put into effect God's plan for consummation.[52] As John weeps since no one is found worthy to open the scroll, he hears a voice: "Weep no more; behold, the Lion of the tribe of Judah, the Root of David, has conquered, so that he can open the scroll" (5:5).

The "Lion of the tribe of Judah" (Gen 49:9–10) and the "Root of David" (Isa 11:1) represent the summation of all the messianic hopes of the Old Testament. But after *hearing* of a Lion in traditional messianic parlance—usually accompanied by militaristic and nationalistic imagery—John turns and shockingly sees quite the opposite: "a Lamb standing, as though it had been slain" (Rev 5:6). Bauckham says that "by juxtaposing the two contrasting images, John has forged a new symbol of conquest by sacrificial death."[53]

---

49. Gerhard Krodel, *Revelation* (ACNT; Minneapolis: Augsburg, 1989), 168; cf. Eugene Boring, *Revelation* (IBC; Louisville: Westminster John Knox, 1989), 102; Mounce, *Revelation*, 138.

50. Elisabeth Schüssler-Fiorenza, *The Book of Revelation: Justice and Judgment* (Philadelphia: Fortress, 1985), 116.

51. Boring, *Revelation*, 103.

52. G. B. Caird, *A Commentary on the Revelation of St. John the Divine* (BNTC; London: Black, 1966), 71; Mounce, *Revelation*, 131.

53. Richard Bauckham, *The Theology of the Book of Revelation* (New York: Cambridge University Press, 1993), 74.

Scholars press their rhetorical limits hoping to capture the immeasurable significance of such an image.[54] According to G. B. Caird, what John sees "constitutes the most impressive rebirth of images he anywhere achieves."[55] "In one brilliant stroke," says Robert Mounce, "John portrays the central theme of NT revelation—victory through sacrifice."[56]

But what exactly is the meaning of this rebirth of images? How do the Lion and the Lamb relate? Eugene Boring provides a helpful taxonomy of interpretations.[57] (1) *First the Lamb, then the Lion.* Although quite popular, Boring says this view "is the polar opposite of the meaning of the text."[58] The Lamb remains slaughtered and, rather than dropping out, "Lamb" is *the* definitive title for Christ from this point forward (used 28 times). (2) *Lamb to Christians, Lion to others.* This view simply does not take into account that there are positive attributes of the Lion (see Gen 49:9–10) and negative attributes of the Lamb ("the wrath of the Lamb," Rev 6:16). (3) *The Lamb is really a Lion.* This view relies on Jewish ideas of a messianic warrior lamb, and though correctly recognizing the power of the Lamb, this view still neglects the fact that the Lamb is slain and is based on Jewish texts widely considered to be late interpolations.[59]

I propose the following alternative: *the Lion redefined by the Lamb.*[60] This interpretation upholds both the lion-ness and the lamb-ness of Christ and highlights their integration throughout Revelation. Both aspects are present in this first mention of the Lamb, for he is both slain and yet has seven horns and eyes. The perfect participle of "slain" (ἐσφαγμένον) indicates the continuing effects of the finished work of Christ's death. As Oecumenius claimed centuries ago, "Even after the resurrection the Lord carried about the trophies of death—the imprint of the nails, his life-giving body made red by his blood . . . for this reason he was seen in the vision 'as though slain.'"[61]

---

54. For example, the juxtaposition of the two images has been called "the central fact of New Testament Theology" (George Eldon Ladd, *A Commentary on the Revelation of John* [Grand Rapids: Eerdmans, 1972], 87); "the central paradox of the gospel" (Graeme Goldsworthy, "The Gospel in Revelation," in *The Goldsworthy Trilogy* [Carlisle, UK: Paternoster, 2000], 169); and "the central paradox and mystery of the Christian faith" (Vern Poythress, *The Returning King: A Guide to the Book of Revelation* [Phillipsburg, NJ: Presbyterian & Reformed, 2000], 109).

55. Caird, *Revelation*, 73.

56. Mounce, *Revelation*, 132.

57. Boring, *Revelation*, 108–11.

58. Ibid., 109.

59. Ibid., 110.

60. This title is largely in line with Boring, although his title ("The 'lion' is really the lamb") could imply that the lion aspect of Christ drops out completely (ibid.).

61. Oecumenius, "Commentary on the Apocalypse," in *Traditio Exegetica Graeca* (Louvain: Peeters, 1991), 8:115–16. Oecumenius's commentary on Revelation has traditionally been dated to the tenth century, but has more recently been dated to the seventh or sixth century.

Boring concludes, "Crucifixion was not an incident which once happened in the cosmic career of the Messiah and then was superseded by the resurrection and exaltation; it is the definitive act which stamps its character on the identity of the Christ."[62]

The background of the "slain Lamb" is both the Passover lamb of the exodus (Exod 12:6; cf. 1 Cor 5:7; 1 Pet 1:18–19) and Isaiah's servant (who is "like a lamb [ἀμνός in LXX] that is led to the slaughter," Isa 53:7), therefore showing that Christ's sacrifice effects both victory and atonement.[63] However, although the Lamb remains slain, he has seven horns (indicating fullness of power) and seven eyes (indicating fullness of knowledge)—he is "the power of God and the wisdom of God" (1 Cor 1:24). The continuing nature of both aspects (lion and lamb) can be seen simply in John's choice of vocabulary throughout the Apocalypse. For just as "Lamb" is the key christological noun for Christ, "conquer" (νικάω)—normally, a property of the Lion—is the most significant verb.[64] The Lamb conquers (Rev 3:21; 5:5; 17:14), as do those who follow him (2:7, 11, 17, 26; 3:5, 12, 21; 12:11; 15:2; 21:7).

Both images of Lion and Lamb are necessary for understanding Christ in Revelation, although the imagery of the Lamb takes priority in the rest of the book. Joseph Mangina rightly concludes, "Christ really is and never ceases to be the Lion of the tribe of Judah. He is indeed a figure of power, but his power is realized precisely in the self-giving love he displays at the cross."[65] The key feature in the integration of these two images, therefore, is that the Lion represents the aim or goal of Christ, whereas the Lamb depicts the means of achieving such a goal. Vernard Eller argues that Christ's "suffering death is his victory; his *modus operandi* . . . always is that of the Lamb, but the consequences, the results, always are a victory that belongs to the character of the Lion."[66] As Augustine says, "He endured death as a lamb; he devoured it as a lion." He is the Lamb and the Lion "because in being slain he slew death."[67]

As is the pattern throughout Revelation, John's vision (Rev 5:1–8) is interpreted by a hymn (5:9–10, 12–13). The Lamb is worthy to take the scroll (to enact God's sovereign purposes) because by his blood he ransomed a people

---

62. Boring, *Revelation*, 109.

63. For further evidence about these backgrounds, see G. K. Beale, *The Book of Revelation: A Commentary on the Greek Text* (NIGTC; Grand Rapids: Eerdmans, 1999), 351.

64. Boring, *Revelation*, 111.

65. Joseph Mangina, *Revelation* (BTCB; Grand Rapids: Brazos, 2010), 88.

66. Vernard Eller, *The Most Revealing Book of the Bible: Making Sense Out of Revelation* (Grand Rapids: Eerdmans, 1974), 80.

67. Augustine, *Sermon 375A: On the Sacraments* (397), WSA 10:330.

and made a kingdom. Mounce demonstrates the logic of the text, showing that the Lamb is worthy to open the scroll for three reasons: "He was slain (a historical fact), he purchased people for God (the interpretation of that fact), and he made them to be a kingdom and priests (the result of the fact)."[68]

Once again, the exodus imagery is explicit. However, not only did Christ fulfill God's promises to Israel (making them a kingdom of priests), he also shared the spoils with people "from every tribe and language and people and nation" (Rev 5:9). Furthermore, Christ's redemptive death fulfills not only the purposes of the exodus, but also restores humanity to their original task of reigning and serving in Eden. "To be a Christian is to be both king and priest, but with a sovereignty and priesthood derived from Christ, as his were derived from God."[69] The creation mandate to rule over the earth (Gen 1:28) clearly echoes in the last line of the hymn: "and they shall reign on the earth" (Rev 5:10).

Finally, it should be noted that, as powerful as this passage is, it makes no mention of what/who God's people are ransomed *from*. The parallel from Rev 1:5 ("freed us *from our sins*"), however, does provide a clear referent. Furthermore, the exodus imagery, as well as the prevalence of spiritual warfare throughout Revelation, begs for further explanation regarding the place of Satan and demons in Christ's victorious sacrifice. It is this question—namely, how sin and Satan relate in Christ's redeeming work and in making a kingdom of priests—that is addressed in Rev 12:10–11.

THE BLOOD OF CHRIST AND THE DEFEAT OF SATAN (REV 12:10–11)

The heavenly victory of Michael and his angels over Satan and his angels (Rev 12:7–9) has its basis in Christ's victory on the cross (5:5, 9–10). Caird summarizes the meaning of the heavenly battle: "Michael's victory is simply the heavenly and symbolic counterpart of the earthly reality of the Cross. Michael, in fact, is not the field officer who does the actual fighting, but the staff officer in the heavenly control room, who is able to remove Satan's flag from the heavenly map because the real victory has been won on Calvary."[70] Likewise, the saints' victory over Satan is also rooted in Christ's cross: "They have conquered by the blood of the Lamb" (12:11). These passages reveal not only *that* Christ and his followers conquer Satan, but *how* they do so. Before

---

68. Mounce, *Revelation*, 135.
69. Caird, *Revelation*, 77.
70. Ibid., 153–54.

discussing their way of conquering, however, I must explain the background to this battle and Satan's specific role within it.

Many scholars have noted the Jewish *legal* background to the battle depicted in Revelation, which has significant implications for understanding the nature of Christ's victory over Satan.[71] Caird summarizes well, saying that "although John depicts the battle between Michael and Satan in military terms, it was essentially a legal battle between opposing counsel, which resulted in one of them being disbarred."[72]

The themes of truth and falsehood are prevalent throughout Revelation, depicting the world as a type of courtroom, contrasting the deceit of the evil forces (Rev 12:9; cf. 20:2–3, 7–8; 13:14; 19:21) with the true testimony of "Jesus Christ, the faithful witness" (1:5) and his followers (14:5).[73] Within this courtroom context, Satan is the "accuser of our brothers" (12:10), a type of legal prosecutor with a one-track passion for condemning the guilty. But he is also the "deceiver of the whole world" (12:9), who from the beginning (Gen 3:1–5) has tempted all of humanity to exchange the truth of God for a lie (Rom 1:25). If this is a legal battle, and Satan is the "accuser" and "deceiver," how then do Christ and his saints conquer Satan?

The means by which Satan is defeated are suffering and witness; first by Christ, then by Christians. Jesus combats Satan as the "deceiver" with truth, for just as Satan is the "deceiver of the whole world" (Rev 12:9), Christ is the "faithful and true witness" (3:14). Richard Bauckham says this title "refers primarily to the witness which Jesus bore to God during his life on earth and to his faithfulness in maintaining his witness even at the cost of his life."[74] Because Jesus was always a faithful witness to the truth, Satan's deception proved to be an inept weapon.

More importantly, Christ has conquered Satan as the "accuser" by removing any basis of accusation and therefore stripping him completely of his accusatory force over believers. The removal of his power is the meaning of Satan's being "thrown down" from heaven to earth (Rev 12:9–10). Because Christ's blood has freed Christians from their sins and made them kings and priests for God (1:5b–6), Satan no longer has any place to accuse them before God. As Gerhard Krodel attests, "The accuser of our sisters and brothers on earth has been disbarred from heaven's court."[75] Although before Christ's

71. See, e.g., Beale, *Revelation*, 661–62.
72. Caird, *Revelation*, 155.
73. Bauckham, *The Theology of the Book of Revelation*, 73, 91.
74. Ibid., 72.
75. Krodel, *Revelation*, 243.

death, Satan's accusations were, in a sense, right accusations (sinners are guilty), the cross has removed sin and its effects from followers of Christ and therefore neutered Satan's accusations. He is left to a curtailed version of accusation and deception on earth, though with no less voracity "because he knows that his time is short!" (12:12).

The pattern in Revelation is that Christ has conquered on the cross (Rev 5:5, 9–10), will conquer finally in the consummation (17:14), and is conquering in between through his saints (3:21; 12:11; 15:2). Since it is *Christ's* victory, the saints participate in the same way Christ achieved it, through witness and suffering. The basis of their victory is the blood of Christ alone—"they have conquered him by the blood of the Lamb" (12:11)—but, as Bauckham says, "the messiah does not wage war alone: he leads the army of Israel against the enemies of Israel."[76]

The saints conquer primarily by witnessing to Christ's decisive victory on the cross: "They have conquered him by the blood of the Lamb *and by the word of their testimony*" (Rev 12:11, italics mine). This witness to the truth exposes the falsity of Satan's lies and the emptiness of his accusations. If Satan has already been defeated by the blood of the Lamb, the saints need only to witness to the eternal truthfulness of this event.

Second, the saints share in Christ's victory over Satan by sharing in Christ's victorious suffering. Although Christ's suffering alone is redemptive (the saints do not ransom), their deaths are a continual witness to the efficacy of Christ's death. As Beale says, "The suffering of Christians is a sign, not of Satan's victory, but of the saints' victory over Satan because of their belief in the triumph of the cross, with which their suffering identifies them."[77]

SUMMARY

These passages from Revelation enlighten the relationship between the kingdom of Christ and the blood of his cross in three ways. First, Christ's atoning work on the cross results in the people of God being made a kingdom (Rev 1:5b–6). Second, the Lion-like victory was achieved through Lamb-like means (5:5–6). By the blood of Christ, people of all nations have been ransomed from sin and made to be kings and priests (5:9–10) in the pattern and fulfillment of the exodus (Exod 19:6). Third, the establishment of God's kingdom entails the defeat of Satan by Christ and his followers (Rev 12:10–

---

76. Bauckham, *The Theology of the Book of Revelation*, 68.
77. Beale, *Revelation*, 663. For an explanation of Christ's followers triumphing through sacrificial death in Rev 7:4–14, see Bauckham, *The Theology of the Book of Revelation*, 77.

11). In what is primarily a legal battle, Christ, by shedding his blood, paid the penalty for sin and therefore defeated Satan by disarming him of his accusatory force. Though the final defeat is yet to come, Christians continue to conquer Satan, exposing his deception by witnessing to Christ's obedient life and the true efficacy of his death.

These representative passages from Colossians and Revelation reveal how the New Testament integrates the kingdom of Christ and the blood of the cross. Having followed the unfolding story of the kingdom and atonement through the story line of Scripture, I can now synthesize my findings in the next chapter.

CHAPTER FIVE

SUMMARY: THE KINGDOM ESTABLISHED BY THE CROSS

IN THIS CHAPTER I bring together, clarify, and advance the previous observations from the Old and New Testaments. Seeking to understand the unity of the diverse biblical witness to the kingdom and the cross naturally provides a transition to part 2, where I extend my findings into specific conversations in systematic theology.

KINGDOM–CROSS INTERPLAY IN THE OLD AND NEW TESTAMENTS

The Old Testament (especially Isaiah 40–55) provides the proper framework for understanding the kingdom–cross interplay in the New Testament.[1] The significance of the Old Testament is especially evident in Israel's story of victory through sacrifice, concepts such as covenant and temple, and fulfillment in Christ.

THE STORY OF VICTORY THROUGH SACRIFICE

Genesis 1–2 presents a project aimed at God's glorious reign over all the earth through the vicegerency of his servants. After the fall, the kingdom project graciously continues, but it will now come through the "seed" of a

---

1. For the influence of the Isaianic new exodus in the New Testament, see Richard Beaton, *Isaiah's Christ in Matthew's Gospel* (Cambridge: Cambridge University Press, 2002); Watts, *Isaiah's New Exodus in Mark*; Peter Mallen, *The Reading and Transformation of Isaiah in Luke-Acts* (New York: T&T Clark, 2008); David Pao, *Acts and the Isaianic New Exodus* (Grand Rapids: Baker Academic, 2002).

woman who, though being wounded, will crush the head of the serpent (Gen 3:15). The victory and suffering introduced in the *protoevangelium* develop throughout the story of Israel into *royal* victory and *atoning* suffering. As various "seeds" fail to bring about the fulfillment of God's design on earth, the prophets point forward to an eschatological seed who will bring about this royal victory *through* atoning suffering. The high point of this prophecy is Isaiah, who tells of the victory of God's kingdom coming through the suffering of his servant (Isa 52:13–53:12).

The New Testament does not present an isolated story of Jesus, but one that is the fulfillment of *this* story—Jesus is the "yes" to every promise of the Old Testament (2 Cor 1:20). Jesus is the promised seed (Gal 3:16) and the prophesied servant (Luke 22:37), who crushes the serpent and restores the Edenic harmony between God and his people, as well as their commission to Edenize the earth for the glory of God. From the bruised heel (Gen 3:15) to the reigning Lamb (Rev 22:1), the Bible is a redemptive story of a crucified Messiah who will establish God's kingdom on earth through his atoning death on the cross. This unfolding story of victory through sacrifice is the tapestry in which kingdom and cross are interwoven.

COVENANT AND THE KINGDOM–CROSS INTERPLAY

Covenant and kingdom are inseparable in the Old Testament, and their link provides key insight into the kingdom–cross interplay. Covenant is the binding relationship between a king and his servants and is therefore at the heart of the coming kingdom of God. Redemptive-historically, God administers his kingdom through the covenants. As Gentry and Wellum have demonstrated, "the saving reign of God—God's kingdom—will occur with the coming of the Messiah and the inauguration of a new covenant which will bring to fulfillment all the previous covenants."[2]

The new covenant of God's kingdom is itself brought about by the blood of Christ as the Passover lamb. At the institution of the Lord's Supper, Jesus reimagines the exodus tradition around himself as the Passover lamb and the fulfillment of the prophesied new covenant with these words, "This is my blood of the covenant, which is poured out for many for the forgiveness of sins" (Matt 26:28; cf. Luke 22:20; 1 Cor. 11:25; also Exod 24:8; Jer 31:31–34; Zech 9:11). Christ's blood seals a new covenant, which is the relational aspect of the coming reign of God over the new creation. "By his cross work, he has inaugurated the new covenant."[3] The kingdom is established at the cross,

---

2. Gentry and Wellum, *Kingdom through Covenant*, 595.
3. Ibid., 662; cf. 691.

where Jesus sheds his blood as the mediator of the new covenant, thereby restoring the right relationship between the divine king and his servants.

TEMPLE AND THE KINGDOM–CROSS INTERPLAY

In the creation narrative, Eden is depicted as a temple and its priest-kings receive the task of expanding God's kingdom.[4] This connection between temple and kingdom is replicated in the kingdom of Israel, where the temple—as the permanent center of the kingdom—functions as the dwelling place of the holy king *and* as the means of atonement and forgiveness for the servants of the king. In other words, God's reigning over and through his people (kingdom) is inseparable from his dwelling with them (temple). The temple represents the presence of the king and the purity of his servants.

The Davidic covenant takes these two historical elements and grafts them together in the coming of the Messiah; for when God establishes the Davidic kingdom, the king is to build a temple for God (2 Sam 7:13). It is no surprise, therefore, that Jesus' proclamation of the coming of God's kingdom (Mark 1:14–15) entailed his own replacement of the temple (John 2:19). It is fitting that on the cross Jesus is depicted as king (Mark 15:32), and the destruction of the old temple is indicated by the tearing of the veil (15:38). "The king and the temple will be one in Christ Jesus. The representative of the people who makes the people righteous (the king) will be the presence of God dwelling in and with the people (the temple)."[5] The two aspects of the temple (the dwelling place of the king and the place of sacrifice for sinners) come together in Christ and his cross.

THE PROMISES OF THE KINGDOM FULFILLED IN THE CROSS

The relationship of the kingdom and the cross in redemptive history is further clarified by observing that various elements of the coming kingdom find their fulfillment in the cross (although certainly not the cross alone). As I argued in the introduction, the coming of God's kingdom entails victory over evil, forgiveness of sins, and a new exodus. The logic is simple. (1) The establishment of the kingdom is dependent on the defeat of evil, forgiveness of sin, and a new exodus. (2) Each of these is accomplished primarily through Christ's death on the cross. (3) The cross, therefore, is where the kingdom is established. I will briefly review Christ's victory and new exodus, followed by a more sustained clarification of the forgiveness of sins.

---

4. Beale, *The Temple and the Church's Mission*, 66–70.
5. Levering and Dauphinais, *Holy People, Holy Land*, 82.

Victory over Evil

Although it is certainly unexpected that a battle could be won through suffering, Scripture is clear and repetitious that it is through Christ's *death* that Satan has been defeated (John 12:31; Col 2:13–15; Heb 2:14; Rev 12:10–11). "The cross represents the climactic victory of the kingdom of God. God's rule was disrupted by human rebellion and all that came with it: demonic power, sickness, suffering, pain, and death—every kind of evil. The root of all opposition to God's rule was human rebellion, and that could be destroyed *only* at the cross."[6]

New Exodus

We have seen in Mark's gospel that all of Christ's work is to be interpreted within the framework of the new exodus. As the Passover lamb and Suffering Servant, Jesus brings his people out of slavery by ransoming them into the kingdom of God. Beyond Mark, Christ's death as a new exodus is evident, wherever it is discussed, in terms of "redemption" (Rom 3:24; Eph 1:7; Titus 2:14; Heb 9:12).

Forgiveness of Sins

The kingdom promise of the forgiveness of sins also finds its resolution at the cross, for it is there, by the blood of Christ, that atonement is made and sin is forgiven (Matt 26:28; Rom 3:25; Eph 1:7; Heb 9:22; 1 John 2:2; 4:10). The forgiveness of the kingdom comes at the cost of the king. Forgiveness of sins and the wrath of God—particularly as aspects of the coming of God's kingdom—have often been neglected or rejected and thereby allow me to distinguish my proposal. Since the forgiveness of sins entails the removal of God's wrath,[7] I will look at each of these two aspects in turn. The main point is that Jesus' death brings the kingdom both by bearing God's wrath and forgiving sins.[8]

---

6. Craig Bartholomew and Michael Goheen, *The Drama of Scripture: Finding Our Place in the Biblical Story* (Grand Rapids: Baker Academic, 2004), 165, italics theirs.

7. Christopher J. H. Wright, "Atonement in the Old Testament," 76.

8. Although the wrath of God is a prevalent theme in Scripture, its meaning in general and significance for Christ's atoning work in particular is greatly contested. I offer three clarifying points. First, wrath is not an essential attribute of God but rather an expression of his holiness in confrontation with sin (see D. A. Carson, "The Wrath of God," in *Engaging the Doctrine of God: Contemporary Protestant Perspectives* [ed. Bruce L. McCormack; Grand Rapids: Baker Academic, 2008], 49). Second, God's wrath is not incompatible with his love but arises for the purpose of protecting what he loves (see Boersma, *Violence, Hospitality, and the Cross*, 49). Third, God's wrath is not univocal to human wrath. Whereas human wrath is often characterized by short tempers and mixed motives, God's wrath is always in line with his loving and

The Wrath of God and the Coming of God's Kingdom

The wrath-bearing nature of Jesus' death is essential for the coming of the kingdom.[9] In the Old Testament, the coming of God's kingdom entailed the pouring out of his wrath: "With wrath poured out I will be king over you" (Ezek 20:33; cf. Ps 59:13; Jer 10:10). Eschatologically, the prophets spoke of the day of Yahweh as the coming of both wrath and mercy under the kingship of Yahweh. More specifically, Isaiah's vision of the new exodus culminating in God's reign from Jerusalem entailed the *removal of God's wrath* from God's people (Isa 51:22). Yet, did Jesus bear God's wrath on the cross? The following passages from Mark's gospel alone indicate that he did.

1. Jesus predicts he will be "rejected (ἀποδοκιμασθῆναι)" (Mark 8:31), a word which "is almost always used in the Septuagint for God's rejection of Israel and as an equivalent for his wrath (Jer. 6:30; 7:29; 8:9; 14:19)."[10]

2. Jesus predicts he will be "delivered over (παραδοθήσεται) to the nations" (Mark 10:33; cf. 15:1), a phrase which in the Old Testament is equivalent to being handed over to the wrath of God (Lev 26:32–33, 38; cf. Ps 106:41; Ezra 9:7; Hos 8:10 LXX).

3. Jesus' interpretation of his death as drinking the "cup" (Mark 10:38–39; 14:36) is an Old Testament symbol of God's wrath (Ps 11:6; 75:8; Isa 51:17, 22; Ezek 23:31–34; Hab 2:16).

4. Jews and Romans agreed that to die by crucifixion is to die under God's curse.[11]

5. Just as Jesus was mocked throughout the crucifixion, "the mockery suffered by the righteous in the Psalms can be viewed as the wrath of God (e.g., Ps 39; 79; 102)."[12]

6. The darkness during the crucifixion (Mark 15:33) represents God's wrath (Exod 10:21; Amos 8:9–10; Mark 13:24).

7. To be forsaken by God (Mark 15:34) is to be under the wrath of God.[13]

---

holy character (Exod 34:6–7; see S. Duby, "The Cross and the Fulness of God: Clarifying the Meaning of Divine Wrath in Penal Substitution," *SBET* 29 [2011]: 165–76). Based on these three points, I can therefore speak of the priority of God's love and the necessity of God's wrath to safeguard his love in light of sin.

9. Although N. T. Wright acknowledges this aspect of Jesus' death, it plays little role in his telling of the story of redemption or in his way of connecting kingdom and cross. See, e.g., Wright, *How God Became King*, 207.

10. Bolt, *The Cross from a Distance*, 50.

11. See Deut 21:22–23 and Martin Hengel, *Crucifixion in the Ancient World and the Folly of the Message of the Cross* (Philadelphia: Fortress, 1977), 33–38, 84–85.

12. Bolt, *The Cross from a Distance*, 125.

13. Ibid., 133–34.

8. Jesus died, which is significant because "death itself is the manifestation of God's wrath."[14]

Having shown that the pouring out of God's wrath is a key element in the coming of the kingdom and that Jesus bore the wrath of God on the cross, we can conclude that Jesus' bearing of God's wrath on the cross is an essential component of the coming of God's kingdom.

Forgiveness of Sins and the Coming of God's Kingdom

The forgiveness of sins is a key element in the coming of the kingdom of God. At the forefront of Isaiah's vision for a new exodus culminating in God's reign over the earth is the forgiveness of sins (Isa 40:2; 43:25; 44:22; cf. 33:24), echoing the great revelation of the royal redeeming God who is "merciful and gracious . . . forgiving iniquity and transgression and sin" (Exod 34:6–7). Just as the kingdom of Israel required the sacrificial system to atone for and forgive sin, the coming kingdom of God would deal with sin once and for all.

It is also important to note that the forgiveness of sins was not an isolated aspect of the kingdom of God but deeply intertwined with the rest. Isaiah 40:1–2 and Zech 13:1–2 both place the forgiveness of sins and the defeat of evil side by side, being brought about respectively by "him whom they have pierced" (Zech 12:10) and by him who was "pierced for our transgressions" (Isa 53:5). In Mark, "the announcements of John (1:4–5) and Jesus (2:5–10) speak of an era of forgiveness that will be brought about by the death of the servant, as the Old Testament expected and as Mark's narrative will demonstrate has come about in Jesus."[15] God's kingdom includes the forgiveness of sins because its king "has authority on earth to forgive sins" (Mark 2:10).

The role of forgiveness in the kingdom of God provides an opportunity to distinguish my position from that of N. T. Wright. Wright's aversion for anything abstract or ahistorical leads him to reject any interpretations that "focus on piety (the *sense* of forgiveness) or the abstract theology (the *fact* of forgiveness, or the belief in it) of Jesus' hearers."[16] According to Wright, forgiveness is not about remedying individual guilt or God's bestowing of a private blessing, but rather "*forgiveness of sins is another way of saying 'return from exile.'*"[17] Wright correctly argues that Israel's exile is a result of her sins,

---

14. Ibid., 133.
15. Ibid., 72; cf. idem, "'. . . With a View to the Forgiveness of Sins': Jesus and Forgiveness in Mark's Gospel," *RTR* 57 (1998): 53–69.
16. Wright, *Jesus and the Victory of God*, 268, italics his.
17. Ibid., italics his; Wright defends this position in ibid., 268–74.

but then wrongly assumes that forgiveness of sins, therefore, must be the same thing as return from exile. Wright's logic seems off. If exile is a result of sin, then would not return from exile be a result of dealing with the sin problem?

Wright argues his point by listing several passages relating forgiveness of sins and return from exile, but where the passages simply speak of inseparability, Wright assumes equation.[18] The result is that Wright collapses forgiveness of sins into return from exile, thereby losing the significance of individual forgiveness.[19] Contrary to Wright, I believe that forgiveness of sins (by means of atonement) is a distinctive element within the return from exile.[20] Furthermore, as we saw in Isaiah, the atoning suffering of the servant (Isa 52:13–53:12) is the means of achieving a new exodus from slavery and for God's kingdom. If sin is the problem that creates the need for a new exodus and restoration of God's reign on earth, then the forgiveness of sins is central to bringing about that solution.

In sum, the coming of the kingdom entails victory, forgiveness, and a new exodus, all of which find their fulfillment at the decisive moment of Christ's death on the cross.

CONCLUSION

The integration of atonement and kingdom must begin with and be shaped throughout by the Old Testament. Only with the proper understanding of the promises of God in the Old Testament can we understand their fulfillment in the New Testament. Apart from the story of Adam and Israel, the concepts of atonement and kingdom will inevitably lose their biblical moorings and fall victim to eisegesis. Furthermore, to understand atonement and kingdom in the Old Testament is to interpret them within the matrix of themes such as of covenant, temple, law, and Messiah.

---

18. Ezra 9:6–15; Neh 9:6–37; Isa 40:1–2; 43:25–44:3; 52–55; Jer 31:31–34; 33:4–11; Lam 4:22; Ezek 36:24–26, 33; 37:21–23; Dan 9:16–19.

19. Others have demonstrated that Wright omits the significance of forgiveness of sins in Romans, Galatians, and Luke: Mark Seifrid, "Unrighteous by Faith: Apostolic Proclamation in Romans 1:18–3:20," in *Justification and Variegated Nomism: The Paradoxes of Paul* (ed. D. A. Carson, Mark Seifrid, and Peter O'Brien; Grand Rapids: Baker Academic, 2004), 2:123; Peter O'Brien, "Was Paul a Covenantal Nomist?" in *Justification and Variegated Nomism*, 2:293; Josh Chatraw observes that Wright has helpfully restored the corporate aspect of forgiveness, but in correcting a weakness, he has swung the pendulum completely to the other side and neglected individual forgiveness altogether ("Balancing Out [Wright]: Jesus' Theology of Individual and Corporate Repentance and Forgiveness in the Gospel of Luke," *JETS* 55 [2012]: 299–322).

20. Watts asserts, "Yahweh's granting of forgiveness was the sine qua non of Israel's release from exile" ("Mark," 132).

The Distinct and Inseparable Roles of the Kingdom and the Cross

The atoning death of Christ and the coming of God's kingdom, properly conceived as eschatological events, are bound together by the one grand narrative of which they take part. Yet while part of the *same* story, kingdom and cross clearly play *different* roles. This point is significant, for acknowledging differences is the first step to understanding relation; distinction precedes unity. Furthermore, acknowledging the difference of roles encourages integration rather than competition. Kingdom and cross need not vie for position because they represent different facets of God's redemptive mission.

The Kingdom Is Telic

The kingdom of God is God's redemptive reign through Christ and his reconciled servant-kings over the new creation, which entails victory over evil, forgiveness of sins, and a new exodus. The salient point, regarding the role of the kingdom in redemptive history, is the expectation that the kingdom is the *final* goal of history, the *telos* of creation and redemption—"it is the kingdom of God toward which all history moves."[21]

The *telic* nature of the kingdom is especially evident in the "two age" schema of Second Temple Judaism, which forms the foundation of New Testament eschatology and, as Oscar Cullmann argues, the substructure of redemptive history.[22] This "two age" schema was standard in Jewish apocalyptic literature: "The Most High made not one age but two" (*4 Ezra* 7:50). The New Testament referred to these eons (αἰῶνες) with such names as "the present evil age" (Gal 1:4; cf. Rom 12:2; 1 Cor 1:20; 2:6–8; 3:18; 2 Cor 4:4)[23] and "the age to come" (Matt 12:32; Mark 10:30; Luke 18:30; Heb 6:5 cf. Eph 1:21). The key here is that Jews and Christians in New Testament times directly identified the kingdom of God with "the age to come."[24] The coming of the kingdom is the coming of the end, when God finally puts all things right under his reign. The kingdom is *telic*.

---

21. Bright, *The Kingdom of God*, 92.
22. Oscar Cullmann, *Christ and Time: The Primitive Christian Conception of Time and History* (Philadelphia: Westminster, 1964), 37.
23. Also, the "present age" (1 Tim 6:17; Titus 2:12; Heb 9:9) or "this age" (Matt 12:32; cf. 13:39, 40, 49; 24:3; Luke 20:34).
24. I. Howard Marshall, "Kingdom of God (of Heaven)," *ZEB*, 3:914; cf. idem, "The Hope of a New Age: The Kingdom of God in the New Testament," *Themelios* 11 (1985): 5–15; Lunde, *Following Jesus, the Servant King*, 190; Gentry and Wellum, *Kingdom through Covenant*, 598–99.

THE CROSS IS CENTRAL

Christ's atoning death is an eschatological event in an unfolding drama of redemption. The role of the cross in this story is clearly seen in the gospel accounts of the passion. Not only do they portray the cross as an eschatological event, but they reveal the position of the cross in the broader story. Matthew, for example, encompasses the moment of Christ's death with numerous signs that the end of the age has come. Darkness covers the land as a sign of apocalyptic judgment (Matt 27:45; cf. Exod 10:22; Isa 13:9–16; Jer 4:27–28; 15:9; Joel 2:10; Amos 5:18, 20; 8:9–10). The temple veil is torn in two, marking the destruction of the temple and universal availability of God's presence (Matt 27:51; cf. 24:2; John 4:20–24). The earth quakes as a sign of God's end-time judgment (Matt 27:51; cf. Isa 24:18–20; Jer 51:29; Ezek 38:20; Matt 24:7). The resurrection of the dead recalls the hope for the end-time resurrection of the dead (Matt 27:52; cf. Dan 12:1–2; Zech 14:4–5; John 11:24). Lastly, a *Gentile* confesses Jesus as the Son of God, which for Matthew is a sign of the universal scope of the gospel in the last days (Matt 27:54; cf. 8:5–13; 21:43; 22:1–14).

In the two-age eschatological timeline, the cross plays a central role. As Moo claims, the primary significance of these signs is that "the death of Jesus constitutes a decisive event in the eschatological Day of the Lord, a turning point in which God intervenes for both judgment and salvation."[25] Daniel Gurtner, in his detailed exposition of the torn veil, concludes that "the *velum scissum* reveals, in part, the eschatological nature of Jesus' death. It serves to reveal (in the special material) that Jesus' death inaugurates a turning of the ages depicted graphically in Ezekiel 37."[26] In other words, the cross is not only the *end* of one age, but is itself the very *transition* to another.[27] The conclusion from Matthew's account, and evident in all three Synoptic Gospels, is that Christ's atoning death represents the *turn of the ages*, the transition from "the present evil age" to "the age to come."[28]

The eschatological understanding of the cross as the turn of the ages is also attested to outside the Gospels. For Paul, the cross demonstrates that the end of the ages has broken into the middle of history, for the old has passed and the new has come (Gal 1:3–4; 3:13–16; 6:14–16; Eph 2:14–16).[29] The

---

25. Moo, *The Old Testament in the Gospel Passion Narratives*, 344.
26. Daniel Gurtner, *The Torn Veil: Matthew's Exposition of the Death of Jesus* (SNTSMS 139; Cambridge: Cambridge University Press, 2007), 183.
27. Moo, *The Old Testament in the Gospel Passion Narratives*, 338–39; Herman Ridderbos, *Matthew's Witness to Jesus Christ: The King and the Kingdom* (London: Lutterworth, 1958), 87; Bright, *The Kingdom of God*, 231.
28. Mark and Luke also report many of the end-time signs. McKnight says that Mark "saw in the death of Jesus the turn of the ages" (*Jesus and His Death*, 359).
29. Ibid., 350.

author of Hebrews declares that Christ "has appeared once for all at the end of the ages to put away sin by the sacrifice of himself" (Heb 9:26). This sacrifice is a "decisive shift" in the ages.[30] The cross of the resurrected Christ, therefore, falls precisely in the middle of the two ages of redemptive history, and it is in this capacity that we can speak of the *centrality* of the cross.

The redemptive-historical centrality of the cross between the two ages has led various scholars to refer to the cross (in proper relation to the resurrection) as the "turning point,"[31] "midpoint,"[32] "pivot-point,"[33] or "omega-point."[34] The cross, therefore, is the climactic midpoint of redemptive history, the hinge on which the eons turn. As Hays says, "By placing the *cross* in the middle, we are reminded that the death of Jesus is the climax and pivot-point of the eschatological drama."[35] In sum, the cross is *central*, in that it is the climactic turning point from "the present evil age" to "the age to come."

SUMMARY

The kingdom and the cross are not in contradiction and need not even be upheld in tension. Each represents a different facet of God's mission; they play different roles in the story of redemption. The kingdom is telic. The cross is central. Shockingly, the end-time reign of God on earth has broken in at the midpoint of history in the crucifixion of Christ. Furthermore, the cross not only falls between the ages, it is the hinge on which ages turn. The significance lies not simply in Jesus' death as a historical fact, but in what God accomplished through it. Jesus died "for our sins" (1 Cor 15:3), with implications for all the world.

THE GREAT EXCHANGE EFFECTS THE GREAT TRANSITION

The cross does not merely fall between the two ages of redemptive history; rather, it causes the very shift from one to the other. By dealing with humanity's sin, God reconciles his servant-kings to himself and reestablishes his

---

30. Craig Koester, *Hebrews: A New Translation with Introduction and Commentary* (AB; New York: Doubleday, 2001), 185.

31. R. T. France, *Matthew: Evangelist & Teacher* (NTP; Downers Grove, IL: InterVarsity Press, 1998), 197; Ridderbos, *Paul*, 66.

32. William Dumbrell, *The Search for Order: Biblical Eschatology in Focus* (Grand Rapids: Baker, 1994), 346; Cullmann, *Christ and Time*, 17.

33. Bright, *The Kingdom of God*, 231.

34. Richard Gaffin, *"By Faith, Not by Sight": Paul and the Order of Salvation* (Bletchley, UK: Paternoster, 2006), 6.

35. Hays, *The Moral Vision of the New Testament*, 199, italics his.

reign through them over the earth. In other words, the great exchange *effects* the great transition.[36] Paul opens his letter to the Galatians by speaking of Christ as the one "who gave himself for our sins to deliver us from the present evil age" (Gal 1:4). He does not merely assert that Christ's *death* delivered us from the present age, but that his death *for our sins* has accomplished this eschatological feat.[37] This is the language of atonement.[38] Galatians 6:14–16 also reveals that the cross is essential for the eschatological new creation, thereby providing an inclusio with 1:4 where Christ's atoning death is the causative turning point from the evil age to the age to come, the broken creation to the new creation.[39]

At the center of this inclusio (Gal 3:10–14) is the clearest explanation of *how* Christ's atoning death brings about the transition to the new age. Galatians 3:13 presents one of the most forthright statements of Christ's atoning death in all of Scripture: "Christ redeemed us from the curse of the law by becoming a curse for us" (cf. 2 Cor 5:21). In short, Jesus takes the place of sinners, bearing the curse of the law (God's wrath) and thereby bringing about redemption. It is, as Luther famously called it, "the wondrous exchange."[40] What is fascinating and often overlooked, however, is the verse that follows, which strongly ties the substitutionary-atoning death of Christ to the age of blessings promised to Abraham (Gal 3:14; cf. Gen 12:1–3).

Furthermore, the two themes of verses 13 and 14 are not merely set beside one another but linked with the explanatory "so that" (Gal 3:14). Christ suffered as a substitute "*so that* in Christ Jesus the blessing of Abraham might come to the Gentiles" (3:14, italics mine). The link between the two verses is even more apparent by the thematic connection between blessing and curse. Christ bore the curse (3:13) so that the promise of blessing might be fulfilled (3:14). In sum, Christ's death "for our sins" delivers us from the "evil age" and

---

36. Some who have sought to recover the eschatological nature of the cross (the great transition) have done so at the expense of "atonement theology" that focuses on what happens between God and humanity (the great exchange) (e.g., Wright, *Jesus and the Victory of God*, 541, 588, 592; idem, *How God Became King*, 176, 196, 244). This dichotomy is unfortunate because, as will be demonstrated below, atonement theology and a redemptive-historical understanding of the cross are not at odds; rather, the latter is dependent on the former.

37. Emphasizing the eschatological nature of Christ's death should not come at the expense of the weight of sin. As African scholar Samuel Ngewa says about Gal 1:4, "We must begin by acknowledging that sin exists and that it must be dealt with" (*Galatians*, ABCS [Nairobi, Kenya: Hippo, 2010], 10).

38. Hans Dieter Betz, *Galatians: A Commentary on Paul's Letter to the Churches in Galatia* (Hermeneia; Philadelphia: Fortress, 1979), 41.

39. Thomas Schreiner, *Galatians* (ZECNT; Grand Rapids: Zondervan, 2010), 77.

40. Luther, *Von der Freiheit eines Christenmenschen* (1520), WA 7:25, 34; the original German for this phrase is *fröhlich Wechsel*.

thereby brings about the new age of God's reign. The great exchange on the cross of Christ effects the great transition to the kingdom of God. But this great transition does not mean that the other aspects of Christ's work are not essential and important. In fact, upholding the centrality of the cross can only be done by properly relating it to Christ's incarnation, life, resurrection, and ascension.

GOD'S KINGDOM ESTABLISHED BY CHRIST'S CROSS
THE MEANING OF "ESTABLISH"

The primary thesis of part 1 is that the kingdom of God is established on earth by the atoning death of Christ on the cross. The establishment of the kingdom is the *decisive moment* within the broader movement of the *coming* of the kingdom. In the Old Testament, the word "establish" (כּוּן) is used frequently in relation to earthly kingdoms and specifically to the messianic kingdom, being paired fifty-seven times with "king/kingdom" (מֶלֶךְ/מַמְלָכָה). "Establish" (כּוּן) technically means to "set up," "fix," or "make firm,"[41] therefore rarely connoting God's bringing something into existence but rather signifying "the fixity of what he has done."[42] David, for example, is anointed as king three times (1 Sam 16:13; 2 Sam 2:3–4; 5:3), but his reign is not said to be "established" (כּוּן) until he has defeated the inhabitants of Jerusalem (2 Sam 5:12; cf. 5:6–11).[43] This victory is when his kingdom is "made firm," "fixed," or "established," despite the fact that he had already been a king for at least seven years (5:5).

More specifically, God promises to "establish" the messianic kingdom (2 Sam 7:12–14; Isa 9:6–7). While the definition still holds, the meaning of establishing the messianic kingdom is enhanced as it unfolds in Scripture: the messianic kingdom is established by God rather than people (2 Sam 7:12–13; 1 Chr 14:2; 17:12–14; 22:10; 28:7; 2 Chr 17:5; Isa 9:7), on earth as it already is in heaven (Job 38:33; Ps 9:7; 93:2; 103:19), for eternity rather than one generation (2 Sam 7:16; 1 Kgs 2:45; 1 Chr 17:12–14; 22:10; 28:7; Isa 9:7), and by justice, righteousness, and steadfast love (Isa 9:7; 16:5; cf. Prov 16:12; 25:5). Each of these characteristics of the coming kingdom of the Messiah can be seen in two of the most explicit messianic prophecies:[44]

---

41. BDB, 465–67.
42. *TWOT*, 1:964.
43. *TDOT*, 7:100.
44. According to John Watts, 2 Sam 7:11–16 is the most foundational messianic text, and Isa 9:6–7 is the highest ranking (*Isaiah 1–33* [WBC; Waco, TX: Word, 1985], 137).

When your days are fulfilled and you lie down with your fathers, I will raise up your offspring after you, who shall come from your body, and I will *establish* [כוּן] his kingdom. He shall build a house for my name, and I will *establish* [כוּן] the throne of his kingdom forever. I will be to him a father, and he shall be to me a son. (2 Sam 7:12–14a, italics mine)

Of the increase of his government and of peace there will be no end, on the throne of David and over his kingdom, to *establish* [כוּן] it and to uphold it with justice and with righteousness from this time forth and forevermore. The zeal of the LORD of hosts will do this. (Isa 9:7, italics mine)

Clearly, the Old Testament speaks of a time when the messianic kingdom will be "established" by God on earth for all eternity with righteousness, justice, and love. To say, therefore, that the cross "establishes" God's reign is to affirm Christ's death as the decisive moment when God's reign is irreversibly fixed on earth as it is in heaven, within the broader movement of the coming of God's kingdom in Christ's life, death, resurrection, ascension, Pentecost, and the second coming.

THE CROSS WITHIN THE BROADER SPECTRUM OF CHRIST'S WORK

Defining the cross as the *decisive* moment in the coming of God's kingdom is meant to imply that it is not the *only* moment. In fact, the cross is inseparable from the other aspects of Christ's work and incomprehensible apart from them.[45] The kingdom of God is present through Christ's incarnation, glimpsed in his miracles/exorcisms, explained by his teaching, established in his death, inaugurated by his resurrection, and advanced through his ascension and his sending of the Spirit, and it will be consummated at his second coming.

The connection between the cross and resurrection is particularly significant. Although these events are inseparably located at the turning point of redemptive history, the resurrection is the "firstfruits" of the new creation (1 Cor 15:20; cf. Col 1:15; Rev 3:14), while the cross is what brings about the transition and therefore the tree that produces the fruit.[46] It is in this sense that the cross is the *establishment* of the kingdom and the resurrection its *inauguration*. Consider the following analogy: in the race for the American presidency, the elected candidate wins the election in November

---

45. I am here focusing on the redemptive-historical centrality of the cross. For a discussion on the centrality of the cross in the doctrine of the atonement, see below, pp. 214–20.

46. For further discussion about the connection between the cross and resurrection, see below, pp. 218–20.

but is not officially inaugurated until January. There is a distinction between *accomplishing* the victory and officially *implementing* its outcome. So it is with Christ's death and resurrection. Through his atoning death, Christ has accomplished victory over evil, forgiveness of sins, and a new exodus—"It is finished" (John 19:30). Yet, if Jesus remains in the tomb, all is for naught (1 Cor 15:17). By his resurrection Jesus has inaugurated the end-time reign of God through his servant-kings over a new creation.

THE KINGDOM AND THE CROSS ARE MUTUALLY INTERPRETIVE

God's kingdom is qualified by the cross *and* Christ's death is characterized by God's reign. Unfortunately, the relationship between kingdom and cross is often characterized by a one-way influence. As we saw in Mark's account, however, the cross is the apex of Jesus' kingdom mission and the kingdom is the aim of the cross. Mark did not cover up suffering with glory; he showed that God's glory is even more glorious as it saves through his paradoxically wise means of suffering. One need not choose between the kingdom and the cross, for the cross is royal and the kingdom is cruciform. N. T. Wright, in speaking of all four Gospels, correctly demonstrates the mutuality between the kingdom and the cross:

> The fact that the kingdom is redefined by the cross doesn't mean that it isn't still the kingdom. The fact that the cross is the kingdom-bringing event doesn't mean that it isn't still an act of horrible and brutal injustice, on the one hand, and powerful, rescuing divine love, on the other. The two meanings are brought into dramatic and shocking but permanent relation.[47]

REIGNING BY SERVING

The kingdom and the cross are often held apart because Christ as king and Christ as servant are seemingly incompatible. Is it coherent to speak of one as king *and* servant, as one who reigns *and* serves? To begin with, Scripture's general usage of the terms king and servant are not incompatible. Abraham's servant is the ruler of his household (Gen 24:2). David is a servant and a king (2 Sam 7:8). In Isaiah, we saw that the messianic king accomplishes his royal task as a servant (Isa 52:13–53:12). In Mark, Jesus maintains his royal prerogative but says he will rule not by wielding worldly power, but by serving (Mark 10:42–45). Jesus does not stop reigning in order to serve.

---

47. Wright, *How God Became King*, 220.

Rather, he reigns *by* serving. Although "reigning by serving" may initially sound contradictory, a closer look reveals that not only is it coherent, it is the wisdom of God.

To reign is to exercise royal power in order to effectively achieve the desired goal, whether by forceful or servile means.[48] God's reign in the Old Testament, for example, is not characterized primarily by its forcefulness but by its effectiveness. The herald's proclamation, "Your God reigns!" is based on the achievement of securing peace, happiness, and salvation (Isa 52:7). The psalmist says God's power is displayed in giving an inheritance to his people (Ps 111:6), emphasizing the result (the *telos*) of the accomplishment, not the means. Therefore, if one equates reigning with forcing, then surely reigning by serving is unintelligible. But if reigning is measured more by its effectiveness (in achieving its goal) rather than its forcefulness (the means), it makes sense to say that Jesus reigns by serving.

Jesus' way of reigning by serving can be seen in the mockers' request for Jesus to display his kingship by coming down from the cross (Mark 15:29–32). According to Eduard Schweizer, "It would be an astonishing miracle indeed if Jesus were to come down from the cross, but this would prove only that he was a superman—not that he was Messiah and King of Israel."[49] Jesus reigns not by coming down from the cross to save himself, but by staying on the cross to save others. He reigns by saving, and the greatest act of salvation is on the cross. Jesus' messianic mission was to bring the kingdom, and to the extent that he did so on the cross, one can truly say that Jesus reigns by serving.[50]

THE STORY OF CHRIST CRUCIFIED (HEBREWS 2:5–10)

The "big picture" of the kingdom and the cross in redemptive history is presented succinctly in Heb 2:5–10. This passage sets forth the primary message of Hebrews by discussing God's royal intent for creation, its apparent failure due to human sin, and its true realization in Christ's death on the cross.[51] The unit opens by quoting Psalm 8, which itself is a commentary on Genesis

---

48. Graham Tomlin defines power as "the capability to influence people or situations and to transform them" (*The Power of the Cross: Theology and the Death of Christ in Paul, Luther and Pascal* [PBTM; Carlisle, UK: Paternoster, 1999], 313). To reign is, in Tomlin's words, to "get things done," which focuses on the end rather than the means (ibid., 99).

49. Eduard Schweizer, *The Good News According to Mark* (trans. Donald H. Madvig; Richmond, VA: Knox, 1970), 350.

50. Reigning by serving, however, does not rule out the more traditional understanding of reigning through force or judgment. See below, pp. 239–43.

51. Koester, *Hebrews*, 97.

1, to affirm that God created people for glory and dominion over the earth (2:6–8). A simple glance at the world, however, reveals that God's blueprint for his kingdom has not been realized (2:8b). But while all those under Adam have fallen short of their royal destiny, there is a new Adam—Jesus—who has been "crowned with glory and honor because of the suffering of death" (2:9).

There are two remarkable features to this statement. First, God's design for humankind finds its realization in Jesus Christ. What the world was created for, and what was lost in Adam and Israel, has been regained in Christ. Second, the way the Son of Man accomplishes this act of restoration, this putting everything in subjection, is unthinkably through "the suffering of death" (Heb 2:9). The author of Hebrews anticipates the reader's shock at the idea of regaining dominion through suffering, and therefore follows up with the statement that it was "fitting" for God to act in this manner (2:10).[52] He then clarifies the fittingness of Christ's suffering by saying that he was made "perfect through suffering" (2:10).

"Christ's suffering," Koester explains, "was not an end in itself, for 'through' suffering he was brought to glory, so that those who follow him might look forward to sharing in the glory and honor for which God created them (Heb 2:5–9)."[53] Interestingly, the verb used for being made perfect (τελειῶσαι) is sometimes used for death and other times for glorification. It is this "complex 'moment' in which death and exaltation are combined."[54] "The cross is 'glory and honor,'" says Chrysostom.[55] In sum, Jesus, as the new Adam, has restored God's design for creation and regained the crown of glory and honor (2:7) for humanity through his death on the cross.

THE WISDOM OF CHRIST CRUCIFIED (1 CORINTHIANS 1:18–2:5)

In part 1, I have described the relationship between the kingdom and the cross as it unfolds in the theology of the Bible. Along this story line we have seen high points of prophecy (the servant-king of Isaiah), fulfillment (the crucified king of Mark), and reflection (the blood of the cross and the kingdom of Christ in Col 1:13–20 and Rev 5:5–10). As we prepare to move from an emphasis on the story of the gospel (biblical theology) to the logic of the gospel (systematic theology), the biblical concept of wisdom provides

---

52. Koester defines "fitting" as "morally congruent . . . with God's character and aims" (ibid., 226).

53. Ibid., 236.

54. Harold Attridge, *The Epistle to the Hebrews: A Commentary on the Epistle to the Hebrews* (Hermeneia; Philadelphia: Fortress, 1989), 147.

55. Chrysostom, *Homilies on Hebrews*, NPNF[1] 14:383.

a fitting transition. Although wisdom has been latent throughout the biblical witness as a connector between kingdom and cross, Paul brings it to the fore with his portrayal of Christ crucified as the wisdom and power of God (1 Cor 1:18–2:5).

What has been implicit throughout Scripture is revealed explicitly in 1 Cor 1:18: power through weakness is the wisdom of God, "for the word of the cross is folly to those who are perishing, but to us who are being saved it is the power of God." In 1 Cor 1:18–2:5, Paul contrasts human wisdom with the "deepest logic of the gospel,"[56] demonstrating that "Christ crucified" is "the power of God and the wisdom of God" (1 Cor 1:23–24). The natural person looks at the cross through the wisdom of the world and sees folly. The spiritual person looks at the cross through the wisdom of God and sees power. In support of his thesis that the cross is the power and wisdom of God, Paul refers to two Old Testament passages (Isa 29:14; Jer 9:23–24), both of which "depict God as one who acts to judge and save his people in ways that defy human expectation."[57] The cross shatters all (fallen) human notions of power and reveals a God who "chose what is foolish in the world to shame the wise" (1 Cor 1:27).

How, then, does the divine wisdom of Christ crucified inform our understanding of kingdom and cross? Although the idea of a "Messiah crucified" seems an oxymoron, in the wisdom of God the promised anointed one of Israel has established God's kingdom by means of the cross. Paul uses power and wisdom, which are traditionally royal characteristics (Ps 145:11; Dan 2:37), to define the message of the cross. In fact, Paul uses "power" to describe both the cross (1 Cor 1:18) and the kingdom (4:20). In a similar way, in the book of Revelation the slain Lamb is praised for his power and wisdom (Rev 5:12). The kingdom of God comes in power, but the power of the gospel is Christ crucified.

God created the world with wisdom, so it should be no surprise that he would also redeem it with wisdom (Prov 8:22–31; Col 1:15–20; 2:3). God promised in Isaiah that he would destroy the wisdom of the wise (Isa 29:14), and Jesus confronted such human wisdom in his disciples who sought a kingdom without a cross (Mark 8:29–33). Finally, God put his wisdom on display as he sent his Son to the cross to be crucified for the sins of the world. Throughout redemptive history, it has been God's wise plan of establishing his kingdom through the crucifixion of his Messiah.

---

56. Richard Hays, *First Corinthians* (IBC; Louisville: Westminster John Knox, 2011), 26.
57. Ibid.

Wisdom is necessary in order to understand atonement and kingdom not only in the story of redemption but also in the logic of redemption. The kingdom is established on the cross—but what is the nature of the kingdom? Who is this Jesus? And in what way is his death redemptive? To apprehend how atonement and kingdom relate, I must answer each of these questions, seeking not only to understand the doctrines themselves, but how they inter-relate. Therefore, I now turn to the doctrines of Christ, the atonement, and the kingdom of God.

SYSTEMATIC
THEOLOGY

CHAPTER SIX

CHRIST: THE KING ON THE CROSS

IN PART 1 I discussed the relation between atonement and kingdom as it unfolds in the story of redemption history, specifically focusing on the Bible's theology in its own terms, concepts, and contexts. Just as theology emerges from the story of redemption, I now shift in emphasis from the unfolding story of redemption to the logical coherence of redemption, although the two are mutually informing. Part 2 extends the study from biblical to systematic theology, focusing on the key doctrines involved and broadening the conversation by engaging with theologians from church history and contemporary theology.

At the most basic level, the kingdom and the cross are held together by the Christ. Therefore, the doctrines of Christology, atonement, and kingdom must each be properly understood, especially in relation to one another. I will discuss each of these doctrines in turn.

In this chapter, I approach Christology. While Scripture presents Christ as king before and on the cross, the kingship of Christ on the cross has been downplayed by the overcategorization often used in the doctrines of the two states of Christ (humiliation and exaltation) and the three offices of Christ (prophet, priest, and king). Unfortunately, the atoning death of Jesus has often been relegated solely to the state of humiliation and the office of priest, which makes impossible any connection between Jesus' kingship and his death. I will, therefore, argue for the kingship of Christ on the cross, followed by a reconsideration of the doctrines of the states and offices of Christ in light of Scripture and theology.

THE KINGSHIP OF CHRIST ON THE CROSS

Jesus was declared king in his birth (Matt 2:2); anointed as king and empowered by the Spirit for his kingly mission at his baptism (Matt 3:13–17);

149

recognized as king in his ministry by his disciples (John 1:49; 6:15), his enemies (John 19:14), and himself (Luke 23:2); and ultimately entered Jerusalem
to die on the cross with the acclamation, "Your king is coming to you" (Matt
21:5). During his trial, Jesus spoke of "my kingdom" (John 18:36); received
a crown of thorns (John 19:2); and was presented for crucifixion with the
announcement, "Behold your king!" (John 19:14). Although mocked as king
by the soldiers and Pharisees, the sign above his head—"The King of the
Jews" (Mark 15:26)—ironically expressed a truth recognized by the criminal
beside him (Luke 23:42) and the centurion below (Mark 15:39). Jesus rose
from the dead, being declared king to a broken creation (Rom 1:3–4) and
inaugurating his kingdom as the firstfruits of the new creation (1 Cor 15:20–
25). He ascended into heaven, where he sat down at the right hand of God,
demonstrating the completion of his earthly task (Ps 110:1; Heb 10:11–12)
and continuing his reign on earth through his Spirit (Acts 2:33).

Throughout his incarnation, life, death, resurrection, and ascension, Jesus
is king. There is, however, still a process of Jesus' *becoming* king, a development in his kingship. In order to further explore the kingship of Jesus, two
areas must be addressed: the distinction between Jesus' divine and human
kingship, and the Old Testament *process* of becoming king.

JESUS THE KING

As the divine Son of God, Jesus *is* king—yesterday, today, and forever.
"Enthronement," says Webster, "cannot mean acquiring an honour or juris-
diction not previously possessed; indeed, the kingly rule of the Son is not
some accidental status or role external to his being, but rather is what he
is: he is king."[1] However, as God promised David, the one to establish the
kingdom would be a Son of God *and* a descendant of David (2 Sam 7:12–
14). As a human, a second Adam, a descendant of David, Jesus came in the
likeness of sinful flesh with the task of restoring human vicegerency over
all the earth. Therefore, while Jesus *is* king as the divine Son of God, his
human kingship is a process of establishing his Father's throne on earth
as it is in heaven. Thus, his human kingship is grounded in his divine
kingship.

The Old Testament provides the proper background for the process of
becoming a king. In biblical times, becoming a king was a process, the high
points of which were anointing and enthronement (or establishing the king's

---

1. John Webster, "One Who Is Son: Theological Reflections on the Exordium to the Epistle to
the Hebrews," in *The Epistle to the Hebrews and Christian Theology* (ed. Richard Bauckham et
al.; Grand Rapids: Eerdmans, 2009), 91; cf. 82, 92.

throne with victory).[2] In the Old Testament, "royal anointing is part of the more comprehensive act of enthronement . . . with various parts."[3] The anointing, however, "is the most important or the most distinctive of the individual acts."[4] The reason anointing is *the* distinctive act in the enthronement process is because it is what affects the *identity* of the anointed one.[5] To be anointed *as king* is to be authorized by God as the chosen ruler, bringing about a "change of status"[6] (highly significant for a discussion on the *states* of Christ). However, this new identity as king is for a purpose, "a specific commission is given to the king with his anointing."[7] In other words, anointing the king serves the greater purpose of establishing his kingdom.

This background reveals several features of Christ's human kingship. First and foremost, Jesus' baptism is his public anointing to kingship. Jesus is declared to be God's beloved Son, the anointed one of Psalm 2. Although his rule will be misunderstood, rejected, and even hidden, from this point forward Jesus *is* king. Furthermore, as in the Old Testament, Jesus' anointing to kingship carries with it a commission. In the baptism, Jesus is not only declared the royal Son of God, he is also empowered by the Holy Spirit to carry out his messianic mission of establishing God's kingdom (Mark 1:9–11; cf. 2 Sam 7:12–14; Psalm 2; Isa 42:1). Jesus, therefore, approached the cross as king seeking to establish his kingdom. As Horton says, "Jesus embraced the cross precisely as a king embraces a scepter."[8]

Although Jesus *is* king before the cross, there yet remains something to be done for his kingship. As the second Adam, sent to restore God's mediatorial reign on earth, Jesus must dethrone the unrightful king of the fallen creation in order to establish his throne over the new creation. As I have argued above, the cross is the decisive moment where Jesus established God's kingdom on earth "because of" and "through suffering" (Heb 2:9–10). I conclude, then, as we saw in Mark, that Jesus' baptism is his anointing to kingship and his crucifixion is his enthronement over the new creation.

In sum, before the cross Jesus is king in at least two senses: (1) as the divine Son of God in union with the Father and (2) as the human publicly anointed as king in his baptism. Yet before the cross Jesus is *not* king in the

---

2. See earlier discussion on "establishing" the kingdom, pp. 139–40.

3. Franz Hesse, "מָשַׁח and מָשִׁיחַ in the Old Testament," in *TDNT*, 9:498.

4. Ibid.; cf. Tryggve Mettinger, *King and Messiah: The Civil and Sacral Legitimation of the Israelite Kings* (Lund: Gleerup, 1976), 185.

5. To be anointed is to be anointed *king* ("They anointed David king" 2 Sam 2:4; 5:3).

6. John Walton, Victor Matthews, and Mark Chavalas, eds., *The IVP Bible Background Commentary: Old Testament* (Downers Grove, IL: InterVarsity Press, 2000), 327; cf. 305.

7. Hesse, "מָשַׁח and מָשִׁיחַ in the Old Testament," 499.

8. Horton, *Lord and Servant*, 254.

two senses: (1) he has yet to definitively defeat Satan and establish God's kingdom; and (2) he has yet to restore human vicegerency. The way I have proposed to understand these different facets of Jesus' kingship is by arguing that Jesus approaches the cross as king seeking to establish his kingdom. There is an "already and not yet" quality to his kingship. Before the cross, he is already king, but he is yet to establish his kingdom.

CROSS AND RESURRECTION

The kingship of Christ on the cross challenges the dominant view that Jesus became king in the resurrection or session.[9] This view is difficult to square with the biblical evidence of Christ's kingship before and on the cross as well as the theological grounding of Christ's kingship in his eternal relation with the Father and Spirit. The resurrection is not the beginning, but the revelation of Christ's kingship and the inauguration of his kingdom on earth. As Barth said, "His resurrection revealed Him as the One who reigns in virtue of His death."[10] Jesus' death is not a defeat that needs to be made right by the resurrection, but a victory that needs to be revealed and implemented in the resurrection. Likewise, Christ's session is not the beginning of his reign but the completion of his earthly task and continuation of his reign through the Spirit. It is, according to Webster, "the repetition in time of his eternal being."[11] Jesus is raised from the dead and seated on the throne not *in order to* be king, but *as* king.

JESUS REIGNS FROM THE CROSS

Just as the person and work of Christ are inseparable, to say that Jesus *is* king on the cross is also to say that he *reigns* from the cross. The reign of Christ from the cross emphasizes the *active* nature of his atoning death. Active and passive obedience, while often wrongly divided among Christ's life and death, are complementary aspects throughout Christ's work.[12] The cross, therefore, is the pinnacle of Christ's obedience (Phil 2:6–8) in both its passive and active aspects. He obediently fulfills his mission of bringing the kingdom (active) by means of obediently suffering as a servant (passive). Jesus himself interprets laying down his life as an act of authority (John 10:18); although he suffers at the hands of others, Jesus does so sovereignly because he has

---

9. See, e.g., Wolfhart Pannenberg, *Jesus—God and Man* (trans. Lewis Wilkins and Duane Priebe; 2nd ed.; Philadelphia: Westminster, 1977), 365–77.

10. Karl Barth, *Church Dogmatics: The Doctrine of Reconciliation* (vol. IV/2; ed. G. W. Bromiley and Thomas Torrance; trans. G. W. Bromiley; Edinburgh: T&T Clark, 1958), 291.

11. Webster, "One Who Is Son," 92.

12. John Murray, *Redemption Accomplished and Applied* (Grand Rapids: Eerdmans, 1978), 20–25.

voluntarily given his own life: "No one takes it from me, but I lay it down of my own accord" (John 10:18; cf. 19:30). Despite being bound, he is in complete control, for at any moment he could have appealed to his Father to send legions of angels (Matt 26:53).

The fathers of the early church championed the kingship of Christ in all things, especially his atoning death on the cross.[13] Justin Martyr promoted the mantra, "The Lord hath reigned from the tree."[14] Irenaeus says, "He whom the Jews had seen as a man, and had fastened to the cross, should be preached as the Christ, the Son of God, their eternal King."[15] The widespread understanding of Jesus as "the immortal king, who has suffered on our behalf,"[16] is exemplified in early artistic portrayals of the crucifixion, which often place on Jesus' head a golden crown.[17] This tradition of Christ reigning from the cross was also preserved through the theologically rich hymnody of the early church. Examining these hymns reveals how the early fathers understood and articulated the implications of the kingship of Christ on the cross.

The *Vexilla Regis*, by Venantius Fortunatus (530–609), is sung by Roman Catholics on the Feast of Exaltation of the Cross:

Abroad the regal banners fly,
Now shines the cross's mystery:
Upon it life did death endure,
And yet by death did life procure. . . .
That which the prophet-king of old
Hath in mysterious verse foretold
Is now accomplished, whilst we see
God ruling the nations from a tree[18]

Written hundreds of years after Justin Martyr, the hymn still upholds the theme of Christ reigning from the tree. Jesus' life-bringing death is understood as the accomplishment of the reign of God, the fulfillment of prophecy.

The Orthodox Church, by contrast, has preserved a hymn sung on Good Friday, from the Byzantine *Lenten Triodion*:

---

13. See Per Beskow, Rex Gloriae: *The Kingship of Christ in the Early Church* (Stockholm: Almqvist & Wiksell, 1962).

14. Justin Martyr, *First Apology* 41 (*ANF* 1:176).

15. Irenaeus, *Against Heresies* 3.12.6 (*ANF* 1:432).

16. From the Sibylline books, quoted in Alois Grillmeier, *Christ in Christian Tradition* (trans. John Bowden; Atlanta: John Knox, 1975), 71.

17. Richard Viladesau, *The Beauty of the Cross: The Passion of Christ in Theology and the Arts from the Catacombs to the Eve of the Renaissance* (New York: Oxford University Press, 2008), 111.

18. Quoted in Paul Gavrilyuk, "God's Impassible Suffering in the Flesh: The Promise of Paradoxical Christology," in *Divine Impassibility and the Mystery of Human Suffering* (ed. James Keating and Thomas Joseph White; Grand Rapids: Eerdmans, 2009), 130.

Today he who hung the earth upon the waters is hung upon the cross;
He who is king of the angels is arrayed in a crown of thorns;
He who wraps the heaven in clouds is wrapped in purple mockery;
He who in Jordan set Adam free receives blows upon his face;
The bridegroom of the Church is transfixed with nails.[19]

This hymn reveals the paradoxical nature of Christ's kingship on the cross. Rather than diminishing the royalty of Christ's kingship or softening the severity of his death, this hymn upholds both in a way that makes Christ's majesty more splendid and his death more appalling.

Te Deum from the fourth century remains a part of Catholic liturgy today. Its second article states:

Thou art the King of Glory, O Christ;
Thou art the everlasting Son of the Father.
When Thou tookest upon Thee to deliver man,
Thou didst not abhor the Virgin's womb:
When Thou hadst overcome the sharpness of death,
Thou didst open the kingdom of heaven to all believers.
Thou sittest at the right hand of God in the glory of the Father;
We believe that Thou shalt come to be our Judge.
We therefore pray Thee help Thy servants
Whom Thou hast redeemed with Thy precious Blood.[20]

Tying together many of the themes discussed thus far, *Te Deum* eloquently places them within the great story of Christ's descent and ascent. The king becomes incarnate for the purpose of delivering humanity and does so by redeeming them with his blood, thereby opening the kingdom of heaven.

The sixth-century hymn "Sing My Tongue" eloquently summarizes my argument about the paradoxical nature of Christ's kingship on the cross within the history of redemption.[21] While the lengthy hymn tells the story of Christ's obedience on the tree in Golgotha, recapitulating Adam's disobedience on the tree in Eden, it speaks of Christ as both the "dying King" and the "lamb upon the altar of the cross." It is within the expansive vision of God's reign in the Old and New Testaments that Christ the king reigns on the cross by offering himself as a sacrificial lamb.

19. Mother Mary and Kallistos Ware, trans., "The Service of the Twelve Gospels," in *The Lenten Triodion* (South Canaan, PA: Saint Tikhon's Seminary Press, 2001), 587.
20. Francis Pott, *The Hymn Te Deum Laudamus* (London: Rivingtons, 1884), 1.
21. Philip Schaff, ed., *Christ in Song: Hymns of Immanuel* (London: Sampson Low, Son, and Marston, 1870), 125–28.

THE TWO STATES OF CHRIST: HUMILIATION AND EXALTATION

The idea of the kingship of Christ on the cross often finds resistance because it does not fit within the common understanding of the two-state doctrine, which places the cross as an act of humiliation preceding exaltation.[22] Wayne Grudem's definition is representative: "The doctrine of 'the twofold state of Christ' is the teaching that Christ experienced *first* the state of humiliation, *then* the state of exaltation."[23] Having divided Christ's work into two successive temporal categories, Grudem then typically allocates Christ's incarnation, suffering, death, and burial to the state of humiliation, and his resurrection, ascension, session, and parousia to the state of exaltation.[24]

The problem with this interpretation, as neat as it is categorically, is that it does not take into account the whole witness of Scripture. While at times Scripture certainly presents humiliation and exaltation in terms of a general progression (Acts 2:33–36; Phil 2:6–9; 1 Pet 1:10–11; Heb 2:9–10), it also reveals a more organic and overlapping relation between the two states (John 12:23–33; Rev 5:5–6). After a brief historical survey of the doctrine of the two states, I will explore what we can learn from that history—both through its insights and blind spots.

A BRIEF HISTORY OF THE DOCTRINE OF THE STATES OF CHRIST

The systematic distinction between Christ's states of humiliation and exaltation was first used by the Lutherans in the late sixteenth century and developed in the ensuing debates with the Reformed. The Lutherans, seeking to uphold the union of Christ's two natures by means of the *communicatio idiomatum*, interpreted the exaltation of the human nature of Christ as the revelation of his previously possessed *divine* glory.[25] The Reformed criticized the Lutherans for wrongly divinizing Christ's humanity and therefore sought

---

22. Kingship in the Bible is intricately bound up with glorification (Ps 24:7–10; Dan 4:30; 5:18; Luke 19:38; 1 Tim 1:17) and exaltation (1 Sam 2:10; Ps 47:2; Dan 4:17). In other words, God/Christ is exalted and glorified as king.

23. Grudem, *Systematic Theology*, 620, italics mine; cf. idem, "States of Jesus Christ," *EDT*, 1052–54.

24. For similar treatments, see Millard Erickson, *Christian Theology* (2nd ed.; Grand Rapids: Baker Academic, 1998), 788–97; Louis Berkhof, *Systematic Theology* (Grand Rapids: Eerdmans, 1979), 331–55.

25. For a survey of the Lutheran view of the two states, see Marvin Hoogland, *Calvin's Perspective on the Exaltation of Christ in Comparison with the Post-Reformation Doctrine of the Two States* (Kampen: Kok, 1966), 11–44.

to explain the exaltation in terms of Christ's newly gained *human* glory.[26] In short, for Lutherans, exaltation is the revelation of previously possessed divine glory. For the Reformed, exaltation is the reward of newly acquired human qualities for prior obedience.

One of the strongest developments in the Reformed tradition was not merely arguing for a temporal transition from humiliation to exaltation but defining the relationship in terms of cause or reward. Bavinck, for example, says, "The entire state of exaltation from the resurrection to his coming again for judgment is a reward for the work that he accomplished as the Servant of the Lord in the days of humiliation."[27] Humiliation is "the meritorious cause of the exaltation."[28] Although the two-states doctrine has persisted at some level in Reformed theology,[29] it was put into disrepute by Schleiermacher in the nineteenth century.[30] Because Schleiermacher rejected the preexistence of Christ, it made no sense to speak of Christ's life in terms of humiliation.[31] "Accordingly," says Schleiermacher, "we are perfectly entitled to set this formula aside; it may justly be entrusted to history for safe keeping."[32] Barth also rejected the traditional distinction between humiliation and exaltation, although, as we will see, for quite different reasons.[33]

EXALTATION IN AND THROUGH HUMILIATION

In response to the common understanding of exaltation *after* humiliation, I propose that the proper view is exaltation *in* humiliation within a broader progression of exaltation *through* humiliation. "Exaltation *in* humiliation" breaks down the typical dichotomy by demonstrating that Christ is exalted supremely in his redemptive suffering, the apex of which is his death on the cross. "Exaltation *through* humiliation" maintains a general progression from humiliation to exaltation while at the same time showing how they overlap and are interrelated.

The argument will be based on Scripture and theology and will draw from Calvin and Barth in order to revise the interpretation of humiliation and exaltation as strictly successive temporal states. Calvin and Barth both differ from the linear schema and offer a middle way between the Reformed and Lutheran positions, affirming the simultaneity of humiliation and exal-

---

26. For a survey of the Reformed development of the two states, see ibid., 45–94.

27. Bavinck, *Sin and Salvation in Christ*, 433.

28. Ibid., 434.

29. Some use the doctrine as a framing device for the work of Christ (e.g., Berkhof, *Systematic Theology*, 331–55), and others as an individual doctrine (e.g., Grudem, *Systematic Theology*, 620).

30. Schleiermacher, *The Christian Faith*, 473–75.

31. Ibid., 475.

32. Ibid.

33. Barth, *CD* IV/1, 133; *CD* IV/2, 106, 110, 135–36.

tation with the idea that Jesus is humbled in his divinity and exalted in his humanity. Though I will draw from both in arguing for exaltation in humiliation, I will part ways with Barth—who ultimately dismisses the doctrine—and follow Calvin in maintaining a broader temporal progression.

EXALTATION IN HUMILIATION: INTEGRATING THE STATES

The primary mistake of the standard view of the states of Christ is that it polarizes humiliation and exaltation. The simplistic view of humiliation *then* exaltation simply does not do justice to the breadth of Scripture's witness—namely, that Christ is exalted before the resurrection and humble after the crucifixion. Not only do humiliation and exaltation overlap in Christ's work, but they both find their apex in his atoning death. Below, I will break down the dichotomy of "humiliation *then* exaltation" by showing that Christ is exalted before the resurrection and remains humble after the crucifixion, and that the overlap of humiliation and exaltation finds its apex at the cross.

Exaltation before the Resurrection

From the cradle to the cross the life of Jesus is clearly one of humiliation. However, Scripture reveals, and the eye of faith perceives, that even during his time of humiliation he is being exalted, glorified, and enthroned as king. The most common and explicit way Scripture speaks of Christ's pre-Easter exaltation is with the language of glorification. Far from being reserved for his resurrection and ascension, the glory of Christ is displayed from the moment of the incarnation, for as John declares, "The Word became flesh . . . and we have seen his glory" (John 1:14). Though hidden to sinful eyes, "He *is* the radiance of the glory of God" (Heb 1:3, italics mine). In Cana Jesus "manifested his glory" through his first "sign" (John 2:11) and through the transfiguration he "received honor and glory from God the Father" (2 Pet 1:17).

In the transfiguration, where the disciples "saw his glory" (Luke 9:32), they were given a preview of what would be fully revealed in the resurrection. Jesus himself says, "My Father . . . glorifies me" (John 8:54) and later speaks of "the glory that you have given me" and even "my glory" (17:22, 24). Finally, Jesus refers to his own death as "the hour . . . for the Son of Man to be glorified" (12:23) and "lifted up" (12:32), thereby combining glorification and exaltation and centering them on the cross. As Paul would later say, they "crucified the Lord of glory" (1 Cor 2:8). Clearly in Scripture, Christ is glorified and exalted as king before the resurrection.

Rightly understanding the person of Christ is essential for his pre-Easter exaltation. In accordance with Chalcedonian Christology, Jesus is not only truly God and truly man, but his two natures are *united* in his one person (the hypostatic union). This means, first of all, that he as the God-man *is* exalted and glorious in his divinity. The majestic glory of Christ's divinity, though "concealed and not exerting its force,"[34] was by no means absent from his person during his ministry on earth.[35] His humanity need not be subsumed into his divinity (the Lutheran tendency) nor treated in isolation from his divinity (the Reformed tendency) but in union with it. As the eternal Son of God he does not need to be exalted, but as the incarnate Son of God he is exalted for us.

Christ is also exalted before the resurrection in his human nature. Although truly human, Jesus was not just *any* human. According to Calvin, Christ was the human who was exalted above every other human because he was completely "without sin" (Heb 4:15) and uniquely empowered by the Holy Spirit, which was evident in his miracles and proclamation of the kingdom.[36] Barth discusses the exaltation of the human nature of Christ under the title "the royal man," highlighting an often-overlooked point: Christ's kingship is attributed primarily to his humanity.[37] God's rule over the earth is mediatorial, and Christ is the second Adam and the Son of David, who will establish God's kingdom and restore his people to their proper place of dominion over the earth.

Humiliation after the Cross

Not only is Christ exalted before the resurrection, he remains humble after the cross. Although his atoning sacrifice is finished (John 19:30) and need not be repeated (Heb 9:26), his identity and reign continue to be shaped by his servant form and work on the cross. Even after his resurrection, he remains the crucified one (Mark 16:6) and appears to his disciples in his glorified state still bearing the scars from the cross (John 20:27). When John is granted a vision into the heavenly throne room, he shockingly sees Christ as a slaughtered lamb still being praised for his redemptive death (Rev 5:5–12). Even after his ascension and session, he remains a humble king who intercedes on behalf of his people (Rom 8:34), graciously gives the gift of the Holy Spirit (Acts 2:33), and will ultimately hand the kingdom over to the Father (1 Cor 15:24).

---

34. John Calvin, *Calvin's Commentaries*, comment on John 12:27.
35. This line of thought goes against kenotic Christologies, which argue that Christ emptied himself of divine attributes. For a survey of kenotic Christologies, see Sarah Coakley, "*Kenōsis* and Subversion: On the Repression of 'Vulnerability' in Christian Feminist Writing," in *Powers and Submissions: Spirituality, Philosophy and Gender* (Malden, MA: Blackwell, 2002), 3–39.
36. *Calvin's Commentaries*, comments on Matt 4:1; John 3:39; 5:30.
37. Barth, *CD* IV/2, 156–268.

Calvin says Christ's kingship remains humble because his kingdom still "lies hidden in the earth, so to speak, under the lowness of the flesh."[38] Marvin Hoogland elaborates Calvin's view: "In so far as the Kingdom or Church of Christ is not yet fully glorious in the world, the glory of Christ Himself is not yet complete, and in this sense His humiliation is not yet a matter of the past."[39] Barth concurs: "Neither the Gospels nor the New Testament as a whole see and know and attest the risen and living and exalted man Jesus except as the man who had this end and outcome, whose story is finally the story of His passion."[40]

The Overlap of Humiliation and Exaltation in Christ

Based on this evidence, any strictly successive interpretation of the two states—"humiliation *then* exaltation"—must be rejected. Temporally, there is overlap. More importantly, as aspects of Christ's person and work, humiliation and exaltation are deeply intertwined. Barth speaks of the "inter-connexion" between humiliation and exaltation and helpfully shifts the emphasis from temporal succession to christological simultaneity: "The exaltation of the Son of Man begins and is completed already in and with the happening of the humiliation of the Son of God; and conversely . . . the exaltation of the Son of Man includes in itself the humiliation of the Son of God, so that Jesus Christ is already exalted in his humiliation and humiliated in His exaltation."[41]

How can these apparently contradictory aspects be simultaneous in Christ? The key for Calvin and Barth is that Jesus is the God-man who is simultaneously humbled in his divinity and exalted in his humanity.[42] According to Barth, "As God he was humbled to take our place, and as man he is exalted on our behalf."[43] Furthermore, the simultaneous humiliation and exaltation of Christ is not a contradiction because Christ always humbles himself (Phil 2:8; cf. Luke 14:11) and is exalted by the Father (Phil 2:9; cf. Acts 2:33).

In other words, Christ is not in two static states of humiliation and exaltation but is constantly humbling himself and being exalted by the Father. Calvin adds that Christ is able to retain his exalted status because he takes on the form of a servant *voluntarily*.[44] In other words, Christ sovereignly accepts a mission of servitude. I conclude with Thomas Torrance that "we are not to

---

38. Calvin, *Institutes*, 2.16.17.
39. Hoogland, *Calvin's Perspective*, 192.
40. Barth, *CD* IV/2, 250.
41. Ibid., 110.
42. Hoogland, *Calvin's Perspective*, 214–15.
43. Barth, *CD* IV/1, 141; for Calvin's view, see Hoogland, *Calvin's Perspective*, 125.
44. *Calvin's Commentaries*, comments on John 19:12; Phil 2:6–7.

think of the humiliation and exaltation of Christ simply as two events following one after the other, but as both involved in appropriate measure at the same time all through the incarnate life of Christ."[45]

The Majestic Glory of the Cross

The humiliation and exaltation of Christ, in both their temporal and christological dimensions, come to an apex on the cross of Christ. While in the Roman world, the cross was an instrument of shame and humiliation,[46] Jesus declared it to be his glorious exaltation. The glory of the cross is most explicit in the gospel of John when Jesus, speaking of his death, says, "The hour has come for the Son of Man to be glorified" (John 12:23). He continues, revealing that the glorification is also exaltation: "And I, when I am lifted up from the earth, will draw all people to myself" (12:32). Although such language initially sounds more fitting for the ascension or session, in the next verse Jesus makes it clear that he is referring to being "lifted up" in his death.

Lest the reader mistake this verse as a mere blip in Jesus' mission or John's theology, this "hour" of suffering and glory is on the mind of Jesus from the beginning of his ministry (John 2:4), is used by John to focus the mission of Jesus to Golgotha (7:30; 8:20; 13:1), and culminates the night before the crucifixion when Jesus prays, "Father, the hour has come" (17:1). Within this movement to the cross, Jesus speaks of his being "lifted up" on three separate occasions (3:14; 8:28; 12:32). For John, everything is moving toward this climactic hour, when Jesus, being "lifted up" on the cross, is truly being enthroned in glory. The cross becomes not only the center of redemptive history, but the fulcrum on which the logic of the world is turned upside down. Shame is transformed into glory, humiliation is exaltation, foolishness is wisdom, and the cross is the throne from which Christ rules the world. Based on these passages in John, Barth concludes that "the exaltation of the One who humiliated Himself in obedience (Phil 2:9) is not the divine act towards this man which takes place after His humiliation, but that which takes place in and with His humiliation."[47] Calvin writes, "In all the creatures, indeed, both high and low, the glory of God shines, but *nowhere has it shone more brightly than in the cross.*"[48]

Interestingly, many proponents of the strictly successive view acknowl-

---

45. Thomas Torrance, *Atonement: The Person and Work of Christ* (ed. Robert Walker; Downers Grove, IL: InterVarsity Press, 2009), 210; cf. Horton, *Lord and Servant*, 254.

46. Hengel, *Crucifixion in the Ancient World,* 46–50.

47. Barth, *CD* IV/2, 256.

48. *Calvin's Commentaries*, comment on John 13:31, italics mine.

edge John's picture of the glory and exaltation of the cross, but then simply ignore or cast it aside as a glitch in the otherwise neat categories of humiliation *then* exaltation.[49] A closer look, however, reveals that John is not merely a wild card in an otherwise uniform system; he is onto something more broadly attested in Scripture.[50] What John states explicitly—Christ is exalted on the cross—Mark says through irony (Mark 15) and Paul through concepts of wisdom/foolishness and power/weakness (1 Cor 1:18–25). Martin Hengel says, "The '*doxa*' of the Son of God cannot be separated from the shame of his cross," a truth he finds not only in John but in Paul, Mark, and Hebrews.[51]

How could Christ be exalted *in* humiliation? First, his suffering is glorious because it accomplishes salvation. Exaltation is "the bright side" of humiliation, says A. B. Bruce, for "while it is a humiliation to die, it is glorious to die for others."[52] Second, Christ is exalted in humiliation because his humiliating death reveals the glorious character of God. Calvin aptly explains Christ's exaltation in humiliation:

> For the death of the cross, which Christ suffered, is so far from obscuring his high rank, that in that death his high rank is chiefly displayed, since there his amazing love to mankind, his infinite righteousness in atoning for sin and appeasing the wrath of God, his wonderful power in conquering death, subduing Satan, and, at length, opening heaven, blazed with full brightness.[53]

Exaltation *in* humiliation is foolishness to the human eye, but to the eye of faith it is the wisdom of God. According to Calvin, "Since only weakness appears in the cross, death, and burial of Christ, faith must leap over all these things to attain its full strength."[54] The servant form of Christ both hides and reveals his kingship. It veils his majesty because people look at a man dying a criminal's death and would never assume him to be a king. Yet his servant form also reveals his majesty, for his sovereignty can be expressed in servitude. As Webster says, "The 'humiliation' of the Word is thus by no means the contradiction of his exaltation; it is, rather, the chosen mode of his exaltation."[55] How, then, can Christ's kingship be hidden and revealed?

---

49. See, e.g., Bavinck, *Sin and Salvation in Christ*, 423.
50. Indeed, this pattern is the pattern that we traced in the unfolding story of the Old Testament. See above, pp. 53–67.
51. Martin Hengel, *The Cross of the Son of God* (London: SCM, 1986), 85.
52. A. B. Bruce, *The Humiliation of Christ: In Its Physical, Ethical, and Official Aspects* (Grand Rapids: Eerdmans, 1955), 30.
53. *Calvin's Commentaries*, comment on John 13:32.
54. Calvin, *Institutes*, 2.16.13.
55. John Webster, *Word and Church: Essays in Church Dogmatics* (New York: T&T Clark, 2001), 137.

It is hidden to fallen eyes, yet by faith one sees the gracious majesty of God in the crucified Christ.

EXALTATION THROUGH HUMILIATION: MAINTAINING THE BROADER PROGRESSION

Thus far I have argued against a strictly linear understanding of the two states and sought to replace it with a view that acknowledges the temporal overlap and places at the forefront the christological simultaneity of humiliation and exaltation. In short, Christ's exaltation is not simply *after* but also *in* his humiliation. Exaltation *in* humiliation, however, does not rule out a broader movement from humiliation to exaltation. Such a progression is irrefutable in light of Scripture. Peter, for example, speaks of "the sufferings of Christ and the *subsequent* glories" (1 Pet 1:11, italics mine). The author of Hebrews says Christ was made "perfect through suffering" (Heb 2:10).

Statements such as these indicate that although the states are tightly intertwined throughout Christ's work, there is an irreversible transition that takes place at the resurrection of Christ. Perhaps it is a transition from exalted humiliation to humble exaltation, but a transition nonetheless. The resurrected Christ is no longer "in the likeness of sinful flesh" (Rom 8:3). He will never offer himself as a sacrifice again (Heb 9:26). His majesty is no longer veiled (Rev 1:10–18). Taking this transition into account along with what has been argued above, we can say that the doctrine of the two states of Christ is properly interpreted as exaltation *in* humiliation within the broader framework of exaltation *through* humiliation. Below, I will demonstrate the validity of this temporal progression by discussing the new glory of Christ's resurrection and the significance of Christ's exaltation as "for us."

We have argued against the dominant position in contemporary Reformed theology by appealing to two of its tradition's greatest theologians—Calvin and Barth. At this point, however, in maintaining the place of an overall progression, I part ways with Barth, whose critique of the successive view of the two states causes him to interpret it solely in terms of christological simultaneity (Christ is at once humbled and exalted).[56] The matter at hand is the fundamental difference between the Lutheran and Reformed positions on the states. For the Lutherans, the exaltation of Christ is a *revelation* of his previously held divine glory, whereas for the Reformed it is the *acquiring* of new glory in his human nature. The genius of Calvin is that before these reactionary debates led to such polarized positions, Calvin was able to

---

56. Barth, *CD* IV/1, 133; *CD* IV/2, 106, 110, 135–36.

uphold both aspects of exaltation.[57] Exaltation is a revelation of previously held divine glory *and* the acquiring of new human glory.[58] Although Calvin's view on the states was certainly not systematized, I will follow him in order to move beyond the Lutheran/Reformed dichotomy.

Revelation of Previous Glory

For Calvin, the resurrection is the revelation of Christ's previously held glory *and* his newly acquired human glory. Before speaking of the new glory, however, it must be emphasized that for Calvin, the revelation of Christ's previously held glory is the primary emphasis. In Hoogland's words, "The honor which comes to Christ in His new exaltation is the honor which is displayed in His death."[59] Calvin, therefore, is closer to the Lutheran view, but because it is a matter of emphasis, he differs with the Reformed only formally rather than materially. The key here for Calvin, though, is that the *revelation* of the previously held glory is itself a new glory. Such a move is possible because revelation is not merely revelatory but effective. In the much later words of Gustaf Aulén, the resurrection "reveals . . . *and realizes* the victorious deed contained in his finished work."[60] In other words, not only is the kingship of Christ revealed, but the kingdom of Christ is inaugurated.

Exalted as a Human "For Us"

Regarding the revelation of Christ's new human glory, Calvin does not dwell on how this affects Christ himself, noting primarily the glorification of his physical body.[61] The key is that Christ's human exaltation is ultimately "for us." According to Hoogland, "the 'for us' appears in Calvin's view to be fully as significant for the resurrection as it is for the death of Christ, and thus as significant for the exaltation as for the humiliation of Christ."[62]

This point stands in contrast to the later Reformed view that Christ's exaltation is primarily *his* reward for humiliation. Calvin asks, "What need was

---

57. Hoogland, *Calvin's Perspective*, 206, 215–16.

58. This argument does not deny the basic continuity between Calvin and Reformed orthodoxy on the states of Christ (see ibid., 206; Richard Muller, *Christ and the Decree: Christology and Predestination in Reformed Theology from Calvin to Perkins* [Durham, NC: Labyrinth, 1986], 10) but rather within broad agreement with later Reformed orthodoxy, Calvin shared the Lutheran emphasis on the exaltation of Christ primarily as the revelation of divine glory, even during his life and death.

59. Hoogland, *Calvin's Perspective*, 175.

60. Gustaf Aulén, *The Faith of the Christian Church* (Philadelphia: Muhlenberg, 1948), 245, italics mine.

61. Hoogland, *Calvin's Perspective*, 156.

62. Ibid., 180.

there for God's only Son to come down in order to acquire something new for himself?"[63] Yet while Calvin says Christ merited nothing for himself,[64] Bavinck claims that he did.[65] Is this an irreconcilable difference? Is Christ's exaltation *either* for himself *or* for us? I contend that there is a third way that can uphold Calvin's and Bavinck's concerns. Although Scripture certainly implies that humiliation is the cause of exaltation, or exaltation the reward of humiliation (Isa 53:10–12; Matt 23:12; Phil 2:9; Heb 2:10), the ultimate aim of Christ's exaltation is "for us." In other words, the exaltation that Christ acquired in himself was not because *he* needed to be exalted but because *we* need to be exalted; it was "for us." He acquired glory "for himself" as a king *so that* it could be given "for us" in his kingdom.

Douglas Farrow sheds further light on the "for us" of Christ's exaltation. According to Farrow, Christ enters into the human cycle of descent and ascent, and where humanity has fallen short of its destiny of ascent to God, Christ has fulfilled it as a second Adam and thereby leads humanity upward toward their original purpose of vicegerency with God over the earth.[66] In Farrow's words, "Through his own U-shaped history (baptism, death, resurrection, and ascension) Jesus recapitulates the entire experience of fallen man."[67] The salient feature is that Christ is exalted "for us"; his exaltation is the recapitulatory precursor for our exaltation. Farrow asserts, "Jesus' destiny is our destiny; or rather that, in reaching our destiny, he has reached it not only for himself but also for us."[68]

Jesus was not exalted because he was in need of glory or royal status, but *so that* he might pour out the Holy Spirit for the building up of his church (Acts 2:33–36; Eph 4:8–12). While Phil 2:9 is often referenced for the exaltation of Christ, many neglect the following verses that reveal the purpose of the exaltation: "*so that* at the name of Jesus every knee should bow . . . and every tongue confess that Jesus Christ is Lord" (Phil 2:10–11, italics mine). Christ's exaltation as *king* is ultimately aimed at his work of advancing his *kingdom* on earth as it is in heaven, for "his ascent to heaven, like his ascent to the cross, is a journey undertaken on behalf of God's people and with a view to the realization of their kingdom hopes."[69]

---

63. Calvin, *Institutes*, 2.17.6.
64. Ibid.
65. Bavinck, *Sin and Salvation in Christ*, 433.
66. Douglas Farrow, *Ascension and Ecclesia: On the Significance of the Doctrine of the Ascension for Ecclesiology and Christian Cosmology* (Grand Rapids: Eerdmans, 1999), 15–40; idem, "Ascension," *DTIB*, 65–67; idem, *Ascension Theology* (New York: T&T Clark, 2011), 1–14.
67. Farrow, "Ascension," 67.
68. Farrow, *Ascension Theology*, 10.
69. Farrow, *Ascension and Ecclesia*, 23.

CONCLUSION

I have argued against a strictly linear view of exaltation *after* humiliation and for an understanding that focuses on exaltation *in* humiliation within the broader progression of exaltation *through* humiliation. This way of understanding the states of Christ highlights the kingship of Christ on the cross, for it was during those dark, shameful hours that Christ's majestic glory shined forth to the world.

THE THREEFOLD OFFICE OF CHRIST: PROPHET, PRIEST, AND KING

Although the content of the *munus triplex* (threefold office) originates in Scripture[70] and is common throughout the history of the church,[71] it was Calvin who established the threefold office as a theological category to interpret and systematize the work of Christ.[72] Calvin employed the *munus triplex* in order to uphold the unity and wholeness of Christ's multifaceted work.[73] Most notably, he interpreted the *death* of Christ in terms of God's revelation (prophet), reconciliation (priest), and reign (king).

As the *munus triplex* became widespread for interpreting the work of Christ,[74] however, Calvin's original purposes and inferences have customarily been altered. I will argue that the *munus triplex* has been overcompartmentalized, and the kingship of Christ on the cross has been both misplayed and downplayed, resulting in a reductionistic understanding of the cross. This claim will be corroborated by tracing broad trends in major theologians who are representative of their times and traditions. Although space does not

---

70. Prophet (Deut 18:15; Luke 4:18–21; 13:33; Acts 3:22); priest (Ps 110:4; Heb 3:1; 4:14–15; 5:5–6; 6:20; 7:26; 8:1); and king (Ps 2:6; 45:6; 110:1–2; Isa 9:6–7; Luke 1:33; John 18:36–37; Heb 1:8; 2 Pet 1:11; Rev 19:16).

71. Geoffrey Wainwright discovers in the tradition of the church the following references to Christ's threefold office: Eusebius ("Christ . . . the only High Priest of the universe, the only King of all creation, and of prophets the Father's sole supreme Prophet"); John Chrysostom ("Christ was to have three dignities: King, Prophet, Priest"); Thomas Aquinas ("One is a lawgiver, another is a priest, another is a king; but all these concur in Christ as the fount of all grace"); Martin Bucer ("Christ was anointed, so that he might be our king [*rex*], teacher [*doctor*], and priest [*sacerdos*] forever") (*For Our Salvation: Two Approaches to the Work of Christ* [Grand Rapids: Eerdmans, 1997], 104, 110–11).

72. Calvin, *Institutes*, 2.15.

73. John Frederick Jansen, *Calvin's Doctrine of the Work of Christ* (London: Clarke, 1956), 17, 45.

74. Ludwig Schick shows the use of the *munus triplex* in Catholicism (*Das dreifache Amt Christi und der Kirche: Zur Entstehung und Entwicklung der Trilogien* [New York: Peter Lang, 1982]); John Deschner demonstrates the same in the theology of John Wesley (*Wesley's Christology: An Interpretation* [Grand Rapids: Francis Asbury, 1988]); Wainwright shows the same in Eastern Orthodoxy (*For Our Salvation*, 113).

permit an exhaustive study of the use of the *munus triplex* since Calvin, the most radical shifts occurred within nineteenth-century liberalism and the ensuing response of the conservative Reformed; these will therefore be the focus of this survey. What Calvin employed for the sake of wholeness has too often been used as a means for reductionism, and Calvin's royal emphasis on the cross as the "triumphal chariot"[75] has been neglected even within his own tradition.

CALVIN ON THE MUNUS TRIPLEX AND THE KINGSHIP OF CHRIST ON THE CROSS

Calvin's use of the *munus triplex* includes two key features. First, Calvin used the *munus triplex* as an instrument to uphold the unity and wholeness of Christ's work,[76] cautioning that "they who separate one office from the other, rend Christ asunder, and subvert their own faith."[77] Thus, Calvin does not structure his discussion of the work of Christ by assigning each specific work to one corollary office. Rather, in his *Institutes* 2.15, Calvin summarizes the role of each office and then discusses the works of Christ in the following two chapters, appealing back to different aspects of Christ's offices. For example, Calvin describes in 2.15 that it is the kingship of Christ that accounts for victory over the devil,[78] and then in 2.16, when discussing the death of Christ, he declares that it is on the cross that Christ achieves this royal triumph.[79]

Calvin's emphasis on the unity and wholeness of Christ's work leads naturally to the second highlighted feature of his understanding of the *munus triplex*: the kingship of Christ on the cross. For Calvin, the office of king consists of two primary roles: (1) victory over Satan, sin, and death,[80] and (2) governing and ruling over the spiritual kingdom.[81] The key to the first role is that Christ is already king while on the cross. Jansen says, "Calvin does not attempt to fix any time in the life of Christ when he began to reign, for the kingdom comes in Him. He is king—he does not become king. Accordingly, Calvin avoids the tendency of later Protestant dogmatics which confined

---

75. Calvin, *Institutes*, 2.16.6; Calvin often spoke of the cross as "a magnificent chariot" to express the victory of Christ's death (see, e.g., *Calvin's Commentaries*, comment on Luke 23:16).

76. The *munus triplex* also upholds the unity of the person and work of Christ, as well as the unity of the Old and New Testaments.

77. *Calvin's Commentaries*, comment on Gen 14:18.

78. Calvin, *Institutes*, 2.15.4.

79. Ibid., 2.16.6.

80. "As is his Kingly reign, Christ's judgment is both present and future. He conquered the powers of evil in His cross" (*Calvin's Commentaries*, comment on Ps 15:1).

81. According to Calvin, God is "a King of infinite power to secure our salvation, and to protect us by his guardian care" (ibid., comment on Gen 14:18)

the kingly office to the state of exaltation."[82] In addition to the priestly and prophetic aspects of Christ's death, Calvin understands the cross as a royal conquest by which Christ the king triumphs over Satan, sin, and death.

NINETEENTH-CENTURY LIBERAL THEOLOGY

Liberal theology in the nineteenth century attempted to mediate the apparent conflict between the assumptions of post-Enlightenment modernity and historic Christian orthodoxy. At the forefront of this movement were German theologians Friedrich Schleiermacher and Albrecht Ritschl, both of whom appropriated the *munus triplex* for articulating the work of Christ.

Schleiermacher not only uses the *munus triplex* but, like Calvin, argues for the primacy of the office of king within the broader framework of all three offices being united in Christ's person.[83] Yet, despite the initial similarities, Schleiermacher's use of the *munus triplex* marks a radical divergence from the Reformation understanding. He openly states that he is appropriating the *munus triplex* to his already established theological conclusions—Christ's redemptive activity "assumes believers into the power of His God-consciousness"[84]—for the sake of preserving continuity with Christian tradition.[85]

Clearly the *munus triplex* is flexible as a framework and can be used to reach extremely differing conclusions—in this case, the definition of the kingship of Christ. Schleiermacher's primary emphasis for the *regium munus* is the corporate life of the community, the church.[86] Although he discusses the royal office under the title "The Work of Christ," Schleiermacher's explanation of kingship is much more ecclesiological and, in this case, subjective. Willem Adolph Visser 't Hooft characterizes Schleiermacher in this way: "Christ is no longer the main actor in the dramatic history of world salvation; He is the inspiration of a community of souls."[87]

Another major divergence in Schleiermacher's version of the kingship of Christ is that he does not appropriate the royal office to the death of Christ. The kingship of Christ *on the cross* was a dominant motif in the early church and a prominent theme for Calvin as well.[88] For Schleiermacher, however, Christ's death is only spoken of under the priestly office. Limiting Christ's

---

82. Jansen, *Calvin's Doctrine of the Work of Christ*, 86.

83. Schleiermacher, *The Christian Faith*, 438–40; Calvin, *Institutes*, 2.15.2.

84. Schleiermacher, *The Christian Faith*, 425.

85. Ibid., 439.

86. Ibid., 444.

87. Willem Adolph Visser 't Hooft, *The Kingship of Christ: An Interpretation of Recent European Theology* (New York: Harper, 1948), 18.

88. Robert Peterson, *Calvin's Doctrine of the Atonement* (Phillipsburg, NJ: P&R, 1983), 46.

death only to the priestly office will prove to be a continual problem throughout the modern historical development of the *munus triplex.*

Ritschl, like Schleiermacher, appropriates the *munus triplex* for his own theological system and argues for the primacy of the kingship of Christ. However, Ritschl sharply criticizes the use of the term "office" (opting for "vocation" instead) because its legal association is supposedly not fitting for a kingdom defined by love rather than law.[89] Whereas Schleiermacher uses kingship to emphasize the community of believers, Ritschl believes theology ultimately serves ethics; therefore, he speaks of the kingship of Christ in moral terms. Ritschl's doctrine of the *regium munus* is entirely subjective, focusing not on what God has done through Christ but on what the people of God are called to do in society. It is telling that Ritschl's theology greatly influenced Rauschenbusch's thinking and was eventually embodied in the social gospel of the early 1900s.

The most troubling feature of Ritschl's use of the *munus triplex,* however, is his treatment of Christ's atoning death. Although Schleiermacher errs by not associating the kingship of Christ and the cross, Ritschl tragically sets the two at odds. Christ's vocation, according to Ritschl, was not to provide a substitutionary atonement for his people but to establish the kingdom of God as a transnational community of love. Absent from Ritschl's understanding of the office of priest and king are the concepts of wrath, judgment, expiating the guilt of sin, and sacrifice. Gerald McCulloh, in his monograph on Ritschl's use of the *munus triplex,* says that for Ritschl, "reconciliation is to be deduced from the love of God and not controlled by notions of wrath or justice."[90] After thoroughly examining Ritschl's doctrine of reconciliation within the *munus triplex,* McCulloh concludes that Ritschl ultimately strays from the biblical and doctrinal foundations of the *munus triplex* and allows his ethical and epistemological concerns to dictate his theology.[91]

This brief survey of Schleiermacher's and Ritschl's uses of the *munus triplex* identifies some of the major trends in how nineteenth-century liberals understood the kingship of Christ. Although the *munus triplex* was widely used and Christ's kingship the most celebrated office, there was a great deviation from Calvin's understanding of that kingship. First of all, the nineteenth-century liberals did not relate the kingship of Christ to Christ's death on

---

89. Ritschl, *Justification and Reconciliation,* 433.
90. Gerald McCulloh, *Christ's Person and Life-Work in the Theology of Albrecht Ritschl: With Special Attention to* Munus Triplex (Lanham, MD: University Press of America, 1990), 68.
91. Ibid., 145–205.

the cross, which is a far cry from Calvin's view of the cross as a "triumphal chariot," or as the early church referred to it, "the trophy of the cross."[92] The death of Christ was almost exclusively relegated to the priesthood of Christ and often stripped of themes, such as God's holiness and wrath.

The second major trend of this movement is that Christ's kingship was understood in almost completely subjective terms. In an attempt to please Enlightenment thinking, there was little room for a supernatural king ruling from heaven, so the focus was placed on the community of the king and its ethics. Furthermore, with modernity's elevation of reason and science, no attention was given to the biblical theme of Christ's victory over Satan and demons on the cross (Col 2:14–15). As a result, the emphasis was not on Christ reigning; it was on his teaching about a moral, communal kingdom. In other words, while the nineteenth-century liberals claim the kingship of Christ as primary, they actually present Christ as a prophet whose primary work is teaching about the morals of the kingdom. Jansen concludes, "The Jesus of Ritschl and Harnack was clad in prophetic garments but stripped of his kingly and priestly vestments."[93]

NINETEENTH-CENTURY REFORMED THEOLOGY

Nineteenth-century liberalism sparked a strong conservative response from Reformed theologians passionate about preserving the tradition and theology of Calvin. One of their most influential and representative theologians was Princeton Seminary president Charles Hodge. Hodge witnessed the influence of German theological liberalism during his own graduate studies in Germany and grew deeply disturbed with Schleiermacher's theology in particular. While Hodge and Schleiermacher both use the *munus triplex* to articulate the work of Christ, Hodge's *Systematic Theology* marks a drastic shift in interpretation,[94] focusing almost exclusively on the priestly office of Christ and downplaying the royal and prophetic offices.

The disproportion of offices, in fact, is the most notable feature of Hodge's use of the *munus triplex*. In his *Systematic Theology,* Hodge uses the *munus triplex* to explain the work of Christ, allotting 2 pages for the office of prophet, 131 pages for the office of priest, and 12 pages for the office of king.[95] Hodge has reacted to the liberal tendency of ignoring the harsh themes of the cross (wrath, penalty, justice, propitiation, etc.) by making them dominate

---

92. Calvin, *Institutes*, 2.16.6; Tertullian, *The Five Books Against Marcion* 4.20 (*ANF* 3:379).
93. Jansen, *Calvin's Doctrine of the Work of Christ*, 20.
94. Charles Hodge, *Systematic Theology* (3 vols.; Grand Rapids: Eerdmans, 1968).
95. Ibid., 2:462–609.

the entirety of Christ's work. However, as much as Hodge emphasizes the cross, he fails to address Christ's death in his treatment of the royal office.[96] Hodge limits Christ's work on the cross solely to the office of priest.

Heinrich Heppe is another nineteenth-century Reformed theologian who attempted to use the *munus triplex* in conjunction with Calvin. Although Heppe agrees with Calvin that the kingly role of the Messiah involves the guidance of the church, his overall use of the *munus triplex* includes its own distinct contours. While many had already relegated the cross solely to the priesthood of Christ, Heppe systematized the three offices chronologically according to Christ's life, death, and ascension, building on what Heinrich Heidegger had called the "order of execution."[97] According to Heppe, Christ "came forward first as teacher, then consummated the high-priestly sacrifice, and is now active as king."[98]

Not only does this "order of execution" relegate the death of Christ to the office of priest, but it further redefines the relation between the priesthood and kingship of Christ. Heppe claims that the royal office upholds and applies what was accomplished in the priestly offices. He refers to Russen, who says, "Christ's kingly office is the power of applying everything which he has merited to the salvation of those for whom he merited and of warding off what is contrary."[99] By defining kingship as the application of what Christ accomplished on the cross, Heppe implies that Christ's kingship did not actually accomplish anything itself. Once again, this reflects a deviation from Calvin's understanding of the cross as the royal victory of Christ, the place where he defeats Satan and demons.

Although nineteenth-century Reformed theologians like Hodge and Heppe reacted sharply against the theological liberalism of their day, they ironically committed a similar mistake regarding the use of the *munus triplex*. Whereas Schleiermacher and Ritschl misplay the office of king by redefining it in subjective/prophetic terms, Hodge and Heppe swing the pendulum to the other side and downplay the royal office altogether. Both sides, however, fail to address the kingship of Christ on the cross. Whether kingship is defined as communal morality or guidance from heaven, neither definition includes Calvin's (and Scripture's) emphasis on the cross as the royal triumph of God.

---

96. Interestingly, Hodge successfully explicates Christ's victory over Satan and demons on the cross, yet he does so within his treatment of Christ's priestly work (ibid., 2:516–20).

97. Heinrich Heppe, *Reformed Dogmatics: Set Out and Illustrated from the Sources* (trans. Ernst Bizer; Grand Rapids: Baker, 1978), 454.

98. Ibid., 452.

99. Ibid., 482.

TWENTIETH-CENTURY RECOVERY OF KINGSHIP?

In 1948 Visser 't Hooft recognized the compartmentalized state of the *munus triplex,* warning that such reductionism would result in nothing less than a truncated gospel:

> A one-sided emphasis on the prophetic ministry leads inevitably to moralism and rationalism: Christ becomes a great teacher of ideas and principles, but his work, past, present and future, disappears from the horizon. And exclusive emphasis on the priestly function leads to pietism and mysticism: Christ is the Lamb of God, but His piercing word and His victory over sin and death are not taken seriously. The full concentration on the Kingship of Christ leads to utopianism and apocalypticism. Christ is the glorious King, but it is forgotten that His victory is the invisible victory of the Word and that in this world the road to glory is the way of the Cross.[100]

Furthermore, the Dutch theologian lamented the neglect of the royal office: "The priestly and prophetic ministries of Christ have been strongly worked out but ... the kingly office has been obscured."[101]

Heeding this twofold call for a fuller account of the *munus triplex* and a robust articulation of the kingship of Christ was the Swiss theologian Emil Brunner. Regarding the *munus triplex,* Brunner writes, "In his Word he is both Reconciler and King; in his sovereignty, He is both Revealer and the Sacrificial Lamb; in his Priesthood, he is both the One who proclaims the Name of God, and asserts God's glory and God's Sovereignty."[102] Brunner also understood the cross as the pinnacle of each of Christ's three offices. Regarding the kingship of Christ on the cross, Brunner asserts, "His sufferings and his death are not only the fulfillment of the revelation of the hidden God, not only the reconciliation of the angry God, but they are also the most perfect mark of the power of One who triumphs in the act of defeat."[103] Although Brunner's use of the *munus triplex* and his understanding of the kingship of Christ on the cross are congruous with Calvin, it is sadly a case of the exception proving the rule.[104] Furthermore, the fact that Brunner's

---

100. Visser 't Hooft, *The Kingship of Christ,* 12.

101. Ibid., 13.

102. Brunner, *The Doctrine of Creation and Redemption,* 274.

103. Emil Brunner, *The Mediator: A Study of the Central Doctrine of the Christian Faith* (Philadelphia: Westminster, 1947), 559.

104. An earlier exception to the rule is Bavinck, who claims, "There have always been one-sided tendencies in the Christian church which saw in Him only the prophet, like the rationalists, or which occupied itself solely with His priestly passion, like the mystics, or which would hear of Him only as a king, like the Chiliasts. But we need a Christ who is all three at once. We need a prophet who proclaims God to us, a priest who reconciles us with God, and a king who in the name of God rules and protects us" (*Sin and Salvation in Christ,* 335); Barth also

Christology has had little long-standing impact in theology only exacerbates the problem that Visser 't Hooft addressed.[105]

Where has this historical development left us today? Unfortunately, the trend continues to be the compartmentalized version of the *munus triplex* with the death of Christ relegated to the priestly office alone. Louis Berkhof's *Systematic Theology*, a standard among Reformed theologians, sustains Hodge's unbalanced treatment of the *munus triplex* as well as the explication of the death of Christ only in terms of the priestly office.[106] Postliberal theologian Robert Sherman argues that the kingship of Christ is the central aspect of the atonement, yet hardly even mentions the death of Christ in his entire chapter on the subject.[107]

To summarize, Calvin's understanding of the *munus triplex* has commonly been overcompartmentalized, and the kingship of Christ on the cross has been both misplayed and downplayed. The pendulum-swinging reductionism demonstrated in the nineteenth century and beyond must be combated with theology that embraces the fullness of Christ's work on behalf of sinners who desperately need the revelation, reconciliation, and reign of Christ. The kingship of Christ on the cross must be taken seriously in a way that is both faithful to the biblical witness, yet not exclusive or dominating toward other aspects of Christ's work. Gerald Bray captures the essence of what must be recovered, while also showing the importance of the offices for the broader task of integrating kingdom and cross:

> Jesus of Nazareth was the king of the Jews, but he was also the high priest who paid the price for the sins of the people by sacrificing himself on a cross. . . . The reign of Christ on earth was not the result of human conquest but of a divine self-revelation that went against all the normal canons of kingship. The king did not come to "live forever" as the salutation to the Persian monarchs went (Neh. 2:3), but to die and to rise again to a new and different kind of life.[108]

resists relegating Christ's death to his priestly office, regarding "His cross [as] the dominating characteristic of his royal office" (*CD* IV/2, 292).

105. Despite the fact that Brunner was one of the most influential theologians in America during the twentieth century, his theology has gone into a virtual eclipse. Brunner is now largely referred to simply as a footnote in the development of dialectical theology or as a useful foil in explaining Barth's rejection of natural theology. Furthermore, Brunner's Christology as a whole is highly problematic, evidenced by the fact that he rejects the virgin birth and the bodily resurrection of Christ. See Paul King Jewett, *Emil Brunner: An Introduction to the Man and His Thought* (Downers Grove, IL: InterVarsity Press, 1961), 36.

106. Berkhof, *Systematic Theology*, 356–412.

107. Robert Sherman, *King, Priest, and Prophet: A Trinitarian Theology of Atonement* (New York: T&T Clark, 2004), 116–68.

108. Gerald Bray, "The Kingdom and Eschatology," in *The Kingdom of God*, 210.

CONCLUSION

Jesus is king on the cross, establishing God's kingdom on earth as it is in heaven. As Barth said, it is "supremely in His cross that He acted as the Lord and King of all men, that He maintained and exercised His sovereignty."[109] This understanding of the kingship of Christ on the cross demands a reconsideration of the commonly overcompartmentalized doctrines of the states and offices of Christ. Though both doctrines are helpful inasmuch as they distinguish aspects of Christ's person and work, they do more harm than good when they relegate Christ's death only to his priestly office and humble state.

We would do well to return to the roots of these doctrines, especially as expressed by Calvin, in seeking to integrate rather than divide the aspects of Christ's work. Horton seems to reflect Calvin's thought, and thereby pave a way forward, by expressing the proper relation between the states and offices of Christ as they express his kingship: "While there is a general progression from the state of humiliation to exaltation and from prophet to priest to king, they are all present simultaneously in the unity of Christ's person and work. Even as he was hanging on the cross in dereliction as the enemy of God and humanity, Christ was winning our redemption as our conquering King."[110] On the cross, as a prophetic-priestly king, Christ is exalted in his humiliation.

The firm lines drawn between these aspects of Christ's work have made it difficult to understand how the kingdom and the cross relate in Christ's ministry and mission. The cross is neither the failure of Jesus' messianic ministry nor simply the prelude to his royal glory, but the apex of his kingdom mission—the throne from which he rules and establishes his kingdom. May we ever follow Calvin's exhortation to imitate the penitent thief on the cross who "adores Christ as a King while on the gallows, celebrates His kingdom in the midst of shocking and worse than revolting abasement, and declares him, when dying, to be the author of life."[111]

Having shown that Jesus is king on the cross who is exalted in his humiliation, I must now give more attention to what Christ's death accomplished *for us*. This leads to the doctrine of the atonement, which although the source of many a debate, is central for my argument.

---

109. Barth, *CD* IV/2, 291.
110. Horton, *The Christian Faith*, 524.
111. *Calvin's Commentaries*, comment on Luke 23:42.

CHAPTER SEVEN

ATONEMENT: EXPANSIVE PARTICULARITY

THE AIM OF the following two chapters is to better understand the nature of Christ's atonement for the sake of answering the broader question of the relation between Christ's atoning death and the coming of God's kingdom. In the next chapter (chapter 8), I will set out to accomplish the ambitious goal of reconciling penal substitution and *Christus Victor* (two aspects of Christ's accomplishment that are most relevant to this project). In this chapter, I will lay the necessary groundwork in order to have a constructive conversation at all. We need an approach to the doctrine of the atonement that avoids the pitfalls of reductionism and relativism.

CHRISTUS VICTOR OR PENAL SUBSTITUTION

The cross of Christ is the great jewel of the Christian faith, which can be examined in its dimensions, but as a whole only admired. Two dimensions of the atonement that shine brightly through the pages of Scripture and the tomes of church history are Christ's victory over Satan, demons, and death, and the satisfaction of God's wrath leading to the forgiveness of sins.[1] Built around these biblical dimensions are two atonement theories: *Christus Victor* and penal substitution. Unfortunately, what was once held together is now frequently torn asunder, resulting in the false dichotomy of Christ as *either*

---

1. Horton sees these as being the two primary biblical-theological categories for the atonement (*The Christian Faith*, 493–501).

victor *or* penal substitute. How, then, do these two dimensions of Christ's work relate, and can the theories built around them be reconciled?[2]

My goal is to integrate *Christus Victor* and penal substitution for the ultimate purpose of properly relating the kingdom and the cross. God's kingdom entails the defeat of evil and forgiveness for sinners, so *Christus Victor* and penal substitution are both significant aspects to Christ's kingdom-establishing work on the cross. While the connection between *Christus Victor* and the kingdom of God is obvious and noted by many, I will demonstrate that a biblical understanding of the coming of God's kingdom requires a doctrine of the atonement that includes both *Christus Victor and* penal substitution in their proper relation. After laying methodological groundwork for atonement theology in general, I will survey recent construals of these two theories and ultimately propose a way forward: *Christus Victor* through penal substitution.

Because my primary task is to integrate *Christus Victor* and penal substitution, I must (for lack of space) assume basic definitions of each. The following are standard definitions from leading proponents of each theory.

Christus Victor: "Christ—*Christus Victor*—fights against and triumphs over the evil powers of the world, the 'tyrants' under which mankind is in bondage and suffering, and in Him God reconciles the world to Himself."[3]

Penal substitution: "Jesus Christ, our Lord, moved by a love that was determined to do everything necessary to save us, endured and exhausted the destructive divine judgment for which we were otherwise inescapably destined, and so won us forgiveness, adoption and glory."[4]

The controversy surrounding penal substitution, including an onslaught of critiques[5] and defenses[6] as well as the diversity of versions, requires a few

---

2. Alan Spence is right to point out that theories, understood as self-contained explanations of the whole of Christ's work, cannot be reconciled (*The Promise of Peace: A Unified Theory of Atonement* [London: T&T Clark, 2006], 3). However, as I will demonstrate below, the vast majority of atonement theology in church history has not set forth exclusive atonement "theories" in this sense. My aim, therefore, is to understand the relationship of the biblical dimensions, drawing from various historical theories as needed. I am not setting forth my own theory, but seeking to clarify the relationship of two prevalent aspects of Christ's work.

3. Aulén, *Christus Victor*, 20.

4. Packer, "What Did the Cross Achieve?" 25.

5. For a sample of the critiques against penal substitution, see Joel Green and Mark Baker, *Recovering the Scandal of the Cross: Atonement in New Testament and Contemporary Contexts* (Downers Grove, IL: InterVarsity Press, 2000), 23–32; Joel Green, "Must We Imagine the Atonement in Penal Substitutionary Terms?" in *The Atonement Debate*, 153–71; Heim, *Saved from Sacrifice*; Belousek, *Atonement, Justice, and Peace*; J. Denny Weaver, *The Nonviolent Atonement* (Grand Rapids: Eerdmans, 2001).

6. For defenses of penal substitution that have listened carefully to the critics and offered helpful nuances, see Hans Boersma, *Violence, Hospitality, and the Cross*, 153–81; Stephen Holmes, *The Wondrous Cross: Atonement and Penal Substitution in the Bible and History* (Bletchley, UK: Paternoster, 2007); idem, "Can Punishment Bring Peace? Penal Substitution Revisited," *SJT*

clarifying comments. Though further defining and defending of penal substitution would require another project itself, I offer three points of theology that frame my approach.

First, penal substitution must be understood within the broader spectrum of Christ's multifaceted accomplishment on the cross. Not only did Jesus bear the penalty of condemnation and death by taking the place of sinners on the cross, but he defeated Satan, sin, and death (Col 2:15), demonstrated the love of God (Rom 5:8), and much more. Penal substitution is essential, but it is not everything.

Second, penal substitution must be presented as the outcome of God's love. Although penal substitution rightly highlights God's wrath and Jesus' propitiation, if it were not for God's unfailing love there would be no atonement.[7] As 1 John 4:10 says, "In this is love, not that we have loved God but that he loved us and sent his Son to be the propitiation for our sins."

Third, penal substitution must be understood within a trinitarian framework. Augustine's notion of God's inseparable operation (*opera Trinitatis ad extra indivisa sunt*) is helpful, for though one can distinguish between the acts of Father, Son, and Spirit in the event of the cross, atonement is ultimately the work of the one God.[8] A trinitarian framework safeguards against the depiction of the cross as a mere exchange between an angry father and a loving son.[9] The Father and the Son, rather, are united in the atoning mission—the

---

58 (2005): 104–23; Henri Blocher, "The Sacrifice of Jesus Christ"; Kevin Vanhoozer, "The Atonement in Postmodernity: Guilt, Goats, and Gifts," in *The Glory of the Atonement*, 367–404; Graham Cole, *God the Peacemaker*, 239–42; Michael Horton, *Lord and Servant*, 157–270. For a catalogued response to the various critiques of penal substitution, see S. Jeffery, Michael Ovey, and Andrew Sach, *Pierced for Our Transgressions*, 205–336; cf. Garry Williams, "Penal Substitution: A Response to Recent Criticisms," in *The Atonement Debate*, 172–91.

7. For the relationship between God's love and wrath, see above, p. 131 fn. 8. Also see Calvin's helpful discussion on the primacy of love in the doctrine of the atonement (*Institutes*, 2.16.4); Holmes says, regarding Calvin, "Here, in the classical account of penal substitution, the first note is necessarily grace, God's love towards his sinful creatures. His wrath burns, it is true, but that is not the basic reality. Any discussion of penal substitution which asserts that the basic reality is the wrath of God is a caricature" ("Can Punishment Bring Peace? Penal Substitution Revisited," 112)

8. We must, therefore, be able to speak generally of the "self-substitution of God," as Stott does (*The Cross of Christ* [Downers Grove, IL: InterVarsity Press, 1986], 133), or in Barth's words, "The judge judged in our place" (*CD* IV/1, 211). This notion, of course, demands further trinitarian and christological nuance. See Stephen Holmes, *The Wondrous Cross*, 95–101.

9. Hence, the now famous critique of penal substitution as "cosmic child abuse" (Brown and Parker, "For God So Loved the World," 26). This critique fails to acknowledge the trinitarian framework of the cross. The Father and Son are united in their purpose, as clearly displayed in Jesus' willingness to go to the cross (John 10:18). The "cosmic child abuse" argument also undermines basic Christian beliefs, such as the sovereignty of God over the cross (Acts 2:23) and the possibility of redemptive suffering (Isa 52:13–53:12). Regarding redemptive violence/suffering, see above, p. 59 fn.19. For a more thorough response to the "child abuse" critique, see Jeffery, Ovey, and Sach, *Pierced for Our Transgressions*, 228–33.

Father motivated by love (John 3:16) and the Son voluntarily giving his life in complete harmony with the purposes of the Father (10:18).[10]

EXPANSIVE PARTICULARITY: AVOIDING REDUCTIONISM AND RELATIVISM

Before discussing *Christus Victor* and penal substitution in more detail, I must consider more generally how the various dimensions of the atonement relate to the event of the crucifixion itself. In other words, how does atonement theology account for the multiplicity of metaphors used in Scripture to ascribe meaning to Christ's death? In my view, atonement theology has been plagued by two opposing errors: reductionism and relativism. I will examine these and propose a way forward, which I call "expansive particularity."

REDUCTIONISM

THE PROBLEM OF REDUCTIONISM

When theologians choose between two biblical truths, the fullness of truth is reduced to a fraction of reality. More often than not, however, this reductionism arises not only from truly difficult paradoxes in Scripture (e.g., divine sovereignty and human responsibility), but from the pendulum-swinging that has plagued theological debates throughout church history.[11] This reactionary reductionism has particularly characterized atonement theology. Aulén's landmark work, *Christus Victor*, divided the rich history of atonement theology into three rather simple theories: the "classic view" (*Christus Victor*), the "Latin view"[12] (satisfaction), and the subjective view (moral influence). Aulén argued exclusively for the "classic view" as *the* view of Scripture and the majority of church history.

Aulén had dropped a bombshell on the playground of atonement theology, and along with the liberal downplay of sin and the wrath of God (and hence penal substitution), his work provoked a strong conservative reaction that

---

10. There are two other common critiques of penal substitution that must also be acknowledged, both related to the issue of justice. First is the issue of whether God's justice is retributive or restorative. I believe this "either/or" approach sets up a false dichotomy, for God's justice can only truly be restorative if it is retributive (see Henri Blocher, "God and the Cross," in *Engaging the Doctrine of God*, 139). Second is the claim that it would be unjust for God to transfer the penalty of one person onto another undeserving person. This critique can be answered with a theology of corporate responsibility and union with Christ (Romans 5). See Holmes, *The Wondrous Cross*, 95–100; Boersma, *Violence, Hospitality, and the Cross*, 177–78.

11. McGrath, *The Genesis of Doctrine*, 35–36.

12. This is Gustaf Aulén's term for the view of atonement that has been dominant in the West.

focused so intently on propitiation as the center of the atonement that it pushed all other aspects to the fringes, if not completely out of the picture. Although few of its defenders would forthrightly say that penal substitution is the only aspect of Christ's work, even Leon Morris (a staunch defender of penal substitution) acknowledges a type of functional reductionism among its advocates.[13]

This reductionism, however, not only applies to penal substitution and *Christus Victor*, but is equally present in certain subjective theories. According to Ritschl, Christ's suffering "served as a means of testing His faithfulness to His vocation—this and nothing else."[14] Morris's critique of this statement is perceptive, saying that it is only the last four words that are objectionable.[15] Narrow theories such as this are to be appreciated for what they affirm but critiqued for what they deny. The unfortunate result of these historical debates is their devastating dichotomizing effect: on the cross, Jesus *either* bore the wrath of God *or* defeated Satan *or* set an example to follow.

The problems with this "either/or" reductionism are apparent. To reject the breadth of the biblical witness is to reject the authority of the Bible itself. Christ's accomplishment *is* multidimensional and is *revealed* in diverse ways as well.[16] To reduce Christ's atoning work to one aspect is to truncate the gospel and diminish God's glory in salvation.

REDUCTIONISM AND REVISIONIST HISTORY

Such one-sidedness in atonement theology is unheard of in the vast majority of church history. Although this claim might sound shocking ("What about Anselm and Abelard?"), I believe such resistance is based on the revisionist history so common in secondary literature on the atonement.[17] Surveys of the doctrine of the atonement typically sweep through church history,

---

13. "Upholders of the penal theory have sometimes so stressed the thought that Christ bore our penalty that they have found room for nothing else. Rarely have they in theory denied the value of other theories, but sometimes they have in practice ignored them" (Leon Morris, *The Cross in the New Testament*, 401).

14. Ritschl, *Justification and Reconciliation*, 480; for a contemporary version of such a subjective *simpliciter* view, see Andrew Park, *Triune Atonement: Christ's Healing for Sinners, Victims, and the Whole Creation* (Louisville: Westminster John Knox, 2009).

15. Morris, *The Cross in the New Testament*, 396.

16. McIntyre lists thirteen different models of soteriology (*The Shape of Soteriology: Studies in the Doctrine of the Death of Christ* [Edinburgh: T&T Clark, 1995], 26–52).

17. The influence of Aulén's *Christus Victor* goes well beyond its proposal of one particular view of the atonement. It has also set the standard for categorizing the history of the doctrine of the atonement. Many scholars, however, have shown Aulén's historical work to be far from accurate. See Sten Hidal, "En segrande *Christus victor*? Auléns analys av ett forsoningsmotiv i backspegeln," *Svensk teologisk kvartalskrift* 86 (2010): 171–76; Blocher, "*Agnus Victor*," 74–77; Timothy George, "The Atonement in Martin Luther's Theology," in *The Glory of the Atonement*, 268; McIntyre, *The Shape of Soteriology*, 43.

assigning to the early church the "ransom theory"; Anselm, the "satisfaction theory"; Abelard, the "exemplarist theory"; and Calvin, the "penal substitution theory"—all the while implying, if not saying explicitly, that each is a self-contained theory that excludes all other aspects of the atonement.[18] The problem with this historical summary, as heuristically convenient as it may be, is that it is simply not true. The following examples are cursory but sufficient evidence to demonstrate that such neat divisions are misleading.

While it is true that figures throughout the history of the church have emphasized certain aspects of the atonement and even built theories around them, they have done so within a broader acknowledgment of Christ's multifaceted work.[19] The early fathers unanimously upheld the breadth of Christ's accomplishment.[20] Augustine clearly cannot be pigeonholed into one theory.[21] Anselm, often depicted as *the* culprit of a narrowly juridical view of the atonement, defies such categorization. Anselm's multifaceted view of sin called for a multifaceted atonement, which, beyond satisfying the honor of God, restored the goodness of all creation.[22] In his *Cur Deus Homo*, Anselm speaks of the cross as Christ's demonstration of love, recapitulation, and victory over evil—all before even mentioning satisfaction:

> For God has shown the magnitude of his love and devotion towards us by the magnitude of his act in most wonderfully and unexpectedly saving us. . . . For it was appropriate that, just as death entered the human race through a man's disobedience, so life should be restored through a man's obedience; and that, just as the sin which was the cause of our damnation originated from a woman, similarly the originator of our justification and salvation should be born of a woman. Also that the devil who defeated the man whom he beguiled through the taste of a tree, should himself similarly be defeated by a man through tree-induced suffering which he, the devil, inflicted. There are many other things too.[23]

---

18. For a typical example, see Bruce Demarest, *The Cross and Salvation: The Doctrine of Salvation* (FET; Wheaton, IL: Crossway, 1997), 147–68.

19. "The Christian church has always expressed its understanding of redemption with the help of a number of metaphors" (Colin Gunton, *The Actuality of Atonement: A Study of Metaphor, Rationality and the Christian Tradition* [London: T&T Clark, 1988], 53).

20. Joseph Mitros, "Patristic Views of Christ's Salvific Work," *Thought* 42 (1967): 415–47.

21. Rowan Greer, "Christ the Victor and the Victim," *CTQ* 59 (1995): 1–30.

22. Anselm, "Why God Became Man," in *Anselm of Canterbury: The Major Works* (ed. Brian Davies and G. R. Evans; OWC; Oxford: Oxford University Press, 2008), 265, 270, 307–8; see also Stephen Holmes, "The Upholding of Beauty: A Reading of Anselm's *Cur Deus Homo*," *SJT* 54 (2001): 189–203.

23. Anselm, "Why God Became Man," 268; Anselm also gives more sustained treatments of recapitulation and victory (ibid., 268–74, 307–9) and demonstration of love/example (ibid., 331, 349, 353).

Many scholars have highlighted similarities between Anselm and the early fathers,[24] and Gunton is right to conclude that "Anselm does not put all of his eggs in the basket of satisfaction."[25]

Thomas Aquinas is rarely given attention in atonement discussions, because he is usually thought to follow Anselm's "satisfaction theory" with only a few minor adjustments. Like Anselm, however, Aquinas's understanding of the atonement was much more than satisfaction, although certainly not less.[26] The breadth of the atonement for Aquinas can be seen in the following statement from his account of Christ's decent into hell: "First of all, because he came to bear our penalty in order to free us from penalty. . . . Secondly, because it was fitting when the devil was overthrown by the passion. . . . Thirdly, that as he showed forth his power on earth by living and dying, so also he might manifest it in hell, by visiting it and enlightening it."[27]

Peter Abelard, though his understanding of the atonement was definitively subjective, also included objective aspects, even propitiation.[28] In the Reformation, it is clear (contra Aulén) that Martin Luther upheld various aspects of the atonement.[29] Calvin, often credited for the first expression of penal substitution, is said by Robert Peterson to uphold the fullness of the atonement by interpreting Christ as the obedient second Adam, victor, legal substitute, sacrifice, merit, and example.[30] Stephen Edmondson concludes that "Calvin has been able to develop a more robust picture of Christ's Gospel than many on the market today."[31]

Finally, perhaps one of the greatest examples of revisionist history is a con-

---

24. K. McMahon, "The Cross and the Pearl: Anselm's Patristic Doctrine of Atonement," *TSR* 91 (2001): 57–70; David Bentley Hart, *The Beauty of the Infinite: The Aesthetics of Christian Truth* (Grand Rapids: Eerdmans, 2003), 366.

25. Gunton, *Actuality of Atonement*, 93.

26. See Adam Johnson, "A Fuller Account: The Role of 'Fittingness' in Thomas Aquinas' Development of the Doctrine of the Atonement," *IJST* 12 (2009): 302–18.

27. Thomas Aquinas, *Summa Theologica* (trans. Fathers of the English Dominican Province; New York: Benziger Bros, 1947), 3.52.1; quoted in Johnson, "A Fuller Account," 303; see also Aquinas's further treatment on Christ's death as satisfaction (*ST* 3.46.2), ransom (*ST* 3.48.4; 3.49.2), and example (*ST* 3.46.3).

28. Peter Abelard, "Exposition of the Epistle to the Romans (An Excerpt from the Second Book)," in *A Scholastic Miscellany: Anselm to Ockham* (ed. and trans. Eugene Fairweather; LCC; Philadelphia: Westminster, 1956), 279. There is no doubt, however, that Abelard's understanding of propitiation was deficient. Abelard was also open to the atonement as redemption from the devil, if indeed the devil's authority was subservient to God's (ibid., 281); Thomas Williams has recognized that Abelard's understanding of the atonement went beyond exemplar *simpliciter* ("Sin, Grace, and Redemption," in *The Cambridge Companion to Abelard* [ed. Jeffrey Brower and Kevin Guilfoy; CCP; Cambridge: Cambridge University Press, 2004], 267).

29. George, "The Atonement in Martin Luther's Theology."

30. Peterson, *Calvin's Doctrine of the Atonement*; see also Jansen, *Calvin's Doctrine of the Work of Christ*, 40.

31. Stephen Edmondson, *Calvin's Christology* (Cambridge: Cambridge University Press, 2004), 12.

temporary one—namely, the way in which penal substitution advocates are regularly portrayed in terms of "doctrinal isolationism," which Garry Williams describes as "an inability to look beyond itself."[32] Although this critique may be valid at a popular level in the church, it is surely far from accurate in describing the most prominent contemporary proponents of penal substitution. James Denney, widely known as an early twentieth-century champion of penal substitution, repeatedly called for the inseparability of penal substitution and moral influence, carefully grounding the latter in the former.[33]

In his seminal essay, "What Did the Cross Achieve? The Logic of Penal Substitution," J. I. Packer certainly argues for the centrality of penal substitution, but he intentionally does so in a nonreductive way. According to Packer, penal substitution "denies nothing asserted by the other two views save their assumption that they are complete. It agrees that there is biblical support for all they say, but it goes further."[34] Moreover, Packer is aware of the dangers of having a one-track approach that often results from reactionary debates and warns his readers of this pitfall.[35] Morris's passion for penal substitution can only be matched by his insistence on the diversity and fullness of Christ's accomplishment.[36] Stott explicitly states the importance of upholding the various aspects of Christ's atoning work, evident in the structure of *The Cross of Christ*.[37] In sum, the revisionist history common in atonement literature has fueled the either/or reductionism prevalent in recent atonement debates.

RELATIVISM
THE TREND OF RELATIVISM

In contemporary atonement theology, there has been widespread recognition of the dangers of reductionism, igniting a trend of championing the plurality of Christ's atoning work. This movement from polarization to pluralization is to

---

32. Garry Williams, "Penal Substitution," 173; Williams himself is a staunch advocate of penal substitution. For his response to the accusation of doctrinal isolationism, see ibid., 183–88.

33. James Denney, *The Death of Christ: Its Place and Interpretation in the New Testament* (New York: Armstrong and Son, 1904), 179–89, 331–34; for a similar contemporary argument, see Jason Hood, "The Cross in the New Testament: Two Theses in Conversation with Recent Literature (2000–2007)," *WTJ* 71 (2009): 281–95.

34. Packer, "What Did the Cross Achieve?" 20. Furthermore, argues Packer, "It is a pity that books on the atonement so often take it for granted that accounts of the cross that have appeared as rivals in historical debate must be treated as intrinsically exclusive" (ibid., 21).

35. Ibid., 26.

36. Morris, *The Cross in the New Testament*, 365–93.

37. According to Stott, "All three of the major explanations of the death of Christ contain biblical truth and can to some extent be harmonized. . . . Jesus Christ is successively the Saviour, the Teacher and the Victor, because we ourselves are guilty, apathetic and in bondage" (*The Cross of Christ*, 229–30).

be received, of course, inasmuch as it recognizes the many metaphors in Scripture and the more holistic views of church tradition. However, the reaction to reductionism coupled with the postmodern suspicion of totalitizing has often led to a type of relativism that seeks only to uphold diversity at the expense of order and integration. The declaration of this approach reads, "All metaphors are created equal," and therefore ensures that there is "no metaphor left behind."

Perhaps the greatest representative of this trend is Joel Green and his "kaleidoscopic view."[38] Green argues that all theories of the atonement are needed (except, ironically, penal substitution) and that one metaphor should not be privileged over another.[39] The advantage to this theory, according to Green and others, is that depending on one's cultural setting, they can choose the aspect of the atonement that most applies to their particular context.

THE DANGER OF RELATIVISM

Although I wholeheartedly accept the multidimensional approach to the atonement, I have three concerns with this relativistic trend. First, the eager acceptance of all of the biblical metaphors has often been strangely paired with the rejection of penal substitution.[40] The focus here is methodology, so I will not provide a defense for penal substitution. The salient point is methodological inconsistency. The rejection of penal substitution is not merely dismissal of a "theory" that has been present at least since the Reformation and in some form since the early church;[41] it is avoiding (or drastically reinterpreting) the major biblical theme of the wrath of God.[42]

Second, the emphasis on upholding diversity has often come at the cost of unity, particularly the task of integrating and ordering the different dimensions of the atonement. Peter Schmiechen, for example, seeks to protect the fullness of the atonement by simultaneously upholding ten different theo-

---

38. Joel Green, "Kaleidoscopic View," in *The Nature of the Atonement,*157–85; cf. Joel Green and Mark Baker, *Recovering the Scandal of the Cross.*

39. Joel Green, "Kaleidoscopic View," 175; Spence finds a similar trend earlier in Dillistone (*The Promise of Peace*, 56).

40. Joel Green, "Must We Imagine the Atonement in Penal Substitutionary Terms?" 153–71; Peter Schmiechen, *Saving Power: Theories of Atonement and Forms of the Church* (Grand Rapids: Eerdmans, 2005); Chalke and Mann, *The Lost Message of Jesus.*

41. For penal substitution in the early church, see Michael Vlach, "Penal Substitution in Church History," *MSJ* 20 (2009): 199–214; Garry Williams, "Penal Substitutionary Atonement in the Church Fathers," *EvQ* 83 (2011): 195–216; Jeffery, Ovey, and Sach, *Pierced for Our Transgressions*, 161–83. For a counterargument, see Derek Flood, "Substitutionary Atonement and the Church Fathers: A Reply to the Authors of *Pierced for Our Transgressions*," *EvQ* 82 (2010): 142–59.

42. The foundation of this argument is Dodd's work, which reinterpreted the wrath of God as (only) passive and nonpersonal (*The Bible and the Greeks* [London: Hodder & Stoughton, 1935], 82–95). For a response, see Morris, *The Apostolic Preaching of the Cross*, 144–213.

ries.[43] Stephen Holmes, who wants to keep penal substitution as one of many aspects, argues for a "multiple models" approach, which seeks to imitate the "biblical practice, where . . . a lot of different pictures are piled up on top of one another with no real shape or order."[44] Spence laments this trend, observing the seeming simplicity of the way atonement theology is thought to be done: catalog the metaphorical terms, study the backgrounds of each, and then simply uphold diversity as did the New Testament authors. The "fatal, but apparently unnoticed flaw," says Spence, is that Scripture itself integrates the different dimensions of the atonement (e.g., Rom 3:24–25).[45]

Third, the emphasis on plurality turns into relativism when the various atonement dimensions merely become alternative options to be chosen according to context. Certainly all theology is to be contextualized. In fact, the recent recognition of global theology may provide the greatest potential for atonement theology in centuries. However, the key question is whether the diversity of different cultures provides a deeper understanding of Christ's multifaceted work on the cross or just more alternatives for how to understand it. The trend being traced here assumes that the different aspects of the atonement provide alternative options that can be applied as needed, depending on the cultural context. McKnight illustrates this strategy with a golf analogy: there are fourteen clubs in the bag, and depending on the situation, the golfer pulls out the appropriate one.[46]

Others go further and, echoing the attempts of Schleiermacher and Ritschl in years past, observe that modern people do not think in the traditional Christian categories of sin and guilt, and therefore suggest redefining the significance of Christ's death accordingly.[47] For Green and Baker, because the New Testament language of Christ's accomplishment is metaphorical and the meanings of metaphors are bound to their cultures, they argue that some biblical metaphors simply will not be suitable for today's culture and should be replaced with new ones.[48]

---

43. Schmiechen, *Saving Power*, 2.
44. Holmes, *The Wondrous Cross*, 78.
45. Spence, *The Promise of Peace*, 55–56.
46. McKnight, *A Community Called Atonement*, xiii.
47. Alan Mann, *Atonement for a "Sinless" Society: Engaging with an Emerging Culture* (Milton Keynes, UK: Paternoster, 2005); Theodore Jennings, *Transforming Atonement: A Political Theology of the Cross* (Minneapolis: Fortress, 2009).
48. Green and Baker, *Recovering the Scandal of the Cross*, 111, 114. The metaphorical nature of New Testament atonement language is often called on by those who critique sacrificial (and especially penal substitutionary) depictions of the atonement. For a defense of the significance of metaphor, see Janet Soskice, *Metaphor and Religious Language* (New York: Oxford University Press, 1985); Gunton, *Actuality of Atonement*; Henri Blocher, "Biblical Metaphors and the Doctrine of the Atonement," *JETS* 47 (2004): 629–45; Boersma, *Violence, Hospitality, and the Cross*, 99–114.

The problem with this relativistic pick-your-metaphor approach is not the straightforward emphasis on contextualization. Again, contextualization is an indispensable part of doing theology. The problem is that this emphasis has come at the expense of seeking how the metaphors fit together into a coherent, unified understanding of Christ's accomplishment. As Spence says, "The quest for theological truth has subtly shifted to the search for religious relevance."[49] If a sinful person does not *feel* guilty (perceived need) before God, does that mean that he or she *is* not guilty (actual need)?

This argument is not merely another defense for penal substitution. May we, living in a "sophisticated" culture that largely does not believe in supernatural demonic beings, completely avoid the biblical truth that these very beings are part of the problem and therefore their defeat part of the solution? Certainly not. Considering that the default mode of human sinful nature is utterly Pelagian, a truly felt-need approach will ultimately end up being a self-help, moral improvement program in place of the good news of what *God* has accomplished in Christ.

Contextualization is needed, but it is not enough to contextualize a sliver of Christ's multifaceted work. Trevor Hart succinctly critiques such a pick-your-metaphor approach, pointing toward my constructive proposal:

> The plurality of biblical imagery does not seem to be intended purely or even primarily as a selection box from which we may draw what we will according to our needs and the pre-understanding of our community. . . . The metaphors are not to be understood as exchangeable, as if one might simply be substituted for another without net gain or loss, but complementary, directing us to distinct elements in and consequences of the fullness of God's saving action in Christ and the Spirit.[50]

A better way is to see the diversity of various cultures as fostering a deeper understanding of Christ's atoning work, and conversely, the diversity of the atonement as providing various *entry points* into a full-orbed understanding of Christ's work on the cross.

EXPANSIVE PARTICULARITY

The history of Christian theology demonstrates the difficulty of upholding the *breadth* of the "whole counsel of God" (Acts 20:27) and giving special

---

49. Spence, *The Promise of Peace*, 55.
50. Trevor Hart, "Redemption and Fall," in *The Cambridge Companion to Christian Doctrine*, ed. Colin Gunton (Cambridge: Cambridge University Press, 1997), 190; cf. Stott, *The Cross of Christ*, 168.

attention to the *particulars* that are "of first importance" (1 Cor 15:3). Unfortunately, one often comes at the expense of the other, resulting in either reductionism (particularity without breadth) or relativism (breadth without particularity). I propose a way forward for atonement methodology that avoids both errors of reductionism and relativism by employing the tools of theological integration, order, and rank. The result is what I have called "expansive particularity": *expansive* because it avoids reductionism and *particular* because it evades relativism.

The atoning work of Christ is grand and glorious; its accomplishment is as wide-reaching as the sin to which it provides a remedy. The various images presented in Scripture, along with nearly two thousand years of the church's reflection on their significance, make clear that one can never exhaust the fullness of this many-splendored work. Anything less than an expansive account of the atonement falls short of Scripture's presentation of the glory of God in the cross of Christ.

The sum, however, is incomprehensible without its parts. Comprehensiveness is not enough without coherence. In other words, the expansiveness of the whole is only properly attended to as one rightly understands the particular parts and how they each contribute to the whole. For this task, we need the tools of integration, order, and rank.

INTEGRATION

Returning to Hart's critique above, the various biblical metaphors for the atonement are not interchangeable (different ways of saying the same thing),[51] but complementary (saying differing things about different aspects of the same thing). We need not, therefore, simply uphold the various images but integrate them (Is this not the task of theology in the first place?).[52]

Take, for example, redemption and reconciliation. Are these simply different ways of saying the same thing, one from the sphere of commerce and the other from friendship? Certainly not. Redemption speaks of a release from bondage by the payment of a ransom price (focusing on what one is saved from and how this is achieved), whereas reconciliation is the bringing together of alienated parties (focusing on the resulting state). Clearly the two

---

51. Robert Peterson, for example, says, "The six pictures do not talk of six different realities. Rather, they are six different ways of talking about the same reality—the salvation that Christ accomplished" (*Salvation Accomplished by the Son: The Work of Christ* [Wheaton, IL: Crossway, 2012], 556).

52. See A. N. Williams, *The Architecture of Theology: Structure, System, & Ratio* (New York: Oxford University Press, 2011); one of Williams' arguments throughout is that theology is inherently systematic.

could overlap (one could be redeemed from slavery and into a reconciled relationship), but they are very different.

More broadly (and obviously), Christ's victory over Satan and his forgiveness of people's sins are not different ways of saying the same thing, but different aspects of Christ's work. The danger of interpreting the various images as different ways of saying the same thing is that it flattens out the multidimensionality of the atonement, shifting the weight of diversity from Christ's objective accomplishment to our subjective understanding of it, from theology to epistemology. These distinctions, therefore, must be made not for the purpose of division but integration.

Integrating the different metaphors of Christ's atoning work is necessary because Scripture itself does so. The metaphors are "closely intertwined," says Blocher, and "seem to flow naturally into one another."[53] Although many examples could be given (Rom 5:6–9; Eph 1:5–7; Col 2:13–15; Rev 5:9), three will suffice.

- In Rom 3:24–25, Paul interweaves three different metaphors from three different spheres of life, all seamlessly in the same thought. He speaks of those who "are justified [law court] by his grace as a gift, through the redemption [commerce] that is in Christ Jesus, whom God put forward as a propitiation [cult] by his blood, to be received by faith."
- Hebrews 2:14–18 speaks of Christ's life and death in terms of victory, propitiation, and moral influence.
- Revelation 12:9–11 combines cultic, military, and legal metaphors.

Beyond metaphors, some of Scripture's most explicit statements of the objective accomplishment in substitutionary atonement also contain the subjective emphasis of following Christ's example (Mark 10:31–45; John 13:1–17; 1 Pet 2:21–25).[54] In 1 John 4:10–11 the declaration of Jesus as the "propitiation for our sins" is immediately followed by the exhortation that "if God so loved us, we also ought to love one another."

Perhaps the task of integrating atonement metaphors can be corroborated by the concept of "fittingness," which has been commonly employed in atonement discussions throughout church history. While Athanasius and Anselm use the term primarily to explore the reason (or necessity) of the incarnation and atonement, Aquinas, according to Adam Johnson, "uses it to bring together the various theories of his day into a fuller account of the

---

53. Blocher, "Biblical Metaphors and the Doctrine of the Atonement," 640.
54. Thomas Schreiner, "Penal Substitution View," in *The Nature of the Atonement*, 96.

atonement."[55] Aspects of the atonement are not to be merely upheld in a state of coexistence; they must be "fit" together into a coherent whole. This fittingness requires not only cohesion but proper ordering.

ORDER

Bringing the atonement metaphors into a unity requires more than merely a melting pot of meaning. There must be a particular ordering, the *right* way in which they fit together. For example, there are objective and subjective aspects of the atonement, but placing them in the right order is crucial for a proper understanding of the atonement as a whole. As Luther said, "When you have Christ as the foundation and chief blessing of your salvation, then the other part follows: that you take him as your example."[56] More recently, Miroslav Volf says, "The cross will serve best as the model if it has first served as the *foundation*."[57]

This proper order, however, has been reversed in much of modern liberal theology (Schleiermacher and Ritschl) and particularly in contemporary views that come close to being subjective *simpliciter*.[58] Just as with these broader categories of objective and subjective, the proper order must also be discerned for the individual metaphors of atonement. Although Scripture does not provide an exhaustive or definitive ordering of the metaphors (how they properly fit), it is also not silent on the matter.

RANK

Finally, and perhaps most controversially, the concept of theological rank is necessary for expansive particularity. Within the broader framework of "the whole counsel of God" (Acts 20:27), Jesus' "seek first" (Matt 6:33) and Paul's "of first importance" (1 Cor 15:3) imply that there are certain doctrines that have more theological significance than others. The Reformers understood this concept of "theological rank" and therefore made a threefold distinction between *articuli fundamentales* ("fundamental articles"), *articuli fundamentales secundarii* ("secondary fundamental articles"), and *articuli non-fundamentales* ("non-fundamental articles").[59]

---

55. Johnson, "A Fuller Account," 303.
56. Luther, *A Brief Instruction On What To Look For and Expect In the Gospels* (1522) *LW* 35:120.
57. Miroslav Volf, *Exclusion and Embrace: A Theological Exploration of Identity, Otherness, and Reconciliation* (Nashville: Abingdon, 1996), 22, italics his.
58. Park, *Triune Atonement*; Paul Fiddes, *Past Event and Present Salvation: The Christian Idea of Atonement* (Louisville: Westminster John Knox, 1989).
59. Richard Muller, *Dictionary of Latin and Greek Theological Terms: Drawn Principally from Protestant Scholastic Theology* (Grand Rapids: Baker, 1985), 45–46.

In atonement theology, however, many scholars such as Green and Baker have made clear that there is no place for privileging one aspect of the atonement over the others.[60] Although this sentiment is certainly pleasing to postmodern ears, it has two major problems. First, it is impossible in practice. No one can talk about everything at once. Practically speaking, the scholar is confined by a page limit and the pastor by the five minutes available to answer a genuine question. We have to start somewhere. We have to end somewhere. And we will inevitably emphasize certain features throughout. Green and Baker cannot escape this reality, and actually contradict themselves by eventually saying that it *is* permissible to privilege one aspect over the others for the sake of cultural relevance.[61] So whether it is Schmiechen's ten aspects or McIntyre's thirteen, it is simply impossible to give equal attention to each.[62]

The second problem with trying to avoid any theological rank is that Scripture itself sets the precedent of privileging certain metaphors. Paul did not keep a running tab of his metaphors so he could make sure they all received equal treatment, nor did any of the other biblical authors. Consider, for example, the relatively undeveloped metaphor of Christ's death as a grain of wheat that is buried and produces much fruit (John 12:24). This is a fascinating metaphor that brings out aspects of the atonement that are often neglected. However, should the "grain of wheat" metaphor receive equal attention as the "sacrificial lamb" metaphor in understanding and presenting the atonement? Certainly not.

But *why* not? This appeals to and brings into the discussion the idea of criteria. How does one decide what gets privileged? Everyone inevitably operates with a type of theological rank, but rarely are they explicit about criteria. The most straightforward and comprehensive account of criteria for theological rank in the doctrine of the atonement has been set forth by Blocher, of which I offer a brief summary:[63]

1. Frequency: regularity, development, and relation to other metaphors
2. Linguistic intentionality: how literally the author intends to use the metaphor
3. Genre: the more didactic genres offer greater conceptual clarity

Based on these criteria, Blocher puts forth five main schemes for understand-

---

60. Green and Baker, *Recovering the Scandal of the Cross*, 86.
61. Ibid., 98.
62. Schmiechen, *Saving Power*; McIntyre, *The Shape of Soteriology*.
63. Blocher, "Biblical Metaphors and the Doctrine of the Atonement," 639.

ing the atonement: sacrificial, judicial, redemptive, polemic (victory/warfare), and Passover.[64] Of the theories that emerge from these schemes, perhaps the two most important, and at least the most controversial, are penal substitution and *Christus Victor*.

THE PROBLEM: CHRISTUS VICTOR VERSUS PENAL SUBSTITUTION

I will now trace the recent development of the relationship of penal substitution and *Christus Victor* from hostility to compatibility, ultimately setting up for a proposal of integration.

CHRISTUS VICTOR VERSUS PENAL SUBSTITUTION

While many proponents of *Christus Victor* outright reject penal substitution, defenders of penal substitution often ignore *Christus Victor*. Sinclair Ferguson demonstrates that, in spite of Scripture's insistence that Jesus came to destroy the works of the devil (1 John 3:8), systematic theologians in the Reformed tradition have largely ignored this aspect of Christ's work:

> Turretin, in his exposition of the work of Christ in *Institutio Theologiae Elencticae*, topic 14, does not concern himself with the issue. Charles Hodge divides the theories of the atonement into five groups (*Systematic Theology*, 3 Vols. [New York, 1872–73], 2:563–91), but deals with the effect of the atonement on Satan only under the heading "The Doctrine of Some of the Fathers." In this he is followed by B. B. Warfield (*The Person and Work of Christ* [Philadelphia: Presbyterian and Reformed, 1952], 356ff.), as well as by Berkhof, who lists seven views of the atonement, including the "Ransom-to-Satan" view; but his own exposition makes no reference to the effect of the cross on Satan (*Systematic Theology* [Grand Rapids: Eerdmans, 1939], 384–99).[65]

Why has such a clear biblical theme been neglected in this tradition? Ferguson offers three reasons.[66] First, the medieval debates between Anselm(ians) and Abelard(ians), focusing so intently on satisfaction and exemplarist theories, greatly shaped the nature of the discussions for most of the second millennium. Second, although the seventeenth century saw a greater awareness

---

64. Ibid., 640.

65. Ferguson, "*Christus Victor et Propitiator*," 172. Gaffin also admits the neglect of the victory theme in his own Reformed and evangelical tradition ("Atonement in the Pauline Corpus," 141).

66. Ferguson, "*Christus Victor et Propitiator*," 172–73.

in spiritual warfare, the emphasis was placed on *Christians'* battle with Satan rather than on *Christ's* victory over Satan. Third, and probably most important, the victory theme was neglected because of an overreaction to the early church's faulty view of *how* Christ accomplished victory over the devil—namely, through deception.

It is not only the Reformed tradition, however, that has neglected the victory theme. Schleiermacher explicitly states that God's plan of salvation has nothing to do with the devil.[67] Adolf von Harnack declared, "It is not a question of angels and devils, thrones and principalities, but of God and the soul, the soul and its God."[68] Ironically, conservatives *and* liberals have for the most part neglected Christ's victory over Satan. Although many liberal theologians have championed Christ's victory on the cross, they have often abandoned the belief in Satan and demons as real spiritual entities. Conservatives, by contrast, have fought for the reality of demonic beings, yet neglected their defeat in Christ's work on the cross.

Aulén emerged from this context and addressed it his landmark work, *Christus Victor*. Aulén should be applauded for bringing about an awakening of a theme that is not only key in the Gospels and Paul's letters, but is present throughout the entirety of Scripture's narrative from Gen 3:15 forward.[69] However, along with Aulén's revitalization of the victory theme came a glaring critique of satisfaction theories of the atonement, and it is for this dual reason that he is the key figure in the debate between *Christus Victor* and penal substitution, a hero to some and a villain to others. Aulén's thesis is straightforward: "Christ—*Christus Victor*—fights against and triumphs over the evil powers of the world, the 'tyrants' under which mankind is in bondage and suffering, and in Him God reconciles the world to Himself."[70]

The responses to Aulén have been many, both laudatory and critical. However, one ought not approach Aulén with an "all or nothing" mentality. A key distinction must be made, rather, between Aulén's positive case (the motif of victory in the atonement) and negative case (the critique of the Latin

67. Schleiermacher, *The Christian Faith*, 163.
68. Adolf von Harnack, *What is Christianity?* (trans. Thomas Saunders; Philadelphia: Fortress, 1986), 56.
69. For contemporary works that highlight the victory theme in Scripture, see Tremper Longman and Daniel Reid, *God Is a Warrior* (Grand Rapids: Zondervan, 1994); Gregory Boyd, *God at War: The Bible & Spiritual Conflict* (Downers Grove, IL: InterVarsity Press, 1997); Youssouf Dembele, "Salvation as Victory: A Reconsideration of the Concept of Salvation in the Light of Jesus Christ's Life and Work Viewed as a Triumph over the Personal Powers of Evil" (Ph.D. diss., Trinity Evangelical Divinity School, 2001); Phillip Bethancourt, "Christ the Warrior King: A Biblical, Historical, and Theological Analysis of the Divine Warrior Theme in Christology" (Ph.D. diss., Southern Baptist Theological Seminary, 2011).
70. Aulén, *Christus Victor*, 20.

view).[71] Aulén's positive case for Christ's victory is helpful in terms of restoring a key biblical theme, but it does not go far enough.

Michael Ovey affirms Aulén's positive case and proposes two extensions and one qualification. The first extension corrects the demythologizing elements in Aulén's understanding of the demonic and therefore restores the original force of Christ's victory over the powers.[72] The second extension emphasizes the victory of the cross as a *just* victory rather than a mere application of force. The just nature of God's character and victorious salvation, therefore, demands the resolution for which only penal substitution can provide.[73] The qualification to Aulén's positive case highlights his neglect of sin in Christ's victorious work. Without dealing with sin, Aulén's account falls short of providing a full remedy for the problem necessitating atonement. Aulén's negative case is the rejection of the Latin view, at the heart of which is satisfaction of God's justice. His critique revolves around the central criterion of divine continuous action, which Ovey rejects because it is appealed to inconsistently, applied to distorted versions of the Latin view, and—most devastatingly—because it is based on a Christology that is incongruous with Chalcedon.[74]

In sum, Ovey affirms Aulén's positive case of victory in the atonement with the extensions and qualification and rejects his negative case that critiques the Latin view. Ovey's solution points toward my own proposal below, but the salient feature at this point is his ability to expose Aulén's false dichotomy between victory and satisfaction. To affirm victory one need not abandon satisfaction. As we will see, the former depends on the latter. Aulén's influence on atonement theology is immeasurable, especially evident in the stream of theologians who have propagated and developed his theory of *Christus Victor* over and against penal substitution.[75]

CHRISTUS VICTOR AND PENAL SUBSTITUTION

In light of the trend from reductionism to relativism, the relationship between *Christus Victor* and penal substitution has been expressed recently as a "both/and": *Christus Victor and* penal substitution.[76] Under the banner of multidimensionality, many have sought to uphold both aspects of the atonement,

---

71. Michael Ovey, "Appropriating Aulén? Employing *Christus Victor* Models of the Atonement," *Churchman* 124 (2010): 297–330.
72. Ibid., 306–8.
73. Ibid., 308–11.
74. Ibid., 313–23.
75. See, e.g., Boyd, "*Christus Victor* View"; Weaver, "Narrative *Christus Victor*."
76. Gunton, *Actuality of the Atonement*; Holmes, *The Wondrous Cross*.

though without moving toward an understanding of how they fit together. While this stance is common today, Ferguson traces such a trend as far back as Origen,[77] and it can be seen explicitly in the Heidelberg Catechism Question 1: "Jesus Christ, who with His precious blood has fully satisfied for all my sins, and redeemed me from all the power of the devil." Blocher says Calvin falls largely in this category, although he at least hinted at a way forward for integrating the two dimensions.[78]

CONCLUSION

We have seen that Christ's accomplishment is a multifaceted work that calls for integration, order, and rank. *Christus Victor* and penal substitution—two of many theories, but the ones that most directly relate to this project—have unfortunately often been pitted against one another. While it is good that some have sought to uphold the two theories in tension, it is not enough. Holding two aspects of Christ's work in balance will not suffice when integration is possible. Therefore, in the next chapter I will present my case for the proper integration: *Christus Victor* through penal substitution.

---

77. Ferguson, "*Christus Victor et Propitiator*," 173.
78. Henri Blocher, "The Atonement in John Calvin's Theology," in *The Glory of the Atonement*, 289–91.

CHAPTER EIGHT

ATONEMENT: RECONCILING CHRISTUS VICTOR AND PENAL SUBSTITUTION

THE GOAL OF this chapter is to integrate *Christus Victor* and penal substitution, which is not only essential for a biblical understanding of the atonement but is crucial in relating the kingdom and the cross. Inasmuch as the coming of God's kingdom entails God's defeat of evil and reconciliation of humanity, *Christus Victor* and penal substitution are both essential aspects to Christ's kingdom-establishing work on the cross. Unfortunately, as we have seen, *Christus Victor* and penal substitution have often been placed in opposition or, at best, upheld in tension.

Rejecting "*Christus Victor versus* penal substitution" and not settling for "*Christus Victor and* penal substitution," I propose "*Christus Victor through* penal substitution." My constructive proposal is not completely new, but one that has been neglected in recent history; I hope to recover it and further develop it. Others have made contributions in this direction, especially Blocher and Ferguson.[1] In this chapter, I will build on their work, going deeper into the Scriptures and back to the theological tradition of the church, and thereby move the conversation forward. The relationship between *Christus Victor* and penal substitution will be defined by answering five questions:

---

1. Blocher, "*Agnus Victor*"; Ferguson, "*Christus Victor et Propitiator*"; see also Cole, *God the Peacemaker*; Boersma, *Violence, Hospitality, and the Cross.*

1. What is the problem?
2. Who is Satan?
3. How does Christ conquer Satan?
4. When does Christ's victory decisively happen?
5. Why does Christ conquer Satan?

Each question will be answered by interacting with Scripture, tradition, and contemporary theology.

WHAT IS THE PROBLEM?

The way one defines a problem will significantly shape its solution. In medicine, a misdiagnosis will not only detract from the remedy but can actually precipitate deadly consequences. So it is with theology. Although in atonement theology much more attention is given to the solution than the problem, it is the (often assumed) definition of the problem from which the differences actually stem. Therefore, in order to answer the question, "What did Christ accomplish on the cross?" one must first answer, "What is the condition of the human situation that is so desperately in need of remedy?" As British poet Lord Byron once said, "The commencement of atonement is the sense of its necessity."[2]

SIN AND ITS EFFECTS

Christians define the problem beneath every problem of this world as sin, along with its effects.[3] Two aspects deserve emphasis: (1) sin is multifaceted in its essence and its effects, and (2) sin at its core is against God. Before specifically addressing the "problems" to which penal substitution and *Christus Victor* propose solutions, I will first highlight the importance of these two preliminary points.

First, reductionistic views of sin lead to reductionistic views of atonement. Conversely, a multifaceted view of sin will lead to a multifaceted view of atonement. Whereas Anselm famously prodded liberal theology to consider the *weight* of sin, I would ask a similar question of reductionistic theology: "Have you considered the *complexity* of sin?" The complexity of sin must be

---

2. Baron George Noël Gordon Byron, *The Works of Lord Byron: Complete in One Volume* (London: John Murray, 1841), 187.
3. Sin and its effects can be distinguished but not ultimately separated. According to Sklar, there was a clear understanding in the Old Testament and ancient Near East that "there is a sin-disaster connection . . . with the disaster coming as God's judgment for the sin" (*Sin, Impurity, Sacrifice, Atonement*, 11).

recognized in its essence (i.e., rebellion, mistrust, pride, etc.) and its effects (i.e., alienation, slavery, ignorance, etc.). The Old Testament alone uses over fifty different Hebrew words for sin, revealing what African theologian John Pobee calls the "many-sidedness of sin."[4] Christopher J. H. Wright discusses the multifaceted ramifications of sin—demonstrating that in the Old Testament, sin has the following "devastatingly wide range of effects":[5]

- a relationship that has been broken: the relational aspect
- the disturbance of *shalom*: the social aspect
- rebellion against authority: the covenantal aspect
- guilt that necessitates punishment: the legal aspect
- uncleanness and pollution: the ritual aspect
- shame and disgrace on oneself and/or on God: the emotional aspect
- an accumulating burden: the historical aspect
- death: the final aspect

I would add to Wright's list that there is an *eschatological* aspect to sin and its effects, culminating in a "sinful kingdom" (Amos 9:8) or "domain of darkness" (Col 1:13). Murray is right when he writes: "We must view sin and evil in its larger proportions as a kingdom that embraces the subtlety, craft, ingenuity, power, and unremitting activity of Satan and his legions."[6] The far-reaching effects of sin extend into every inch of the *cosmos* and even shape our understanding of time: the old age—under Adam—is dominated by the law, flesh, and death, whereas the new age—inaugurated by the second Adam—is marked by grace, the Spirit, and life.[7] This eschatological framework for sin serves as a reminder that sin is not merely existential separation from God; it is banishment from Eden, exile from the promised land, and ultimately the forsakenness Jesus experienced on the cross. Therefore, we need not only reconciliation with God, we need also a new king who will usher in a new kingdom.

Second, sin at its core is against God. Although theologians have long sought to define the essence of sin as rebellion, pride, or mistrust, each of these is ultimately aimed at God and is a rejection of God. Perhaps the clearest example in Scripture is from David, who commits adultery against his wife, murders one of his own soldiers, and then prays *to the Lord*: "Against you, you only, have I sinned" (Ps 51:4). Cornelius Plantinga helpfully com-

---

4. John Pobee, *Toward an African Theology* (Nashville: Abingdon, 1979), 107.
5. Wright, "Atonement in the Old Testament," 71. The following list is from pp. 69–71.
6. Murray, *Redemption Accomplished and Applied*, 50.
7. Stott, *The Cross of Christ*, 246.

bines both of the above points, revealing the Godward essence of sin: "All sin has first and finally a Godward force" as well as the breadth of its resulting effects—"sin is culpable shalom-breaking."[8]

ENMITY WITH GOD AND BONDAGE TO SATAN

Having laid this foundation for the nature of sin, I can now discuss specifically the problems to which *Christus Victor* and penal substitution propose solutions. The core problem for *Christus Victor* is that humans are in bondage to the powers of evil. For penal substitution, the problem is that humans have enmity with God, entailing both divine wrath and human guilt. Yet, how do these two obstacles to reconciliation relate? Are humans victims of Satan or violators of God's law, or both? Does one take precedence over the other?

First and foremost, both theories present aspects of the problem that are clearly taught in Scripture. Humans in their fallen state are in the "domain of darkness" (Col 1:13) and under "the power of the evil one" (1 John 5:19; cf. 2 Cor 4:4; Eph 2:2). Yet, Scripture equally asserts that God's wrath remains on every unregenerate person (Rom 1:18–3:20; Eph 2:3; 5:6; Col 3:6; Rev 6:16). As Barth says, humans are "the responsible author but also the poor victim of sin."[9] Ephesians 2:2–3 brings both aspects together (amidst even more aspects of sin), describing humans as both "following the prince of the power of the air" and "by nature children of wrath."

WHAT IS THE PRIMARY PROBLEM?

Establishing the validity of both problems in Scripture leads to the key question: Is one prior or foundational to the other? As demonstrated above, order matters. Some have argued that bondage to Satan is the primary problem, resulting in a fractured relationship with God. Youssouf Dembele, for example, says that "sin is Satan's work" and therefore claims, "Satan and his works stand as the most simple and irreducible expression of the negative situation from which humankind needs to be saved."[10] Sherman claims that "humans are separated from God because we are held in bondage to 'powers and principalities' opposed to God."[11] Gregory Boyd goes even further, arguing that it is evil's corruption of all creation—of which humanity is only a small part—

---

8. Cornelius Plantinga, *Not the Way It's Supposed to Be: A Breviary of Sin* (Grand Rapids: Eerdmans, 1995), 13–14. In a similar way, McKnight argues for a "hyper-relational" view, where sin "is active corruption in all directions" and yet "begins in rebellion against God" (*A Community Called Atonement*, 22–23).

9. Barth, *CD* IV/1, 138.

10. Youssouf Dembele, "Salvation as Victory," 252, 254.

11. Sherman, *King, Priest, and Prophet*, 160.

that is the primary problem. According to Boyd, "Neither evil nor its cure is first and foremost about human beings at all. Rather, it is . . . primarily about free willing agents ('the powers') whose cosmic power and influence dwarf the free agency of human beings."[12] For Boyd, then, not only is the human problem derivative of the Satan problem, but the latter is ultimately more significant than the former.

The approaches of Dembele, Sherman, and Boyd are plagued with exegetical, theological, and pastoral problems. First, regarding Dembele's claim, it is exegetically and theologically unwarranted to attribute human sin primarily to Satan. It is true, of course, that Satan's rebellion preceded human rebellion and that "the devil has been sinning from the beginning" (1 John 3:8). However, the responsibility in Scripture is always placed first and foremost on humanity, regardless of whether they are tempted (as was Adam) or in bondage (as are all under Adam). Romans 5:12 could not be any clearer: "Sin came into the world through one man . . . and so death spread to all men because all sinned." The reign of Satan therefore is parasitic to the reign of sin (Rom 5:21). As George Smeaton says, "Sin was the ground of Satan's dominion, the sphere of his power, and the secret of his strength."[13] Sin, in other words, gives the devil a foothold (Eph 4:26–27). Satan tempts people to sin, deceives them of the effects of sin, accuses them of the guilt of sin, and thereby leads them to death—the wages of sin.

After the fall in Eden, God cursed the serpent (Gen 3:15), but he first held Adam responsible ("Where are you?" 3:9), as well as Eve ("What is this that you have done?" 3:13). Dembele, therefore, gets it backward. As Blocher points out, "Temptations . . . require the self-determination of human will to give birth to sin."[14] So while Satan certainly had an influence, it was *Adam* who brought sin to humanity. Satan tempted Adam before the fall, but it was not until *Adam* sinned that Satan gained dominion over Adam (and his progeny). Only because Adam rejected God as king did Satan become his ruler. Adam, who had been created in the image of God to rule over every beast of the earth (1:26, 28), had failed at his task and was now ruled by the craftiest of all the beasts (3:1).

The biblical witness testifies that what was true of Adam is also true of every descendent of Adam: bondage to Satan is the consequence of rejecting the dominion of God. The fact that Satan's rebellion preceded human

---

12. Boyd, *God at War*, 242.
13. George Smeaton, *The Apostles' Doctrine of the Atonement* (Grand Rapids: Zondervan, 1957), 307–8.
14. Blocher, "Agnus Victor," 82.

rebellion does not mean that human *bondage* did as well. Bondage to Satan is a *result* of rebelling against God and the enmity that follows. The prefall rebellion of Satan does, however, show that human sin and Satan's influence are deeply intertwined.

THE COMMUNITY AND THE COSMOS

Boyd's argument that "salvation is the liberation of the whole world process of which I am only a small part"[15] raises the question of the proper places of the cosmos and the community in God's redemptive purposes—an important issue for relating *Christus Victor* and penal substitution. For Boyd, redemption aims at the broader cosmic scale of God's creation, with no special focus on humanity. Accordingly, Boyd defines the solution primarily as Christ's victory over the powers and only derivatively as reconciliation of humans.

The dilemma, however, with Boyd's description of "the problem" is that it does not square with the order built into creation and therefore its corruption. Clearly, God has cosmic purposes in creation (Psalm 148; Col 1:15–20); yet, there is also a priority given to humanity as the special focus of God's work. In Genesis 1–2, only humans are made in the image of God, and their creation is the apex of all God's creation, bringing forth the unprecedented "very good" (Gen 1:31).[16] Furthermore, Rom 8:19–23 makes clear that creation being "subjected to futility" and in "bondage to corruption" is ultimately tied to the brokenness of humanity. A fractured relationship between God and humanity results in the shattered *shalom* of creation. The movement of corruption is not from cosmos to community, but from community to cosmos. As humans go, creation goes. The implications for soteriology are immense. Christ's salvation is aimed at both the church and the cosmos, but in proper order. The church is the *focus* of salvation; the cosmos, the *scope* of salvation. As Robert Letham says, Christ's "church is to be the spearhead of a renovated and restored cosmos."[17]

VIOLATORS AND VICTIMS

A final critique of this position is a pastoral one. This view of the problem essentially makes people victims that need to be saved *from* the problem rather than sinners who are *part of* the problem. Again, we need not set up an either/or; people are victims *and* violators. But the sole emphasis on the

---

15. Boyd, *God at War*, 267; Boyd favorably quotes James Kallas here.
16. For an exegetical argument for the special place of humans in Genesis 1–2, see Gentry, "Kingdom through Covenant," 22–23.
17. Robert Letham, *The Work of Christ* (Downers Grove, IL: InterVarsity Press, 1993), 211.

problem as bondage to Satan removes the weighty biblical emphasis on the guilt and brokenness of humans themselves.

BONDAGE TO SATAN AS A RESULT OF ENMITY WITH GOD

The positive case, therefore, for rightly understanding the relationship between these two problems of bondage and alienation can be stated as follows: humans are in bondage to Satan *because* they have rejected God as king; they are in the kingdom of Satan *because* they have been banished from the kingdom of God. Enmity with God—entailing God's wrath on humans and human guilt before God—is therefore the root problem.[18] Bondage to Satan is derivative of the God-human problem, for as soon as distance comes into the relationship, a third party is then able to creep in, which is precisely what Satan did and continues to do.

The most common way that Scripture speaks of sinning against God is by breaking his law, as is especially clear in 1 John 3:4: "Everyone who makes a practice of sinning also practices lawlessness; sin is lawlessness." The key here is that Scripture not only describes sin as being against God (breaking *God's* law) but does so primarily with judicial language (breaking God's *law*). Bavinck demonstrates well the multifaceted nature of sin and yet the particular emphasis on judgment: "The punishments that God has ordained for sin in this life are guilt, pollution, suffering, death, and the dominion of Satan. Guilt is the first and heaviest punishment."[19] So while both problems of enmity and bondage are clearly found in Scripture, the right order is imperative: bondage to Satan *is a result of* enmity with God.

WHO IS SATAN?

If Satan is the "ruler of this world" (John 12:31) and "the whole world lies in the power of the evil one" (1 John 5:19), what is the nature of his reign and how does he exercise such power? Surely it is not by sheer force, for every ruler reigns through means, and only Yahweh is omnipotent. Our answers to these questions are significant, for they not only further define the problem but also point forward to *how* Christ overcomes Satan's dominion. Below, I will demonstrate biblically that the means by which Satan rules are (1) tempta-

---

18. Brunner speaks of "divine wrath as the objective correlate to human guilt. This, then, is the obstacle which alienates us from God. . . . This separation is an objective reality, the two-fold reality of human guilt and divine wrath" (*The Mediator*, 445).

19. Bavinck, *Sin and Salvation in Christ*, 170.

tion, (2) deception, and (3) accusation, all of which result in (4) death. These are the "works" (1 John 3:8) or "schemes" (Eph 6:11) of the devil.

Although these different schemes of Satan are often discussed individually, the following unifying point has been overlooked: each of these "schemes" is an instrument of Satan's *words*. Satan rules through his word—his tempting, deceiving, accusing word—which leads to death. The idea of ruling by speaking is actually basic to nearly every concept of kingship: a king speaks and his will is done.

The Bible, of course, portrays God's reign in such a way. Genesis 1–2 depicts God as a king who reigns through his word (cf. Psalm 93); he speaks and creation comes into existence. The contrast could not be any starker. God rules over his kingdom of light through his truthful word that brings life; Satan rules over his kingdom of darkness through his deceitful word that brings death. As speech-act theory has been appropriated by many to better understand how God acts by speaking, a similar approach is needed to better understand the way in which Satan exercises power over sinners.[20]

One preliminary point is necessary. When speaking of Satan's "power," one must acknowledge that only Yahweh is omnipotent (Isa 40:25–26), which therefore makes an absolute dualism impossible. In other words, Satan's power is exercised under the sovereignty of God and is used for his purposes. Just as God used the wicked nation of Assyria to bring *his* judgment on Israel (Isa 10:5–19), and just as he permitted Satan to afflict Job (Job 2:6), so does God grant Satan power for his greater purposes.

THE TEMPTER

Satan is "the tempter" (Matt 4:3; 1 Thess 3:5), and he accomplishes his purposes through his tempting word. It is this tactic that perhaps most broadly defines his activity. From Adam and Eve in Eden to Jesus in the wilderness, Satan seeks to entice, allure, and persuade humans to sin against God. Clinton Arnold observes that "Satan's ability to prevent or sever a relationship with God comes through his power to incite sin and transgression."[21]

This point significantly reveals the limits to Satan's power, for he cannot force humans to sin. Blocher explains that "temptation is suggestion. It

---

20. Vanhoozer briefly discusses the metaphysics of Satan as a liar in *Remythologizing Theology: Divine Action, Passion, and Authorship* (Cambridge: Cambridge University Press, 2010), 342–46. Following Augustine's notion of evil as the privation of the good, Vanhoozer says Satan's deception is "the corruption of true communicative agency." He concludes that "Satan can do nothing with words but gesture vainly. Satan's communicative agency is nothing but a conjuring trick with words" (ibid., 344).

21. Clinton Arnold, "Satan, Devil," *DLNT*, 1080.

requires, in order to succeed, to find what it cannot create: the formally free consent of the human person."[22] It is sin that is ultimately destructive in this world (Rom 6:23), so Satan schemes in order to draw humans into self-destructive decisions. Since he cannot force people to sin, he tempts them by making sin seem attractive.

THE DECEIVER

Satan is "the deceiver of the whole world" (Rev 12:9), and he wields his power through his deceptive word. He is "a liar and the father of lies" (John 8:44); he "disguises himself as an angel of light" (2 Cor 11:14) and "has blinded the minds of the unbelievers" (4:4). Deception, in fact, has been his tactic since the beginning (11:3). When Satan seeks to attack the church, he does so by inspiring deviant teaching—"teachings of demons" (1 Tim 4:1)—requiring churches to "test the spirits to see whether they are from God" (1 John 4:1; cf. 2:18–27). In opposition to the Lord who speaks truth (Isa 45:19), Satan accomplishes his purposes through deceit.

THE ACCUSER

Satan is "the accuser" (Rev 12:10), and he achieves his purposes through his accusatory word. "Satan" is the transliteration of the Hebrew שָׂטָן, which literally means adversary, but in its usual legal context, the corresponding verb שָׂטַן means to stand against or accuse.[23] As Rev 12:9–11 reveals, the war that Satan wages against Christ and his people is essentially a legal battle.[24] The drama of Scripture, says Horton, is a "courtroom drama."[25] Zechariah 3:1–5 previews a scene to this courtroom drama, with the high priest Joshua standing in filthy garments "and Satan [שָׂטָן] standing at his right to accuse [שָׂטַן] him" (3:1). The opening of Job provides a glimpse into a heavenly courtroom, where Satan presents himself before the Lord in order to accuse Job and the integrity of his devotion.

The surprising feature of this aspect of Satan's power (considering that he is the "deceiver") is that he is right in his accusation, appealing to the holy standard of God's justice. His weapon is the law; for as soon as it is broken, he is ready to accuse the guilty and call for the proper sanctions according to God's justice. As Beale explains, "The devil's accusation is based on the correct presupposition that the penalty of sin necessitates a judgment of spiritual

---

22. Blocher, "*Agnus Victor*," 82.
23. Ibid.
24. Beale, *Revelation*, 661–63.
25. Horton, *The Christian Faith*, 408.

death and not salvific reward."[26] Luther, based on a similar understanding, offered surprising counsel in response to Satan's accusations:

> When the devil throws our sins up to us and declares we deserve death and hell, we ought to speak thus: "I admit that I deserve death and hell. What of it? Does this mean that I shall be sentenced to eternal damnation? By no means. For I know One who suffered and made a satisfaction in my behalf. His name is Jesus Christ, the Son of God. Where he is, there I shall be also."[27]

It should be noted, however, that although Satan appeals to God's righteous standard, he is far from a righteous accuser. His name itself (שָׂטָן) is a reminder that he is not only an accuser but a slanderer. He accuses not for the sake of upholding justice to the praise of a holy God but as part of his mission to "steal and kill and destroy" (John 10:10).

THE DEATH-BRINGER

Satan's tempting, deceiving, and accusing words ultimately lead to death. He "has the power of death" (Heb 2:14), and it is to this end that all of Satan's activity is aimed (John 10:10).[28] Satan's power of death, however, must be understood properly. The statement in Heb 2:14 about Satan having "the power of death" must be interpreted within its immediate context, as well as the broader biblical witness regarding death. First and foremost, only God has the ultimate power over life and death (1 Sam 2:6). As noted above, any "power" that Satan has is given by God. Second, Satan's "power of death" in Heb 2:14 is revealed in the next verse to be a power that works through inciting the *fear* of death. In other words, Satan's "power of death" is exercised by subjecting sinners to slavery through fear of their sins' consequences.

Furthermore, to speak of Satan bringing sinners directly to death is to leave out the key piece of the puzzle—sin. Spence observes that "a victory perspective tends to consider death as an entity in its own right."[29] This idea is precarious, however, for death "came into the world through human sin and is ultimately related to divine judgment. . . . Sin and death are thus inextricably linked."[30]

---

26. Beale, *Revelation*, 659.

27. Martin Luther, *Luther: Letters of Spiritual Counsel* (ed. and trans. Theodore Tappert; Vancouver, BC: Regent College Publishing, 2003), 85.

28. Bolt says the power of death is Satan's "major function" and laments the fact that it is regularly overlooked or denied in demonology ("Towards a Biblical Theology of the Defeat of the Evil Powers," in *Christ's Victory Over Evil: Biblical Theology and Pastoral Ministry* [ed. Peter Bolt; Nottingham, UK: Apollos, 2009], 67).

29. Spence, *The Promise of Peace*, 17.

30. Ibid.

Paul develops this connection between sin and death most clearly in Romans 5–7. Death came into the world through sin, "and so death spread to all men because all sinned" (Rom 5:12), a passage that reveals a clear sin–death connection (cf. 6:16, 23; 7:11, 13). Sin results in death, however, because God's judgment follows human sin and brings about condemnation (5:16). Death is not merely an alien force that God must defeat, but is a penalty from God himself and comes about as a consequence of enmity with God. First Corinthians 15 corroborates this understanding of the sin–death connection, which is why, according to Spence, "Paul's twofold question 'Where, O death, is your victory? Where, O death, is your sting?' must not be interpreted rhetorically. It does have an answer and Paul provides it. 'The sting of death is sin and the power of sin is the law.'"[31] One does not defeat death simply by defeating death. Death must be defeated by overcoming sin.

GENESIS 3

All of the aspects of Satan's power over sinners are present in Genesis 3, which "can be taken as a paradigm for the way the devil has worked throughout the ages."[32] By opposing God, the *speaking* serpent sets up a contest between the word of God and the word of Satan. Whose word will Adam and Eve obey? Whose reign will they serve? Through his word, Satan tempts ("You will be like God" 3:5) and deceives ("You will not surely die" 3:4), leading to accusation—though not his own—("The woman whom you gave . . ."; "The serpent deceived me . . ." 3:12–13) and resulting in the curse of death (3:19).

HOW DOES CHRIST CONQUER SATAN?

Here—in turning from problem to solution, from sin to atonement—we come to the heart of the matter. Scripture is clear that Christ *does* in fact defeat Satan (Col 2:15; Rev 12:10), but *how* does he accomplish this victory? That is the question and, as we will see, its answer will provide the key to reconciling *Christus Victor* and penal substitution.[33]

---

31. Ibid.

32. Bolt, "Towards a Biblical Theology of the Defeat of the Evil Powers," 69.

33. I are not the first, of course, to explain the "how" of Christ's victory over Satan. The means of victory is the thrust of Gregory's fishhook theory ("An Address on Religious Instruction," 301), Augustine's mouse-trap theory (*Sermon 263*, 220), and more recently Boyd's version of *Christus Victor* ("*Christus Victor* View," 37). Rene Girard, and those who follow him, argue that Christ defeats evil by exposing it (*I See Satan Fall Like Lightning* [New York: Orbis, 2001]; Heim, *Saved from Sacrifice*).

Thus far I have identified (1) the relation between the two problems—bondage to Satan *as a result of* enmity with God—and (2) the nature of Satan's dominion as an unrightful king who rules through his tempting, deceiving, accusing, death-bringing word. My answer to the "how" question will begin by responding to each of these. First, in response to the (properly ordered) problem—enmity with God leading to bondage to Satan—Christ liberates people from Satan by dealing with the root problem, their enmity with God. Second, because Satan attacks through his tempting, deceitful, and accusing word, God defeats him through his obedient, truthful, and suffering Word. Third, though often overlooked, Jesus' humanity is especially significant for his victory. Fourth, essential to Christ's victory is the role of Christians between the cross and the consummation.

A FITTING REMEDY: CHRISTUS VICTOR THROUGH PENAL SUBSTITUTION

The order of the human sinful condition (bondage to Satan *because of* enmity with God) is determinative for the order of its remedy (*Christus Victor through* penal substitution). Theologically, if the God-human problem is the root of the Satan-human problem, then resolving the former must be the means of dealing with the latter. How is Satan defeated? Christ defeats Satan (*Christus Victor*) by removing the ground of Satan's accusation, which Jesus does by paying the penalty for sin (penal substitution). God's justice has been upheld and sinners have been forgiven: he is both the "just and the justifier" (Rom 3:26). Ferguson summarizes the way in which Christ's work toward humanity relates to his victory over Satan:

> A comprehensively biblical exposition of the work of Christ recognizes that the atonement, which terminates on God (in propitiation) and on man (in forgiveness), also terminates on Satan (in the destruction of his sway over believers). And it does this last precisely because it does the first two.[34]

Christus Victor apart from penal substitution, therefore, does not explain why Christ had to suffer in order to conquer Satan and actually undermines the victory. According to Kathryn Tanner, "*Christus Victor* is not a model

---

34. Ferguson, "*Christus Victor et Propitiator*," 185; cf. Packer, who asserts, "Christ's death had its effect first on God, who was hereby propitiated (or, better, who hereby propitiated himself), and only because it had this effect did it become an overthrowing of the powers of darkness" ("What Did the Cross Achieve?," 20); Stott concurs, saying, "Is not his payment of our debts the way in which Christ has overthrown the powers? By liberating us from these, he has liberated us from them" (*The Cross of Christ*, 234–35).

at all in that it fails per se, to address the question of the mechanism of the atonement. Christ is battling the forces of evil and sin on the cross but how is the battle won?"[35] In the words of Garry Williams, "Deny penal substitution and *Christus Victor* is hamstrung."[36] Or, as Cole says, "*Christus Victor* needs the explanatory power of substitutionary atonement."[37]

How does the theological argument above (*Christus Victor* through penal substitution) fare with Scripture? There are several passages that strongly suggest such a synthesis.

HEBREWS 2:5–18

Hebrews 2:5–18 is a theological whirlwind on the person and work of Christ. Jesus is the second Adam (2:5–10), the high priest (2:17), the pioneer of salvation (2:10), and a true "flesh and blood" human (2:14, 17). Through his death, he has achieved victory over the devil (2:14), propitiation for sins (2:17), and a moral influence (2:18). Most important, the author of Hebrews declares that Christ took on flesh so "that through death he might destroy the one who has the power of death, that is, the devil" (2:14). What is it about this death that could make it the cause of victory?

The key is that "death" in the broader context of Hebrews is Christ's sacrificial, once-for-all, sin-bearing death (Heb 9:26–28). Even closer in context, 2:17 says that Christ came "to make propitiation for the sins of the people," which he would do by offering his own blood (9:14). Therefore, based on the context of 2:14, we can say that it is the *sacrificial and propitiatory* death of Jesus that defeats the devil.

But how does this cultic interpretation of Christ's death shed light on the way in which the devil is defeated? Christ's sacrificial death purifies the sinner's conscience (Heb 9:14) so that "we now have confidence to enter the holy places by the blood of Jesus" (10:19). This boldness before God that flows from forgiveness of sin is the antithesis of the "fear of death," which the devil wields as his weapon (2:15). Moreover, the word for "destroy" in 2:14 (καταργήσῃ) also includes the meaning of depriving something of its power (Rom 3:31; Eph 2:15).[38] Christ destroys the devil by depriving him of his power through his sacrificial death, thereby reconciling sinners and restoring his design for the world.

---

35. K. Tanner, *Christ the Key* (Cambridge; Cambridge University Press, 2010), 253.
36. Williams, "Penal Substitution," 187.
37. Cole, *God the Peacemaker*, 184.
38. Koester, *Hebrews*, 231.

COLOSSIANS 2:13–15[39]

Colossians 2:13–15 contains two of Scripture's most explicit statements on penal substitution (2:13–14) and *Christus Victor* (2:15), and as we will see, they are intricately related. Beginning with *Christus Victor*, 2:15 is the foundational text for almost every understanding of Christ's victory over evil. It is straightforward: Christ "triumphed" over the powers. The triumph, however, is also, according to earlier in the verse, a disarming. How does Christ disarm and therefore triumph over the powers? Colossians 2:13–14 provides the explanatory power, the "how" of *Christus Victor*: Christ disarmed and triumphed over the powers through his debt-cancelling, trespass-forgiving, legal-demand-satisfying death on the cross. Smeaton captures the essence of this exchange:

> When the guilt of sin was abolished, Satan's dominion over God's people was ended; for the ground of his authority was the law which had been violated, and the guilt which had been incurred. This points the way to the right interpretation, for all the mistakes have arisen from not perceiving with sufficient clearness how the triumph could be celebrated on His cross.[40]

Although Col 2:13–15 is not a full explanation of penal substitution, there is a great emphasis on the legal framework of Christ's death and his accomplishment of cancelling a debt on behalf of sinners. Christ's military victory over the powers (triumphing) is therefore achieved through forensic means (cancelling a debt).

REVELATION 12:9–11

Revelation 12:11 declares that Satan has been "conquered . . . by the blood of the Lamb."[41] Like the passages above, the context explains *how* Christ's blood effects the downfall of Satan. Although the final outcome is presented in military language ("conquered"), the entire conflict is depicted essentially as a legal battle, a courtroom drama climaxing in the removal of Satan's authority to rightfully accuse.[42] Satan is the legal prosecutor ("the accuser of our brothers," 12:10) who seeks to condemn the guilty for breaking the law. Satan's

---

39. This section builds on our previous exegesis of Col 2:13–15. See above, pp. 112–19.
40. Smeaton, *The Apostles' Doctrine of the Atonement*, 307–8.
41. This passage is speaking more broadly of Christ's victory on the cross as it is implemented by Michael and his angels in heaven (Rev 12:7–9) and by Christians on earth (12:10–11). My focus here is on the nature of the foundational event of Christ's victory on the cross; the other aspects are discussed elsewhere. See above, pp. 124–26; and below, p. 211.
42. Caird, *Revelation*, 155; Beale, *Revelation*, 661–62.

accusatory power, however, is undone because Christ has freed Christians from their sins (1:5–6), thereby removing the basis of Satan's accusations.

Furthermore, referring to Christ's death by "the blood of the Lamb" is to employ the language of sacrificial, substitutionary atonement. Therefore, John speaks of Christ's sacrificial death (cultic) as conquering the devil (military) by removing Satan's power of accusation (legal). Although this passage does not spell out penal substitution in its fullness, it appeals to the two primary categories of penal substitution (cultic and legal) to describe the means by which Christ achieves victory.

1 JOHN 3:4–9

First John 3:8 is a classic text for *Christus Victor*: "The reason the Son of God appeared was to destroy the works of the devil." Yet reading this verse in context reveals that victory does not exclude substitutionary atonement but depends on it. This victory statement comes in the broader context of a discussion on sin—namely, that "sin is lawlessness" and Christ "appeared to take away sins" (3:4–5). I. Howard Marshall claims that "sin" in this context is not "a matter of isolated peccadilloes" but a rebellion against God and siding with the devil.[43] It should not be a surprise, therefore, that Christ appeared "to take away sins" (3:5) and "to destroy the works of the devil" (3:8). Matthew Jensen identifies the parallel structure here, concluding that the parallels "should be read together and interpreted in the light of each other. Thus the destruction of the devil's work should be understood in terms of taking away sins."[44]

Furthermore, although "taking away sins" does not explicitly say how Christ does so, there are clear echoes from John's gospel of "the Lamb . . . who takes away the sin of the world" (John 1:29), as well as the description within 1 John of Christ's death as "the propitiation for . . . the sins of the whole world" (1 John 2:2; 4:10; cf. 1:7).[45] Lastly, 3:8 does not simply say that Christ came to "destroy the devil" but rather to "destroy *the works* of the devil" (italics mine). This distinction is significant because the work of the devil is ultimately to entice sinners; he schemes at tempting humans to sin, deceiving them regarding the effects of sin, and accusing them of the guilt of

---

43. I. Howard Marshall, *The Epistles of John* (NICNT; Grand Rapids: Eerdmans, 1978), 176–77.

44. Matthew Jensen, "'You Have Overcome the Evil One': Victory Over Evil in 1 John," in *Christ's Victory Over Evil*, 114.

45. Marshall, *Epistles of John*, 177; Stephen Smalley, *1, 2, 3 John* (rev. ed.; WBC; Nashville: Nelson, 2007), 148–49.

sin. Through his sacrificial death, Jesus undoes the effects of sin and thereby destroys the works of the devil.

SUMMARY: CHRISTUS VICTOR THROUGH PENAL SUBSTITUTION

"*Christus Victor* through penal substitution" broadly summarizes the thrust of the above passages. There are, however, two specific patterns that must be made explicit. First, each passage presents a straightforward statement of Christ's victory over Satan along with a forensic and/or cultic explanation of the means of such a victory. The basic point is that penal substitution and *Christus Victor* are doing different things in the explanation of the cross. Penal substitution explains the means of victory—or how Christ's suffering disarms Satan—and is usually depicted in cultic and/or forensic terms. *Christus Victor* explains the effect of Christ's accomplishment on Satan and his dominion over sinners. These two aspects of the atonement need not compete, for they are explanations of different (yet inseparable) aspects of Christ's work.

Second, contrary to Aulén, who argues for Christ's victory over and against God's justice,[46] the forensic framework of these passages (especially Col 2:13–15 and Rev 12:9–11) makes clear that Christ's victory was achieved in accordance with God's standard of justice.[47] In other words, Jesus' conquest of the devil was not *just* a victory; it was a *just victory*.

This combination of justice and victory is well attested in the Old Testament, which speaks regularly of God's throne being established in righteousness and his victories won in justice (Ps 97:2). In the New Testament, Jesus speaks of Satan's defeat as judgment (a justice concept; John 12:31; 16:11), and God is praised specifically for the way in which justice is upheld in victory (Rev 19:1–2). Romans 3:21–26, although not specifically addressing victory, repeatedly makes the point that Christ's propitiatory work on the cross was "to show God's righteousness . . . so that he might be just and the justifier" (3:25–26). Ovey captures the importance of this issue:

> If we exclude justice considerations from God's victory, what is the nature of that victory? It becomes difficult to see it as resting on anything other than power: it would not necessarily be immoral, of course, but it would at best be amoral. . . . The risk here is that God's victory becomes naked power. Justice concepts tell us not merely that God is powerful, but that his reign is just.[48]

---

46. Aulén, *Christus Victor*, 90–91.
47. God acting in accordance with justice should not be construed in terms of God being bound by an external standard or law. Rather, because the law is a reflection of God's character, acting in accordance with justice is God being true to himself.
48. Ovey, "Appropriating Aulén?" 309.

The need for justice in victory, therefore, leads to the synthesis of *Christus Victor* and penal substitution for which I have been arguing—"justice concepts pose the questions that penal substitution is designed to answer, and which victory . . . on its own does not."[49]

We have seen that penal substitution is the "how" of *Christus Victor*. It has not been argued, however, that penal substitution alone provides all the resources for explaining how Christ is victorious over Satan. There are other essential aspects of Christ's work that are inseparable from penal substitution that have often been neglected and yet are at the heart of Christ's way of conquering. The next three points draw out each of these aspects.

COUNTERATTACK: THE WORKS OF SATAN AND THE WAYS OF JESUS

From the beginning of creation, God has been on a mission to establish his reign over all the earth. Humanity fell, Satan launched his own kingdom project, and God's kingdom mission has now become a redemptive one that requires counterattacks to the thwarts of Satan. Satan is the serpent-king who rules through temptation, deception, and accusation—resulting in death. Jesus is the servant-king who rules through obedience, truth, and suffering—resulting in life.

SATAN THE TEMPTER—JESUS THE OBEDIENT ONE

From the wilderness (Matt 4:1–11) to Gethsemane (26:36–46) and ultimately on the cross (27:40), Jesus resisted the temptation of the devil and chose obedience to the Father. The obedience of Christ, as a counterattack to Satan's temptation, is incredibly important for understanding Christ's atoning work; Murray even calls it "*the* unifying or integrating principle" of atonement theology.[50]

The well-known distinction between Christ's active and passive obedience is helpful, but must be appropriated carefully.[51] Such a distinction should *not* be used to designate certain periods of Christ's life to one aspect or the other (i.e., that Christ's life is active obedience and his death is passive obedience). It may, of course, be used to describe different *aspects* of Christ's work. Christ was active in everything he did, including his suffering, and yet he was also always submissive to the Father's will.[52] The proper use of

---

49. Ibid., 310.

50. Murray, *Redemption Accomplished and Applied*, 19, italics mine.

51. See ibid., 20–24.

52. According to Bavinck, "Christ's active and passive obedience . . . always coincide in the life and death of Christ" (*Sin and Salvation in Christ*, 395); cf. Murray, *Redemption Accomplished and Applied*, 21.

the active/passive distinction is in line with what Bavinck calls the twofold demand of God's law: "For the demand posed by God to fallen humanity was twofold: one, that humans would keep the law perfectly, and two, that they would redress the violation of it by punishment."[53] Christ's obedience therefore meets this twofold demand by fulfilling the law (active obedience) and paying the penalty for breaking the law (passive obedience). As Murray puts it, "He perfectly met both the penal and the preceptive requirement of God's law."[54]

The obedience of Christ has two specific payoffs for this discussion. First, as Horton claims, "the Reformed emphasis on the active obedience reconciles the Greek emphasis on recapitulation and incarnation and the Latin emphasis on the cross."[55] While the cross is central and penal substitution is crucial for understanding it, neither makes any sense unless understood as the culmination of Christ's obedient life. Christ humbled himself in the incarnation, "becoming obedient to the point of death, even death on a cross" (Phil 2:8). Obedience holds Christ's life and death together in his work of atonement (Rom 5:19), thereby avoiding the mistake of locating atonement solely in the cross.[56] Furthermore, active obedience affords a link between penal substitution and *Christus Victor*, for "Christ brings not only forgiveness, but fulfillment of God's design for an obedient humanity."[57]

SATAN THE DECEIVER—JESUS THE TRUE AND FAITHFUL WITNESS

While Satan is "the deceiver" who "has blinded the minds of the unbelievers" (2 Cor 4:4), Jesus is "the truth" (John 14:6) who "gives light to everyone" (1:9). Jesus overcomes the deceiver through truth, exposing his testimony as false, his assertions as lies, and his promises as empty. Jesus is the "faithful and true witness" (Rev 3:14), who in the courtroom drama defeats Satan as the legal prosecutor by exposing his testimony as false. Satan was wrong. Adam did die, and all of his progeny with him. Whereas Satan reigns by his deceitful word, Jesus reigns by bearing witness to the truth (John 18:37). As Satan continues to lie in order to entice sinners into slavery, Jesus declares: "I am . . . the truth" (14:6), and "the truth will set you free" (8:32).

---

53. Bavinck, *Sin and Salvation in Christ*, 394.
54. Murray, *Redemption Accomplished and Applied*, 22.
55. Horton, *Lord and Servant*, 173; cf. Boersma, *Violence, Hospitality, and the Cross*, 126 n. 45.
56. Among others, Calvin and Bavinck warned against such a mistake (Calvin, *Institutes*, 2.16.5; Bavinck, *Sin and Salvation in Christ*, 378).
57. Horton, *The Christian Faith*, 502.

SATAN THE ACCUSER—JESUS THE PROPITIATOR

Christ's removal of Satan's accusatory power is the most deadly blow delivered to Satan and is the central thrust of penal substitution's explanatory power regarding Christ's victory. Although this aspect of Christ's work has been mentioned several times thus far, its importance demands a more comprehensive treatment.

Satan is "the accuser," standing against sinners to accuse them day and night before God (Zech 3:1; Rev 12:10). As a courtroom prosecutor, he zealously declares, "Guilty!" and calls for the proper penalty for sin—death. This scheme of Satan is his strongest because, unlike his other schemes, its power is derived from the fact that it appeals to God's holy standard: the law. In other words, Satan is right. Sinners are guilty before the holy Judge and fully deserve the sentence of God's wrath and, ultimately, death. Sinners are left speechless, unable to rebut Satan's accusations and therefore are enslaved by his accusatory power.

This is where Jesus comes in and changes everything. As Satan spouts his accusatory words—wielding the weapon of the law—they are rendered ineffective on Jesus, who is without sin and fulfills the law in every aspect of his life.[58] For this reason, Jesus alone can say, Satan "has no claim on me" (John 14:30). In a shocking move, the sinless, law-keeping, covenant-fulfilling Messiah voluntarily takes on himself the sins of the world, bearing the curse of the law—namely, God's wrath and, ultimately, death (2 Cor 5:21; Gal 3:13).

As the propitiation for sins (Rom 3:25), Jesus bears the wrath of God in the place of sinners, thereby satisfying God's justice and expiating the sin of God's people. As a result of Christ's penal substitutionary atonement, Satan's accusatory word is silenced, for his weapon of the law has been rendered ineffective by Christ's covenant-keeping life and curse-bearing death. When Paul asks the rhetorical question, "Who shall bring any charge against God's elect?" (Rom 8:33), the answer is clearly no one (including Satan), for those who have put their faith in Christ are declared innocent (Rom 8:1). Satan's being "thrown to the earth" in Rev 12:9 (cf. Luke 10:17–20), therefore, means that Satan has been disbarred from the heavenly court because his accusatory word is rendered ineffective by Christ's substitutionary death.[59]

Before Christ's death, God permitted Satan a place in the heavenly court to accuse God's people (Job 1:6–12; 2:1–6; Zech 3:1–2). Beale explains further how Satan has lost his place because of Christ's death: "The death and

---

58. The law, of course, is not an abstract code of conduct external to God but a reflection of God's own eternal character.

59. Krodel, *Revelation*, 243.

resurrection of Christ have banished the devil from this privilege formerly granted him by God, because . . . the devil no longer had any basis for his accusations against the saints, since the penalty that they deserved and that he pleaded for had at last been exacted in Christ's death."[60] By satisfying God's justice and forgiving sinners, Christ has rendered Satan's accusation ineffective and therefore broken the accusatory power that Satan held sway over Christians.

SATAN THE DEATH-BRINGER—JESUS THE LIFE-GIVER

Although death is ultimately a result of God's judgment on sin (Rom 6:23), Satan has an instrumental role in leading the sinner down this path. It is in this sense that he is a "murderer" (John 8:44) and has "the power of death" (Heb 2:14). Yet while Satan comes "to steal and kill and destroy," Jesus came so that sinners "may have life and have it abundantly" (John 10:10). Sin is the ground of Satan's dominion, and by atoning for sin, Jesus undoes Satan's authority to reign. In light of the sin–death connection, Jesus reverses the decay of death by undoing the effects of sin. Paul can mock death itself ("O death, where is your sting?" 1 Cor 15:55) because Jesus, by atoning for sin, has removed the sting of death. He conquered death through death (Heb 2:14), and where the reign of death is defeated, the reign of grace prevails, which results in life (Rom 5:21).

THE WEAPONRY OF THE BATTLE (EPHESIANS 6:10–20)

Finally, in discussing Christ's counterattacks to the schemes of the devil, it is fitting to mention briefly the significance of Paul's discussion of the "armor of God" in Eph 6:10–20. Although this passage is addressing Christians' role in resisting the devil, it can be applied to Christ as the head of the body and the commander of God's army. In other words, this passage can offer a perspective on *how* Christ and Christians wage war on, and ultimately defeat, Satan.

First and foremost, this battle is not against "flesh and blood," but rather against the "spiritual forces of evil" (Eph 6:12). The outcome, therefore, is not to be determined by which side has the greatest strength or power (if it were, there would be no real battle since God is omnipotent). Rather, this war is advanced on the spiritual battlefield of sin and salvation, bondage and liberation. The weaponry of this battle is not the strength of arms or valor of swords but truth, righteousness, the gospel of peace, faith, salvation, the word of God, prayer, and perseverance (6:14–18). These are the weapons with

---

60. Beale, *Revelation*, 659.

which Christ defeated the devil and has invited his followers to use as they continue to "stand against the schemes of the devil" (6:11).

VICTORIOUS HUMANITY

Aulén's insistence that Christ's victory on the cross was a *divine* victory has invited one of the most common and devastating critiques: he leaves little room for the humanity of Christ in his victory; that reflects a departure from Chalcedonian Christology.[61] Unfortunately, Aulén is not alone. Many Reformers attributed Christ's victory almost completely to his divinity;[62] according to Horton, "there has been a widespread tendency throughout church history to treat the victory of Christ almost exclusively as the victory of *God*."[63]

Scripture, however, is clear that Christ's humanity is essential to both his sacrificial and victorious work. The one mediator between God and humanity is "the *man* Christ Jesus" (1 Tim 2:5, italics mine). According to Hebrews, Christ's humanity is essential for both his victory over the devil (Heb 2:14) and his work of propitiation (2:17). The most comprehensive way the significance of Christ's humanity is expressed in Scripture is through Christ's work as a second Adam (Rom 5:12–21): "For as by one *man*'s obedience the many were made sinners, so by the one *man*'s obedience the many will be made righteous" (Rom 5:19, italics mine).

Jesus is fully God and fully man, but as the second Adam, he has been given an essentially human task. He comes as a human to set right what Adam set wrong, recapitulating in himself the story of Adam and Israel but keeping the covenant where previously broken (e.g., Matt 4:1–11). Christ had to be fully human in order to save us because he had to fulfill the covenant as our representative, make an offering of atonement on our behalf, and bear the penalty in our place. "This meritorious human life," says Horton, "is not merely a necessary prerequisite of a sacrificial offering, but part and parcel of that offering."[64]

A proper understanding of the humanity of Christ makes room for the place of the Holy Spirit in the work of Christ. Whereas much of the tradi-

---

61. Eugene Fairweather, "Incarnation and Atonement: An Anselmian Response to Aulén's *Christus Victor*," *CJT* 7 (1961): 167–75; John McIntyre, *St. Anselm and His Critics: A Re-Interpretation of the* Cur Deus Homo (Edinburgh: Oliver and Boyd, 1954), 197–99; Ovey, "Appropriating Aulén?" 317–23.

62. For Luther's view, see David Brondos, *Fortress Introduction to Salvation and the Cross* (Minneapolis: Fortress, 2007), 93.

63. Horton, *Lord and Servant*, 171, italics his.

64. Ibid., 172.

tion has attributed Christ's power to his divinity, Spence argues instead that the emphasis should be on the "Spirit-empowered human nature of Christ."[65] Jesus is, after all, the Messiah—the Spirit-anointed son of David who as a human mediates God's royal power to all the earth. The intention here is clearly not to create a Nestorian dichotomy between the humanity and divinity of Christ but rather, as Gunton says, to recognize that the cross is "a divine victory only because it is a human one."[66]

THE VICTORY OF CHRIST AND CHRISTIANS

God defeats Satan through Christ *and* Christians. Although Christ's work on the cross is a finished work, it still needs to be appropriated and consummated. Christians do not contribute to Christ's atoning, victorious work, but they are taken up into it. Paul says to his fellow Christians, "the God of peace will soon crush Satan under *your* feet" (Rom 16:20, italics mine). John writes to his "young men" that "*you* have overcome the evil one" (1 John 2:13–14, italics mine). Beyond using the "armor of God" (Eph 6:10–20), the clearest statement on *how* Christians are involved in the defeat of Satan comes in Rev 12:11: "And they [Christians] have conquered him [Satan] by the blood of the Lamb and by the word of their testimony, for they loved not their lives even unto death." As argued above, the army of Christians defeats Satan in the same way that their commander does—through witness and suffering.[67]

First, Christians conquer Satan through their witness ("the word of their testimony," Rev 12:11) to Christ's victorious achievement on the cross. While Satan's power of accusation has been curtailed, deception remains as a crucial scheme. A Christian witness to the truth of Christ's victory, therefore, exposes Satan's lies as false and portends his inevitable demise. Second, Christians take part in Christ's victory by sharing in his victorious suffering ("for they loved not their lives even unto death," Rev 12:11). Although paradoxical, it should be no surprise that a kingdom established by suffering would be advanced through similar means (1 Pet 5:6–11).

WHEN DOES CHRIST'S VICTORY DECISIVELY HAPPEN?

While the doctrine of the atonement is often understood as the answer to the question of what Christ accomplished on the cross, theologians have for-

---

65. Spence, *The Promise of Peace*, 34.
66. Gunton, *Actuality of Atonement*, 59.
67. See above, p. 126.

tunately regained an appreciation for the breadth of Christ's atoning work. Others, however, have pushed further, shifting the point of gravity from the cross to another "moment" in the work of Christ. Below, I will briefly survey the strongest arguments scholars have offered for the centrality of different "moments" in Christ's atoning work (i.e., the incarnation, the life of Jesus, the resurrection, and the ascension). My argument is that while all the work of these scholars is to be appreciated for providing a more holistic understanding of Christ's atoning work, the centrality of the cross in Scripture and theology is undeniable. The "when" question also provides further clarity on "how" Christ accomplishes victory.

INCARNATION

According to Thomas Torrance, the incarnation—more specifically the moment of the hypostatic union—is the defining moment of Christ's atoning work. Torrance's theology is greatly shaped by Gregory's famous maxim, "The unassumed is the unhealed," which for Torrance seems to automatically mean that the act of assuming *is* the healing.[68] In the person of Christ, argues Torrance, God has brought together humanity and divinity; "it is that oneness which constitutes the heart of the atonement."[69] Torrance can therefore say, "Jesus IS the atonement," and all of Christ's atoning work, including his death, is an outworking of this hypostatic union.[70]

LIFE

The life of Jesus is a popular option as the central aspect of Jesus' atoning work. The most theologically developed argument can be found in Tanner's work, which presents a "grace perfecting nature" schema where union with God is the goal and the incarnation is the means.[71] Tanner weighs in on atonement debates, arguing for an "incarnational view of the atonement" that takes a radical departure from traditional descriptions of the cross in an attempt to do justice to the criticisms of feminist and womanist theologians.[72] Tanner rejects any forensic or propitiatory understanding of the cross, rede-

---

68. Torrance asserts, "In his incarnation Christ not only took upon himself our physical existence from God, but in taking it into himself he at the same time healed it" (*Atonement*, 70).
69. Ibid., 75.
70. Ibid., 94; cf. 125.
71. Kathryn Tanner, *Jesus, Humanity and the Trinity: A Brief Systematic Theology* (Edinburgh: T&T Clark, 2001); Tanner, *Christ the Key*.
72. Tanner, *Christ the Key*, 262. Chapter 6 in *Christ the Key*, titled, "Death and Sacrifice," is a reprint of her previous essay, "Incarnation, Cross, and Sacrifice: A Feminist-Inspired Reappraisal," *AThR* 86 (2004): 35–56.

fines sacrifice in terms of communal harmony, and argues for the incarnation as "the primary mechanism of atonement."[73] Though there is much overlap with Torrance's emphasis on the unity of divinity and humanity in Christ, Tanner goes further by arguing for Christ's life over against his death:

> Death itself is an impediment to the mission and not its positive culmination in any obvious way. If the mission of God continues, that is despite Jesus' death and not thanks to it . . . it would presumably have been better—a sign of the kingdom's having already come—if the suffering and crucifixion of Jesus had never happened.[74]

RESURRECTION

Although many contend for the centrality of the resurrection for the atonement,[75] Weaver's "Narrative *Christus Victor*" is the most relevant for this discussion, arguing for "victory through the resurrection."[76] Weaver's argument "is grounded in assumptions of nonviolence" and therefore rules out any possibility of God willing Jesus' death.[77] In the grander vision of Jesus' mission to make present the reign of God, his death is no longer interpreted positively as salvific but negatively as opposition. Similar to Tanner's claims, people are not saved *by* the cross but *from* the cross (suffering, evil, etc.).

According to Weaver, the death of Jesus, like that of Martin Luther King Jr., was "a by-product of faithfulness rather than the goal of his actions."[78] How, then, does Jesus achieve this nonviolent victory? Weaver asserts, "His death did not pay off or satisfy anything. On the contrary, it was a product of the forces of evil that opposed Jesus and opposed the reign of God. The real saving act of and in and with Jesus is his resurrection."[79]

ASCENSION

Faustus Socinus seems to have separated atonement from Christ's death altogether, interpreting the cross only as an example and locating Christ's sacrificial atonement in his postresurrection/ascension offering of himself in

---

73. Tanner, *Christ the Key*, 252.
74. Ibid., 251.
75. Sherman, *King, Priest, and Prophet*, 116–68; Thomas Finger, "*Christus Victor* and the Creeds: Some Historical Considerations," *MQR* 72 (1998): 43; Robert Jenson, *The Triune God*, vol. 1 of *Systematic Theology* (New York: Oxford University Press, 1997), 179–206.
76. Weaver, "Narrative *Christus Victor*," 20; cf. idem, *The Nonviolent Atonement*, 21–22.
77. Ibid., 25.
78. Ibid.
79. Ibid., 26.

heaven.[80] Although Socinus' argument has not been adopted because of his largely unorthodox theology, David Moffitt has recently come to a similar conclusion, at least in regards to the book of Hebrews.[81] In his view, atonement is not accomplished on the cross but in the heavenly sanctuary, where the resurrected Jesus presents his life (not death) on the altar: "His death sets the sequence into motion. His appearance before God in heaven effects atonement."[82]

THE CENTRALITY OF THE CROSS IN THE ATONEMENT

While Christ's incarnation, life, resurrection, and ascension are all vastly important, Scripture presents Christ's death on the cross as the high point of his atoning work. By declaring, "It is finished" just before his death (John 19:30), Jesus himself revealed the definitive nature of his crucifixion. When the New Testament authors sought to explain Christ's setting right what sin had made wrong, they regularly recalled Christ's cross (e.g., Eph 2:16) or blood (e.g., 1 Pet 1:19), both representing his death: "Christ *died* for our sins" (1 Cor 15:3, italics mine); "we were reconciled to God by the *death* of His Son" (Rom 5:10, italics mine). Paul could summarize his entire message under the simple yet powerful phrase, "Christ crucified" (1 Cor 1:23; cf. 2:2). Furthermore, the fact that the Old Testament sacrificial system and especially Isa 52:13–53:12 provide the primary background for understanding Christ's atoning work surely suggests an emphasis on the death of Christ as the slain Lamb and Suffering Servant.

The centrality of the cross in Christ's atoning work has certainly been maintained throughout most of church history. According to McKnight, "When a theory of atonement contends that the cross is not central to the plan of the atoning God, that theory dissolves the only story the church has ever known."[83] Athanasius says the cross is "the very centre of our faith."[84] While the early church did indeed put a great emphasis on Christ's incarnation, when talking specifically about Christ's atoning and victorious work, they consistently emphasized the cross. Even amidst the various disagreements

---

80. Faustus Socinus, *De Jesu Christo servatore: Hoc est cur & qua ratione Iesus Christus noster seruator sit* (Rakow: Rodecius, 1594); idem, *Prælectiones theologicæ* (Racoviæ: Sebastiani Sternacii, 1609). For a partial translation of Socinus in English, see Alan Gomes, "Faustus Socinus' *De Jesu Christo Servatore*, Part III: Historical Introduction, Translation and Critical Notes" (PhD diss., Fuller Theological Seminary, 1990).

81. David Moffitt, *Atonement and the Logic of Resurrection in the Epistle to the Hebrews* (Leiden: Brill, 2011).

82. Ibid., 294.

83. McKnight, *A Community Called Atonement*, 61.

84. Athanasius, *On the Incarnation* (Crestwood, NY: St. Vladimir's Seminary Press, 2002), 48.

throughout church history on atonement theories, whether Anselm, Abelard, or Aulén, they all agreed that it was primarily at the cross where Christ accomplished his task.

To call the cross *central*, of course, does not mean that it is the *only* moment of the atonement but the most definitive. The cross must be *central* but never *solo*. Calvin demonstrates well the centrality of the cross within a holistic understanding of Christ's atoning work:

> How has Christ abolished sin? . . . He has achieved this for us by the whole course of his obedience. . . . In short, from the time when he took on the form of a servant, he began to pay the price of liberation in order to redeem us. Yet to define salvation more exactly, Scripture ascribes this as peculiar and proper to Christ's death.[85]

Each of the scholarly contributions regarding Christ's incarnation, life, resurrection, and ascension are helpful inasmuch as they seek to recover a holistic understanding of Christ's atoning work and clarify the specific role that each plays. We need an expansive view that encompasses all of Christ's work, but in a way that still upholds the particular significance of each aspect through integration, order, and rank. The cross must be upheld as central within the broader framework of Christ's work *and* related to each of these various aspects. How, then, does each aspect relate to the cross?

Christ's incarnation and hypostatic union are foundational for the doctrine of atonement, for as the early church recognized, Jesus had to be fully God and fully human to be the Mediator and Savior. Christ's life and ministry are essential to his atoning work. He not only paid the penalty for our breaking the law, but he kept the covenant and fulfilled the law in our place as well. Furthermore, Christ's preaching, healings, exorcisms, and miracles clarify that Christ's intentional journey to the cross was not an end in and of itself but the means by which he would accomplish his greater goal of reconciling sinners, defeating evil, and establishing God's kingdom on earth as it is in heaven.[86]

Relating Christ's death to his resurrection is of particular importance, for these two are often paired together (Mark 8:31; Rom 6:5) and as such are said to be "of first importance" (1 Cor 15:3–4). If Jesus is the crucified and

---

85. Calvin, *Institutes*, 2.16.5.
86. For a helpful discussion of Jesus' miracles, healings, and exorcisms in relation to the kingdom of God, see Clinton Arnold, "The Kingdom, Miracles, Satan, and Demons," in *The Kingdom of God*, 153–78. According to Arnold, "Jesus' miracles, exorcisms, and healings declare the intervention of God's kingly rule in a world marred by sin, disease, and the oppressive mayhem of the Evil One" (ibid., 159).

resurrected one, is it justifiable to uphold the centrality of the cross for the atonement? Calvin helpfully argues that while Christ's death and resurrection are inseparable,[87] their roles must be differentiated in Christ's broader work of salvation:

> Therefore we divide the substance of our salvation between Christ's death and resurrection as follows: through his death, sin was wiped out and death extinguished; through his resurrection, righteousness was restored and life raised up, so that—thanks to his resurrection—his death manifested its power and efficacy in us.[88]

The cross and the resurrection are doing different things, and it is more appropriate to speak of the cross as the center of atonement. "Without the shedding of blood there is no forgiveness of sins" (Heb 9:22).

The cross is central for the doctrine of the atonement because, as P. T. Forsyth says, "it is there that He atones, expiates, reconciles."[89] Propitiation, redemption, conquering Satan, and so forth form the language of the doctrine of the atonement, and all of these are accomplished primarily on the cross. The centrality of the cross in the doctrine of atonement does not take away from the resurrection but rather seeks to locate its significance in the right place. First Corinthians 15 holds cross and resurrection together, but Christ's death is "for our sins" (15:3), whereas his resurrection is the beginning of the new creation (15:20).

What, then, of the resurrection? The typical Reformed answer has been that the resurrection is the vindication of Christ. The resurrection *reveals* that Jesus is who he said he was and accomplished what he said he would. As Bavinck says, "The resurrection is . . . the 'Amen!' of the Father upon the 'It is finished!' of the Son."[90]

Yet while the resurrection as the vindication of Christ is to be affirmed, there is more. First, if Jesus has not been raised from the dead, the salvation that he achieved cannot be applied to those in need (cf. 1 Cor 15:17). As Denney says, "There can be no salvation from sin unless there is a living Saviour: this explains the emphasis laid by the apostle on the resurrection. But the Living One can only be a Saviour because He has died: this explains

---

87. Calvin asserts, "So then, let us remember that whenever mention is made of his death alone, we are to understand at the same time what belongs to his resurrection. Also, the same synecdoche applies to the word 'resurrection': whenever it is mentioned separately from death, we are to understand it as including what has to do especially with his death" (*Institutes*, 2.16.13).

88. Ibid., 2.13.16.

89. Peter Forsyth, *God the Holy Father* (London: Independent, 1957), 40–41.

90. Bavinck, *Sin and Salvation in Christ*, 442; see also Bavinck's eightfold meaning of the resurrection (ibid.).

the emphasis laid on the Cross."[91] If all the benefits of salvation are found in union with Christ, it is the *resurrected* Christ to whom we are united.

Second, and most important, Christ's resurrection is the beginning of the new creation.[92] Although this aspect of the resurrection is clear in Scripture (1 Cor 15:35–49; Eph 1:15–23; Col 1:15–20; Rev 3:14), the contemporary preoccupation with interpreting Christ's resurrection in terms of apologetics (he really did rise from the dead) has clouded the primary theological meaning: the end-time resurrection of the dead has begun in the resurrected body of Jesus. The resurrection constitutes Christ as the "life-giving Spirit" (1 Cor 15:45). In sum, although the cross and resurrection are inseparable and both are at the center of God's salvation in Christ, the doctrine of atonement specifically hinges on Christ's death on the cross.

The ascension of Christ is also important for his atoning work. The atoning value of Christ's offering in the heavenly sanctuary (Heb 9:11–14) need not be set against Christ's atoning accomplishment on the cross but rather can show the breadth of Christ's atoning work—specifically, just as in the Old Testament sacrificial system, atonement was a process.[93] Furthermore, it is the resurrected and ascended Christ who sends his Spirit to continue his work on earth. *"Pentecost belongs to the atonement,"* says Torrance, "for the presence of the Spirit is the actualisation amongst us of the new or redeemed life."[94] As Horton says, "The pouring out of 'the blood of the new covenant' (Matt 26:28) is the presupposition of the pouring out of the Spirit at Pentecost (Acts 2)."[95]

Christ's second coming is also included because it is the consummation of his atoning-victorious work on the cross, not a further step beyond it. In sum, the atonement achieved by Christ encompasses his work from conception to consummation and centers on his crucifixion.

WHY DOES CHRIST CONQUER SATAN?

Christ does not defeat Satan for the sake of defeating Satan. In other words, his accomplishment of victory serves an even greater aim—reconciliation. Although penal substitution deals with enmity with God and *Christus Victor* with bondage to Satan, both address barriers to the great need of reconciliation between God and the world. Gregory of Nazianzus said the aim of

---

91. Denney, *The Death of Christ: Its Place and Interpretation in the New Testament*, 123.

92. Ridderbos, *Paul*, 57; N. T. Wright, *The Resurrection of the Son of God* (Christian Origins and the Question of God; Minneapolis: Fortress, 2003), 712.

93. For a constructive proposal of the role of the ascension in Christ's atoning work, see Farrow, *Ascension Theology*, chap. 7, titled, "Ascension and Atonement."

94. Torrance, *Atonement*, 178, italics his.

95. Horton, *Lord and Servant*, 177.

Christ's victory was "that God, by overcoming the tyrant, might set us free and reconcile us with Himself through His Son."[96]

Aulén could not be any clearer about the goal of reconciliation: "It cannot be too strongly emphasized that when this [the defeat of the devil] has been done, atonement has taken place; for a new relation between God and the world is established by the fact that God has delivered mankind from the powers of evil, and reconciled the world to Himself."[97] The goal of reconciliation with God, therefore, helps reconcile Christ's propitiatory and victorious work, for both remove barriers in service of the greater aim of a reconciled people in a renewed kingdom.

Reconciliation, however, proves to be penultimate, for the ultimate aim of God's atoning work is—as in all things—the glory of God. If God created people for his glory (Isa 43:6–7), chose Israel for his glory (Jer 13:11), redeemed Israel from slavery in Egypt for his glory (Exod 14:4, 18), sustained Israel in the wilderness for his glory (2 Sam 7:23), and restored Israel from exile for his glory (Ezek 36:22–23), is it any surprise that he has atoned for sin and defeated Satan *for his glory*? This is precisely the testimony of Scripture: propitiation, redemption, forgiveness, and victory are all ultimately for the glory of God, for his name's sake, and "to the praise of his glorious grace" (Eph 1:6; cf. Exod 14:4, 18; Ps 79:9; Isa 43:25; 48:9–11; Rom 3:24–25; 1 John 2:12). Gunton helpfully points out that worship is at the heart of the sacrificial system itself.[98] Christ's sacrifice is not only atonement for sin but an offering of praise to God, which then enables others to join in their created purpose of worshiping God.[99]

All the different dimensions of Christ's work on the cross, especially penal substitution and *Christus Victor*, are united as they serve the greater aim of reconciliation for the glory of God.

BEYOND RHETORIC

I have answered the question of how penal substitution and *Christus Victor* relate, but one controversial issue remains: Is one the central or overarching metaphor for the doctrine of the atonement? I will provide a taxonomy of how this question has been answered and then briefly suggest a way forward.

---

96. Quoted in Aulén, *Christus Victor*, 42.

97. Ibid., 30. It is for this reason that Aulén demands that Christ's victory does belong in the doctrine of atonement. According to Aulén, Christ's victory is "atonement in the full sense of the word, for it is a work wherein God reconciles the world to Himself, and is at the same time reconciled" (ibid., 4).

98. Colin Gunton, "Atonement: The Sacrifice and the Sacrifices, From Metaphor to Transcendental?" in *Father, Son, and Holy Spirit: Essays Toward a Fully Trinitarian Theology* (New York: T&T Clark, 2003), 181–200.

99. Ibid., 198.

According to its advocates, penal substitution is the "center,"[100] "heart,"[101] "foundation,"[102] "basis,"[103] "big idea of atonement,"[104] "anchor of all other theories,"[105] "essence of the atonement,"[106] "normative soteriological theory,"[107] " *modus operandi* of the different understandings of the cross,"[108] and the "underlying principle present in all the other [theories] and the factor that makes them cohere."[109] *Christus Victor* proponents, no less grandiose, claim Christ's victory as "the ultimate metaphor,"[110] "a unifying framework,"[111] "dominant,"[112] "the heart,"[113] "the central content for the whole interpretation of the Cross,"[114] or "the central theme in atonement theology, around which all the other varied meanings of the cross find their particular niche."[115]

I fear that claims such as "this theory is *the center* of the atonement" are too often rhetorical ways of basically saying, "My theory is better than yours," rather than well-thought-out theological explanations that seek to uphold and integrate the essential aspects of penal substitution and *Christus Victor*. I agree wholeheartedly that penal substitution is central. But what does that mean? And what does it imply about *Christus Victor*? It could be taken positively, that *Christus Victor* is the scope of the atonement, or negatively, where it is merely pushed to the periphery.

The confusion can be seen in the different approaches by Blocher and Boersma. Both theologians agree that penal substitution is the "how" of *Christus Victor*, yet based on this synthesis, each makes an opposite claim. For Boersma, penal substitution is "subordinate" because it is a means toward

---

100. Blocher, "The Sacrifice of Jesus Christ," 31; Cole, *God the Peacemaker*, 238; Stott, *The Cross of Christ*, 159; Williams, "Penal Substitution," 187; Jeffery, Ovey, and Sach, *Pierced for Our Transgressions*, 211.

101. Donald Bloesch, *Jesus Christ: Savior and Lord,* vol. 4 of *Christian Foundations* (Downers Grove, IL: InterVarsity Press, 1997), 158; Blocher, "The Sacrifice of Jesus Christ," 31.

102. Jarvis Williams, "Violent Atonement in Romans: The Foundation of Paul's Soteriology," *JETS* 53 (2010): 583.

103. Blocher, "The Sacrifice of Jesus Christ," 31.

104. Demarest, *The Cross and Salvation*, 171.

105. Schreiner, "Penal Substitution View," 93.

106. Letham, *The Work of Christ*, 174–75.

107. Mark Chan, "The Gospel and the Achievement of the Cross," *ERT* 33 (2009): 30.

108. I. Howard Marshall, *Aspects of the Atonement: Cross and Resurrection in the Reconciling of God and Humanity* (London: Paternoster, 2007), 51.

109. I. Howard Marshall, "The Theology of the Atonement," in *The Atonement Debate*, 50.

110. Boersma, *Violence, Hospitality, and the Cross*, 181.

111. Boyd, "*Christus Victor* View," 24.

112. Finger, "*Christus Victor* and the Creeds," 32.

113. N. T. Wright, *Evil and the Justice of God* (Downers Grove, IL: InterVarsity Press, 2006), 95.

114. Karl Heim, *Jesus, the World's Perfecter: The Atonement and the Renewal of the World* (Edinburgh: Oliver and Boyd, 1959), 70–71.

115. Wright, *Evil and the Justice of God*, 114.

an end—*Christus Victor*.[116] Blocher, however, claims that penal substitution is primary because *Christus Victor* depends on it as the means.[117] The recognition of instrumentality should not lead to the conclusion that either penal substitution or *Christus Victor* is subordinate, but to the idea that they play different roles. Proponents on each side need to stop talking past one another, replace reductionistic rhetorical claims with holistic theological explanations, and recognize that each aspect plays an essential role in Christ's atoning work.

Conceptually, penal substitution addresses the "how" of the atonement and *Christus Victor* addresses its effects on Satan, demons, and death—both within the broader aim of reconciliation for the glory of God. Inasmuch as *Christus Victor* is seen not merely as a victory over Satan but as the establishment of God's kingdom—the recovery of its Edenic reality and commission—*Christus Victor* provides the broader context for penal substitution. Metaphorically, perhaps we can tease out the "heart" language. If penal substitution is the *heart* of the atonement, pumping life into the other aspects, then perhaps *Christus Victor* is the *heel*, crushing the head of the serpent and reversing the curse barring humanity from its Edenic kingdom. But let us not forget that we need a heart *and* a heel. A heart without a heel stands no chance in battle. But a heel without a heart has no power to conquer.

This is not to say that there is no place for priority in the doctrine of the atonement, but that it must be given in a way that upholds and integrates the other aspects of Christ's work.[118] As I have argued above, Paul's "of first importance" (1 Cor 15:3) demonstrates that there is a place for dogmatic rank in theology.[119] Therefore, with these qualifications, and based on the above groundwork of defining the relationship between penal substitution and *Christus Victor* (i.e., *Christus Victor* through penal substitution, where the latter focuses on the means and the former on the effects toward Satan), I believe that the place of priority belongs to penal substitution in at least two senses.

First, in terms of theology, penal substitution has priority because of its explanatory power. Since systematic theology engages explicitly with doctrine

---

116. Boersma, *Violence, Hospitality, and the Cross*, 182.

117. Blocher, "The Sacrifice of Jesus Christ," 31.

118. According to James Beilby and Paul Eddy, this pursuit is in line with the tradition of the church: "From the patristic period onward, Christian theologians generally acknowledged the rich diversity of ways that the manifold aspects of the atonement can be expressed while at the same time they sought to identify the heart of the atonement—the primary image that most powerfully and completely expresses the crux of the saving work of Christ" ("Atonement," in *Global Dictionary of Theology* [ed. W. Dyrness and Veli-Matti Kärkkäinen; Downers Grove, IL: InterVarsity Press, 2008], 85).

119. For my discussion on dogmatic rank, see above, pp. 187–89.

and theory, the fact that penal substitution explains the "how" of *Christus Victor* gives it priority in the doctrine of the atonement. Penal substitution does not do everything, but it provides insight into many of the other aspects of the atonement, especially *Christus Victor.*

Second, penal substitution has priority in the sense that it is more directly related to the God-human relationship, which is the special focus of creation, fall, and redemption. In other words, penal substitution *directly* addresses the root problem between God and humanity (wrath/guilt), whereas *Christus Victor* addresses the *derivative* problem of human bondage to Satan. However, I must once again be clear that maintaining this type of priority for penal substitution does not imply that it does everything. Penal substitution is necessary but not sufficient for understanding the doctrine of the atonement in its entirety.

CONCLUSION

How, then, does this synthesis of "*Christus Victor* through penal substitution" help answer the primary question of the relationship between the kingdom and the atonement? The answer, in short, is that penal substitution and *Christus Victor* (in their proper relation) are *both* essential for a right understanding of the coming of God's kingdom.

The connection between *Christus Victor* and the kingdom of God is rather obvious, for divine victory is ultimately royal victory and aimed at God's kingdom. The first sentence of Aulen's *Christus Victor* further reveals the link: "The central idea of *Christus Victor* is the view of God and the Kingdom of God as fighting against evil powers ravaging in mankind."[120] It is only natural, then, that scholars have appealed to *Christus Victor* as the way to connect the kingdom and the cross. The cross is the victory of the kingdom of God. Yes, this is certainly right. Christ is victorious on the cross, and his victory is none other than the establishment of the kingdom of God. But what I have demonstrated in this chapter is that the victory of the cross is dependent on the vicarious suffering of the Christ. Therefore, a fuller connection of the kingdom and the cross acknowledges not only Christ's victory but Christ's means of victory—penal substitution. On the cross, Jesus bears the penalty of sin by taking the place of sinners, thereby defeating Satan and establishing God's kingdom on earth. There are at least three reasons why penal substitution must be attached to *Christus Victor* in connecting kingdom and cross.

---

120. Aulén, *Christus Victor*, ix; see also Gunton, who says, "Notions of victory and the reassertion of God's kingly authority belong together" (*Actuality of Atonement*, 59).

First, if our sins have not been dealt with, the coming of God's kingdom is *not* good news. Christ's victory over Satan, demons, and death is a glorious accomplishment, but if our sins have not been atoned for, we remain under God's wrath and outside his kingdom. *Christus Victor* alone implies that humans are merely victims of Satan who must be rescued from the problem rather than sinners who are part of the problem. But even with Satan defeated and shackles broken, only those whose penalty has been paid can enter the kingdom of God as citizens.

Second, penal substitution is crucial to the story line of Scripture culminating in the kingdom of God. *Christus Victor* has recently been acclaimed by scholars who have sought to recover the eschatological framework of the cross. From Gen 3:15 forward, the victory of Christ is crucial to the story. Yes, but this argument is usually made in opposition to penal substitution, which is depicted as the result of abstract, ahistorical systematic theology. The problem with this interpretation is that penal substitution should be understood within the story of redemption. The concepts of sin and the wrath of God are woven throughout the unfolding story of Israel, culminating in the song of the Suffering Servant (Isa 52:13–53:12). As Cole says, "If we remove the wrath theme from Scripture, its storyline is eviscerated."[121]

Third, penal substitution is imperative for upholding the justice of the coming of God's kingdom. The irony is thick: though the kingdom of God and a penal substitutionary interpretation of the cross both appeal strongly to the concept of justice, the two are rarely associated.[122] The Old Testament declares, "Righteousness and justice are the foundation of his [the Lord's] throne" (Ps 97:2), and it prophesies that the Messiah will establish and uphold his kingdom with justice and righteousness (Isa 9:7; cf. Ps 89:14; Jer 23:5). So if the kingdom is established with justice, where is the justice of God revealed in its fullest? It is revealed at the cross, where Jesus was "put forward as a propitiation . . . to show God's righteousness" (Rom 3:24–25).[123]

---

121. Cole, *God the Peacemaker*, 75; cf. D. A. Carson, "The Wrath of God," 11.

122. Part of the problem is that there are different views of justice—namely, whether it is restorative or retributive. As mentioned above (see p. 177 fn. 10), I believe justice must be retributive to truly be restorative. More specifically, in the words of Boersma, "Restorative justice can only function if we are willing to include the notion of punishment" (*Violence, Hospitality, and the Cross*, 10).

123. Moo explains the thrust of this statement within the context of Rom 3:21–26: "This clause makes an important contribution to our understanding of the 'internal' mechanism of the atonement, explaining the necessity of Christ's propitiating work in terms of the requirements of God's holy character. God's past restraint in punishing sins with the full measure of punishment they deserved calls into question his fair and impartial 'justice,' or holiness, creating the need for this justice to be 'satisfied,' a satisfaction rendered by the propitiatory sacrifice of Christ" (*The Epistle to the Romans* [NICNT; Grand Rapids: Eerdmans, 1996], 238).

In other words, penal substitution upholds God's justice in atonement, which is an essential aspect of the coming of the kingdom of God. The coming of the kingdom, including the defeat of evil and the salvation of his people, must be in accordance with God's just character.

So, to the *Christus Victor* proponents I would say that if you lose penal substitution, you lose the kingdom. Boersma expresses the danger of over-looking the wrath of God in order to emphasize the love of God: "Ironically, by cutting out the wrath and violence of God in an attempt to hold up his love, we end up losing the very thing we are trying to safeguard: the restoration of shalom and, therefore, the enjoyment of the presence of God's love."[124] And to the penal substitution advocates, I would say that the justice of God has broader application than the justification of individuals. Gunton appropriately cautions against a bifurcation of justification and justice:

> It is a mistake to interpret the legal metaphor in a narrowly personalistic or individualistic way. The centre is undoubtedly the justification of sinners, but they are seen in the context of a world which stands or falls with them. . . . The justification of the sinner, then, is only a part of what is meant by the justice of God, which is conceived more broadly in terms of the transformation of the whole created order, as the outcome—as we shall see—of God's loyalty to his creation.[125]

The establishment of the kingdom will be a great victory that is accomplished with justice. Hence, we need an accomplishment that is both victorious and upholds the justice of God: *Christus Victor* through penal substitution.

In this chapter we have seen the royal nature of the atonement. In the next chapter we will see the cruciform nature of the kingdom. This will round out the picture of Jesus the crucified king.

---

124. Hans Boersma, "Violence, the Cross, and Divine Intentionality: A Modified Reformed View," in *Atonement and Violence* (ed. John Sanders; Nashville: Abingdon, 2006), 65.
125. Gunton, *Actuality of Atonement*, 102–3.

CHAPTER NINE

KINGDOM: THE CRUCIFORM REIGN OF GOD

IN THE PREVIOUS three chapters, we have seen how the coming kingdom of God shapes the meaning of Christ's person and work. Jesus is king on the cross—atoning for sin, defeating evil, and thereby establishing his kingdom on earth. Yet, having previously asserted that kingdom and cross are mutually enriching, what can we now say about the kingdom in light of the cross? In this chapter, I will set forth a constructive proposal for the way in which the kingdom is shaped by the cross: it is the *cruciform* kingdom of God. After presenting a case for the cruciform kingdom of God, I will advance the argument in dialogue with Jürgen Moltmann, focusing primarily on the doctrine of God and briefly on the way in which God advances the kingdom in between the already and not yet.[1]

THE CRUCIFORM KINGDOM OF GOD

Christ's atoning death on the cross creates a community of ransomed people living under the reign of God (Rev 1:6). Inasmuch as God's kingdom is founded by the cross, entered through the cross, and shaped by the cross, it is truly a cruciform kingdom. Thus far I have focused on the *establishment*

---

1. Moltmann is the primary interlocutor here because he has incorporated the kingdom of God into systematic theology as much as or more than any other theologian. He also presents the kingdom in a way that integrates rather than excludes the cross. Regarding the focus on the doctrine of God, although the expansive motif of the kingdom should shape all of theology (as shown in the two previous chapters), it is especially relevant for the doctrine of God because the kingdom of God is first and foremost a statement about God—that he is king.

of God's kingdom through the cross of Christ, but here I seek to identify the *nature* of the kingdom and the way in which it *advances*. God's kingdom is a cruciform kingdom, and just as it was established and inaugurated by Christ's death and resurrection, it will be advanced by God's reign over and through those whom the Spirit unites to Christ in his death and resurrection.

LUTHER'S THEOLOGY OF THE CROSS

The cruciform nature of God's kingdom draws on a concept latent throughout this project—namely, Luther's theology of the cross.[2] Against the backdrop of medieval scholasticism, Luther derided "theologians of glory" who sought to know God apart from his revelation in the gospel of Jesus Christ, claiming instead that "*CRUX sola est nostra theologia*" ("the cross alone is our theology").[3] The cross is the standard by which all theology must be judged. Luther's theology of the cross therefore focuses on the cross as God's chosen means not only of *salvation* but also of *revelation*.[4] It is through the lowly means of Christ's death on a cross that God saves sinners *and* reveals himself. Walther von Loewenich summarizes five essential aspects of Luther's theology of the cross:

1. The theology of the cross as a theology of revelation stands in sharp antithesis to speculation.
2. God's revelation is an indirect, concealed revelation.
3. Hence God's revelation is recognized not in works but in suffering.
4. This knowledge of God who is hidden in his revelation is a matter of faith.
5. The manner in which God is known is reflected in the practical thought of suffering.[5]

How, then, does the theology of the cross apply to the kingdom of God? Luther hinted toward the idea of a cruciform kingdom, speaking of "the

---

2. For Luther's clearest explication of the theology of the cross, see his *Heidelberg Disputation* (1518), *LW* 31:35–70, especially theses 19–24. For a commentary on this text, see Gerhard Forde, *On Being a Theologian of the Cross: Reflections on Luther's Heidelberg Disputation, 1518* (Grand Rapids: Eerdmans, 1997). For the historical and theological background, see Alister McGrath, *Luther's Theology of the Cross: Martin Luther's Theological Breakthrough* (New York: Blackwell, 1985).

3. Luther, *Operationes in Psalmos* (1519–1521), *WA* 5:176. Gerhaard Forde makes the important point that in Luther's theology of the cross, "cross" is "shorthand for the entire narrative of the crucified and risen Jesus" (*On Being a Theologian of the Cross*, 1).

4. Tomlin, *The Power of the Cross*, 115.

5. Walther von Loewenich, *Luther's Theology of the Cross* (Minneapolis: Augsburg, 1976), 22. This summary is agreed upon by McGrath (*Luther's Theology of the Cross*, 149–50) and Tomlin (*The Power of the Cross*, 114).

kingdom of faith in which the cross of Christ holds sway"[6] and noting that in the "kingdom (which consisteth in nothing else but strengthening the weak, healing the sick, and encouraging the faint hearted), the holy cross shall not be wanting."[7] According to Luther, the fact that "this King does not rule without the cross"[8] means "this must be a kingdom of the cross."[9] Unfortunately, Luther never discussed the cruciform nature of the kingdom in a sustained manner, which is precisely what I will do, seeking to extend Luther's theology of the cross into the doctrine of God's kingdom.

THE CRUCIFORM NATURE OF THE KINGDOM

There are five primary ways that the way a theology of the cross applies to the kingdom of God. First, the theology of the cross reveals the great continuity between the means of establishing and advancing God's kingdom on earth. According to Graham Tomlin, "The fundamental insight lying at the heart of the theology of the cross is the notion that God acts in the present in continuity with the way he has acted in the past."[10] Therefore, continues Tomlin, "Just as God revealed himself, and worked salvation through a crucified Messiah, God still works in and through what is to conventional human understanding, weak, powerless and apparently irrational rather than through what is strong, powerful and reasonable."[11] This paradox is evident in the apostles' ministry of power through weakness (1 Cor 1:26–31), which was patterned after Christ himself (1 Cor 1:18–25).[12] This continuity between Christ and Christians, however, is not based solely on the imitation of Christ but first and foremost on union with Christ.[13] The crucified-resurrected Christ advances his kingdom through those whom the Spirit unites to Christ in his death and resurrection.

Second, the theology of the cross clarifies the *hidden* nature of the kingdom of God during "this present age." Central to the theology of the cross is the idea that "the revelation of God in the cross lies *abscondita sub contrario*,

---

6. Luther, *Operationes in Psalmos* (1519–1521), *WA* 5:128.

7. Martin Luther, "John X. From the 11th to the 16th verses, inclusive," in *A Selection of the Most Celebrated Sermons of M. Luther and J. Calvin: Eminent Ministers of the Gospel, and Principal Leaders in the Protestant Reformation* (New York: Bentley, 1829), 111.

8. Luther, *The Interpretation of the Second Psalm* (1532), *LW* 12:66.

9. Luther, *Lectures on Zechariah* (1526), *LW* 20:304.

10. Tomlin, *The Power of the Cross*, 278.

11. Ibid., 279.

12. Ibid., 11–107; Timothy Savage, *Power through Weakness: Paul's Understanding of the Christian Ministry in 2 Corinthians* (New York: Cambridge University Press, 1996).

13. This appeal to union with Christ follows J. Todd Billings critique of "incarnational ministry" in *Union with Christ: Reframing Theology and Ministry for the Church* (Grand Rapids: Baker Academic, 2011), 123–67.

so that God's strength is revealed under apparent weakness, and his wisdom under apparent folly."[14] Remarkably, the idea that the cross is *abscondita sub contrario* overlaps with the way the Reformers spoke of the kingdom of God as "concealed under the cross and under opposition" (*tectum sub cruce et sub contrario*).[15] In short, between Christ's resurrection and return, the kingdom of God is hidden beneath the cross. It is, as the Reformers called it, the "servant's form of the kingdom."[16] This second point overlaps with the first, for the power-through-weakness of the king and his kingdom is also power-hidden-by-weakness to a sinful world.

Third, God's kingdom will not be hidden by the cross forever, a statement that requires a distinction between the kingdom in "this present age," where God's rule is hidden, and "the age to come," where it is unveiled. The Reformers referred to this distinction as the kingdom of grace (*regnum gratiae*) and the kingdom of glory (*regnum gloriae*).[17] I can, however, speak of both forms of the kingdom as cruciform, although in different ways. The kingdom is *forever* cruciform in the sense that the cross ever remains the basis of the kingdom and will always shape its existence. In *this age* (between the first and second coming of Christ), however, the kingdom is cruciform particularly in the sense that it is advanced by taking up the cross and hidden to fallen eyes beneath the weakness and foolishness of the cross. As Horton says, "Like its Lord during his earthly ministry, at present this kingdom has a glory that lies hidden under the cross."[18]

Fourth, although the royal power of God is hidden under the cross, it is recognized by faith for those who have eyes to see. In the theology of the cross, the emphasis on divine revelation is inseparable from human faith. The cross, which is foolishness and weakness to the world, is revealed by God and received by people in faith to be the wisdom and power of God. Only by faith (not by worldly wisdom) can the kingdom be perceived in the cross of Christ.

Finally, the theology of the cross reveals that the coming of the kingdom does not render the cross obsolete. Certainly, Christ's sacrificial death is "once for all" and need not be repeated (Heb 9:26), but it forever remains the

---

14. McGrath, *Luther's Theology of the Cross*, 165.
15. Quoted in Jürgen Moltmann, *Theology of Hope: On the Ground and the Implications of a Christian Eschatology* (trans. James Leitch; Minneapolis: Fortress, 1993), 223. Calvin, for example, says that "although [Jesus] now reigns in heaven and earth, yet hitherto his reign is not clearly manifested, but, on the contrary, is obscurely hidden under the cross, and is violently assailed by enemies" (*Calvin's Commentaries,* comment on 2 Timothy 4:1).
16. Heinrich Heppe and Ernst Bizer, *Die Dogmatik der evangelisch-reformierten Kirche* (Neukirchen: Moers, 1958), 557; quoted in Moltmann, *The Trinity and the Kingdom*, 210.
17. Horton, *Lord and Servant*, 258.
18. Horton, *The Christian Faith*, 537.

founding act and shaping factor for the kingdom and therefore reaches into eternity. The risen and ruling Christ still appeared to his disciples bearing the scars from the cross (John 20:27), and John's glimpse into the throne room of heaven centered on Christ reigning *as the Lamb who was slain* (Rev 5:6).

JÜRGEN MOLTMANN: A CRUCIFORM KINGDOM WITHOUT A KING?

Jürgen Moltmann is one of the most significant contemporary systematic theologians and is especially relevant to this discussion because he (1) integrates the kingdom of God into his theology as much as any systematic theologian and (2) argues specifically for the cruciform nature of the kingdom.[19] At the heart of Moltmann's theology is the hope of the kingdom found in the resurrection of the crucified Christ. The way these themes have developed and fit together in Moltmann's thought can be seen in some of his most influential works.

Theology of Hope (1964) was Moltmann's first major contribution, arguing that "from first to last, and not merely in the epilogue, Christianity is eschatology"—an eschatology that gives hope for the kingdom, grounded in the resurrection of the Messiah.[20] In *The Crucified God* (1972), Moltmann continues his focus on hope for the kingdom, but with a drastic shift in emphasis to the cross of Christ as the revelation of God (better, God's becoming) and therefore the answer to the question of theodicy.[21] Moltmann's radicalized theology of the cross[22] demands a complete rethinking of the kingdom, and especially its God, which Moltmann fully provides in

---

19. For an overview of Moltmann's theology, see Richard Bauckham, *Moltmann: Messianic Theology in the Making* (Basingstoke, UK: Pickering, 1987); idem, *The Theology of Jürgen Moltmann* (Edinburgh: T&T Clark, 1995). Moltmann himself says Bauckham's two books are "far and away the best accounts of my theology" ("The World in God or God in the World?" in *God Will Be All in All: The Eschatology of Jürgen Moltmann* [ed. Richard Bauckham; Edinburgh: T&T Clark, 1999], 35). For an extensive bibliography on Moltmann up to 2001, see James Wakefield, *Jürgen Moltmann: A Research Bibliography* (Lanham, MD: Scarecrow, 2002). For more recent engagements with Moltmann, see Tim Chester, *Mission and the Coming of God: Eschatology, the Trinity and Mission in the Theology of Jürgen Moltmann and Contemporary Evangelicalism* (PTM; Waynesboro, GA: Paternoster, 2006); Poul Guttesen, *Leaning into the Future: The Kingdom of God in the Theology of Jürgen Moltmann and in the Book of Revelation* (PTMS; Eugene, OR: Pickwick, 2009); Sung Wook Chung, *Jürgen Moltmann and Evangelical Theology: A Critical Engagement* (Eugene, OR: Pickwick, 2012).
20. Moltmann, *Theology of Hope*, 16.
21. Jürgen Moltmann, *The Crucified God: The Cross of Christ as the Foundation and Criticism of Christian Theology* (New York: Harper & Row, 1974).
22. Moltmann himself acknowledges taking the theology of the cross far beyond Luther (ibid., 72–73). For a comparison of Luther and Moltmann on the theology of the cross, see Burnell Eckardt Jr., "Luther and Moltmann: The Theology of the Cross," *CTQ* 49 (1985): 19–28.

The Trinity and the Kingdom (1981). Below, I will present an overview of his understanding of the cruciform kingdom followed by an evaluation and constructive proposal.

The Kingdom of God according to Moltmann

The kingdom of God is a constant throughout Moltmann's writings, but rarely does he pause to explain its content. In one such instance he says, "The eschatological fulfilment of the liberating lordship of God in history is termed the kingdom of God. The Greek word *basileia* can mean both the actual rule of God in the world, and the universal goal of that divine rule."[23] In this definition, Moltmann grants much flexibility in his understanding of the kingdom. Its meaning can be as specific as "the liberating lordship of God"[24] or as broad as "God in all things and all things in God."[25] Certainly, he uses the kingdom to capture the thrust of his entire project: "The kingdom of God is the perfected *perichoretic* unity of God and world."[26]

Timothy Harvie attempts to summarize Moltmann's definition of the kingdom, but says the *importance* of the kingdom for Moltmann's theology is only matched by the *ambiguity* of its actual content.[27] There are, however, at least two basic themes that prevail in Moltmann's understanding of the kingdom. First, the kingdom is thoroughly christological, especially in Jesus' embodiment of the kingdom toward the poor and oppressed.[28] Second, in the words of Poul Guttesen, "the kingdom functions as a symbol of hope for humanity."[29]

The Cruciform Nature of the Kingdom according to Moltmann

The cruciform nature of the kingdom is a key feature of Moltmann's theology. Based on the Reformation idea that the kingdom is hidden in its opposite, Moltmann writes, "The coming lordship of God takes shape here in

---

23. Jürgen Moltmann, *The Church in the Power of the Spirit: A Contribution to Messianic Ecclesiology* (Minneapolis: Fortress, 1993), 190.
24. Ibid.
25. Jürgen Moltmann, *Sun of Righteousness, Arise! God's Future for Humanity and the Earth* (Minneapolis: Fortress, 2010), 32.
26. Ibid., 30.
27. Timothy Harvie, *Jürgen Moltmann's Ethics of Hope: Eschatological Possibilities for Moral Action* (Burlington, VT: Ashgate, 2009), 39–40. Harvie says this ambiguity is because "Moltmann uses the notion of the Kingdom of God as a foil to critique societal situations he perceives to be unjust, but less often will employ the notion to offer a positive description of the content of the Christian hope" (ibid., 40).
28. Ibid., 54.
29. Guttesen, *Leaning into the Future*, 14; cf. Geiko Müller-Fahrenholz, *The Kingdom and the Power: The Theology of Jürgen Moltmann* (trans. John Bowden; Minneapolis: Fortress, 2001), 221.

the suffering of the Christians," and "the kingdom of God was seen in the form of the lordship of the crucified one."[30] Because the cross is the "basis" and "form" of the coming kingdom, Moltmann argues that "the crucified Christ does not disappear when the fulfilment comes, but rather becomes the ground for redeemed existence in God."[31] Moltmann could not be any clearer on the cruciform nature of the kingdom: "In the history of sin and death the kingdom of freedom takes on the form of the crucified Christ."[32]

CRUCIFORM KINGDOM WITHOUT A KING?

Clearly, Moltmann argues for a cruciform kingdom. But in what sense does the cross shape the kingdom? For Moltmann, a radical theology of the cross demands a "revolution in the concept of God"[33]—the king of the kingdom. This "revolution" began for Moltmann in *The Crucified God*, but was fully developed in *The Trinity and the Kingdom*.[34] The doctrine of God is especially pertinent for the kingdom because the kingdom of God "tells us more about *God* (the fact that he reigns) than about anything else."[35]

In *The Trinity and the Kingdom*, Moltmann sets up his entire discussion as an answer to the following "theological problem":

> What is the relation of the trinitarian history of God, the Father, the Son and the Spirit, which the New Testament relates, to God's sovereignty? My own teachers, Karl Barth and Karl Rahner, decided the question in favour of the sovereignty of the One God. . . . I myself have proposed instead that the question be decided in favour of the Trinity.[36]

Moltmann sets up a dichotomy between God as king (monotheistic monarchianism) and God as Trinity (social Trinity). *Either* God is a single authoritative ruler *or* a community of fellowship. Moltmann strongly argues for the latter, thereby "overcoming the notion of a universal monarchy of the one God," for "it is impossible to form the figure of the omnipotent, universal monarch, who is reflected in earthly rulers out of the unity of this Father, this Son and this Spirit."[37]

Why does Moltmann present such a stark contrast between these two

---

30. Moltmann, *Theology of Hope*, 222, 223.
31. Moltmann, *The Crucified God*, 106, 185, 266.
32. Moltmann, *The Trinity and the Kingdom*, 211.
33. Moltmann, *The Crucified God*, 152.
34. Chapter six in *The Crucified God* is Moltmann's theology of the cross applied to the doctrine of God. *The Trinity and the Kingdom* is in its entirety Moltmann's doctrine of God.
35. Gentry and Wellum, *Kingdom through Covenant*, 596, italics theirs.
36. Moltmann, *The Trinity and the Kingdom*, viii.
37. Ibid., 197.

interpretations of God? His own experience as a prisoner of war, along with the pressing awareness of oppression in the third world, have proven to be determinative throughout Moltmann's theology. Moltmann believes the notion of a divine king enables and legitimates oppressive rulers and hierarchical structures on earth,[38] and "it is only when the doctrine of the Trinity vanquishes the monotheistic notion of the great universal monarch in heaven, and his divine patriarchs in the world, that earthly rulers, dictators and tyrants cease to find any justifying religious archetypes any more."[39] According to him, such a view of the kingship of God (monotheistic monarchianism) does not originate from Scripture but in patriarchal cultures and Greek philosophy.[40]

Moltmann, therefore, could not be any clearer about his solution: the cross demands a redefinition of the doctrine of God as the community of freedom and fellowship *to the exclusion of* the idea of God as king:

> The *basileia* only exists in the context of God's fatherhood. In this kingdom God is not the Lord; he is the merciful Father. In this kingdom there are no servants; there are only God's free children. In this kingdom what is required is not obedience and submission; it is love and free participation.[41]

> In friendship the distance enjoined by sovereignty ceases to exist. . . . God does not want the humility of servants or the gratitude of children forever. He wants the boldness and confidence of friends, who share his rule with him.[42]

What Guttensen calls the "disappearance of God's sovereignty" has been a constant in Moltmann's thought, but it has become increasingly prevalent throughout his career.[43] One of the main factors steering Moltmann in this direction is the emphasis on mutual and reciprocal friendship between God and humanity, for it is the apex of the trinitarian history of God. Following Joachim of Fiore, Moltmann sees a progression from the kingdom of the Father to the kingdom of the Son to the kingdom of the Spirit, in which one's relationship to God progresses from fear to servitude to friendship.[44] The argument moves toward what Moltmann describes as the ultimate goal for God and humanity: friendship and freedom. He claims, "Friendship with God is the highest stage of freedom."[45]

---

38. Ibid., 191–92.
39. Ibid., 197.
40. Ibid., 130–31, 165.
41. Ibid., 70.
42. Ibid., 221.
43. Guttesen, *Leaning into the Future*, 102–3.
44. Moltmann, *The Trinity and the Kingdom*, 205. Moltmann does not follow Joachim in that the three kingdoms are assigned to three distinct and successive stages of history (ibid., 209).
45. Ibid., 206.

The emphasis on freedom is why Moltmann understands the kingdom as the "*liberating* lordship"[46] of Christ and says, "*The Trinitarian doctrine of the kingdom is the theological doctrine of freedom.*"[47] Moltmann rejects the kingship of God, ultimately because it is contrary to his understanding of the kingdom of freedom where there is no longer a distinction between king and servant. Hence, Moltmann asserts, "Where the great Lord of the universe reigns, there is no room for liberty."[48]

In sum, we have seen that Moltmann's radical theology of the cross requires "fundamental changes in the doctrine of God"[49]—namely, the rejection of the idea that God is king.[50] The conclusion is not only ironic but devastating: in the midst of his passion for the cruciform kingdom of God, Moltmann eclipses the kingship of God.[51]

EVALUATION OF MOLTMANN

In assessing Moltmann's contribution to this discussion on the cruciform kingdom of God, I will offer several strengths and weaknesses of his approach, which will then lead to further advancing my own constructive proposal.

MOLTMANN'S STRENGTHS

There are two primary strengths of Moltmann's proposal. First, in an age of systematic theology that has largely ignored or misplaced the kingdom of

---

46. Ibid., 210, italics mine.
47. Ibid., 218, italics his.
48. Ibid., 203; Moltmann is here favorably quoting Ernst Bloch.
49. Ibid., 134.
50. Moltmann is not alone in rejecting the kingship of God. Sallie McFague argues that kingship is an outdated concept that was helpful during one era of the church but should be retired today (*Models of God: Theology for an Ecological, Nuclear Age* [Philadelphia: Fortress, 1987], 29). Rauschenbusch and the social gospel movement, despite emphasizing the kingdom of God, sought to replace the idea of God as king with that of God as Father (*A Theology for the Social Gospel*, 174–75). A similar critique is made of one contemporary American movement (Todd Miles, "A Kingdom without a King? Evaluating the Kingdom Ethic[s] of the Emerging Church," *SBJT* 12 [2008]: 88–103). Many open theists have also sought to do away with the kingship of God, or at least the primacy of its place. Boyd says the cosmos is "more of a democracy than it is a monarchy" (*God at War*, 58). John Sanders says, "Indeed the reading of the Old Testament legitimately provides for a world-ruling messiah, but God simply chose differently in Jesus" (*The God Who Risks: A Theology of Providence* [Downers Grove, IL: InterVarsity Press, 1998], 300); Alfred North Whitehead famously said, "The church gave God the attributes which belonged exclusively to Caesar" (*Process and Reality: An Essay in Cosmology* [New York: Harper & Row, 1960], 342).
51. This discussion of Moltmann's rejection of the kingship of God has relied solely on *The Trinity and the Kingdom*, which, although it is his most sustained treatment of the doctrine of God, was published over thirty years ago. Has Moltmann reconsidered his position in light of persistent criticism (see Randall Otto, "Moltmann and the Anti-Monotheism Movement," *IJST* 3 [2001]: 293–308)? The answer is clearly no. As of 2010, Moltmann maintains his thesis that God is not a universal monarch (*Sun of Righteousness, Arise!*, 85–100).

God, Moltmann provides an excellent example of allowing the kingdom to impact every aspect of his thought. Material conclusions aside, Moltmann is to be commended for the way in which the kingdom formally shapes his Christology and theology proper.

Second, Moltmann has comprehensively and consistently argued for the cruciform nature of the kingdom. While so much kingdom theology has come at the expense of the place of the cross, Moltmann has interwoven the two throughout his work. He clearly depicts that the death of Christ was aimed toward a broader kingdom goal, and the kingdom advances not merely beyond the cross but by the cross. For these achievements, Moltmann is to be greatly commended as one who still provides a much-needed voice in systematic theology today.

MOLTMANN'S WEAKNESSES

Although I could critique Moltmann's theology on many different levels,[52] especially the fact that for him the cross is not so much about atoning for sin but revealing God's becoming,[53] I will focus on Moltmann's doctrine of God, particularly his dethroning of God.[54] Despite arguing vigorously for

---

52. For an excellent survey of recent responses to Moltmann's theology, see Chester, *Mission and the Coming of God*, 91–196.

53. Moltmann's theology has been critiqued for failing to have an adequate soteriology because he ultimately collapses the fall into creation. For Moltmann, salvation is not so much about God's saving the world from sin but about overcoming the godforsaken space in creation and in God himself, which is a result of God creating by making space within himself (Guttesen, *Leaning into the Future*, 55–67; Chester, *Mission and the Coming of God*, 65–72; Douglas Schuurman, "Creation, Eschaton, and Ethics: An Analysis of Theology and Ethics in Jürgen Moltmann," *CTJ* 22 [1987]: 65). Therefore, Moltmann rarely speaks of the cross as atoning but primarily as the revelation of God's fellow-suffering with humanity. Bauckham says that for Moltmann, "the cross does not solve the problem of suffering, but meets it with the voluntary fellow-suffering of love" (*The Theology of Jürgen Moltmann*, 12). Chester says, "The cross does not so much effect atonement as reveal atonement through 'the pain of God'" (*Mission and the Coming of God*, 71–72). Ultimately for Moltmann, the cross is the event of God's becoming. He says, "'God' is not another nature or a heavenly person or a moral authority, but in fact an 'event'" (*The Crucified God*, 247). And again, "One should think of the Trinity as a dialectical event, indeed as the event of the cross" (ibid., 255).

54. Another related aspect of Moltmann's doctrine of God is his rejection of impassibility. For Moltmann, impassibility represents the intrusion of Greek philosophy into Christian theology and makes impossible God's ability to truly love (*The Trinity and the Kingdom*, 21–60). Rahner critiques Moltmann on this point, stating bluntly that "it does not help me to escape from my mess and mix-up and despair if God is in the same predicament" (quoted in Jürgen Moltmann, *History and the Triune God: Contributions to Trinitarian Theology* [New York: Crossroad, 1992], 122). Unfortunately, while Moltmann acknowledges the critique as being at the heart of his theology, he does not directly respond to Rahner's accusation but rather tells the story of his experience in a concentration camp, concluding that "it is on the basis of this experience of God that I believe and think" (ibid., 123). For recent defenses of impassibility, albeit nuanced in different ways, see Thomas Weinandy, *Does God Suffer?* (Notre Dame, IN: University of Notre Dame, 2000); Paul Gavrilyuk, *The Suffering of the Impassible God: The Dialectics of Patristic Thought* (OECS; Oxford: Oxford University Press, 2004); Vanhoozer, *Remythologizing Theology*, 387–468.

the kingdom, Moltmann equally rejects the idea of God as king.[55] Such a rejection is troubling, for, as we have seen, the emphasis of the kingdom is that it is *God's* kingdom. I offer five critiques of Moltmann's rejection of the kingship of God.

First, Moltmann's rejection of the kingship of God does not square with the biblical account and, in fact, undermines precisely what he seeks to uphold. Scripture is emphatic: "The LORD is king" (Ps 10:16). Furthermore, the kingship of God is evident before the fall in creation (Ps 93:1–2) and throughout the history of redemption (Zech 14:9; Mark 1:15), and it is central to the eschatological picture of God in the book of Revelation (Rev 22:1). This biblical witness is not altogether problematic for Moltmann himself, who says, "I take scripture as a stimulus to my own theological thinking, not as an authoritative blueprint and confining boundary."[56] Such an approach is unfortunate, for Scripture reveals that the very thing Moltmann rejects (the kingship of God) is the only thing that can ensure what he seeks to affirm (an eschatological community of peace).[57] The eschatological picture in Rev 22:3–5, where the curse is removed and humans are restored to dominion over the earth, does not come at the expense of God's throne, but is only possible because of it (Rev 22:1). Bauckham also notes that while Moltmann sacrifices God's kingship for the sake of human freedom, in Scripture it is precisely the reign of God that enables the freedom of his people.[58]

Second, Moltmann's rejection of the kingship of God is based on the inaccurate and untenable interconnectedness of monotheism and human monarchianism. To begin with, Moltmann is building on the largely discredited work of Erik Peterson's case for monotheism as a political problem.[59] Randall Otto demonstrates that there is no intrinsic relationship between monotheism and human monarchy. Israel was monotheistic and at times *not* monarchial, and the surrounding nations of Israel were polytheistic and

---

55. Some might quibble with our characterization of Moltmann rejecting (rather than redefining) the kingship of God. However, the statements above make clear that, although Moltmann continues to use the language of kingdom, he opposes any idea of God as king. Therefore, although he is redefining kingdom, he is rejecting God's kingship.

56. Jürgen Moltmann, *Experiences in Theology: Ways and Forms of Christian Theology* (Minneapolis: Fortress, 2000), xxii. For an overview and critique of Moltmann's use of Scripture, see Guttesen, *Leaning into the Future*, 16–37.

57. Guttesen, *Leaning into the Future*, 219.

58. Bauckham, *The Theology of Jürgen Moltmann*, 182.

59. Erik Peterson, *Theologische Traktate* (Munich: Wild, 1951), 45–147. Alfred Schindler demonstrates that Peterson's thesis is "untenable, both in its historical specifics as well as in its systematic generalizations" ("Einführung," in *Monotheisms als politisches Problem? Erik Peterson und die Kritik der politischen Theologie* [ed. Alfred Schindler; Gütersloh: Gütersloher Verlagshaus Mohn, 1978], 12).

monarchial.[60] I concur with Otto's assessment that "relinquishing Christianity as monotheistic is a watershed in the history of theology" and that "unjust exertion of power is better attributed to sinful defiance of God than to monotheistic or trinitarian conceptualizations."[61]

Moltmann's counterproposal of replacing the sovereign God with the social Trinity reveals the same erroneous presuppositions. Moltmann assumes a necessary correlation between God's being (becoming?) and human social structures. In other words, in order to protect the egalitarian nature of human community, he feels it necessary to only speak of God as an egalitarian community. Moltmann's argument wrongly assumes, however, that the goal of *participating* in the triune God is achieved by *imitating* his nature. Guttesen is right to point out that "what human beings are is not predicated first upon *who God is* but whom *he has purposed them to be.*"[62]

Third, Moltmann wrongfully equates authority with domination.[63] Failing to distinguish between authority abused and authority itself, Moltmann rejects all forms of authority or hierarchy. In the kingdom of God, claims Moltmann, "authority and obedience are replaced by dialogue, consensus and harmony."[64] Just as Moltmann elsewhere collapses the ontological distinction between creator and creature (panentheism), here he has done away with the relational distinction between king and servants. In short, Moltmann has failed to acknowledge that when it comes to authority, misuse does not nullify proper use (*abusus non tollit usum*).

Fourth, whereas Moltmann appeals to a two-way relationship between God and humanity in order to do away with God's royal position of authority, the biblical concept of covenant actually upholds God's kingship in relationship with his people.[65] Certainly a covenant is a two-way relationship, but it is a particular kind of relationship—namely, one between a king and his servants. Covenant, therefore, does not obliterate God's royal identity and power but provides the proper context for kingship—kingship that is exercised for the good of his people.

Finally, and most important (as it will strongly distinguish and serve to advance my proposal), Moltmann's rejection of God's kingship is problematic because it fails to acknowledge God's power in salvation *and* judgment.

---

60. Otto, "Moltmann and the Anti-Monotheism Movement," 296.

61. Ibid., 295, 307.

62. Guttesen, *Leaning into the Future,* 106, italics his.

63. Bauckham, *Moltmann,* 135.

64. Moltmann, *The Trinity and the Kingdom,* 202.

65. Moltmann actually employs covenant to erase the distinction between king and servant (*Sun of Righteousness, Arise!,* 91).

Above, I highlighted Moltmann's claim that God rules through self-giving love, and with this I concur. I part ways with Moltmann, however, when he claims that God rules *only* through self-giving love. In other words, many would agree with Moltmann when he says, "God is nowhere greater than in his humiliation."[66] It is another thing, however, to say that God is *only* great in his humiliation. Moltmann makes precisely that argument: "The *sole* omnipotence which God possesses is the almighty power of suffering love."[67] "It is his passionate, passible love that is almighty, *nothing else.*"[68] Guttesen exposes Moltmann's weakness by appealing to the biblical concept of judgment:

> While Moltmann's vision of the way God's rule is oriented toward the free-dom of humanity rightly emphasizes how Jesus radically turns notions of power and rule on their head in his proclamation and own example, this, neither in the Gospels or [sic] elsewhere in Scripture, negates the fact that God not only asserts the right of a sovereign but also exercises this right in decisive acts of judgment and redemption.[69]

Therefore, although Moltmann goes on to speak of the "rule" of God, he has ultimately collapsed the term by equating it solely with suffering love.

This last point provides a fitting transition toward advancing my con-structive proposal. While I have discussed the cruciform nature of the king-dom, we must also carefully seek to understand the king. If the kingdom is cruciform, what then can I say about the kingship of the king? We will see that although the kingdom is certainly a *cruciform* kingdom, it is the cruci-form kingdom of the compassionate and just king.

THE COMPASSIONATE AND JUST KING

God is king (Exod 15:18; Num 23:21; Deut 33:5, 26; Judg 8:23; 1 Sam 8:7; 10:19; 12:12; Ps 93:1; 96:10; 97:1; 99:1).[70] But what kind of king is he? The cross reveals that God is a compassionate king—a shepherd-king who rules

---

66. Moltmann, *The Trinity and the Kingdom*, 119.
67. Ibid., 31, italics mine, cf. 68.
68. Ibid., 197, italics mine.
69. Guttesen, *Leaning into the Future*, 105, cf. 222.
70. Many Old Testament scholars see the kingship/reign of God as the unifying principle of the Old Testament (Bright, *The Kingdom of God*, 7; Edmond Jacob, *Theology of the Old Testament* [New York: Harper & Row, 1958], 37; Eugene Merrill, *Everlasting Dominion: A Theology of the Old Testament* [Nashville: Broadman & Holman, 2006], 129). Likewise, many New Testament scholars make the same claim for the entirety of both testaments (e.g., Ladd, *A Theology of the New Testament*, xi).

by serving.[71] However, the fact that he may rule by serving does not mean that he rules *only* by serving. As a shepherd-king, God reigns not only by laying down his life for his sheep but also by defending them against voracious wolves. He rules through serving *and* guarding. He exercises power through weakness *and* strength. The coming of his kingdom entails salvation *and* judgment. God is the compassionate *and* just king.

THE COMPASSIONATE KING

God's kingship is inseparable from his character. In Psalm 145, where David extols God as king and meditates on the splendor of his majesty, he also praises God for his abundant goodness and righteousness (Ps 145:1–7). This king is "gracious and merciful, slow to anger and abounding in steadfast love" (145:8). It is for this type of kingship that "they shall speak of the glory of your kingdom and tell of your power" (145:11). What kind of king is God? He is a good, righteous, gracious, merciful, and loving king. God's kingship must be understood in light of all his attributes.

Such benevolent kingship is evident in the creation narrative, where the first act of God as the Creator-king is to bless his image-bearers (Gen 1:28). It was the lie of the serpent to portray God's reign as oppressive and tyrannical. After the fall, God's kingship is revealed in the context of his covenant with Abraham and his descendants. Because God is a covenant-king who has bound himself to his people, he is not a disinterested despot capitalizing on his servants but a caring king who seeks the welfare of his people.

Perhaps the greatest image the Old Testament uses to capture the benevolent nature of God's kingship is that of a shepherd (Ezekiel 34).[72] As Goldingay says, "Like kingship, shepherding suggests on one hand absolute authority and the power of life and death, and on the other an obligation to see that the subjects of this authority and power are looked after properly."[73] In this sense, the king is the servant of the people,[74] for "his exaltation above his subjects is inseparable from his selfless devotion to their welfare."[75]

The idea of God as a shepherd-king draws from the interplay between divine and human kingship. This divine/human interplay is important, for if the ques-

---

71. To "reign" or "rule" is to exercise royal power. Tomlin defines power as "the capability to influence people or situations and to transform them" (*The Power of the Cross*, 313); Michael J. Gorman offers a similar definition (*Cruciformity: Paul's Narrative Spirituality of the Cross* [Grand Rapids: Eerdmans, 2001], 269).

72. Walter Brueggemann, *Genesis* (IBC; Atlanta: John Knox, 1982), 33.

73. Goldingay, *Israel's Faith*, 2:63.

74. Moshe Weinfeld, "The King as the Servant of the People: The Source of the Idea," *JJS* 33 (1982): 189–94.

75. Levenson, *The Death and Resurrection of the Beloved Son*, 145.

tion is what kind of king is God, one place to look is in those who bear the image of such kingship. In other words, if humanity is to reflect God's kingship on earth (Gen 1:26–28), then the way in which they are told to reign should also reveal something about the way in which God reigns. The key is, as I have pointed out above, that Adam's commission to rule over the earth in Gen 1:26–28 is defined in 2:15 as serving and guarding.[76] Therefore, a good king does not simply rule *and* serve, but rules *by* serving (cf. Deut 17:14–20). King Rehoboam, for example, rejected the wise counsel of the elders to "be a servant to this people today and serve them" (1 Kings 12:7), which resulted in the division of the kingdom.

In the New Testament, the benevolent kingship of God is seen through the gospel of Jesus Christ. On the way to Jerusalem, Jesus redefines kingship to James and John in terms of service and giving (Mark 10:32–45). Jesus rules by serving, which for him means giving his life as a ransom for many (10:45). In the upper room, Jesus washes his disciples' feet and declares, "You call me . . . Lord, and you are right, for so I am" (John 13:13). He does not say, "I am not Lord, I am a servant." Rather, through his words and actions, he says, "I am Lord and I am showing my authority by washing your feet." Ultimately, as I have demonstrated, Jesus is crucified as the king who rules by serving.

Although Moltmann helpfully captures the ideas of God's self-giving power and ruling by serving, these themes are in no way original to him. In fact, there is a rich tradition in the church of understanding God's power and rule as being displayed supremely on the cross. According to Gregory of Nyssa, "That the omnipotent nature was capable of descending to man's lowly position is a clearer evidence of power than . . . to do great and sublime things."[77] According to Anselm, Christ determined "that the way in which he would demonstrate the exaltedness of his omnipotence should be none other than through his death."[78] Barth argued repeatedly that God's omnipotence "can assume the form of weakness and impotence and do so as omnipotence, triumphing in this form."[79]

THE JUST KING

God is not only a benevolent king; he is a just king. Psalm 89 says that righteousness and justice are the foundation of God's throne, from which steadfast love and faithfulness go forth (Ps 89:14). Kingship by definition

---

76. See above, p. 55, especially n. 7.
77. Gregory of Nyssa, "An Address on Religious Instruction," 300–301.
78. Anselm, "Why God Became Man," 278.
79. Barth, *CD* IV/1, 186–87; cf. 129–30; 158–59, 179–80, 192.

entails authority,[80] and God can assert his righteous authority to save or to judge.[81] Kingship expressed through salvation or judgment does not imply arbitrariness on God's part but rather emphasizes that as king he remains true to his character. He is worthy to be praised as "the King of heaven, for all his works are right and his ways are just" (Dan 4:37; cf. Rev 15:3). Therefore, while God's royal power can assume the form of weakness, it is by no means limited to it.

The just nature of God's kingship can be seen in his exercise of power, judgment of sin, and victory over evil. First, Michael Gorman explains how Paul's reinterpretation of divine power (as being made perfect in weakness) does not rule out the more traditional aspects:

> Paul's reinterpretation of divine power is, therefore, startling, and it should not be underestimated. In it, however, he does not completely deny more traditional understandings of divine power. The power of God is displayed in the creation (Rom. 1:20). The power of God was the source of Jesus' resurrection and will be the source of believers' resurrection (1 Cor. 6:14; cf. Rom 1:4). The power of God is displayed in the extraordinary manifestations of the Spirit both in Paul's ministry (1 Thess. 1:5; 1 Cor. 2:4; 2 Cor. 12:12; Rom 15:19) and in the life of his communities (Gal. 3:5; 1 Cor. 12:10, 28–29).[82]

Second, the just nature of God's kingship is also evident in his judgment of sin, for as a holy king who is committed to protecting the purity of his kingdom, God "will by no means clear the guilty" (Nah 1:3). While this aspect of God's kingship is absent from Moltmann's theology, it is clear in Scripture that the coming of the kingdom entails the "twofold content" of salvation *and* judgment.[83]

Third, God's just kingship is demonstrated in his victory over evil. Whether victory over the nations in the Old Testament or Satan in the New Testament, God must dethrone and destroy the very enemies that seek to prevent his reign of peace. This pattern is set in the exodus, where the kingship of God is proclaimed on account of his victory over his enemies (Exod 15:7, 18).

Finally, the just nature of God's kingship is not relaxed when Jesus comes to bring the kingdom as the Suffering Servant. Rather, it was the mission of

---

80. K. M. Heim, "Kings and Kingship," *DOTHB*, 610.

81. Gerald Bray says, "The right to execute judgment is fundamental to any meaningful rule" ("The Kingdom and Eschatology," 223).

82. Gorman, *Cruciformity*, 280.

83. Ridderbos, *The Coming of the Kingdom*, 20.

the servant to "bring forth justice to the nations" (Isa 42:1; cf. 9:7; Jer 23:5). And while Jesus displayed the kingdom through healing and forgiving, he also maintained that there is no place in God's kingdom for those opposed to the king (e.g., Matt 7:21).

I have demonstrated that God is a benevolent and just king. While Moltmann rightly observes Jesus' qualification of kingship in terms of serving, he wrongfully excludes any notion of God's reign through judgment. At the cross, however, the benevolent and just kingship of God is put on full display, for Christ's death reveals not only the love of God (Rom 5:8) but his justice as well (3:25).

THE TRINITARIAN KINGSHIP OF GOD

One final observation that needs to be made regarding the doctrine of God in relation to the kingdom is that the coming of the kingdom is trinitarian through and through. Against Moltmann's false dichotomy between triunity and sovereignty, the trinitarian nature of God does not undermine his kingship but rather defines it. The cruciform kingdom of the triune God breaks into history when the *Father* sends the *Son* in the power of the *Spirit*. In between the already and the not yet, God advances his kingdom by the *Spirit*, who applies the finished work of the *Son* in order that the kingdom may ultimately be handed over to the *Father*. One need not choose between a relational and sovereign God—"He is the King who cares."[84]

FOLLOWING THE KING BY TAKING UP THE CROSS

So far in this chapter I have discussed the kingdom of God in light of the doctrines of atonement and theology proper. The kingdom is the cruciform kingdom of the compassionate and just king. Yet, since God reigns over and *through* his people, what can be said about the role of Christians in the advancement of the kingdom between the already and the not yet? My answer is threefold: *God* advances his kingdom through the *church* as it conforms to the *cross*.

First, to be clear, the kingdom is not built or advanced by people but is received (Heb 12:28). Contra social gospel theology, the kingdom of God is not the culmination of human potential and effort but the intervention of

---

84. John Feinberg, *No One Like Him: The Doctrine of God* (FET 2; Wheaton, IL: Crossway, 2001), 799.

God's sovereign grace into a sinful and broken world. God's sovereignty does not obliterate human participation or involvement in his royal reconciling of all things but rather protects the foundational truth of the kingdom—that it is *of God*.

Second, God advances his kingdom primarily through *the church*—local congregations of God's reconciled servant-kings.[85] Although the refrain of the kingdom is "The LORD reigns!" (Ps 96:10), the restoration of human vicegerency is an essential harmony in the Bible's royal song. God reigns, but he reigns through those being renewed into the image of their creator. Contra Moltmann, who largely neglects the church in his emphasis on the kingdom, the church is God's means of advancing his kingdom. To talk about the place of the church in the advancement of God's kingdom, the relationship between the church and the kingdom must first be defined.

The church is *not* the kingdom. The kingdom is a more comprehensive notion of God's eschatological reign over the earth, whereas the church is the people of the king between the already and the not yet of the kingdom.[86] Yet, just as they are distinct, the church and the kingdom are also inseparable. The church is a sign of the kingdom, a display to this present evil age of the proleptic reality of God's reign in the age to come. In short, the church is distinct from the kingdom but central to its advancement.

How, then, does God advance his kingdom through the church? The third and most important point is that God advances the kingdom through Christians in the same way he established the kingdom through Christ.[87] As Leslie Newbigin says, "All kingship from Calvary onward is tested and judged by the standard of the true kingship established there."[88] Jesus' initial "follow me" (δεῦτε ὀπίσω μου, Mark 1:17), given as an invitation to the kingdom, is later qualified with the warning: "If anyone would come after me (ὀπίσω μου ἀκολουθεῖν), let him deny himself and take up his cross and follow me" (8:34). In other words, to follow Jesus as king in this age is to take up the cross. Just as Christ crucified is declared to be the power of God (1 Cor 1:23–24), Timothy is charged to "share in suffering for the gospel by the power of God" (2 Tim 1:8).

---

85. My purpose is not to enter into ecclesiology discussions (which would raise many other issues) but to discuss the place and form of the church *within the advancement of the kingdom*.

86. Ridderbos, *The Coming of the Kingdom*, 354; Ladd, *The Presence of the Future*, 262.

87. Christians follow Christ in his example of self-giving love. However, Christians do not atone for sins, but rather witness to Christ's atoning death. Though there is much to be commended in McKnight's *A Community Called Atonement*, he fails to make this distinction between Christ as the one who atones for sin and Christians who witness to this reality.

88. Lesslie Newbigin, *Foolishness to the Greeks: The Gospel and Western Culture* (Grand Rapids: Eerdmans, 1986), 126.

Such *power* to suffer for the gospel and "take up [the] cross" must ultimately be "the power of the Spirit of God" (Rom 15:19). Inasmuch as the coming of the kingdom entails the pouring out of God's Spirit (Isa 32:15–18; Ezek 36:26–30), the kingdom hidden beneath the cross is at the same time the kingdom in the power of the Spirit. The power of the Spirit, however, is a power for Christlike service. Richard Gaffin says, "Just as the Spirit of glory came on Jesus at his Jordan-baptism, opening up before him the way of suffering obedience that led to the cross, so the same Holy Spirit, with which the church was baptized at Pentecost, points it to the path of suffering."[89] The Holy Spirit, therefore, is the mediating link between the presence of the kingdom in Christ and its advancement through Christians. Jesus brought the kingdom as the Spirit-empowered Messiah. The Spirit advances the kingdom by applying the finished work of Christ.

If, as I have argued, the kingdom is advanced by the cross, then it is certainly an *empty* cross. The crucified king is alive, so the kingdom advances not simply by looking back to the cross but by moving forward with the crucified-resurrected king. In Phil 3:10, Paul yearns for Christ that he "may know him and the power of his resurrection, and may share his sufferings, becoming like him in his death." The sequence here may initially seem odd, but it proves to be the logic of advancing the kingdom. Where one would normally expect the order of death-resurrection, Paul inverts the order to show that resurrection power is exercised in order to conform the Christian to the cross of Christ. Gaffin offers the following conclusion regarding this passage:

> It tells us, together with II Corinthians 4:10, 11, that the power of Christ's resurrection is realized just as the fellowship of his sufferings and conformity to his death. It tells us of the forming and patterning power of the resurrection; the resurrection is a conforming energy, an energy that produces conformity to Christ's death. The impact, the impress of the resurrection in Paul's existence, is the cross.[90]

The power of the resurrection conforms individuals and the church as a whole to the cross. God advances his kingdom through his church, though its resurrection power is veiled by weakness and its glory by apparent foolishness. Between Christ's resurrection and return, the kingdom is not only hidden beneath the cross but advanced by the cross. Chester captures the essence of this interplay between the Spirit, the resurrection, and the cross: "Through

---

89. Richard Gaffin, "The Usefulness of the Cross," *WTJ* 41 (1979): 239.
90. Ibid., 234; see also Gorman, who says, "The power of the resurrection operates in the present as the power of conformity to the death of Christ" (*Cruciformity*, 332).

the Holy Spirit we experience the power of the resurrection in order to follow the way of the cross."[91]

Followers of Jesus are bound for glory. But what is true for Christ is true for those who are "in Christ": glory comes through suffering. Paul says that as coheirs with Christ, "we suffer with him in order that we may also be glorified with him" (Rom 8:17). God's power is being made perfect through weakness (2 Cor 12:9). This does not make suffering easy, but it does make it meaningful. God is with us in our suffering, he transforms us through our suffering, and one day he will put an end to our suffering. And this is true not only for God's people, but also for God's creation. "The creation itself will be set free from its bondage to decay and obtain the freedom of the glory of the children of God" (Rom 8:21). For Christ, Christians, and all of creation, the way of glory is the way of the cross.

CONCLUSION

While much theology of the kingdom is done in spite of the cross, I have sought to understand the kingdom in light of the cross. With the help of Luther's theology of the cross, the eye of faith perceives that the wisdom and power of the kingdom are hidden beneath the foolishness and the weakness of the cross. However, the fact that God rules by serving does not mean that he sacrifices his kingship for the sake of service. Contra Moltmann, God is the compassionate and just king, whose kingdom entails salvation and judgment. In this age, God advances his kingdom through the church as it is conformed to the cross. Just as the kingdom was established and inaugurated through Christ's death and resurrection, God advances his kingdom through Christians who have been united to Christ and who by the power of his resurrection are conformed to his cross.

---

91. Chester, *Mission and the Coming of God*, 220.

CROWN OF THORNS

MANY CHRISTIANS EITHER champion the kingdom or cling to the cross; yet Scripture presents a mutually enriching relationship between the two that draws significantly from the story of Israel and culminates in the crucifixion of Christ the king. In short, the kingdom and the cross are held together by the Christ—Israel's Messiah—who brings God's reign on earth through his atoning death on the cross. The kingdom is the ultimate goal of the cross, and the cross is the means by which the kingdom comes. Jesus' death is neither the failure of his messianic ministry nor simply the prelude to his royal glory. His death is the apex of his kingdom mission; the cross is the throne from which Jesus rules and establishes his kingdom. The shocking paradox of God's reign through Christ crucified certainly appears foolish to fallen human logic; however, perceived through faith, it is the power and wisdom of God. This kingdom–cross interplay can be seen in the *story* and *logic* of redemption.[1]

---

1. Readers interested in the way this project relates to the work of N. T. Wright should see my interaction throughout this work on specific issues. In brief, my main idea is congruent with Wright—namely, that Jesus brings the kingdom by way of the cross (see above, pp. 31, 39, 48, 65, 112–19, 141). Our differences lie in the following areas: (1) Method: Wright's scholarly work contributes primarily to discussions in historical Jesus studies; I incorporate biblical and systematic theology (see above, pp. 31–37). (2) Diagnosing the problem: Wright primarily blames the creeds and the Reformers for separating kingdom and cross; I see this division as more of a modern problem (see above, pp. 26–28). In other words, I think church tradition largely bolsters the relationship between kingdom and cross rather than hindering it. (3) Atonement: although Wright acknowledges some form of penal substitution, it plays little role in his telling of the story of redemption or connecting kingdom and cross (see above, pp. 131–34, 138 fn 36, 222). I see penal substitution (as integrated with *Christus Victor*) being essential for relating kingdom and cross (see above, pp. 192–226). Furthermore, Wright equates forgiveness of sins with return from exile and thereby downplays individual forgiveness; I distinguish between the two, while upholding corporate and individual forgiveness (see above, pp. 133–34).

THE STORY OF REDEMPTION

From the beginning (Genesis 1–2), the kingdom of God is the telic vision of God's reign through his vice-regents over all creation, the heart of which is the covenant relationship between the divine king and his image-bearing servants. The fall, therefore, both fractures the covenant relationship between God and his people *and* collapses the project aimed at God's reign over all the earth.

After the fall, the telic vision of the kingdom remains, but in light of sin, it must be achieved in a new way. The first glimmer of hope is embedded within the curse itself, as God tells the serpent that the seed of a woman will crush its head (Gen 3:15). However, the victory of the seed, which will overcome the sin-induced curse and reconcile God's people as servant-kings, will entail suffering for the victor. Henceforth, a pattern emerges in the story of Adam and Israel whereby victory comes through suffering, exaltation through humiliation, and ultimately, kingdom through cross.

God's gracious promise to Abraham in Gen 12:1–3 sets out to reverse the curse of Genesis 3–11 and thereby recover the blessed reality of Genesis 1–2—namely, land and people under God's good reign. The commission to Adam and Eve becomes a promise to Abraham, which is then ensured by a covenant (Gen 15:1–21; 17:1–14), where God binds himself to his people, astonishingly agreeing to take the curse upon *himself* if the covenant is broken (Gen 15:17). The fact that God administers his kingdom through a series of covenants with his people sheds great light on the way in which the kingdom comes. Just as the covenant with Abraham was sealed by sacrifice, the coming of the kingdom is ultimately administered through the *new* covenant, which is ratified by the blood of Christ, "poured out for many for the forgiveness of sins" (Matt 26:28).

In the exodus, God redeems his covenant people by judging the Egyptians (and the Passover lambs in place of the Jews), resulting in the declaration of God as king (Exod 15:7, 18) and Israel as a "kingdom of priests" (19:6). Echoes of Eden abound; but in a sin-stained world, establishing God's kingdom in the promised land must come after the installation of the sacrificial system. Atonement is essential for upholding the purity of the kingdom.

The united monarchy represents the high point of fulfillment in the Old Testament. David is the ideal king, a second Adam who rules on behalf of God with righteousness and justice. David's kingship, however, represents the pattern throughout the Old Testament—namely, that his rise to the throne was one of humiliation and exaltation, and his royalty is characterized by righteous suffering (e.g., Psalm 22). God's covenant with David captures all the previous hopes of Israel and ties them to a future Davidic king (a son of David and a son of God) who will "establish" God's kingdom on earth forever (2 Sam 7:12–14; cf. Ps 89:35). The coming kingdom will also include a temple, which is significantly the place of God's rule *and* atonement for sin. Temple connects atonement and kingdom, for only by means of atonement can unholy people dwell with the holy divine king. Jesus replaces the temple in both senses. He is the dwelling place of God, *and* his death the final and definitive means for atonement (Heb 10:10–14).

Isaiah 52:13–53:12 represents the apex of the development of suffering and victory that began in Gen 3:15, for the song of the Suffering Servant is not only the most forthright explanation of substitutionary atonement but is also strongly tied to its immediate context of the coming of God's kingdom. Isaiah clarifies not only the seed's suffering as *atoning* and victory as *royal* but also the royal victory will come *through* atoning suffering. The kingdom of God ("Your God reigns!" Isa 52:7) is brought about by the atoning suffering of the servant ("he bore the sin of many" Isa 53:12).

Zechariah builds on the Isaianic message that atonement is instrumental in the coming of God's kingdom, telling of a humble king who will rule over the earth as one who redeems his people with the blood of his covenant (Zech 9:9–12). The Old Testament draws to a close with the same vision with which it began: "The LORD will be king over all the earth" (Zech 14:9).

The New Testament presents the story of Jesus as the climax of the story of Israel. Mark's gospel, for example, frames Jesus' ministry in terms of the long-awaited Isaianic new exodus culminating in God's reign over the earth (Isaiah 40–55). Jesus proclaims the kingdom in Galilee (Mark 1:1–8:21) and dies on the cross on Golgotha (11:1–16:8); but on "the way" from one to the other (8:22–10:52), he explains that his kingdom mission will culminate in his atoning death. Jesus is the crucified king who brings the kingdom by "way" of the cross.

In Colossians, the "blood of his cross" (Col 1:20) is the means for Christ's cosmic reconciliation (1:15–20) within the broader context of the eschatological transfer to the kingdom of Christ (1:12–14) with the effect of disarming the evil powers (2:13–15). Hebrews 2:5–10 succinctly captures the "big picture" of the kingdom and the cross, presenting Jesus as a last Adam who has restored God's royal design for creation and regained the "crown of glory and honor" for humanity through his death on the cross. Revelation explicitly says that King Jesus "has freed us from our sins by his blood and made us a kingdom" (Rev 1:5–6). This assertion is later described as a lion-like victory through lamb-like means (5:5–6), which entails the defeat of Satan by Christ and his followers (12:10–11). In sum, from the bruised heel of Gen 3:15 to the reigning Lamb of Rev 22:1, the Bible is a redemptive story of a crucified Messiah who brings the kingdom through his atoning death on the cross.

There are four key points regarding the kingdom and the cross that emerge from this story of redemption. (1) The Old Testament (especially Isaiah 40–55) is the proper framework for understanding the kingdom and the cross. Not only does the story of Adam and Israel provide all the right categories (and how to relate them), but the core promises of the kingdom in the Old Testament find their fulfillment through the cross in the New Testament (i.e., victory over enemies, forgiveness of sin, new exodus).

(2) Kingdom and cross need not vie for position in the story of redemption because they play different roles. The cross is central (in between the ages) and the kingdom is telic (the *telos* of the ages). The glory of God's wisdom, however, is displayed in the manner that the end-time kingdom has broken into the middle of history through the death of the Messiah.

(3) The cross is the causative turning point into the age to come—the kingdom of God. As Paul says, Jesus "gave himself for our sins to deliver us from the present evil age" (Gal 1:4). The great exchange (Christ's death for our sins) effects the great transition (the coming of the kingdom).

(4) Finally, the kingdom of God is established on earth by Christ's atoning death on the cross. *Establish* signals that Christ's atoning death is the decisive moment, though certainly not the only significant moment. God's kingdom was present in Jesus' life, proclaimed in his preaching, glimpsed in his miracles/exorcisms, established by his death, and inaugurated through the resurrection. It is now being advanced by the Holy Spirit and will be consummated in Christ's return.

THE LOGIC OF REDEMPTION

Since the kingdom and the cross are held together by the Christ, the doctrines of Christology, atonement, and kingdom must be properly understood, especially as they mutually inform each other. I therefore discuss the kingship of Christ (Christology) and his death on the cross (atonement), and examine how these inform God's reign over the earth (kingdom).

Jesus is anointed as king at his baptism (Matt 3:13–17); he is recognized as a king throughout his ministry (John 1:49; 6:15); and, as the triumphal entry makes clear (Matt 21:1–11), Jesus approaches the cross *as king* seeking to establish his kingdom. Unfortunately, the kingship of Christ on the cross has been downplayed by the overcategorization commonly employed in the doctrines of the two states of Christ (humiliation and exaltation) and the three offices of Christ (prophet, priest, and king). Christ's death has often been relegated solely to the state of humiliation and the office of priest, thereby making impossible any connection between the kingdom and the cross.

In light of the kingship of Christ on the cross, the states of Christ are best understood not in a strictly successive manner (exaltation *after* humiliation) but as exaltation *in* humiliation within the broader movement of exaltation *through* humiliation. This framework maintains the broader progression from suffering to glory (1 Peter 1:11), but recognizes that Christ's death is at once humiliation *and* exaltation (John 12:32–33). The kingship of Christ on the cross also demands a rethinking of the offices of Christ, whereby firm lines between Christ's priestly and kingly offices are erased, and Christ's death is understood as a priestly *and* kingly act.

The doctrine of the atonement is particularly important for integrating kingdom and cross, for what Christ accomplishes on the cross must be understood in tandem with his proclamation of the kingdom. Contemporary atonement debates have largely pitted *Christus Victor* and penal substitution against one another—the former emphasizing the cross as victory over unrightful rulers, and the latter focusing on the reconciliation of people. However, inasmuch as the coming of God's kingdom entails God's defeat of evil and reconciliation of sinners, *Christus Victor* and penal substitution are both essential aspects to Christ's kingdom-establishing death on the cross.

Therefore, rather than placing *Christus Victor* and penal substitution in opposition, or even upholding both separately, a better way is to recognize that Christ's victory over Satan is accomplished by his paying the penalty for sins—*Christus Victor* through penal substitution. On the cross, Jesus bears the penalty of sin by taking the place of sinners, thereby disarming Satan of his accusatory power and establishing God's kingdom on earth.

Finally, the kingdom of God must be understood in light of the atoning death of Christ the king. Inasmuch as God's kingdom is founded and forever shaped by the cross of Christ, it is truly a *cruciform* kingdom. Though already established and not yet consummated, in this age the kingdom is hidden beneath the foolishness of the cross, although perceived through faith to be the very power and wisdom of God. Furthermore, because the kingdom of God is primarily a statement about *God* (that he reigns), the cruciform nature of the kingdom has significant implications for the doctrine of God. Although the cross reveals that God rules through his self-giving love, it does not require that he rules *only* in such a manner. God is a compassionate *and* just king, who rules by saving *and* judging. God, in Christ, is the shepherd-king who lays down his life for his sheep and guards them against ferocious wolves. Lastly, just as God *established* his kingdom through the humble means of Christ's cross, so does he *advance* his kingdom through Christians who have been united to the resurrected Christ and who by the power of his Spirit are being conformed to the cross.

CROWN OF THORNS

The thief on the cross looked at the man from Nazareth being crucified next to him and said, "Jesus, remember me when you come into your kingdom" (Luke 23:42). Somehow this man conceived of the crucified Jesus as ruling over a kingdom. While the title on Christ's cross—"The King of the Jews"—makes explicit *that* there is a connection between the kingdom and the cross, perhaps the crown of thorns provides the best image for explaining *how* they relate. This is not, after all, the first time that thorns have showed up in the story.

Adam was to be a servant-king in the garden, but because he did not exercise dominion over the ground and the animals, the serpent ruled over him and the ground was cursed by God. Thorns first appear as a direct result and manifestation of the curse (Gen 3:17–18). Jesus comes as the last Adam, the faithful servant-king who not only fulfills Adam's commission of ruling over the earth but removes the curse by taking it onto himself. As Jesus wore the crown of thorns, he bore the curse of God. He is the "[seed] of a woman" who crushed Satan with a bruised heel (Gen 3:15). He is the seed of Abraham who "redeemed us from the curse of the law by becoming a curse for us . . . so that in Christ Jesus the blessing of Abraham might come to the Gentiles" (Gal 3:13–14). The thorns, which were a sign of the curse and defeat of Adam, are paradoxically transformed into a sign of the kingship and victory of Jesus. As Augustine said, the crown of thorns is a symbol that "the kingdom which was not of this world overcame that proud world, not by the ferocity of fighting, but by the humility of suffering."[2]

Jesus is the king who reigns by bearing the curse of the people whom he so loves. The connection between the cross and the curse, however, does reveal that the title given to Jesus during his crucifixion—"The King of the Jews"—was only partially correct. Inasmuch as the task of the Jews was to bring God's blessing to *all the earth* (Gen 12:3) and thereby reverse the curse

---

2. Augustine, *Tractate 116: John:19:1–16*, *NPNF¹* 7:425.

of sin in Genesis 3–11, Jesus—the Jewish Messiah—was claiming his throne not only over Israel but over all the earth. God accomplished his mission of restoring his creation through Jesus as he was enthroned as king on the cross. The kingdom of God comes in power, but the power of the gospel is Christ crucified.

BIBLIOGRAPHY

Abelard, Peter. "Exposition of the Epistle to the Romans (An Excerpt From the Second Book)." Pages 276–87 in *A Scholastic Miscellany: Anselm to Ockham*. Edited and translated by Eugene Fairweather. LCC. Philadelphia: Westminster, 1956.

Ahn, Yong-Sung. *The Reign of God and Rome in Luke's Passion Narrative: An East Asian Global Perspective*. Leiden: Brill, 2006.

Alexander, T. Desmond. "Genealogies, Seed and the Compositional Unity of Genesis." *TynBul* 44 (1993): 25–70.

———. "Royal Expectations in Genesis to Kings: Their Importance for Biblical Theology." *TynBul* 49 (1998): 191–212.

———. *The Servant King: The Bible's Portrait of the Messiah*. Vancouver, BC: Regent College, 2003.

Allis, Oswald Thompson. *The Unity of Isaiah: A Study in Prophecy*. Philadelphia: Presbyterian & Reformed, 1950.

Allison, D. C. *The End of the Ages Has Come*. Philadelphia: Fortress, 1985.

Anderson, Bernhard. "Exodus Typology in Second Isaiah." Pages 177–95 in *Israel's Prophetic Heritage: Essays in Honor of James Muilenburg*. Edited by Bernhard Anderson and W. Harrelson. New York: Harper, 1962.

Anselm. "Why God Became Man." Pages 260–356 in *Anselm of Canterbury: The Major Works*. Edited by Brian Davies and G. R. Evans. OWC. Oxford: Oxford University Press, 2008.

Aquinas, Thomas. *Summa Theologica*. Translated by Fathers of the English Dominican Province. New York: Benziger Bros, 1947.

Arnold, Clinton. "Satan, Devil." Pages 1077–82 in *DLNT*. Edited by Ralph P. Martin and Peter H. Davids. Downers Grove, IL: InterVarsity Press, 1997.

———. *The Colossian Syncretism: The Interface Between Christianity and Folk Belief at Colossae*. Grand Rapids: Baker, 1996.

———. "The Kingdom, Miracles, Satan, and Demons." Pages 153–78 in *The Kingdom of God*. Edited by Christopher Morgan and Robert Peterson. Theology in Community. Wheaton, IL: Crossway, 2012.

Athanasius. *On the Incarnation*. Crestwood, NY: St. Vladimir's Seminary Press, 2002.

Attridge, Harold. *The Epistle to the Hebrews: A Commentary on the Epistle to the Hebrews*. Hermeneia. Philadelphia: Fortress, 1989.

Augustine. *WSA*. Edited by John E. Rotelle. Brooklyn: New City, 1990–2009.

Aulén, Gustaf. *Christus Victor: An Historical Study of the Three Main Types of the Idea of Atonement*. New York: Macmillan, 1969.

———. *The Faith of the Christian Church*. Philadelphia: Muhlenberg, 1948.

Barth, Karl. *The Doctrine of Reconciliation*. Edited by G. W. Bromiley and Thomas Torrance. Translated by G. W. Bromiley. Vol. IV/1. *Church Dogmatics*. Edinburgh: T&T Clark, 1958.

———. *The Doctrine of Reconciliation*. Edited by G. W. Bromiley and Thomas Torrance. Translated by G. W. Bromiley. Vol. IV/2. *Church Dogmatics*. Edinburgh: T&T Clark, 1958.

Barth, Markus, and Helmut Blanke. *Colossians: A New Translation with Introduction and Commentary*. AB. New York: Doubleday, 1994.

Bartholomew, Craig, and Michael Goheen. "Story and Biblical Theology." Pages 144–71 in *Out of Egypt: Biblical Theology and Biblical Interpretation*. Edited by Craig Bartholomew, Mary Healy, Karl Möller, and Robin Parry. Grand Rapids: Zondervan, 2004.

———. *The Drama of Scripture: Finding Our Place in the Biblical Story*. Grand Rapids: Baker Academic, 2004.

Bauckham, Richard. *Moltmann: Messianic Theology in the Making*. Basingstoke, UK: Pickering, 1987.

———. *The Theology of Jürgen Moltmann*. Edinburgh: T&T Clark, 1995.

———. *The Theology of the Book of Revelation*. New York: Cambridge University Press, 1993.

———. "Where is Wisdom to be Found? Colossians 1:15–20 (2)." Pages 129–38 in *Reading Texts, Seeking Wisdom: Scripture and Theology*. Edited by David Ford and Graham Stanton. Grand Rapids: Eerdmans, 2004.

Bavinck, Herman. *Sin and Salvation in Christ*. Vol. 3 of *Reformed Dogmatics*. Edited by John Bolt. Translated by John Vriend. Grand Rapids: Baker Academic, 2003.

Beale, G. K. *A New Testament Biblical Theology: The Unfolding of the Old Testament in the New*. Grand Rapids: Baker Academic, 2011.

———. *The Book of Revelation: A Commentary on the Greek Text*. NIGTC. Grand Rapids: Eerdmans, 1999.

———. *The Temple and the Church's Mission: A Biblical Theology of the Temple*. NSBT. Downers Grove, IL: InterVarsity Press, 2004.

Beaton, Richard. *Isaiah's Christ in Matthew's Gospel*. Cambridge: Cambridge University Press, 2002.

Becker, Jürgen. *Jesus of Nazareth*. New York: de Gruyter, 1998.

Beilby, James, and Paul Eddy. "Atonement." Pages 84–92 in *Global Dictionary of Theology*. Edited by William Dyrness and Veli-Matti Kärkkäinen. Downers Grove, IL: InterVarsity Press, 2008.

Beilby, James, and Paul Eddy, eds. *The Nature of the Atonement: Four Views*. Downers Grove, IL: InterVarsity Press, 2006.

Belcher, Jim. *Deep Church: A Third Way Beyond Emerging and Traditional*. Downers Grove, IL: InterVarsity Press, 2009.

Belousek, Darrin W. Snyder. *Atonement, Justice, and Peace: The Message of the Cross and the Mission of the Church*. Grand Rapids: Eerdmans, 2012.

Berkhof, Louis. *Systematic Theology*. Grand Rapids: Eerdmans, 1979.

Beskow, Per. *Rex Gloriae: The Kingship of Christ in the Early Church*. Stockholm: Almqvist & Wiksell, 1962.

Bethancourt, Phillip. "Christ the Warrior King: A Biblical, Historical, and Theological Analysis of the Divine Warrior Theme in Christology." Ph.D. diss., Southern Baptist Theological Seminary, 2011.

Betz, Hans Dieter. *Galatians: A Commentary on Paul's Letter to the Churches in Galatia*. Hermeneia. Philadelphia: Fortress, 1979.

Beuken, W. A. M. "The Main Theme of Trito-Isaiah 'the Servants of Yhwh.'" *JSOT* 15 (1990): 67–87.

Billings, J. Todd. *The Word of God for the People of God: An Entryway to the Theological Interpretation of Scripture*. Grand Rapids: Eerdmans, 2010.

———. *Union with Christ: Reframing Theology and Ministry for the Church*. Grand Rapids: Baker Academic, 2011.

Bird, Michael. "Mark: Interpreter of Peter and Disciple of Paul." Pages 30–61 in *Paul and the Gospels: Christologies, Conflicts and Convergences*. Edited by Michael Bird and Joel Willitts. London: T&T Clark, 2011.

———. "The Crucifixion of Jesus as the Fulfillment of Mark 9:1." *TJ* 24 (2003): 23–36.

Bird, Michael, and Joel Willitts, eds. *Paul and the Gospels: Christologies, Conflicts and Convergences*. London: T&T Clark, 2011.

Blenkinsopp, Joseph. *Isaiah 56–66: A New Translation with Introduction and Commentary*. AB. New York: Doubleday, 2003.

Blocher, Henri. "*Agnus Victor*: The Atonement as Victory and Vicarious Punishment." Pages 67–91 in *What Does It Mean to Be Saved? Broadening Evangelical Horizons of Salvation*. Edited by John Stackhouse. Grand Rapids: Baker Academic, 2002.

———. "Atonement." Pages 72–76 in *DTIB*. Edited by Kevin J. Vanhoozer. Grand Rapids: Baker, 2005.

———. "Biblical Metaphors and the Doctrine of the Atonement." *JETS* 47 (2004): 629–45.

———. *Evil and the Cross: Christian Thought and the Problem of Evil*. Downers Grove, IL: InterVarsity Press, 1994.

———. "God and the Cross." Pages 125–41 in *Engaging the Doctrine of God: Contemporary Protestant Perspectives*. Edited by Bruce McCormack. Grand Rapids: Baker Academic, 2008.

———. *La doctrine du péché et de la rédemption*. Vaux-sur-Seine, France: EDIFAC, 2000.

———. *Songs of the Servant: Isaiah's Good News*. Downers Grove, IL: InterVarsity Press, 1975.

———. "The Atonement in John Calvin's Theology." Pages 279–303 in *The Glory of the Atonement*. Edited by Charles Hill and Frank James. Downers Grove, IL: InterVarsity Press, 2004.

———. "The Sacrifice of Jesus Christ: The Current Theological Situation." *EuroJTh* 8 (1999): 23–36.

Block, Daniel. "My Servant David: Ancient Israel's Vision of the Messiah." Pages 17–56 in *Israel's Messiah in the Bible and the Dead Sea Scrolls*. Edited by Richard Hess and Daniel Carroll R. Grand Rapids: Baker Academic, 2003.

Bloesch, Donald. *Jesus Christ: Savior and Lord*. Downers Grove, IL: InterVarsity Press, 1997.

Boersma, Hans. *Violence, Hospitality, and the Cross: Reappropriating the Atonement Tradition*. Grand Rapids: Baker Academic, 2004.

———. "Violence, the Cross, and Divine Intentionality: A Modified Reformed View." Pages 47–72 in *Atonement and Violence*. Edited by John Sanders. Nashville: Abingdon, 2006.

Bolt, Peter. "'. . . With a View to the Forgiveness of Sins': Jesus and Forgiveness in Mark's Gospel." *RTR* 57 (1998): 53–69.

———. *Jesus' Defeat of Death: Persuading Mark's Early Readers*. Cambridge: Cambridge University Press, 2003.

———. "Mark 13: An Apocalyptic Precursor to the Passion Narrative." *RTR* 54 (1995): 10–32.

———. *The Cross from a Distance: Atonement in Mark's Gospel*. NSBT. Downers Grove, IL: InterVarsity Press, 2004.

———. "Towards a Biblical Theology of the Defeat of the Evil Powers." Pages 35–81 in *Christ's Victory over Evil: Biblical Theology and Pastoral Ministry*. Edited by Peter Bolt. Nottingham, UK: Apollos, 2009.

Bonhoeffer, Dietrich. "Thy Kingdom Come: The Prayer of the Church For God's Kingdom on Earth." Pages 27–47 in *Preface to Bonhoeffer: The Man and Two of His Shorter Writings*. Edited by John Godsey. Philadelphia: Fortress, 1965.

Borg, Marcus J., and N. T. Wright. *The Meaning of Jesus: Two Visions*. San Francisco: HarperSanFrancisco, 1999.

Boring, Eugene. *Revelation*. IBC. Louisville: Westminster John Knox, 1989.

Borsch, Frederick Houk. *Power in Weakness: New Hearing for Gospel Stories of Healing and Discipleship*. Philadelphia: Fortress, 1983.

Botterweck, G. Johannes, Helmer Ringgren, and Heinz-Josef Fabry, eds. *Theological Dictionary of the Old Testament*. Translated by David E. Green. Grand Rapids: Eerdmans, 1974–2006.

Boyd, Gregory. "*Christus Victor* View." Pages 23–49 in *The Nature of the Atonement: Four Views*. Edited by James Beilby and Paul Eddy. Downers Grove, IL: InterVarsity Press, 2006.

———. *God at War: The Bible and Spiritual Conflict*. Downers Grove, IL: InterVarsity Press, 1997.

Bray, Gerald. "The Kingdom and Eschatology." Pages 207–28 in *The Kingdom of God*. Edited by Christopher Morgan and Robert Peterson. Theology in Community. Wheaton, IL: Crossway, 2012.

Bright, John. *The Kingdom of God: The Biblical Concept and Its Meaning for the Church*. Nashville: Abingdon, 1957.

Brondos, David. *Fortress Introduction to Salvation and the Cross*. Minneapolis: Fortress, 2007.

———. "Why Was Jesus Crucified? Theology, History and the Story of Redemption." *SJT* 54 (2001): 484–503.

Brower, Kent. "Mark 9:1: Seeing the Kingdom in Power." *JSNT* (1980): 17–41.

Brown, Francis, S. R. Driver, and Charles A. Briggs. *A Hebrew Lexicon of the Old Testament with an Appendix Containing Biblical Aramaic*. Oxford: Clarendon, 1977.

Brown, Joanne Carlson, and Rebecca Parker. "For God So Loved the World." Pages 1–30 in *Christianity, Patriarchy, and Abuse: A Feminist Critique*. Edited by Joanne Carlson Brown and Carole Bohn. New York: Pilgrim, 1989.

Bruce, A. B. *The Humiliation of Christ: In Its Physical, Ethical, and Official Aspects*. Grand Rapids: Eerdmans, 1955.

Bruce, F. F. "Christ as Conqueror and Reconciler." *BSac* 141 (1984): 291–302.

Brueggemann, Walter. *Genesis*. IBC. Atlanta: John Knox, 1982.

Brunner, Emil. *The Doctrine of Creation and Redemption*. Vol. 2 of *Dogmatics*. Philadelphia: Westminster, 1950.

———. *The Mediator: A Study of the Central Doctrine of the Christian Faith*. Philadelphia: Westminster, 1947.

Buchanan, George Wesley. "The Day of Atonement and Paul's Doctrine of Redemption." *NovT* 32 (1990): 236–49.

Bultmann, Rudolf. *Jesus Christ and Mythology*. New York: Scribner, 1958.

———. *The History of the Synoptic Tradition*. Translated by John Marsh. New York: Harper & Row, 1963.

Byron, George Noël Gordon, Baron. *The Works of Lord Byron: Complete in One Volume*. London: John Murray, 1841.

Caird, G. B. *A Commentary on the Revelation of St. John the Divine*. BNTC. London: Black, 1966.

Calvin, John. *Calvin's Commentaries*. Translated by Calvin Translation Society. Grand Rapids: Baker, 1999.

———. *Institutes of the Christian Religion*. Edited by John McNeill. Translated by Ford Lewis Battles. LCC. Louisville: Westminster John Knox, 2006.

Camery-Hoggatt, Jerry. *Irony in Mark's Gospel: Text and Subtext*. Cambridge: Cambridge University Press, 1992.

Caneday, Ardel. "Christ's Baptism and Crucifixion: The Anointing and Enthronement of God's Son." *SBJT* 8 (2004): 70–85.

Carey, Holly. *Jesus' Cry from the Cross: Towards a First-Century Understanding of the Intertextual Relationship between Psalm 22 and the Narrative of Mark's Gospel*. New York: T&T Clark, 2009.

Carroll, Daniel. "The Power of the Future in the Present: Eschatology and Ethics in O'Donovan and Beyond." Pages 116–43 in *A Royal Priesthood? The Use of the Bible Ethically and Politically: A Dialogue with Oliver O'Donovan*. Edited by Craig Bartholomew. SHS. Carlisle, UK: Paternoster, 2002.

Carson, D. A. "Matthew." *EBC*. Grand Rapids: Zondervan, 1995.

———. "Systematic Theology and Biblical Theology." Pages 89–103 in *NDBT*. Edited by T. Desmond Alexander and Brian Rosner. Downers Grove, IL: InterVarsity Press, 2000.

———. *The Gospel According to John*. PiNTC. Grand Rapids: Eerdmans, 1991.

———. "The Wrath of God." Pages 37–66 in *Engaging the Doctrine of God: Contemporary Protestant Perspectives*. Edited by Bruce L. McCormack. Grand Rapids: Baker Academic, 2008.

Cassuto, Umberto. *A Commentary on the Book of Genesis*. Vol. 1. Jerusalem: Magnes, 1989.

Chalke, Steve, and Alan Mann. *The Lost Message of Jesus*. Grand Rapids: Zondervan, 2003.

Chan, Mark. "The Gospel and the Achievement of the Cross." *ERT* 33 (2009): 19–31.

Chatraw, Josh. "Balancing Out (Wright): Jesus' Theology of Individual and Corporate Repentance and Forgiveness in the Gospel of Luke." *JETS* 55 (2012): 299–322.

Chester, Tim. *Mission and the Coming of God: Eschatology, the Trinity and Mission in the Theology of Jürgen Moltmann and Contemporary Evangelicalism*. PTM. Waynesboro, GA: Paternoster, 2006.

Childs, Brevard. *Isaiah*. OTL. Louisville: Westminster John Knox, 2001.

Chrupcala, Lesław. *The Kingdom of God: A Bibliography of 20th Century Research*. Jerusalem: Franciscan, 2007.

Chung, Sung Wook. *Jürgen Moltmann and Evangelical Theology: A Critical Engagement*. Eugene, OR: Pickwick, 2012.

Ciampa, Roy. "The History of Redemption." Pages 254–308 in *Central Themes in Biblical Theology: Mapping Unity in Diversity*. Edited by Scott Hafemann and Paul House. Grand Rapids: Baker Academic, 2007.

Clements, Ronald. "Beyond Tradition-History: Deutero-Isaianic Development of First Isaiah's Themes." *JSOT* 31 (1985): 95–113.

Coakley, Sarah. "*Kenōsis* and Subversion: On the Repression of 'Vulnerability' in Christian Feminist Writing." Pages 3–39 in *Powers and Submissions: Spirituality, Philosophy and Gender*. Malden, MA: Blackwell, 2002.

Cole, Graham. *God the Peacemaker: How Atonement Brings Shalom*. NSBT. Downers Grove, IL: InterVarsity Press, 2009.

———. "The Peril of a 'Historyless' Systematic Theology." Pages 55–70 in *Do Historical Matters Matter to Faith? A Critical Appraisal of Modern and Postmodern Approaches to Scripture*. Edited by James Hoffmeier and Dennis Magary. Wheaton, IL: Crossway, 2012.

Collins, Adela Yarbro. *Mark: A Commentary*. Hermeneia. Minneapolis: Fortress, 2007.

Collins, Jack. "A Syntactical Note (Genesis 3:15): Is the Woman's Seed Singular or Plural?" *TynBul* 48 (1997): 139–48.

Conzelman, Hans. *The Theology of St. Luke*. New York: Harper & Row, 1961.

Creach, Jerome. *The Destiny of the Righteous in the Psalms*. St. Louis: Chalice, 2008.

Cullmann, Oscar. *Christ and Time: The Primitive Christian Conception of Time and History*. Philadelphia: Westminster, 1964.

Dalman, Gustaf. *The Words of Jesus.* Translated by D. M. Kay. Edinburgh: T&T Clark, 1902.

Dautzenberg, G. "Psalm 110 im Neuen Testament." Pages 141–71 in volume 1 of *Liturgie und Dichtung.* Edited by H. Becker and R. Kacyznski. St. Ottilien: Eos, 1983.

Davies, John. *Royal Priesthood: Literary and Intertextual Perspectives on an Image of Israel in Exodus 19:6.* JSOTSup 395. London: T&T Clark, 2004.

Davies, W. D., and D. C. Allison. *A Critical and Exegetical Commentary on the Gospel according to Saint Matthew.* 3 vols. ICC. Edinburgh: T&T Clark, 1988–1997.

Demarest, Bruce. *The Cross and Salvation: The Doctrine of Salvation.* FET. Wheaton, IL: Crossway, 1997.

Dembele, Youssouf. "Salvation as Victory: A Reconsideration of the Concept of Salvation in the Light of Jesus Christ's Life and Work Viewed as a Triumph Over the Personal Powers of Evil." PhD diss., Trinity Evangelical Divinity School, 2001.

Dempster, Stephen. *Dominion and Dynasty: A Biblical Theology of the Hebrew Bible.* NSBT. Downers Grove, IL: InterVarsity Press, 2003.

———. "The Servant of the Lord." Pages 128–78 in *Central Themes in Biblical Theology: Mapping Unity in Diversity.* Edited by Scott Hafemann and Paul House. Grand Rapids: Baker Academic, 2007.

Denney, James. *The Atonement and the Modern Mind.* London: Hodder & Stoughton, 1903.

———. *The Death of Christ: Its Place and Interpretation in the New Testament.* New York: A. C. Armstrong and Son, 1904.

Deschner, John. *Wesley's Christology: An Interpretation.* Grand Rapids: Francis Asbury, 1988.

Dewey, Joanna. "Literary Structure of the Controversy Stories in Mark 2:1–3:6." *JBL* 92 (1973): 394–401.

———. *Markan Public Debate: Literary Technique, Concentric Structure, and Theology in Mark 2:1–3:6.* SBLDS 48. Chico, CA: Scholars, 1979.

Diamond, John. "The Interpretation of the Demonic in the Theologies of Gustaf Aulén and Karl Heim." PhD diss., Boston University, 1969.

Dodd, C. H. *According to the Scriptures: The Sub-Structure of New Testament Theology.* London: Nisbet, 1952.

———. *The Bible and the Greeks.* London: Hodder & Stoughton, 1935.

Donahue, S. J. "Temple, Trial, and Royal Christology (Mark 14:53–65)." Pages 61–79 in *The Passion in Mark: Studies on Mark 14–16.* Edited by Werner Kelber. Philadelphia: Fortress, 1976.

Drury, John. *The Parables in the Gospels: History and Allegory.* New York: Crossroad, 1985.

Duby, S. "The Cross and the Fulness of God: Clarifying the Meaning of Divine Wrath in Penal Substitution." *SBET* 29 (2011): 165–76.

Duhm, Bernhard. *Das Buch Jesaia.* KKHS. Göttingen: Vandenhoeck & Ruprecht, 1892.

Dumbrell, William. *Covenant and Creation: A Theology of the Old Testament Covenants.* Grand Rapids: Baker, 1993.

———. *The Faith of Israel: A Theological Survey of the Old Testament.* 2nd ed. Grand Rapids: Baker Academic, 2002.

———. "The Role of the Servant in Isaiah 40–55." *RTR* 48 (1989): 105–13.

———. *The Search for Order: Biblical Eschatology in Focus.* Grand Rapids: Baker, 1994.

Dunn, James. *Jesus Remembered.* Grand Rapids: Eerdmans, 2003.

———. *The Epistles to the Colossians and to Philemon: A Commentary on the Greek Text.* NIGTC. Grand Rapids: Eerdmans, 1996.

Eckardt, Burnell, Jr. "Luther and Moltmann: The Theology of the Cross." *CTQ* 49 (1985): 19–28.

Edmondson, Stephen. *Calvin's Christology.* Cambridge: Cambridge University Press, 2004.

Eisenbise, Kate. "Resurrection as Victory? The Eschatological Implications of J. Denny Weaver's 'Narrative *Christus Victor*' Model of Atonement." *BLT* 53 (2008): 9–22.

Eissler, Tobias. "Die Heilstat Jesu Christi in altkirchlicher, mittelalterlicher und reformatorischer Sicht." Pages 107–37 in *Warum das Kreuz? Die Frage nach der Bedeutung des Todes Jesu.* Edited by Volker Gäckle. Wuppertal: Brockhaus, 1998.

Eller, Vernard. *The Most Revealing Book of the Bible: Making Sense Out of Revelation.* Grand Rapids: Eerdmans, 1974.

Erickson, Millard. *Christian Theology.* 2nd ed. Grand Rapids: Baker Academic, 1998.

Evans, Craig. "Inaugurating the Kingdom of God and Defeating the Kingdom of Satan." *BBR* 15 (2005): 49–75.

Fairweather, Eugene. "Incarnation and Atonement: An Anselmian Response to Aulén's *Christus Victor.*" *CJT* 7 (1961): 167–75.

Farrow, Douglas. "Ascension." Pages 65–68 in *DTIB.* Edited by Kevin Vanhoozer. Grand Rapids: Baker, 2005.

———. *Ascension and Ecclesia: On the Significance of the Doctrine of the Ascension for Ecclesiology and Christian Cosmology.* Grand Rapids: Eerdmans, 1999.

————. *Ascension Theology.* New York: T&T Clark, 2011.

Feinberg, John S. *No One Like Him: The Doctrine of God.* FET. Wheaton, IL: Crossway, 2001.

Fenton. "Paul and Mark." Pages 89–112 in *Studies in the Gospels: Essays in Memory of R. H. Lighfoot.* Edited by D. E. Nineham. Oxford: Blackwell, 1967.

Ferguson, Sinclair. "*Christus Victor et Propitiator*: The Death of Christ, Substitute and Conqueror." Pages 171–89 in *For the Fame of God's Name.* Edited by Sam Storms and Justin Taylor. Wheaton, IL: Crossway, 2010.

Fiddes, Paul. *Past Event and Present Salvation: The Christian Idea of Atonement.* Louisville: Westminster John Knox, 1989.

Finger, Thomas. "*Christus Victor* and the Creeds: Some Historical Considerations." *MQR* 72 (1998): 31–51.

Fishbane, Michael. *Biblical Interpretation in Ancient Israel.* New York: Clarendon, 1985.

Flood, Derek. "Substitutionary Atonement and the Church Fathers: A Reply to the Authors of Pierced for Our Transgressions." *EvQ* 82 (2010): 142–59.

Forde, Gerhard. *On Being a Theologian of the Cross: Reflections on Luther's Heidelberg Disputation, 1518.* Grand Rapids: Eerdmans, 1997.

————. "Robert Jenson's Soteriology." Pages 126–38 in *Trinity, Time, and Church: A Response to the Theology of Robert W. Jenson.* Edited by Colin Gunton. Grand Rapids: Eerdmans, 2000.

Forsyth, Peter. *God the Holy Father.* London: Independent, 1957.

France, R. T. *Divine Government: God's Kingship in the Gospel of Mark.* London: SPCK, 1990.

————. "Kingdom of God." Pages 420–22 in *DTIB.* Edited by Kevin Vanhoozer. Grand Rapids: Baker Academic, 2005.

————. *Matthew: Evangelist & Teacher.* NTP. Downers Grove, IL: InterVarsity Press, 1998.

————. *The Gospel of Mark: A Commentary on the Greek Text.* NIGTC. Grand Rapids: Eerdmans, 2002.

Frei, Hans W. *The Eclipse of Biblical Narrative: A Study in Eighteenth and Nineteenth Century Hermeneutics.* New Haven, CT: Yale University Press, 1974.

Gaffin, Richard. "Atonement in the Pauline Corpus: 'The Scandal of the Cross.'" Pages 140–62 in *The Glory of the Atonement: Biblical, Theological, and Practical Perspectives.* Edited by Charles Hill and Frank James. Downers Grove, IL: InterVarsity Press, 2004.

———. *"By Faith, Not by Sight": Paul and the Order of Salvation*. Bletchley, UK: Paternoster, 2006.

———. "The Usefulness of the Cross." *WTJ* 41 (1979): 228–46.

Galvin, John. "Jesus' Approach to Death: An Examination of Some Recent Studies." *TS* 41 (1980): 713–44.

Gathercole, Simon. "The Gospel of Paul and the Gospel of the Kingdom." Pages 138–54 in *God's Power to Save*. Edited by Chris Green. Downers Grove, IL: InterVarsity Press, 2006.

Gavrilyuk, Paul. *The Suffering of the Impassible God: The Dialectics of Patristic Thought*. The Oxford Early Christian Studies. Oxford: Oxford University Press, 2004.

———. "God's Impassible Suffering in the Flesh: The Promise of Paradoxical Christology." Pages 127–49 in *Divine Impassibility and the Mystery of Human Suffering*. Edited by James Keating and Thomas Joseph White. Grand Rapids: Eerdmans, 2009.

Gentry, Peter. "Kingdom through Covenant: Humanity as the Divine Image." *SBJT* 12 (2008): 16–42.

———. "The Atonement in Isaiah's Fourth Servant Song (Isaiah 52:13–53:12)." *SBJT* 11 (2007): 20–47.

Gentry, Peter, and Stephen Wellum. *Kingdom through Covenant: A Biblical-Theological Understanding of the Covenants*. Wheaton, IL: Crossway, 2012.

George, Timothy. "The Atonement in Martin Luther's Theology." Pages 263–78 in *The Glory of the Atonement*. Edited by Charles Hill and Frank James. Downers Grove, IL: InterVarsity Press, 2004.

Gese, Hartmut. *Vom Sinai zum Zion: alttestamentliche Beiträge zur biblischen Theologie*. Munich: Kaiser, 1974.

Gilkey, Langdon. "Cosmology, Ontology, and the Travail of Biblical Language." *JR* 41 (1961): 194–205.

Girard, Rene. *I See Satan Fall Like Lightning*. New York: Orbis, 2001.

Goldingay, John. *Isaiah*. NIBCOT 13. Peabody, MA: Hendrickson, 2001.

———. *Israel's Faith*. Vol. 2. *Old Testament Theology*. Downers Grove, IL: InterVarsity Press, 2006.

Goldingay, John, and David Payne. *A Critical and Exegetical Commentary on Isaiah 40–55*. ICC. London: T&T Clark, 2006.

Goldsworthy, Graeme. "The Gospel in Revelation." Pages 149–328 in *The Goldsworthy Trilogy*. Carlisle, UK: Paternoster, 2000.

———. "The Kingdom of God as Hermeneutic Grid." *SBJT* 12 (2008): 4–15.

Gomes, Alan. "De Jesu Christo Servatore: Faustus Socinus on the Satisfaction of Christ." *WTJ* 55 (1993): 209–31.

———. "Faustus Socinus' *De Jesu Christo Servatore*, Part III: Historical Introduction, Translation and Critical Notes." PhD diss., Fuller Theological Seminary, 1990.

Gordley, Matthew. *The Colossian Hymn in Context: An Exegesis in Light of Jewish and Greco-Roman Hymnic and Epistolary Conventions*. Tübingen: Mohr Siebeck, 2007.

Gorman, Michael J. *Cruciformity: Paul's Narrative Spirituality of the Cross*. Grand Rapids: Eerdmans, 2001.

———. *Inhabiting the Cruciform God: Kenosis, Justification, and Theosis in Paul's Narrative Soteriology*. Grand Rapids: Eerdmans, 2009.

Grappe, Christian. *Le royaume de dieu: avant, avec et après Jésus*. MB. Genève: Labor et Fides, 2001.

Green, Joel. "Kaleidoscopic View." Pages 157–85 in *The Nature of the Atonement: Four Views*. Edited by James Beilby and Paul Eddy. Downers Grove, IL: InterVarsity Press, 2006.

———. "Must We Imagine the Atonement in Penal Substitutionary Terms?" Pages 153–71 in *The Atonement Debate*. Edited by Derek Tidball, David Hilborn, and Justin Thacker. Grand Rapids: Zondervan, 2008.

Green, Joel, and Mark Baker. *Recovering the Scandal of the Cross: Atonement in New Testament and Contemporary Contexts*. Downers Grove, IL: InterVarsity Press, 2000.

Greer, Rowan. "Christ the Victor and the Victim." *CTQ* 59 (1995): 1–30.

Gregory of Nyssa. "An Address on Religious Instruction." Pages 268–325 in *Christology of the Later Fathers*. Edited by Edward Hardy. LCC. Philadelphia: Westminster, 1954.

Grillmeier, Alois. *Christ in Christian Tradition*. Translated by John Bowden. Atlanta: John Knox, 1975.

Van Groningen, Gerard. *Messianic Revelation in the Old Testament*. Grand Rapids: Baker, 1990.

Groves, J. Alan. "Atonement in Isaiah 53: For He Bore the Sins of Many." Pages 61–89 in *The Glory of the Atonement*. Edited by Charles Hill and Frank James III. Downers Grove, IL: InterVarsity Press, 2004.

Grudem, Wayne. "States of Jesus Christ." Pages 1052–54 in *EDT*. Edited by Walter Elwell. Grand Rapids: Baker, 1989.

———. *Systematic Theology: An Introduction to Biblical Doctrine*. Grand Rapids: Zondervan, 1995.

Gundry, Robert. *Mark: A Commentary on His Apology for the Cross.* Grand Rapids, 2000.

Gunton, Colin. "Atonement: The Sacrifice and the Sacrifices, From Metaphor to Transcendental?" Pages 181–200 in *Father, Son, and Holy Spirit: Essays Toward a Fully Trinitarian Theology.* New York: T&T Clark, 2003.

———. *The Actuality of Atonement: A Study of Metaphor, Rationality and the Christian Tradition.* London: T&T Clark, 1988.

Gurtner, Daniel. *The Torn Veil: Matthew's Exposition of the Death of Jesus.* Cambridge: Cambridge University Press, 2007.

Guttesen, Poul. *Leaning into the Future: The Kingdom of God in the Theology of Jürgen Moltmann and in the Book of Revelation.* PTMS. Eugene, OR: Pickwick, 2009.

Haag, Herbert. *Der Gottesknecht bei Deuterojesaja.* EdF 233. Darmstadt: Wissenschaftliche Buchgesellschaft, 1985.

Hafemann, Scott. *The God of Promise and the Life of Faith: Understanding the Heart of the Bible.* Wheaton, IL: Crossway, 2001.

Hahn, Scott. *Kinship by Covenant: A Canonical Approach to the Fulfillment of God's Saving Promises.* New Haven, CT: Yale University Press, 2009.

Hamilton, James. "The Seed of the Woman and the Blessing of Abraham." *TynBul* 58 (2007): 253–73.

———. "The Skull Crushing Seed of the Woman: Inner-Biblical Interpretation of Genesis 3:15." *SBJT* 10 (2006): 30–54.

Harnack, Adolf von. *What is Christianity?* Translated by Thomas Saunders. Philadelphia: Fortress, 1986.

Harris, R. Laird, Gleason Leonard Archer, and Bruce Waltke, eds. *Theological Wordbook of the Old Testament.* Chicago: Moody Press, 1981.

Hart, David Bentley. *The Beauty of the Infinite: The Aesthetics of Christian Truth.* Grand Rapids: Eerdmans, 2003.

Hart, Trevor. "Redemption and Fall." Pages 189–206 in *The Cambridge Companion to Christian Doctrine.* Edited by Colin Gunton. Cambridge: Cambridge University Press, 1997.

———. "Systematic—In What Sense?" Pages 341–51 in *Out of Egypt: Biblical Theology and Biblical Interpretation.* Edited by Craig Bartholomew, Mary Healy, Karl Möller, and Robin Parry. Grand Rapids: Zondervan, 2004.

Harvie, Timothy. *Jürgen Moltmann's Ethics of Hope: Eschatological Possibilities for Moral Action.* Burlington, VT: Ashgate, 2009.

Hays, Richard. *First Corinthians.* IBC. Louisville: Westminster John Knox, 2011.

————. "Knowing Jesus: Story, History, and the Question of Truth." Pages 41–61 in *Jesus, Paul, and the People of God: A Theological Dialogue with N. T. Wright*. Edited by Nicholas Perrin and Richard Hays. Downers Grove, IL: InterVarsity Press, 2011.

————. *The Moral Vision of the New Testament: Community, Cross, New Creation: A Contemporary Introduction to New Testament Ethics*. San Francisco: HarperSanFrancisco, 1996.

Heim, K. M. "Kings and Kingship." Pages 610–23 in *DOTHB*. Edited by Bill T. Arnold and H. G. M. Williamson. Downers Grove, IL: InterVarsity Press, 2005.

Heim, Karl. *Jesus, the World's Perfecter: The Atonement and the Renewal of the World*. Edinburgh: Oliver and Boyd, 1959.

Heim, S. Mark. *Saved from Sacrifice: A Theology of the Cross*. Grand Rapids: Eerdmans, 2006.

Hengel, Martin. *Crucifixion in the Ancient World and the Folly of the Message of the Cross*. Philadelphia: Fortress, 1977.

————. *The Cross of the Son of God*. London: SCM, 1986.

————. "The Kingdom of Christ in John." Pages 333–58 in *Studies in Early Christology*. Edinburgh: T&T Clark, 1995.

Hengstenberg, Ernst Wilhelm. *Christology of the Old Testament: And a Commentary on the Messianic Predictions*. Edinburgh: T&T Clark, 1861.

Heppe, Heinrich. *Reformed Dogmatics: Set Out and Illustrated from the Sources*. Translated by Ernst Bizer. Grand Rapids: Baker, 1978.

Heppe, Heinrich, and Ernst Bizer. *Die Dogmatik der evangelisch-reformierten Kirche*. Neukirchen: Moers, 1958.

Hesse, Franz. "מָשַׁח and מָשִׁיחַ in the Old Testament." Pages 496–509 in *TDNT*, vol. 9. Edited by Gerhard Kittel and Gerhard Friedrich, translated by Geoffrey Bromiley. Grand Rapids: Eerdmans, 1974.

Hidal, Sten. "En segrande *Christus victor*? Auléns analys av ett forsoningsmotiv i backspegeln." *Svensk teologisk kvartalskrift* 86 (2010): 171–76.

Hodge, Charles. *Systematic Theology*. 3 vols. Grand Rapids: Eerdmans, 1968.

Holmes, Michael, ed. *The Apostolic Fathers in English*. Translated by Michael Holmes. 3rd ed. Grand Rapids: Baker Academic, 2006.

Holmes, Stephen. "Can Punishment Bring Peace? Penal Substitution Revisited." *SJT* 58 (2005): 104–23.

————. "The Upholding of Beauty: A Reading of Anselm's *Cur Deus Homo*." *SJT* 54 (2001): 189–203.

————. *The Wondrous Cross: Atonement and Penal Substitution in the Bible and History*. Bletchley, UK: Paternoster, 2007.

Hood, Jason. "The Cross in the New Testament: Two Theses in Conversation with Recent Literature (2000–2007)." *WTJ* 71 (2009): 281–95.

Hoogland, Marvin. *Calvin's Perspective on the Exaltation of Christ in Comparison with the Post-Reformation Doctrine of the Two States.* Kampen: Kok, 1966.

Hooker, Morna. *From Adam to Christ: Essays on Paul.* Cambridge: Cambridge University Press, 1990.

———. *The Son of Man in Mark: A Study of the Background of the Term "Son of Man" and Its Use in St. Mark's Gospel.* Montreal: McGill University Press, 1967.

———. "Where Is Wisdom to Be Found? Colossians 1:15–20 (1)." Pages 116–28 in *Reading Texts, Seeking Wisdom: Scripture and Theology.* Edited by David Ford and Graham Stanton. Grand Rapids: Eerdmans, 2004.

Horton, Michael. *Covenant and Eschatology: The Divine Drama.* Louisville: Westminster John Knox, 2002.

———. *Lord and Servant: A Covenant Christology.* Louisville: Westminster John Knox, 2005.

———. *The Christian Faith: A Systematic Theology for Pilgrims on the Way.* Grand Rapids: Zondervan, 2011.

Hugenberger, G. "The Servant of the Lord in the 'Servant Songs' of Isaiah: A Second Moses Figure." Pages 105–40 in *The Lord's Anointed: Interpretation of Old Testament Messianic Texts.* Edited by P. Satterthwaite, Richard Hess, and Gordon Wenham. THS. Carlisle, UK: Paternoster, 1995.

Jackson, Howard. "The Death of Jesus in Mark and the Miracle from the Cross." *NTS* 33 (1987): 16–37.

Jacob, Edmond. *Theology of the Old Testament.* New York: Harper & Row, 1958.

Jansen, John Frederick. *Calvin's Doctrine of the Work of Christ.* London: Clarke, 1956.

Jeffery, S., Michael Ovey, and Andrew Sach. *Pierced for Our Transgressions: Rediscovering the Glory of Penal Substitution.* Wheaton, IL: Crossway, 2007.

Jennings, Theodore. *Transforming Atonement: A Political Theology of the Cross.* Minneapolis: Fortress, 2009.

Jensen, Matthew. "'You Have Overcome the Evil One': Victory Over Evil in 1 John." Pages 104–22 in *Christ's Victory Over Evil: Biblical Theology and Pastoral Ministry.* Edited by Peter Bolt. Nottingham, UK: Apollos, 2009.

Jenson, Robert. *The Triune God.* Vol.1 of *Systematic Theology.* New York: Oxford University Press, 1997.

Jewett, Paul King. *Emil Brunner: An Introduction to the Man and His Thought.* Downers Grove, IL: InterVarsity Press, 1961.

Jipp, Joshua. "Luke's Scriptural Suffering Messiah: A Search for Precedent, a Search for Identity." *CBQ* 72 (2010): 255–74.

Johnson, Adam. "A Fuller Account: The Role of 'Fittingness' in Thomas Aquinas' Development of the Doctrine of the Atonement." *IJST* 12 (2009): 302–18.

———. *God's Being in Reconciliation: The Theological Basis of the Unity and Diversity of the Atonement in the Theology of Karl Barth.* New York: T&T Clark, 2012.

Kahler, Martin. *The So-Called Historical Jesus and the Historic, Biblical Christ.* Philadelphia: Fortress, 1964.

Kaiser, Otto. *Der königliche Knecht: eine traditionsgeschichtlich-exegetische Studie über die Ebed-Jahwe-Lieder bei Deuterojesaja.* FRLANT. Göttingen: Vandenhoeck & Ruprecht, 1959.

Kee, Howard Clark. "The Function of Scriptural Quotations and Allusions in Mark 11–16." Pages 165–85 in *Jesus und Paulus.* Edited by E. Ellis and E. Grässer. Göttingen: Vandenhoeck & Ruprecht, 1975.

———. "The Terminology of Mark's Exorcism Stories." *NTS* 14 (1968): 232–46.

Kelber, Werner. *The Kingdom in Mark: A New Place and a New Time.* Philadelphia: Fortress, 1974.

Kim, Seyoon. *The "Son of Man" as the Son of God.* WUNT 30. Tübingen: J. C. B. Mohr, 1983.

Kline, Meredith. *Kingdom Prologue: Genesis Foundations for a Covenantal Worldview.* Overland Park, KS: Two Age, 2000.

Klink, Edward, and Darian Lockett. *Understanding Biblical Theology: A Comparison of Theory and Practice.* Grand Rapids: Zondervan, 2012.

Koester, Craig. *Hebrews: A New Translation with Introduction and Commentary.* AB. New York: Doubleday, 2001.

Krodel, Gerhard. *Revelation.* ACNT. Minneapolis: Augsburg, 1989.

Künzi, Martin. *Das Naherwartungslogion Markus 9.1.* Tübingen: J. C. B. Mohr, 1977.

Ladd, George Eldon. *A Commentary on the Revelation of John.* Grand Rapids: Eerdmans, 1972.

———. *A Theology of the New Testament.* Grand Rapids: Eerdmans, 1974.

———. "The Kingdom of God: Reign or Realm?" *JBL* 81 (1962): 230–38.

———. *The Presence of the Future: The Eschatology of Biblical Realism.* Grand Rapids: Eerdmans, 1974.

Lee-Pollard, Dorothy. "Powerlessness as Power: A Key Emphasis in the Gospel of Mark." *SJT* 40 (1987): 173–88.

Legaspi, Michael C. *The Death of Scripture and the Rise of Biblical Studies.* New York: Oxford University Press, 2010.

Letham, Robert. *The Work of Christ.* Downers Grove, IL: InterVarsity Press, 1993.

Leung, Mavis. *The Kingship-Cross Interplay in the Gospel of John: Jesus' Death as Corroboration of His Royal Messiahship.* Eugene, OR: Wipf & Stock, 2011.

———. "The Roman Empire and John's Passion Narrative in Light of Jewish Royal Messianism." *BSac* 168 (2011): 426–42.

Levenson, Jon. *The Death and Resurrection of the Beloved Son: The Transformation of Child Sacrifice in Judaism and Christianity.* New Haven, CT: Yale University Press, 1993.

Levering, Matthew, and Michael Dauphinais. *Holy People, Holy Land: A Theological Introduction to the Bible.* Grand Rapids: Brazos, 2005.

Lewis, C. S. *Mere Christianity: Comprising The Case for Christianity, Christian Behaviour, and Beyond Personality.* New York: Touchstone, 1996.

Lightfoot, J. B. *Saint Paul's Epistles to the Colossians and to Philemon.* New York: Macmillan, 1900.

Linnemann, Eta. *Studien zur Passionsgeschichte.* Göttingen: Vandenhoeck & Ruprecht, 1970.

Lints, Richard. *The Fabric of Theology: A Prolegomenon to Evangelical Theology.* Grand Rapids: Eerdmans, 1993.

Loewenich, Walther von. *Luther's Theology of the Cross.* Minneapolis: Augsburg, 1976.

Lohse, Eduard. *Colossians and Philemon: A Commentary on the Epistles to the Colossians and to Philemon.* Hermeneia. Philadelphia: Fortress, 1971.

Long, Stephen. "Justification and Atonement." Pages 79–92 in *The Cambridge Companion to Evangelical Theology.* Edited by Daniel Treier and Timothy Larsen. Cambridge: Cambridge University Press, 2007.

Longman, Tremper, and Daniel Reid. *God Is a Warrior.* Grand Rapids: Zondervan, 1994.

Ludlow, Morwenna. "Suffering Servant or King of Glory? Christological Readings of the Old Testament in the Patristic Era." Pages 104–19 in *Christology and Scripture: Interdisciplinary Perspectives.* Edited by Andrew Lincoln and Angus Paddison. London: T&T Clark, 2007.

Lunde, Jonathan. *Following Jesus, the Servant King: A Biblical Theology of Covenantal Discipleship.* Grand Rapids: Zondervan, 2010.

Luther, Martin. "John X. From the 11th to the 16th verses, inclusive." Pages 100–113 in *A Selection of the Most Celebrated Sermons of M. Luther and J. Calvin: Eminent Ministers of the Gospel, and Principal Leaders in the Protestant Reformation*. New York: Bentley, 1829.

———. *Luther: Letters of Spiritual Counsel*. Edited and translated by Theodore Tappert. Vancouver, BC: Regent College Publishing, 2003.

———. *LW*. Edited by Jaroslav Pelikan (vols. 1–30) and Helmut T. Lehmann (vols. 31–55). Philadelphia: Muhlenberg; St. Louis: Concordia, 1955–1986.

———. *WA*. 67 vols. to date. Weimar: Böhlaus, 1883–.

Malbon, Elizabeth Struthers. *Mark's Jesus: Characterization as Narrative Christology*. Waco, TX: Baylor University Press, 2009.

Mallen, Peter. *The Reading and Transformation of Isaiah in Luke-Acts*. New York: T&T Clark, 2008.

Mangina, Joseph. *Revelation*. BTCB. Grand Rapids: Brazos, 2010.

Mann, Alan. *Atonement for a "Sinless" Society: Engaging with an Emerging Culture*. Milton Keynes, UK: Paternoster, 2005.

Marcus, Joel. "Crucifixion as Parodic Exaltation." *JBL* 125 (2006): 73–87.

———. *Mark 1–8: A New Translation with Introduction and Commentary*. AYBC. New York: Doubleday, 2000.

———. "Mark 4:10–12 and Marcan Epistemology." *JBL* 103 (1984): 557–74.

———. *Mark 8–16: A New Translation with Introduction and Commentary*. AYBC. New Haven, CT: Yale University Press, 2009.

———. "Mark—Interpreter of Paul." *NTS* 46 (2000): 473–87.

———. *The Way of the Lord: Christological Exegesis of the Old Testament in the Gospel of Mark*. Louisville: Westminster John Knox, 1992.

Marshall, Christopher. *Faith as a Theme in Mark's Narrative*. Cambridge: Cambridge University Press, 1994.

Marshall, I. Howard. *Aspects of the Atonement: Cross and Resurrection in the Reconciling of God and Humanity*. London: Paternoster, 2007.

———. "Kingdom of God (of Heaven)." Pages 911–22 in vol. 3 of *ZEB*. Edited by Merrill Tenney and Moisés Silva. Grand Rapids: Zondervan, 2009.

———. *The Epistles of John*. NICNT. Grand Rapids: Eerdmans, 1978.

———. "The Hope of a New Age: The Kingdom of God in the New Testament." *Themelios* 11 (1985): 5–15.

———. "The Theology of the Atonement." Pages 49–69 in *The Atonement Debate*. Edited by Derek Tidball, David Hilborn, and Justin Thacker. Grand Rapids: Zondervan, 2008.

Martin, R. P. "Reconciliation and Forgiveness in the Letter to the Colossians." Pages 116–23 in *Reconciliation and Hope: New Testament Essays on Atonement and Eschatology Presented to L. L. Morris on his 60th Birthday*. Edited by Robert Banks. Carlisle, UK: Paternoster, 1974.

Matera, Frank. *The Kingship of Jesus: Composition and Theology in Mark 15*. SBLDS. Chico, CA: Scholars, 1982.

McCartney, Dan. "*Ecce homo*: The Coming of the Kingdom as the Restoration of Human Vicegerency." *WTJ* 56 (1994): 1–21.

McCulloh, Gerald. *Christ's Person and Life-Work in the Theology of Albrecht Ritschl: With Special Attention to* Munus Triplex. Lanham, MD: University Press of America, 1990.

McFague, Sallie. *Models of God: Theology for an Ecological, Nuclear Age*. Philadelphia: Fortress, 1987.

McGrath, Alister. *Luther's Theology of the Cross: Martin Luther's Theological Breakthrough*. New York: Blackwell, 1985.

———. *The Genesis of Doctrine: A Study in the Foundations of Doctrinal Criticism*. Grand Rapids: Eerdmans, 1997.

———. *The Mystery of the Cross*. Grand Rapids: Academie, 1988.

McIntyre, John. *St. Anselm and His Critics: A Re-Interpretation of the* Cur Deus Homo. Edinburgh: Oliver and Boyd, 1954.

———. *The Shape of Soteriology: Studies in the Doctrine of the Death of Christ*. Edinburgh: T&T Clark, 1995.

McKnight, Scot. *A Community Called Atonement*. Nashville: Abingdon, 2007.

———. *Jesus and His Death: Historiography, the Historical Jesus, and Atonement Theory*. Waco, TX: Baylor University Press, 2005.

McMahon, K. "The Cross and the Pearl: Anselm's Patristic Doctrine of Atonement." *TSR* 91 (2001): 57–70.

Meed, James. *Biblical Theology: Issues, Methods, and Themes*. Louisville: Westminster John Knox, 2007.

Merklein, Helmut. "Der Tod Jesu als stellvertretender Sühnetod." Pages 181–91 in *Studien zu Jesus und Paulus*. WUNT 43. Tübingen: Mohr Siebeck, 1987.

Merrill, Eugene. *Everlasting Dominion: A Theology of the Old Testament*. Nashville: Broadman & Holman, 2006.

Mettinger, Tryggve. "Die Ebed-Jahwe-Lieder: Ein fragwürdiges Axiom." *ASTI* (1978): 68–76.

———. *King and Messiah: The Civil and Sacral Legitimation of the Israelite Kings*. Lund: Gleerup, 1976.

Meyer, Paul. "An Exegetical Reflection on Matthew 21:1–11." Pages 277–81 in *The Word in This World: Essays in New Testament Exegesis and Theology.* Edited by J. T. Carroll. Louisville: Westminster John Knox, 2004.

Miles, Todd. "A Kingdom without a King? Evaluating the Kingdom Ethic(s) of the Emerging Church." *SBJT* 12 (2008): 88–103.

Mitchell, David. *The Message of the Psalter: An Eschatological Programme in the Book.* JSOTSup 252. Sheffield: Sheffield Academic, 1997.

Mitros, Joseph. "Patristic Views of Christ's Salvific Work." *Thought* 42 (1967): 415–47.

Moffitt, David. *Atonement and the Logic of Resurrection in the Epistle to the Hebrews.* Leiden: Brill, 2011.

Moltmann, Jürgen. *Experiences in Theology: Ways and Forms of Christian Theology.* Minneapolis: Fortress, 2000.

———. *History and the Triune God: Contributions to Trinitarian Theology.* New York: Crossroad, 1992.

———. *Sun of Righteousness, Arise! God's Future for Humanity and the Earth.* Minneapolis: Fortress, 2010.

———. *The Church in the Power of the Spirit: A Contribution to Messianic Ecclesiology.* Minneapolis: Fortress, 1993.

———. *The Crucified God: The Cross of Christ as the Foundation and Criticism of Christian Theology.* New York: Harper & Row, 1974.

———. *The Trinity and the Kingdom: The Doctrine of God.* New York: Harper & Row, 1981.

———. "The World in God or God in the World?" Pages 35–42 in *God Will Be All in All: The Eschatology of Jürgen Moltmann.* Edited by Richard Bauckham. Edinburgh: T&T Clark, 1999.

———. *Theology of Hope: On the Ground and the Implications of a Christian Eschatology.* Translated by James Leitch. Minneapolis: Fortress, 1993.

Moo, Douglas. *The Epistle to the Romans.* NICNT. Grand Rapids: Eerdmans, 1996.

———. *The Letters to the Colossians and to Philemon.* PiNTC. Grand Rapids: Eerdmans, 2008.

———. *The Old Testament in the Gospel Passion Narratives.* Eugene, OR: Wipf & Stock, 2008.

Moore, Russell. *The Kingdom of Christ: The New Evangelical Perspective.* Wheaton, IL: Crossway, 2004.

Morris, Leon. *The Apostolic Preaching of the Cross.* 3rd rev. ed. Grand Rapids: Eerdmans, 1965.

———. *The Cross in the New Testament.* Exeter, UK: Paternoster, 1965.

Mother Mary, and Kallistos Ware, trans. "The Service of the Twelve Gospels." In *The Lenten Triodion*. South Canaan, PA: Saint Tikhon's Seminary Press, 2001.

Motyer, J. A. *The Prophecy of Isaiah: An Introduction & Commentary*. Downers Grove, IL: InterVarsity Press, 1993.

Motyer, Stephen. "The Rending of the Veil: A Markan Pentecost?" *NTS* 33 (1987): 155–57.

Mounce, Robert. *The Book of Revelation*. NICNT. Grand Rapids: Eerdmans, 1977.

Muller, Richard. *Christ and the Decree: Christology and Predestination in Reformed Theology from Calvin to Perkins*. Durham, NC: Labyrinth, 1986.

———. *Dictionary of Latin and Greek Theological Terms: Drawn Principally from Protestant Scholastic Theology*. Grand Rapids: Baker, 1985.

Müller-Fahrenholz, Geiko. *The Kingdom and the Power: The Theology of Jürgen Moltmann*. Translated by John Bowden. Minneapolis: Fortress, 2001.

Murray, John. *Redemption Accomplished and Applied*. Grand Rapids: Eerdmans, 1978.

Newbigin, Lesslie. *Foolishness to the Greeks: The Gospel and Western Culture*. Grand Rapids: Eerdmans, 1986.

Ngewa, Samuel. *Galatians*. ABCS. Nairobi, Kenya: Hippo, 2010.

Nichols, Stephen. "The Kingdom of God: The Kingdom in Historical and Contemporary Perspectives." Pages 25–48 in *The Kingdom of God*. Edited by Christopher Morgan and Robert Peterson. Theology in Community. Wheaton, IL: Crossway, 2012.

Niebuhr, H. Richard. *The Kingdom of God in America*. New York: Harper & Row, 1937.

North, Christopher. *The Suffering Servant in Deutero-Isaiah: An Historical and Critical Study*. London: Oxford University Press, 1948.

O'Brien, Kelli. *The Use of Scripture in the Markan Passion Narrative*. London: T&T Clark, 2010.

O'Brien, Peter. *Colossians, Philemon*. WBC. Waco, TX: Word, 1982.

———. "Was Paul a Covenantal Nomist?" Pages 249–96 in *Justification and Variegated Nomism: The Paradoxes of Paul*. Vol. 2. Edited by D. A. Carson, Mark Seifrid, and Peter O'Brien. Grand Rapids: Baker Academic, 2004.

Oecumenius. "Commentary on the Apocalypse." In *Traditio Exegetica Graeca*. Louvain: Peeters, 1991.

Orlinsky, Harry. "The So-Called 'Servant of the Lord' and 'Suffering Servant' in Second Isaiah." Pages 1–133 in *Studies on the Second Part of the*

Book of Isaiah. Edited by Harry Orlinsky and N. Snaith. Leiden: Brill, 1967.

Osborne, Grant. *Revelation.* BECNT. Grand Rapids: Baker Academic, 2002.

———. *The Hermeneutical Spiral: A Comprehensive Introduction to Biblical Interpretation.* Downers Grove, IL: InterVarsity Press, 2006.

Oswalt, John. *The Book of Isaiah: Chapters 40–66.* NICOT. Grand Rapids: Eerdmans, 1998.

Otto, Randall. "Moltmann and the Anti-Monotheism Movement." *IJST* 3 (2001): 293–308.

Ovey, Michael. "Appropriating Aulén? Employing *Christus Victor* Models of the Atonement." *Churchman* 124 (2010): 297–330.

Packer, J. I. "What Did the Cross Achieve? The Logic of Penal Substitution." *TynBul* 25 (1974): 3–45.

Pannenberg, Wolfhart. *Jesus—God and Man.* Translated by Lewis L. Wilkins and Duane A. Priebe. 2nd ed. Philadelphia: Westminster, 1977.

Pao, David. *Acts and the Isaianic New Exodus.* Grand Rapids: Baker Academic, 2002.

Park, Andrew. *Triune Atonement: Christ's Healing for Sinners, Victims, and the Whole Creation.* Louisville: Westminster John Knox, 2009.

Patterson, Richard, and Michael Travers. "Contours of the Exodus Motif in Jesus' Earthly Ministry." *WTJ* 66 (2004): 25–47.

Pennington, Jonathan. *Heaven and Earth in the Gospel of Matthew.* NovTSup 126. Boston: Brill, 2007.

———. *Reading the Gospels Wisely: A Narrative and Theological Introduction.* Grand Rapids: Baker Academic, 2012.

Perowne, J. Stewart. *The Book of Psalms.* Grand Rapids: Zondervan, 1976.

Perrin, Nicholas. "Where to Begin with the Gospel of Mark." *CurTM* 35 (2008): 413–19.

Perrin, Norman. "The High Priest's Question and Jesus' Answer (Mark 14:61–62)." Pages 80–95 in *The Passion in Mark: Studies on Mark 14–16.* Edited by Werner Kelber. Philadelphia: Fortress, 1976.

Peterson, Anthony. *Behold Your King.* New York: T&T Clark, 2009.

Peterson, Erik. *Theologische Traktate.* Munich: Wild, 1951.

Peterson, Robert. *Calvin's Doctrine of the Atonement.* Phillipsburg, NJ: P&R, 1983.

———. *Salvation Accomplished by the Son: The Work of Christ.* Wheaton, IL: Crossway, 2012.

Plantinga, Cornelius. *Not the Way It's Supposed to Be: A Breviary of Sin.* Grand Rapids: Eerdmans, 1995.

Pobee, John. *Toward an African Theology.* Nashville: Abingdon, 1979.

Pott, Francis. *The Hymn Te Deum Laudamus.* London: Rivingtons, 1884.

Poythress, Vern. "Kinds of Biblical Theology." *WTJ* 70 (2008): 129–42.

———. *The Returning King: A Guide to the Book of Revelation.* Phillipsburg, NJ: Presbyterian & Reformed, 2000.

Rad, Gerhard von. "Typological Interpretation of the Old Testament." Pages 17–39 in *Essays on Old Testament Hermeneutics.* Edited by Claus Westermann. Atlanta: John Knox, 1963.

Rauschenbusch, Walter. *A Theology for the Social Gospel.* New York: Macmillan, 1917.

Rees, Thomas. *The Racovian Catechism, with Notes and Illustrations, Translated from the Latin to Which Is Prefixed a Sketch of the History of Unitarianism in Poland and the Adjacent Countries.* Lexington, KY: American Theological Library Association, 1962.

Ridderbos, Herman. *Matthew's Witness to Jesus Christ: The King and the Kingdom.* London: Lutterworth, 1958.

———. *Paul: An Outline of His Theology.* Grand Rapids: Eerdmans, 1975.

———. *The Coming of the Kingdom.* Philadelphia: P&R, 1962.

Ritschl, Albrecht. *The Christian Doctrine of Justification and Reconciliation: The Positive Development of the Doctrine.* Clifton, NJ: Reference Book, 1966.

Robertson, O. Palmer. *The Christ of the Covenants.* Grand Rapids: Baker, 1980.

Rosner, Brian. "Salvation, History of." Pages 714–17 in *DTIB.* Edited by Kevin Vanhoozer. Grand Rapids: Baker, 2005.

Rosner, Brian, and Roy Ciampa. *The First Letter to the Corinthians.* PiNTC. Grand Rapids: Eerdmans, 2010.

Ruppert, Lothar. *Der leidende Gerechte: Eine motivgeschichtliche Untersuchung zum Alten Testament und zwischentestamentlichen Judentum.* FzB: Würzburg: Echter, 1972.

Sailhamer, John. *Pentateuch as Narrative.* Grand Rapids: Zondervan, 1992.

Sanders, John, ed. *Atonement and Violence: A Theological Conversation.* Nashville: Abingdon, 2006.

Sanders, John. *The God Who Risks: A Theology of Providence.* Downers Grove, IL: InterVarsity Press, 1998.

Sandys-Wunsch, J., and L. Eldredge. "J. P. Gabler and the Distinction between Biblical and Dogmatic Theology: Translation, Commentary, and Discussion of His Originality." *SJT* 33 (1980): 133–58.

Santos, Narry. *Slave of All: The Paradox of Authority and Servanthood in the Gospel of Mark*. JSNT 237. London: Sheffield Academic, 2003.

Sappington, Thomas. *Revelation and Redemption at Colossae*. Sheffield: JSOT, 1991.

Savage, Timothy. *Power through Weakness: Paul's Understanding of the Christian Ministry in 2 Corinthians*. New York: Cambridge University Press, 1996.

Schaff, Philip, ed. *Christ in Song: Hymns of Immanuel*. London: Sampson Low, Son, and Marston, 1870.

Schick, Ludwig. *Das dreifache Amt Christi und der Kirche: Zur Entstehung und Entwicklung der Trilogien*. New York: Peter Lang, 1982.

Schindler, Alfred. "Einführung." In *Monotheisms als politisches Problem? Erik Peterson und die Kritik der politischen Theologie*. Edited by Alfred Schindler. Gütersloh: Gütersloher Verlagshaus Mohn, 1978.

Schleiermacher, Friedrich. *The Christian Faith*. Edinburgh: T&T Clark, 1986.

Schlosser, Jacques. *Jésus de Nazareth*. Paris: Noesis, 1999.

Schmidt, T. E. "Mark 15.16–32: The Crucifixion Narrative and the Roman Triumphal Procession." *NTS* 41 (1995): 1–18.

Schmiechen, Peter. *Saving Power: Theories of Atonement and Forms of the Church*. Grand Rapids: Eerdmans, 2005.

Schneck, Richard. *Isaiah in the Gospel of Mark I–VIII*. Vallejo, CA: BIBAL, 1994.

Schreiner, Thomas. *Galatians*. ZECNT. Grand Rapids: Zondervan, 2010.

———. "Penal Substitution View." Pages 67–98 in *The Nature of the Atonement: Four Views*. Edited by James Beilby and Paul Eddy. Downers Grove, IL: InterVarsity Press, 2006.

Schultz, Richard. "Servant/Slave." Pages 1183–98 in *New International Dictionary of Old Testament Theology & Exegesis*. Vol. 4. Edited by Willem VanGemeren. Grand Rapids: Zondervan, 1997.

———. "The King in the Book of Isaiah." Pages 141–65 in *The Lord's Anointed: Interpretation of Old Testament Messianic Texts*. Edited by P. Satterthwaite, Richard Hess, and Gordon Wenham. THS. Carlisle, UK: Paternoster, 1995.

Schürmann, Heinz. *Gottes Reich, Jesu Geschick: Jesu ureigener Tod im Licht seiner Basileia-Verkündigung*. Freiburg, Breisgau: Herder, 1983.

———. "Jesu ureigenes Todesverständnis: Bemerkungen zur 'impliziten Soteriologie' Jesu." Pages 202–40 in *Jesus, Gestalt und Geheimnis: Gesammelte Beiträge*. Edited by Klaus Scholtissek. Paderborn: Bonifatius, 1994.

Schüssler-Fiorenza, Elisabeth. *The Book of Revelation: Justice and Judgment.* Philadelphia: Fortress, 1985.

Schuurman, Douglas. "Creation, Eschaton, and Ethics: An Analysis of Theology and Ethics in Jürgen Moltmann." *CTJ* 22 (1987): 42–67.

Schweitzer, Albert. *The Mystery of the Kingdom of God: The Secret of Jesus' Messiahship and Passion.* Translated by Walter Lowrie. New York: Macmillan, 1950.

Schweizer, Eduard. *The Good News According to Mark.* Trans. Donald H. Madvig. Richmond, VA: Knox, 1970.

Seifrid, Mark. "Unrighteous by Faith: Apostolic Proclamation in Romans 1:18–3:20." Pages 105–46 in *Justification and Variegated Nomism: The Paradoxes of Paul.* Vol. 2. Edited by D. A. Carson, Mark Seifrid, and Peter O'Brien. Grand Rapids: Baker Academic, 2004.

Sherman, Robert. *King, Priest, and Prophet: A Trinitarian Theology of Atonement.* New York: T&T Clark, 2004.

Shogren, G. S. "Presently Entering the Kingdom of Christ: The Background and Purpose of Col 1:12–14." *JETS* 31 (1988): 173–80.

Sklar, Jay. *Sin, Impurity, Sacrifice, Atonement: The Priestly Conceptions.* Sheffield: Sheffield Phoenix, 2005.

Smalley, Stephen. *1, 2, 3 John.* Revised ed. WBC. Nashville: Nelson, 2007.

Smeaton, George. *The Apostles' Doctrine of the Atonement.* Grand Rapids: Zondervan, 1957.

Smit, D. J. "Kingdom of God." Pages 566–68 in *DEM.* Edited by Nicolas Lossky. Grand Rapids: Eerdmans, 1991.

Smith, Gary V. *Isaiah 40–66.* NAC 15b. Nashville: Broadman & Holman, 2009.

Socinus, Faustus. *De Jesu Christo servatore: Hoc est cur & qua ratione Iesus Christus noster seruator sit.* Rakow: Rodecius, 1594.

———. *Prælectiones theologicæ.* Racoviæ: Sebastiani Sternacii, 1609.

Soskice, Janet. *Metaphor and Religious Language.* New York: Oxford University Press, 1985.

Spence, Alan. *The Promise of Peace: A Unified Theory of Atonement.* London: T&T Clark, 2006.

Stendahl, Krister. "Biblical Theology, Contemporary." Pages 418–32 in *IDB,* vol. 1. Edited by George Buttrick. New York: Abingdon, 1962.

Stott, John. *The Cross of Christ.* Downers Grove, IL: InterVarsity Press, 1986.

———. *Understanding the Bible.* Grand Rapids: Zondervan, 1984.

Strauss, Mark. *The Davidic Messiah in Luke-Acts: The Promise and Its Fulfillment in Lukan Christology.* Sheffield, England: Sheffield Academic, 1995.

Stromberg, Jake. *Isaiah After Exile: The Author of Third Isaiah as Reader and Redactor of the Book.* Oxford: Oxford University Press, 2011.

Swartley, William. "The Structural Function of the Term 'Way' in Mark." Pages 73–86 in *The New Way of Jesus: Essays Presented to Howard Charles.* Edited by W. Klassen. Newton, KS: Faith and Life, 1980.

Sweeney, Marvin. "On the Road to Duhm: Isaiah in the Nineteenth-Century Critical Scholarship." Pages 243–62 in *"As Those Who Are Taught": The Interpretation of Isaiah from the LXX to the SBL.* Edited by Claire Mathews McGinnis and Patricia Tull. Atlanta: SBL, 2006.

Sykes, Stephen. *The Story of Atonement.* London: Darton, Longman & Todd, 1997.

Tanner, Kathryn. *Christ the Key.* CIT. Cambridge: Cambridge University Press, 2010.

———. "Incarnation, Cross, and Sacrifice: A Feminist-Inspired Reappraisal." *AThR* 86 (2004): 35–56.

———. *Jesus, Humanity and the Trinity: A Brief Systematic Theology.* Edinburgh: T&T Clark, 2001.

Telford, William. *The Theology of the Gospel of Mark.* Cambridge: Cambridge University Press, 1999.

Thüsing, Wilhelm. *Die Erhöhung und Verherrlichung Jesu im Johannesevangelium.* Münster: Aschendorff, 1959.

Tidball, Derek, David Hilborn, and Justin Thacker, eds. *The Atonement Debate: Papers from the London Symposium on the Theology of Atonement.* Grand Rapids: Zondervan, 2008.

Tomlin, Graham. *The Power of the Cross: Theology and the Death of Christ in Paul, Luther and Pascal.* PBTM. Carlisle, UK: Paternoster, 1999.

Torrance, Thomas. *Atonement: The Person and Work of Christ.* Edited by Robert Walker. Downers Grove, IL: InterVarsity Press, 2009.

———. *Divine Meaning: Studies in Patristic Hermeneutics.* Edinburgh: T&T Clark, 1995.

Treier, Daniel. "Biblical Theology and/or Theological Interpretation of Scripture?" *SJT* 61 (2008): 16–31.

———. *Introducing Theological Interpretation of Scripture: Recovering a Christian Practice.* Grand Rapids: Baker Academic, 2008.

Uhlig, Torsten. "Too Hard to Understand? The Motif of Hardening in Isaiah." Pages 62–83 in *Interpreting Isaiah: Issues and Approaches.* Edited by David Firth and H. G. M. Williamson. Downers Grove, IL: InterVarsity Press, 2009.

VandenBerg, Mary. "Redemptive Suffering: Christ's Alone." *SJT* 60 (2007): 394–411.

Vanhoozer, Kevin. "Atonement." Pages 175–202 in *Mapping Modern Theology: A Thematic and Historical Introduction*. Edited by Kelly Kapic and Bruce McCormack. Grand Rapids: Baker Academic, 2012.

———. "Interpreting Scripture Between the Rock of Biblical Studies and the Hard Place of Systematic Theology: The State of the Evangelical (Dis) union." In *Renewing the Evangelical Mission*. Edited by Richard Lints. Grand Rapids: Eerdmans, 2013.

———. *Remythologizing Theology: Divine Action, Passion, and Authorship*. Cambridge: Cambridge University Press, 2010.

———. "The Atonement in Postmodernity: Guilt, Goats, and Gifts." Pages 367–404 in *The Glory of the Atonement*. Edited by Charles Hill and Frank James. Downers Grove, IL: InterVarsity Press, 2004.

———. *The Drama of Doctrine: A Canonical-Linguistic Approach to Christian Theology*. Louisville: Westminster John Knox, 2005.

Vermeylen, Jacques. "L'unité du livre d'Isaïe." Pages 11–53 in *The Book of Isaiah*. Edited by Jacques Vermeylen. BETL. Leuven: Leuven University Press, 1989.

Viladesau, Richard. *The Beauty of the Cross: The Passion of Christ in Theology and the Arts from the Catacombs to the Eve of the Renaissance*. New York: Oxford University Press, 2008.

Visser 't Hooft, Willem Adolph. *The Kingship of Christ: An Interpretation of Recent European Theology*. New York: Harper, 1948.

Viviano, Benedict. *The Kingdom of God in History*. Wilmington, DE: Glazier, 1988.

Vlach, Michael. "Penal Substitution in Church History." *MSJ* 20 (2009): 199–214.

Vögtle, A. "Todesankündigungen und Todesverständnis Jesu." Pages 51–113 in *Der Tod Jesu: Deutungen im Neuen Testament*. Edited by Karl Kertelge. Herder: Freiburg, 1976.

Volf, Miroslav. *Exclusion and Embrace: A Theological Exploration of Identity, Otherness, and Reconciliation*. Nashville: Abingdon, 1996.

Vos, Geerhardus. *Biblical Theology: Old and New Testaments*. Grand Rapids: Eerdmans, 1948.

———. *The Pauline Eschatology*. Grand Rapids: Eerdmans, 1961.

Wagner, J. Ross. "The Heralds of Isaiah and the Mission of Paul: An Investigation of Paul's Use of Isaiah 51–55 in Romans." Pages 193–222 in *Jesus and the Suffering Servant: Isaiah 53 and Christian Origins*. Edited by W. H. Bellinger and William Reuben Farmer. Harrisburg, PA: Trinity Press International, 1998.

Wainwright, Geoffrey. *For Our Salvation: Two Approaches to the Work of Christ*. Grand Rapids: Eerdmans, 1997.

Wakefield, James. *Jürgen Moltmann: A Research Bibliography*. Lanham, MD: Scarecrow, 2002.

Wall, Robert. *Revelation*. NIBC. Peabody, MA: Hendrickson, 1991.

Walsh, Brian, and Silvia Keesmaat. *Colossians Remixed: Subverting the Empire*. Downers Grove, IL: InterVarsity Press, 2004.

Waltke, Bruce. "The Kingdom of God in the Old Testament: Definitions and Story." Pages 49–72 in *The Kingdom of God*. Edited by Christopher Morgan and Robert Peterson. Theology in Community. Wheaton, IL: Crossway, 2012.

Walton, John. *Genesis*. NIVAC. Grand Rapids: Zondervan, 2001.

———. "The Imagery of the Substitute King Ritual in Isaiah's Fourth Servant Song." *JBL* 122 (2003): 734–43.

Walton, John, Victor Matthews, and Mark Chavalas, eds. *The IVP Bible Background Commentary: Old Testament*. Downers Grove, IL: InterVarsity Press, 2000.

Watts, John. *Isaiah 1–33*. WBC. Waco, TX: Word, 1985.

Watts, Rikki. "Consolation or Confrontation: Isaiah 40–55 and the Delay of the New Exodus." *TynBul* 41 (1990): 31–59.

———. *Isaiah's New Exodus in Mark*. Grand Rapids: Baker Academic, 2001.

———. "Mark." Pages 111–249 in *Commentary on the New Testament Use of the Old Testament*. Edited by G. K. Beale and D. A. Carson. Grand Rapids: Baker Academic, 2007.

———. "The Psalms in Mark's Gospel." Pages 25–46 in *The Psalms in the New Testament*. Edited by Steve Moyise and Maarten Menken. London: T&T Clark, 2004.

Weaver, J. Denny. "Narrative *Christus Victor*." Pages 1–32 in *Atonement and Violence: A Theological Conversation*. Edited by John Sanders. Nashville: Abingdon, 2006.

———. *The Nonviolent Atonement*. Grand Rapids: Eerdmans, 2001.

———. "The Nonviolent Atonement: Human Violence, Discipleship and God." Pages 316–55 in *Stricken by God? Nonviolent Identification and the Victory of Christ*. Edited by Brad Jersak and Michael Hardin. Grand Rapids: Eerdmans, 2007.

Webb, Barry. *The Message of Isaiah: On Eagles' Wings*. BST. Leicester: InterVarsity Press, 1996.

Webster, John. "Biblical Theology and the Clarity of Scripture." Pages 352–84 in *Out of Egypt: Biblical Theology and Biblical Interpretation*. SHS.

Edited by Craig Bartholomew, Mary Healy, Karl Möller, and Robin Parry. Grand Rapids: Zondervan, 2004.

———. "One Who Is Son: Theological Reflections on the Exordium to the Epistle to the Hebrews." Pages 69–94 in *The Epistle to the Hebrews and Christian Theology*. Edited by Richard Bauckham, Daniel Driver, Trevor Hart, and Nathan MacDonald. Grand Rapids: Eerdmans, 2009.

———. "Principles of Systematic Theology." *IJST* 11 (2009): 56–71.

———. *Word and Church: Essays in Church Dogmatics*. New York: T&T Clark, 2001.

Weeden, Theodore. "Cross as Power in Weakness (Mark 15:20b–41)." Pages 115–34 in *The Passion in Mark: Studies on Mark 14–16*. Edited by Werner Kelber. Philadelphia: Fortress, 1976.

Wegner, Paul. *An Examination of Kingship and Messianic Expectation in Isaiah 1–35*. Lewiston, NY: Mellen, 1993.

Weinandy, Thomas. *Does God Suffer?* Notre Dame, IN: University of Notre Dame, 2000.

Weinfeld, Moshe. "The King as the Servant of the People: The Source of the Idea." *JJS* 33 (1982): 189–94.

Weiss, Johannes. *Die Predigt Jesu vom Reiche Gottes*. Göttingen: Vandenhoeck & Ruprecht, 1900.

Wenham, Gordon. *Genesis 1–15*. WBC. Waco, TX: Word, 1987.

Westermann, Claus. *Isaiah 40–66: A Commentary*. OTL. Philadelphia: Westminster, 1969.

Whitehead, Alfred North. *Process and Reality: An Essay in Cosmology*. New York: Harper & Row, 1960.

Whybray, R. N. *Isaiah 40–66*. NCB. Greenwood, SC: Attic, 1975.

———. *Thanksgiving for a Liberated Prophet: An Interpretation of Isaiah Chapter 53*. JSOT 4. Sheffield: University of Sheffield, 1978.

Willard, Dallas. *The Divine Conspiracy: Rediscovering Our Hidden Life in God*. San Francisco: HarperSanFrancisco, 1998.

Williams, A. N. *The Architecture of Theology: Structure, System, & Ratio*. New York: Oxford University Press, 2011.

Williams, David. *Paul's Metaphors: Their Context and Character*. Peabody, MA: Hendrickson, 1999.

Williams, Garry. "Penal Substitution: A Response to Recent Criticisms." Pages 172–91 in *The Atonement Debate*. Edited by Derek Tidball, David Hilborn, and Justin Thacker. Grand Rapids: Zondervan, 2008.

———. "Penal Substitutionary Atonement in the Church Fathers." *EvQ* 83 (2011): 195–216.

Williams, Jarvis. "Violent Atonement in Romans: The Foundation of Paul's Soteriology." *JETS* 53 (2010): 579–600.

Williams, Joel. "Is Mark's Gospel an Apology for the Cross?" *BBR* 12 (2002): 97–122.

———. "Literary Approaches to the End of Mark's Gospel." *JETS* 42 (1999): 21–35.

Williams, Michael. "Systematic Theology As a Biblical Discipline." Pages 167–96 in *All For Jesus: A Celebration of the 50th Anniversary of Covenant Theological Seminary*. Edited by Robert Peterson and Sean Michael Lucas. Fearn, UK: Christian Focus, 2006.

Williams, Thomas. "Sin, Grace, and Redemption." Pages 258–78 in *The Cambridge Companion to Abelard*. Edited by Jeffrey Brower and Kevin Guilfoy. CCP. Cambridge: Cambridge University Press, 2004.

Williamson, H. G. M. "Recent Issues in the Study of Isaiah." Pages 21–42 in *Interpreting Isaiah: Issues and Approaches*. Edited by David Firth and H. G. M. Williamson. Downers Grove, IL: InterVarsity Press, 2009.

———. *Variations on a Theme: King, Messiah and Servant in the Book of Isaiah*. Carlisle, UK: Paternoster, 2000.

Williamson, Paul. *Sealed with an Oath: Covenant in God's Unfolding Purpose*. NSBT. Downers Grove, IL: InterVarsity Press, 2007.

Wink, Walter. *Engaging the Powers: Discernment and Resistance in a World of Domination*. Minneapolis: Fortress, 1992.

———. *Naming the Powers: The Language of Power in the New Testament*. Philadelphia: Fortress, 1984.

———. *Unmasking the Powers: The Invisible Forces That Determine Human Existence*. Philadelphia: Fortress, 1986.

Wrede, William. *The Messianic Secret*. Translated by J. Grieg. Cambridge: Clarke, 1971.

Wright, Christopher J. H. "Atonement in the Old Testament." Pages 69–82 in *The Atonement Debate: Papers from the London Symposium on the Theology of Atonement*. Edited by Derek Tidball, David Hilborn, and Justin Thacker. Grand Rapids: Zondervan, 2008.

———. *Knowing Jesus Through the Old Testament*. Downers Grove, IL: InterVarsity Press, 1995.

———. *The Mission of God: Unlocking the Bible's Grand Narrative*. Downers Grove, IL: InterVarsity Press, 2006.

Wright, N. T. *After You Believe: Why Christian Character Matters*. New York: HarperOne, 2010.

———. *Evil and the Justice of God*. Downers Grove, IL: InterVarsity Press, 2006.

————. *How God Became King: The Forgotten Story of the Gospels*. New York: HarperOne, 2012.

————. *Jesus and the Victory of God*. Christian Origins and the Question of God. Minneapolis: Fortress, 1996.

————. *The Challenge of Jesus: Rediscovering Who Jesus Was and Is*. Downers Grove, IL: InterVarsity Press, 1999.

————. *The Crown and the Fire: Meditations on the Cross and the Life of the Spirit*. Grand Rapids: Eerdmans, 1995.

————. *The Epistles of Paul to the Colossians and to Philemon: An Introduction and Commentary*. TNTC. Grand Rapids: Eerdmans, 2002.

————. *The Resurrection of the Son of God*. Christian Origins and the Question of God. Minneapolis: Fortress, 2003.

————. "Whence and Whither Historical Jesus Studies in the Life of the Church?" Pages 115–58 in *Jesus, Paul, and the People of God: A Theological Dialogue with N. T. Wright*. Edited by Nicholas Perrin and Richard Hays. Downers Grove, IL: InterVarsity Press, 2011.

Yarbrough, Robert. "Atonement." Pages 388–93 in *NDBT*. Edited by T. Desmond Alexander and Brian Rosner. Downers Grove, IL: InterVarsity Press, 2000.

————. "The Practice and Promise of Biblical Theology: A Response to Hamilton and Goldsworthy." *SBJT* 12 (2008): 78–86.

Yeago, David. "Crucified Also for Us under Pontius Pilate." Pages 87–106 in *Nicene Christianity: The Future for a New Ecumenism*. Edited by Christopher Seitz. Grand Rapids: Brazos, 2001.

————. "The New Testament and the Nicene Dogma: A Contribution to the Recovery of Theological Exegesis." *ProEccl* 3 (1994): 152–64.

Young, Edward. *The Book of Isaiah: With English Text, with Introduction, Exposition, and Notes*. NICOT. Grand Rapids: Eerdmans, 1965.

SCRIPTURE INDEX

SCRIPTURE INDEX

SUBJECT INDEX

Abraham, 57, 59–60, 63, 64, 138, 248, 252
abscondita sub contrario, 229–30
absolute dualism, 200
abstract theology, 133
accuser, 201–2, 211–12
active/passive distinction, 209–10
Adam and Eve, 55–57, 60, 63, 143, 197,
    200, 203, 241, 248, 252
"age to come," 135, 136, 137, 138, 230,
    244, 250
alienation, 199
"already/not yet" motif, 114, 152, 243
angels, 115, 124–25
anointing, 151
apocalyptic judgment, 136
apologetics, 220
apostles, 229
"arm of the Lord" motif, 72, 77, 78–79,
    80, 85
"armor of God," 212–13
articuli fundamentales, 187
ascension, 216–17, 220
ascetism, 115
Assyria, 200
atonement, 45–49, 85, 134, 138, 204
    centrality of cross in, 217–20
    as Christ's victory over Satan, 17
    contemporary theology of, 48
    defined, 45–46
    dimensions of, 47–49
    doctrine of, 27, 30, 149, 175, 218, 219,
        220, 221–24, 251
    expansive particularity, 174–92
    and incarnation, 17, 215–16
    integrating and ordering dimensions
        of, 182
    and kingdom, 134, 224
    and kingship of Christ, 172
    metaphors, 187
    outcome and means, 46
    and purity of the kingdom, 248
    reconciling *Christus Victor* and penal
        substitution, 193–226
    and redemption, 28

and resurrection, 216, 219–20
satisfaction theories of, 190
substitutionary, 49, 61, 62, 81–82,
    138–39, 168, 186, 207, 249
and suffering, 249
theology of, 138, 175, 194–99, 209
theories, 17, 49, 174
and victory, 63
authority, 238

baptism, Jesus', 90–91, 151
basileia, 234
Beelzebub, 93
biblical studies, 27
biblical theology, 33–37, 51–145
blessing and curse, 138
blood of Christ, 124–26
"blood of the covenant," 104
"blood of the cross," 111–27, 249
    and kingdom of darkness, 115–18
    and kingdom of God, 120
bondage, 76, 81, 95, 196–99, 204
book of comfort, 75
book of judgment, 75
botanical imagery, 70
bridegroom motif, 92

Catholicism, 165
chiasm, 92–93, 95
Chiliasts, 171
Christ. *See also* Jesus
    accepts mission of servitude, 159
    ascension of, 216–17, 220
    atoning death of, 38, 39
    atoning work, 215
    crucifixion, 142–43
    death of (*see* death, Christ's)
    destroys Satan, 169, 174, 186, 203–14,
        220–21, 225, 249–50, 251
    divinity of, 213
    exaltation before the resurrection, 158
    as "faithful and true witness," 125
    human exaltation, 163
    humanity of, 158, 213

293

AUTHOR INDEX